Red Army and Society

RED ARMY AND SOCIETY

A Sociology of the
Soviet Military

ELLEN JONES

Boston
ALLEN & UNWIN
London   Sydney

Allen & Unwin, Inc.,
Fifty Cross Street, Winchester, Mass. 01890, USA

George Allen & Unwin (Publishers) Ltd,
40 Museum Street, London WC1A 1LU, UK

George Allen & Unwin (Publishers) Ltd,
Park Lane, Hemel Hempstead, Herts HP2 4TE, UK

George Allen & Unwin Australia Pty Ltd,
8 Napier Street, North Sydney, NSW 2060, Australia

First published in Great Britain in 1985
Second printing, 1986

Library of Congress Cataloging in Publication Data

Jones, Ellen.
  Red army and society.
Includes index.
1. Sociology, Military – Soviet Union. 2. Soviet Union
– Armed Forces. 3. Manpower – Soviet Union. I. Title.
UA770.J63 1984   306′.27′0947   84-12336
ISBN 0-04-322011-8 (alk. paper)
ISBN 0-04-497016-1

British Library Cataloguing in Publication Data

Jones, Ellen
  Red army and society.
1. Union of Soviet Socialist Republics, *Armilá*
2. Sociology, Military – Soviet Union
I. Title
306′.27′0947   U21.5
ISBN 0-04-322011-8

Contents

List of Abbreviations

KVS	*Kommunist vooruzhennykh sil*
KZ	*Krasnaya zvezda*
NO	*Narodnoye obrazovaniye*
SI	*Sotsiologicheskiye Issledovaniye*
SVE	*Sovetskaya voyennaya entsiklopediya*
SZ	*Svod zakonov SSSR*
TIS	*Tyl i snabzheniye*
VIZh	*Voyenno-istoricheskiy zhurnal*
VES	*Voyennyy entsiklopedicheskiy slovar'*

Acknowledgements

This book evolved from a series of conference papers and drafts that benefited from the advice of colleagues both inside and outside of the government. I am especially indebted to my coworkers in the Defense Department—Jim Reitz, Michael O'Hara, and Christina Shelton—who provided detailed comments and criticisms of the manuscript. Denzil Pritchard, Mitzi Leibst, and Bill Manthorpe read and critiqued earlier versions of selected chapters. Steve Rapowy and Godfrey Baldwin, of the Department of Commerce, provided projections of the Soviet population that formed the base of many of my own estimates. John Collins and Bob Goldich of the Library of Congress assisted me with materials on the U.S. military. Tadeusz Sadowski of the Library's European Law Division provided much-needed help in locating Soviet and East European legal sources.

I also owe a great deal to nongovernment friends and colleagues. Harriet and Bill Scott generously shared ideas, insights, and research material that significantly improved my understanding of the Soviet military. I am indebted as well to John Erickson, whose unfailing enthusiasm for the subject did much to stimulate my own interest. I would also like to express my gratitude to the members of the Network of Women in Slavic Studies, who unfailingly provided encouragement and moral support at a time when it was greatly needed.

Finally, this book would not have been written without the help of Fred Grupp—husband, helpmate, and friend.

To my parents

Introduction

For several hundred years Western visitors have returned from Russia with tales of a culture and system very different from their own. The image of the army that they have brought back is generally an ambivalent one of a massive land army manned by hardy and harshly disciplined soldiers, who are obedient and formidable, but lazy, ignorant, and given to strong drink. Western assessments of both the imperial Russian army and its Soviet counterpart have been dominated by efforts to puzzle out what this inherently contradictory image means in terms of relative military power. The contemporary Soviet military has been analyzed by some as a military institution (and potential threat to the military security of its European neighbors)[1] and by others as a political institution (and potential threat to the political security of the Communist Party leadership).[2]

In this book I examine the Soviet military as a social institution. I began with the assumption that the Soviet military has some characteristics in common with its counterparts in noncommunist states, while others are unique to the society and political culture in which it is embedded. One of the goals of this study is to identify the similarities and differences. This approach facilitates use of the concepts and findings of Western military sociology—a field that has expanded rapidly in the last decade.[3] While many of the findings of Western military sociologists are not directly relevant to the Soviet case, some do have a direct bearing on the Soviet armed forces. It is useful to be reminded, for example, that the USSR is by no means the only modern state whose military manpower management system must cope with ethnic, linguistic, and regional diversity among its troops. Inductee adjustment to the physical rigors and strict discipline of military life is a problem the USSR shares with many other military systems. For this study, the U.S. military provides the primary point of comparison. This reflects the fact that much of the military sociological research on which I have drawn is primarily or exclusively based on the U.S. military system; moreover, no other military organization approaches the Soviet army in size and complexity.

Study of the Soviet military from a sociological perspective must also be undertaken within the broader context of Soviet society and polity. This approach recognizes that the military organization is closely linked to a larger political system and society, and that some of its characteristics are not common to military institutions in other national settings, but rather reflect the culture and system of which it is a part. While some of these characteristics are uniquely Soviet in the sense that they are understood best in the context of Marxist–Leninist ideology or in the particular series of revolutionary events that gave birth to the Bolshevik regime, many of the factors that distinguish the Soviet military from its noncommunist counterparts can be traced to the tsarist period. This approach requires that the Soviet military as a social institution be viewed within a broad historical framework; it also facilitates the application of conclusions drawn from the growing body of literature produced by Soviet sociologists.

The substantive focus of this book is the qualitative aspect of military manpower: procurement and personnel policies and the military and civilian agencies most closely involved in implementing them. This choice was dictated by the fact that military manpower issues have a significant influence in the relations between the armed forces and society. Students of the Soviet Union have examined the political behavior of the Soviet armed forces as a way of understanding civil–military relations. It is argued here that this approach can also be reversed—using an examination of civil–military relations (as reflected in the military manpower system) as a way of explaining the armed forces' political behavior.

The available evidence is far from complete. The caveats that accompany most judgments are meant as reminders that these issues are quite complex. Assessing the personnel policies of any military system is a difficult task. In the Soviet case it is made even more difficult by lack of access to the surveys, official data, and on-site visits that many Western military manpower analysts take for granted. There are two basic sources of data on the Soviet military as a social institution: the Soviet press, and materials drawn from those who have had personal contact with the Soviet armed forces. Both sources suffer from intrinsic weakness.

The Soviet press is after all not independent, but an in-house organ. Many aspects of Soviet military manpower and military–civilian relations are shrouded in the secrecy that pervades all national security issues and receive only guarded discussion in the press. The media are routinely used to manipulate public opinion both at home and abroad. Still, the conventional wisdom that little of value can be gleaned from the press—a particularly popular view among those who lack the time or linguistic skills to exploit it properly—is false. While Soviet journalists and military journalists especially are quite obviously under instructions to emphasize the positive, once one gets past the upbeat insistence on the loyalty and valor of the glorious defenders of the motherland, the military press contains abundant evidence of social problems within the military. Although most references to such issues cheerfully assure the reader that the problem under discussion is only an isolated case, the frequency with which an issue surfaces in the military press and the attention to developing effective remedial programs provide excellent indicators of how serious and widespread a particular problem may be. Abuses of the hazing system, for example, are a recurring theme for the Ministry of Defense's "investigative reporters"—military journalists whose job is to publicize both the problems and the unhappy fate that awaits service personnel who contribute to them. The Soviet press, then, provides one method for getting inside the Soviet military.

The comments of Soviet veterans provide another. Many thousands of the émigrés who left the Soviet Union in the 1970s served in the Soviet military, primarily as conscripts. The personal reminiscences of such men constitute a valuable source of data supplementing the material drawn from Soviet written sources. Although this material has sometimes been portrayed as a realistic counterbalance to the rosy portrait painted by the Soviet military press, in fact the picture of the Soviet military that emerges from émigré evidence is not all that different from that which emerges from a careful reading of the press. Like the stories in the Soviet military press, the eyewitness accounts of former Soviet soldiers are frequently in conflict. Most émigrés seem to agree about the existence of the seniority system (which pits older soldiers against newly drafted conscripts); but they disagree on the consequences for unit solidarity. Similarly, some press accounts of the seniority system warn darkly of the threat it poses to healthy personnel relations, while others point out cheerfully that the skilled officer can exploit the system for control and socialization. Second, as noted above, many of the negative aspects of military life can be pieced together from individual incidents recounted in the military press. The most dramatic examples of corruption, cover-up, and abuses of the disciplinary regulations are found not in the memoirs of former Soviet soldiers, but on the pages of *Red Star*. In short, the two sources of data on the Soviet military supplement one another. Both are incomplete, anecdotal, and subject to predictable biases. Sifting through the mountain of sometimes contradictory evidence is a task guaranteed to instill an appreciation of the complexity of the issue. For these reasons, I have qualified my conclusions. Some of them, particularly those that rest primarily on the findings of Western social research, must remain tentative until further data are available.

This study, then, will isolate those features of the Soviet military manpower system that reflect factors unique to the Soviet system and those that derive from requirements common to armies in industrialized states. This investigation of Soviet military personnel provides a window through which we can observe the broader military system at work: how that system affects and, in turn, is affected by the economic, social, and political life of the country. It is expected that this heuristic approach will contribute both to our understanding of civil–military relations in communist systems and to our knowledge of Soviet politics.

Notes: Introduction

1 The fullest and best treatment of the Soviet armed forces, bringing together detailed data on doctrine, organization, and personalities, is the Scotts' meticulously researched text: Harriet Fast Scott and William F. Scott, *The Armed Forces of the USSR*, 2d ed. (Boulder, Colo.: Westview Press, 1981). Efforts to exploit the insights of Soviet émigrés to assess the human side of Soviet military capability include Richard Gabriel, *The New Red Legions* (Westport, Conn.: Greenwood Press, 1980); and Andrew Cockburn, *The Threat: Inside the Soviet Military Machine* (New York: Random House, 1983). Both authors would have done well to ground their use of émigré material in the basic factual data provided in the Scotts' text. The émigré literature itself is represented by two books by a former Soviet officer writing under the pseudonym of Viktor

Suvorov: *The Liberators: My Life in the Soviet Army* (New York: Norton, 1981), and *Inside the Soviet Army* (New York: Macmillan, 1983). One study that focusses exclusively on personnel is Herbert Goldhamer, *The Soviet Soldier: Soviet Military Management at the Troop Level* (New York: Crane, Russak, 1975). Goldhamer's excellent study is an evaluation of how manpower issues affect Soviet military effectiveness.

2 Edward L. Warner III, *The Military in Contemporary Soviet Politics: An Institutional Analysis* (New York: Praeger, 1978), focusses on the military's role in Soviet policy formation. Several studies discuss why the armed forces have not played an interventionist role in Soviet politics. Two which conclude that the professional military are held in check by an ever-watchful party are: Roman Kolkowicz, *The Soviet Army and the Communist Party: Institutions in Conflict* (Santa Monica, Calif.: Rand, 1966); and Michael J. Deane, *Political Control of the Soviet Armed Forces* (New York: Crane, Russak, 1977). More careful research has shown, however, that the conflictual aspects of the party–military relationship have been overemphasized: Timothy J. Colton, *Commissars, Commanders, and Civilian Authority: The Structure of Soviet Military Politics* (Cambridge, Mass.: Harvard University Press, 1979).

3 Gwyn Harries-Jenkins and Charles C. Moskos, Jr., "Trend report: armed forces and society," *Current Sociology*, vol. 29, no. 3 (Winter 1981), pp. 1–170; and George A. Kourvetaris and Betty A. Dobratz, "The present state and development of sociology of the military," *Journal of Political and Military Sociology*, vol. 4, no. 1 (Spring 1976), pp. 67–105.

1

National Defense Policymaking

In 1967 the Soviet Defense Minister (at that time Marshal Grechko) addressed the legislature (the Supreme Soviet) on a draft law on military manpower policy. The proposed legislation decreased the length of conscript service by one year, expanded basic and specialist training for predraft youth, and decreased educational deferments. The draft law that Grechko presented was the result of a long debate on military service. Opponents of the decreased service term had argued that the reduced terms would degrade military training and combat readiness. Proponents of the decrease had countered with the argument that improved educational levels of the draft pool, coupled with expanded military training programs, would offset the reduction in active duty training time.[1] The formal unveiling of the law at the Supreme Soviet marked the end of this debate. The Supreme Soviet, a rubber-stamp parliament, merely formalized a decision which had already been made elsewhere, probably at Defense Council and Politburo level. The formalization of public policy—in this case through the Supreme Soviet—is the end-product of the policy process. For military issues, the policy output is frequently the only direct evidence of the decisionmaking process. The Western observer is left to puzzle out the antecedents of the decision through indirect indicators and the few hints of policy controversy that surface in the Soviet press.

The 1967 service law and the subsequent modifications of it were political decisions, taken by political actors. In the Soviet Union, as in many other countries, defense decisions—in particular those relating to how the armed forces are manned—are closely connected with larger political and socioeconomic issues. First, many ostensibly civilian issues have direct influence on defense. Decisions on educational policy and Russian-language training, for example, have an effect on the armed forces because such programs affect the draft pool from which the majority of military manpower is drawn. Second, many programs that are designed explicitly for military purposes have a direct effect on related civilian activities. The 1980 cutback in higher education deferments, for instance, had an immediate impact on college admission policies. Third, many agencies charged with implementing military policy are

Red Army and Society

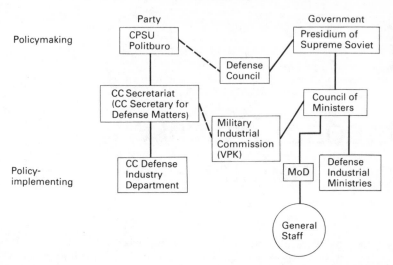

Figure 1.1 *Soviet military–political decisionmaking bodies (formal administrative bodies).*

part of the civilian government. The premilitary training course, for example, is taught in schools subordinate to the civilian educational ministries. Finally, the Ministry of Defense (MoD) itself is involved in a wide variety of adjunct programs (for example, construction, agriculture) that bring it into direct contact with civilian agencies that monitor these activities. Understanding decisions that affect military manpower requires an understanding of how defense decisionmaking fits into the larger framework of Soviet politics: who makes defense policy? How are competing military and civilian resource allocation issues resolved? What is the role of the professional military in this process?

The task of describing the top-level Soviet policy process is complicated by the fact that defense policies, and all other aspects of Soviet policymaking as well, are made and implemented through a dual party–government structure (Figure 1.1), consisting of two parallel hierarchies: the party apparatus of full-time CPSU officials and the much larger state structure of full-time government officials. These parallel networks are linked in several ways. First, key government officials (virtually all of the national and the republic-level managers and most at lower levels) are party members, subject to party directives. Second, Soviet policy is formulated in decision-making committees that have representatives from both party and government hierarchies and serve as institutional links between the two structures. Some, like the Politburo, are formally a part of the party system; others, like the Defense Council, are formally attached to the government. In general, the party leadership has the authority to formulate policy and to oversee its execution. The government's role is to ratify party policy and to implement it.

The National-Level Party Leadership

The relationship between the two components of the dual party–state structure is best described as a partnership, in which the party is the undisputed senior partner. At the apex of the dual system is the Politburo of the CPSU Central Committee—the USSR's top decisionmaking committee. The Politburo contains both full-time government officials and full-time party functionaries. At this writing, five Politburo members (including the General Secretary) are full-time party functionaries assigned to the national-level party apparatus. Four others are regional leaders. The areas currently represented are: Russian Soviet Federal Socialist Republic (RSFSR), Moscow city, Kazakhstan, and the Ukraine. Four Politburo members have full-time posts in the national-level government hierarchy: the chairman and first deputy chairman of the Council of Ministers, the head of the Committee for State Security (KGB) and the Minister of Foreign Affairs. Until Ustinov's death in December 1984, the Ministry of Defense was also represented on the Politburo. Ustinov's successor, Sergey Sokolov, is a professional military officer who, at this writing, is a candidate Polituburo member. Candidate Politburo members represent a similar mix of national-level party functionaries, national-level state officials, and leaders of important regions. This representation by key government officials on the Politburo is often referred to as the dual-hatted or interlocking nature of the Soviet leadership. This characteristic is repeated throughout the Soviet hierarchy. Key government officials at republic and local level are represented in the analogous party decisionmaking committees; and the top provincial party apparatchiks are members of key government committees.[2] These membership patterns are not necessarily institutionalized. Politburo membership, for example, depends on both institutional position and personal political power. Foreign Minister Gromyko, for instance, was named to the top Foreign Ministry position in 1957; he did not become a full Politburo member until 1973.[3]

The Politburo meets as a committee about once a week. Brezhnev reported that the Politburo met 215 times in the five-year interval between the Twenty-fourth and Twenty-fifth Party Congresses; the analogous figure for the five-year interval between the Twenty-fifth and Twenty-sixth Party Congresses was 236, or an average of forty-seven meetings a year.[4] Thanks to the post-Brezhnev decision to publish regular summaries of selected meeting topics, we know a great deal more now about the Politburo agenda than at any time since the 1920s. To be sure, the published reports are highly selective, playing down or ignoring sensitive issues and highlighting those agenda items that depict the Politburo as an effective policy body. Still, the reports do provide the best evidence to date on Politburo agendas. An analysis of the 328 specific agenda items reported between 1 December 1982 and 1 August 1984 suggests that Politburo attention is fairly evenly divided between domestic and foreign policy issues.[5] Many of the domestic issues on the published agendas involved agriculture, consumer concerns, and changes in the management system. While these topics were clearly chosen to depict the leadership as deeply involved in bread-and-butter and efficiency issues, this pattern is probably a valid reflection of larger leadership concerns in 1983–4. The published agenda reports also dramatize the overloading of the Politburo meeting schedule; an average of 4·5 separate issues are reported for each meeting and this represents (according to the reports themselves) but a small portion of the total agenda.

The Politburo sets overall policy in virtually all areas, including defense.[6] Politburo decisions can take several forms; they can be implemented as laws, as resolutions taken in the name of the party's Central Committee (CC), or as joint CC–government decrees. The Central Committee itself, however, does not normally have a great deal of decisionmaking authority. It is an unwieldy body of over 400 members and candidates that meets in plenum only several times per year; its mission is more one of mobilization and socialization than actual policymaking. Central Committee membership is, to be sure, an important measure of both an individual's personal status in the political system and the policy role of the institutions with which they are affiliated. Virtually all major officials from the party and state hierarchy have CC membership or candidate status. On the government side the single largest contingent is from the Ministry of Defense. In 1981, in addition to Ustinov (then Defense Minister), twelve deputies and first deputies, plus twenty-one chiefs of other MoD entities, were given full or candidate CC status.[7]

Although the CC itself does not normally play a major role in the policy process, the CC Secretariat and associated Central Committee staff do. The Central Committee Secretariat is a committee that meets about once a week and apparently operates much like a subcommittee of the Politburo.[8] It consists currently of ten members, headed by General Secretary Gorbachev; and its membership overlaps with that of the Politburo. Unlike the Politburo, all members of the Secretariat are full-time, Moscow-based party officials. The Secretariat's mission (as stipulated in the party statutes) is to oversee party and government appointments and to control the implementation of high-level party decrees.[9] As a collegial decisionmaking body the Secretariat's primary concerns (in addition to personnel appointments) are "ideology" (issues involving the press, culture, and education) and internal party affairs. Basic policies governing media activities within the military are probably discussed in Secretariat meetings. Most CC resolutions on the structure and functions of the military's political hierarchy, as well as those of party and Komsomol organizations within the military, are probably reviewed by the Secretariat.

The individual CC secretaries themselves perform a crucial function in Soviet policymaking that goes well beyond their role as members of the committee. Each secretary handles an informal portfolio of responsibilities. These portfolios are not identified officially and must be inferred from public activities or subsequent Soviet acknowledgements. National security issues within the Secretariat have generally been handled by one CC secretary, who concentrates on defense R&D and production. From 1965 to 1976 this portfolio was held by Marshal Dmitriy Ustinov, who later served as Minister of Defense. Ustinov may also have been involved in military matters outside the defense industry area, as well as internal security and law and order issues.

After Ustinov's 1976 appointment to head the Ministry of Defense, the defense portfolio on the Secretariat was assigned to CC secretary Yakov Ryabov. When Ryabov was demoted and assigned to Gosplan in 1979, the defense post was not filled and some of Ryabov's duties were apparently split up among the remaining secretaries. Gregory Romanov, named to the CC Secretariat in June 1983, has apparently been assigned the Secretariat defense portfolio.[10]

Supporting the CC Secretariat is a staff of perhaps several thousand full-time employees, organized on a functional basis into twenty-two departments covering all aspects of government activity.[11] Many decision drafts that are ultimately reviewed and approved by the Politburo and Secretariat are prepared by the appropriate CC department. The CC departments monitor plan fulfillment by organizations within their areas of responsibility and provide high-level assistance and intervention when necessary to meet plan commitments.[12]

Like other ministries, the MoD coordinates its activities with various entities within the CC staff. In theory, the MoD's major point of contact is the Main Political Administration (MPA).[13] In practice, the MPA, which has been integrated structurally into the MoD itself, operates less as a CC monitor over the MoD and more as a component of the MoD, specializing in educational, recreational, and other personnel-related issues. One CC department with which the MoD has close contact is the Defense Industry Department. It oversees the activities of those government organizations that develop and/or produce weapons and military equipment. Headed by Igor Dmitriyev (a schoolmate and crony of former Defense Minister Ustinov), this department is the primary CC monitor of some nine civilian defense industrial ministries (for example, Ministry of Defense Industry, Ministry of General Machinebuilding).[14] The Defense Industry Department's oversight of development and production brings its staff personnel into frequent contact with the primary consumers—those MoD officials most closely involved in weapon acquisition.

The component of the Central Committee that comes closest to being a monitor of the MoD is the Administrative Organs Department (AOD)—the MoD's primary point of contact on the CC staff. The Administrative Organs Department derives its name from Soviet legal terminology: military, security, police, and judicial entities are assigned to a category of government agencies called "administrative organs."[15] The AOD's basic mission is to oversee activities of the court system; prosecutor's office; the regular and secret police—run by the Ministry of Internal Affairs (MVD) and the Committee for State Security (KGB) respectively; the Ministry of Defense; and the defense society DOSAAF (Voluntary Organization for Cooperation with the Army, Aviation, and Fleet).[16] The AOD serves as the primary CC point of contact for most military-related issues that pass through the CC staff. For example, key personnel appointments within the MoD are screened by the AOD. One former Soviet citizen reported that proposed appointments of MPA officers to division-level political positions require an interview by AOD officials who specialize in military personnel issues.[17]

The AOD also plays a coordinating role for draft decisions on MoD issues that affect other state agencies. For example, overall policy affecting construction projects performed by military units will probably bring MoD construction and billeting officials in close contact with the CC Construction Department (which serves as the primary monitor for the USSR's construction ministries). The MoD's farms and food industry facilities must comply with overall guidance on agricultural programs—an area that is directed by the CC's Agriculture and Food Industry Department. Policy guidance affecting the military's party and Komsomol organizations is probably reviewed by the CC's Organization–Party Department. The CC Culture Department formulates general policy on recreational and cultural programs, including those in the military. Policy guidelines on press campaigns for the MoD's extensive network of journals and newspapers is reviewed by the CC Propaganda Department. The MoD's network of military commissioning schools must comply with general regulations on admission and curriculum formulated by the CC's Science and Educational Institution Department, which probably also plays a coordinating role in Ministry of Defense cooperation with the various educational ministries involved in implementing the premilitary training program. In short, the Ministry of Defense's projects have a direct impact on many civilian agencies. The overlap in responsibilities and authority between the MoD and other government entities creates a need for ongoing interaction between the MoD and its civilian counterparts. The CC staff plays an important role in mediating and controlling that interaction.

National Security Affairs: the Defense Council

The highest government body that specializes in national security issues is the Defense Council, a joint political–military committee "formed" by the Presidium of the Supreme Soviet, which also determines its composition.[18] One Soviet source describes the Council as occupying "an important place in the mechanism of state administration."[19] Another describes it as "a collegial, interoffice organ of state and administration."[20] While the Defense Council is unquestionably a state body, in practice it may operate more as a subcommittee of the Politburo, in the sense that it specializes in a subset of national security issues in the same way the CC Secretariat specializes in socialization and party affairs. The peacetime existence of a high-level policy review board to deal with defense issues has only recently been acknowledged in the Soviet military and administrative press; but Defense Council existence clearly predated the official recognition. A recent Soviet biography of late General Secretary Brezhnev indicates that he served as Defense Council chairman since 1964—suggesting that the Council has been in existence from at least the early 1960s.[21]

Since at least the mid-sixties, the party General Secretary has in practice served as chairman of the Council.[22] The Soviets do not publish an official list of other Defense Council members, but a rough estimate of probable Council members can be derived from an examination of East European analogues. Defense Council missions suggest that the Defense Minister is almost certainly a full member. Both the Romanian and Polish Defense Ministers are members of their respective defense councils; in Poland the Minister of National Defense serves as the deputy chairman of the National Defense Committee for Armed Forces Affairs and Strategic Defense Planning.[23] Legal regulations on the composition of the Romanian Defense Council suggest that Soviet Defense Council membership also includes the chairman of the Council of Ministers (currently Tikhonov), the chief of the General Staff (currently Akhromeyev), and Foreign Minister (currently Gromyko).[24] It is also reasonable to assume, given the Romanian analogue, that those CC secretaries with national security responsibilities are also members. This would include the CC secretary charged with monitoring defense industry (a post probably being filled by Romanov) and the senior CC secretary involved in foreign policy. The head of the Soviet Military–Industrial Commission (currently Smirnov) may also be a member.[25] The paucity of data precludes a more definitive assessment of the membership of the Soviet Defense Council. Until the Soviets see fit to publish an official list any Western estimate of current Council members is speculative.[26]

On the matter of Defense Council functions we have considerably more information since the Soviets have published numerous general descriptions of Defense Council missions. These comments can be amplified through an examination of the more detailed East European descriptions. According to the Soviets, the Defense Council provides top-level coordination for the defense-related activities of government bodies.[27] Defense issues implemented by government bodies and subject to coordination by the Defense Council include:[28]

(1) the review and decision of all major questions relating to maintaining the security of the country, strengthening its defensive capabilities, and developing its military potential;
(2) determination of the basic directions of and plans for military development (including military manpower procurement policy);
(3) direction and coordination of the work of the entire Soviet state apparatus, making sure that defense interests are considered in deciding all matters of state administration.

Another source indicates that "the Defense Council plays an important role in the development of the army and the fleet."[29]

These comments suggest that the Defense Council reviews both military development plans and armed forces development plans. It is necessary to summarize here what is meant by the terms military development (*voyennoye stroitel'stvo*) and armed forces development (*stroitel'stvo vooruzhennykh sil*).[30] The Soviets make a careful distinction between the kinds of responsibility embraced by these two terms and between the various party and government bodies charged with the approval or execution of the planning documents associated with each. "Military development" is the broader term. It includes economic, social–political, and purely military measures taken by a government to enhance its military power. Military development decisions define the organization and mission of the armed forces, basic command structure, and manpower procurement system.[31] As with other aspects of the five-year planning process, military development plans are based on a document embodying overall goals ("basic directions"). In the interwar period the basic guidelines for the first five-year plan for military development (involving a two-year weapons modernization program) were established by a Politburo resolution of 15 July 1929.[32] Given the contemporary Soviet descriptions of the Defense Council's role in determining "the basic directions of military development," it is likely that guidelines for contemporary five-year plans for military development are reviewed in the Defense Council.

Material on defense planning in the interwar period, as well as of contemporary basic directions for civilian five-year plans, suggests that documents embodying basic directions do not contain detailed blueprints for actual programs. Rather the guidelines are a base for the formulation of the five-year plans for military development. For instance, basic guidelines for the first five-year plan for military development identified general areas in which military technology was to be upgraded (for example, large-caliber machine guns); these goals were translated into more detailed objectives in the five-year plan for military development, which was formulated by the Red Army Staff and approved through a joint party–state resolution.[33] Given the references in contemporary Soviet descriptions of the Defense Council to its role in determining plans for military development (as well as the basic directions for those plans), it is likely that the Council also reviews the military development plan itself.

Military development plans are implemented by more detailed planning documents—the armed forces development plans. Armed forces development is a component of military development. Armed forces development includes measures relating to the organizational structure of the military, the balance between the various services and branches of services, weapons procurement, manpower procurement procedures, force deployment, and supply.[34] In the interwar period the goals of the first five-year development plan were defined in further detail by a parallel armed forces development plan, drawn up by the Red Army Staff.[35] Contemporary armed forces development plans are probably drafted in the General Staff, coordinated throughout MoD headquarters and reviewed by the Defense Council. In the interwar period the five-year armed forces development plan was implemented by service-specific development plans; individual programs required by the plan were implemented by joint party–government resolutions. For example, joint CC–Council of Ministers' resolutions were used to organize new technical military academies in the early 1930s.[36] Joint CC–Council of Ministers' resolutions were also used to authorize individual weapon systems development plans.[37] In the interwar period these service-specific development plans were approved by the Council of Labor and Defense—a body described by Soviet sources as the prototype of the contemporary Defense Council.[38] It is likely, therefore, that the contemporary Defense Council reviews service development plans as well as the most important of these implementing resolutions.

Both the historical record and contemporary Soviet descriptions of Defense Council missions, then, suggest that one of the Council's primary tasks is to review planning documents relating to defense. By analogy with the stated functions of East European councils, however, it would suggest that the Soviet Defense Council's role goes well beyond this mission. Both the East German and the Romanian councils are assigned a coordinating role with regard to security—implying that security-related activities of both the KGB and the MVD are directed by the Defense Council.[39] The statutes regulating the Czech State Defense Council specify that the Council approves the basic concept of the operational plan for the defense of the CSSR; if this pattern applies to the USSR, the basic outline for the Soviet operational plan is approved in the Defense Council.[40]

Another probable Defense Council mission is civil defense. Laws and/or regulations on the defense councils in Czechoslovakia, Romania, East Germany, and Poland all include civil defense preparations among defense council missions.[41] If this pattern holds true for the Soviet Union, it is likely that the USSR Defense Council reviews key decisions relating to civil defense. The Defense Council's probable involvement in civil defense issues is also in line with the frequent references in the Soviet press to the Council's role as a vehicle to unify the political, economic, and military leadership of the Soviet Union. This unity is an important aspect of the Soviet defense decision system that the Soviets see as an important prerequisite for effective military development. In effect, the Soviets view this concentration of authority as a way of systematizing and legitimizing the priority of military programs and military interests in all aspects of Soviet society.[42] This mechanism is especially important for those aspects of military policy that have a broad impact on the civilian sector. For example, military manpower policy requires close coordination between the MoD component responsible for premilitary training and the civilian educational system. Major issues affecting premilitary programs in the civilian schools may be reviewed by the Defense Council.

Defense Council missions also include setting general policy relating to military manpower issues. Soviet sources indicate that Defense Council functions extend to direction over those military personnel matters handled in the Main Political Administration.[43] Both the Romanian and the GDR defense councils are closely involved in military mobilization planning.[44] Assuming this pattern holds true for the Soviet Defense Council as well, another of the Council's missions is that of coordinating mobilization planning.

The Defense Council's probable involvement with civil defense and mobilization planning reflects its apparent role in directing defense and security affairs during wartime. Several of the Council's East European counterparts specify that the councils are intended to function in both peace and wartime.[45] In the Soviet case it is not clear whether the Defense Council as constituted in peacetime would provide wartime management, or if (as is more likely) both the missions and the membership will be broadened in a wartime situation. This was certainly the case in past wars. In the Civil War the wartime management function was fulfilled by the Council of Workers' and Peasants'

Defense, also known as the Defense Council, which operated from 30 November 1918 to April 1920. The mission of this civil war Defense Council, which included the Ministers of Transportation and Food Supply, was to mobilize labor and material resources for the needs of the front. During World War II this mission was filled by the State Defense Committee (GKO), formed on 30 June 1941 and headed by Stalin. Until 4 September 1945 when the GKO was disbanded, its resolutions had the force of law. The current Defense Council provides an in-place peacetime body that, the Soviets hope, will facilitate the organizational adjustments necessary in any future war, enhancing their ability to respond rapidly and effectively to a crisis situation.[46]

National-Level Government

As noted above, the dual party government policymaking and management system in the USSR involves procedures to legalize top-level party decisions. The most important and far-reaching of party policies (including military manpower policy) are embodied in laws (*zakony*) approved by the Supreme Soviet.[47] The Supreme Soviet itself is an unwieldy body of about 1,500 deputies that meets infrequently; its role is largely ceremonial and it has no real policymaking authority. The legal acts promulgated in its name, however, are very real for they are the legal enactment of key party decisions. The legal activities of the Supreme Soviet thus provide additional insight into those areas of military policy that the Soviet party leadership considers so crucial as to warrant top-level attention. Supreme Soviet ratification is required for all laws and other major decisions, including nearly all aspects of government activity—economic development, social policy, state structure, national security, and foreign policy.[48] Five-year and annual state plans and budgets, including defense expenditures, are also legalized by the Supreme Soviet. The Supreme Soviet rubber stamp is also required for matters relating to military manpower policy; both the 1967 law governing universal military service and the 1980 amendments to it were legalized through the Supreme Soviet.[49]

The Presidium of the Supreme Soviet is the Supreme Soviet's standing executive committee. Like the Supreme Soviet itself, the Presidium plays a largely symbolic role; but the legal acts that bear the Presidium's approval are important in the process by which party policy is endowed with legal authority. Defense-related questions which require Presidium ratification include:[50]

(1) formation of the Defense Council and approval of its composition;
(2) naming and removal of the high command of the armed forces in the period between Supreme Soviet sessions;
(3) declaration of war;
(4) declaration of martial law;
(5) promulgation of decrees (*ukazy*) on important questions of military development;
(6) announcement of general or partial mobilization;

(7) affirmation of other legal acts of particular importance to the armed forces.

The Presidium, like the Supreme Soviet, ratifies important policy decisions previously reviewed by the party leadership organs. In the area of military manpower policy, for example, the Presidium approved the military disciplinary regulations, the regulations on internal service, and the regulations on warrant officers.[51]

The party's military manpower decisions are implemented by an extensive administrative apparatus formally headed by the Council of Ministers.[52] The Council is again a rather unwieldy body required to meet only once per quarter. It consists of the chairman (currently senior Politburo member Tikhonov); several first deputies and deputy chairmen; the sixty-four all-union and union–republic ministers; twenty state committee chairmen; and each of the fifteen republic Council of Ministers chairmen. As a collective body the Council is clearly too large to provide flexible leadership, and its actual policymaking power is probably quite limited. However, the legal acts taken in its name (Council of Ministers resolutions and decrees) are very important, for they provide the legal authority to execute party policy.

Moreover, Tikhonov (as head of the huge government bureaucracy and a senior Politburo member) and his deputies together wield a great deal of political power and probably have much influence in determining how party policy is executed. As Council chairman Tikhonov conducts meetings of the Council and its Presidium—a sort of "inner" council that includes the Council's deputy chairmen. Tikhonov also reviews top-level personnel appointments that must be formalized by Supreme Soviet *ukaz*, although, as noted below, such appointments are also subject to Politburo or CC Secretariat approval as well. Tikhonov also coordinates the activities of his deputies and first deputies. The deputies constitute, in effect, Tikhonov's closest government advisers. Within their assigned areas they coordinate the activities of ministries and committees, oversee fulfillment of plans and other Council decrees, and review proposals and draft resolutions entered into the Council.

Council authority, as demonstrated by both its legal mission and an examination of the resolutions taken in its name, covers nearly every aspect of government activity.[53] The Council, dominated by Tikhonov and other Presidium members, directs all aspects of Soviet economic development and organizes the management of industry, construction, transportation, and communication. In the national security affairs area the Council provides overall direction for armed forces development and civil defense, and ratifies the annual number of draftees, as well as the number of predraft youth assigned to military specialist training. Also subject to Council approval are resolutions and decrees defining the legal status of various forms of military service. Other defense matters that are subject to the Council of Ministers' rubber stamp include:[54]

(1) direction of the activities of the Ministry of Defense;
(2) formation, when necessary, of committees, main administrations, and other offices to deal with matters of defense development;
(3) determination of the structure, functions, and competence of the central organs of military management;
(4) ensuring that the armed forces are equipped with "all that is necessary" for the fulfillment of their mission;
(5) ensuring that the defense needs of the state will be considered in the formulation of state plans for economic and social development and in the state budget.

The most important administrative measures affecting defense matters are embodied in joint resolutions (*sovmestnye postanovleniye*) of the CPSU Central Committee and the Council of Ministers; party decisions of lesser importance are executed by the Council of Ministers in the form of resolutions and directives.[55] These administrative channels provide the party with a legal mechanism to implement party policy. These channels are supplemented by a control and oversight network—in the case of military programs a redundant and powerful network—designed to guarantee responsiveness to policy direction.

As should be evident, these broad mission statements endow the USSR Council of Ministers with a great deal of decisionmaking authority in the Soviet system. And to the extent that one is careful to distinguish between the "rank-and-file" Council members whose authority is limited primarily to their ministry or committee and the Council leadership (Tikhonov and his closest deputies), on whom most of the real decisionmaking authority devolves, the image conveyed by an analysis of the Council's legal mission and activities is a fairly realistic one. Nor is the influence of the Council leadership limited to civilian issues. Tikhonov, as Council chairman, is probably a Defense Council member. Because defense policy touches so many aspects of the civilian economy and society, close cooperation between government agencies involved primarily in national security affairs (the Ministry of Defense and defense industrial ministries) is absolutely essential. The Council of Ministers leadership is well placed to play a mediating role in the relationship between military and civilian agencies. However, any discussion of the Council's role in the defense policy process would be incomplete without a reminder that it operates in close accord with and subordinate to the top-level party leadership bodies, in particular the Politburo and the CC Secretariat.

Managing the Armed Forces: the Ministry of Defense

Direct management of the Soviet armed forces is the responsibility of the Ministry of Defense. Because the Soviet Ministry of Defense (MoD) is an integral part of a larger government hierarchy, it is helpful to examine how it compares with other Soviet ministries. The Soviets administer all aspects of their economy, as well as social welfare and administrative functions, through a ministerial system. The most highly centralized of Soviet ministries are "all-union" ministries, headquartered in Moscow. The MoD is an all-union ministry. Such ministries manage their assigned sector through "field offices" (factories, in the case of an industrial ministry; military units, in the case of the MoD), which are linked to the Moscow ministry through a direct chain of command. In addition to the MoD, many of the heavy-industry sectors—such as machinebuilding, the defense industry, three out of the four major types of transport, and several of the construction ministries specializing in rail and energy facilities—fall into this most highly centralized category of all-union ministries.

Union–republic ministries represent an intermediate level of centralization. Most of their enterprises are administered through the republic governments and answer to republic ministries that are subordinate both to the republic Council of Ministers and the parent ministry in Moscow. The Ministry of Light Industry and the Ministry of the Food Industry are examples of union–republic ministries. The most decentralized functions are run through republic ministries. These ministries have no parent ministry in Moscow and administer their field offices either directly or through analogous directorates and departments at regional level that are subordinate to both the local government and the parent ministry at republic level. The Ministry of Local Industry and the Ministry of Inland Waterways are examples of sectors administered in this fashion.

These three major types of ministry provide the Soviet system with varying degrees of administrative centralization. A ministry's legal status provides an important clue as to how centralized its management activities are. The MoD's administrative status as an all-union ministry, the most highly centralized of the USSR's management systems, is a reflection of the high level of attention accorded high-priority sectors. It also has an important effect on how the MoD relates to the republic and regional governments that help it procure manpower. Constitutional recognition of the MoD's all-union nature is of fairly recent vintage. Until 1978 the MoD retained its formal legal status as a union–republic ministry. In fact none of the republics had a republic Ministry of Defense, and the MoD operated as a highly centralized all-union ministry. The 1978 change was thus a legal recognition of administrative reality.

Like its civilian counterparts, the MoD is a product of frequent reorganization. The current military management arrangement—one centralized ministry in charge of all five services—is but one of a long series of organizational arrangements. The MoD's bureaucratic progenitor, the Commissariat for Military Affairs, was organized in late 1917; but by early 1918 it was split into two independent organizations, one for military affairs, and one for naval affairs.[56] By 1923 the two bodies were unified again into a Commissariat of Military and Naval Affairs.[57] In 1934 this organization was reorganized into the Commissariat of Defense; but naval matters once again came under separate administration with the establishment of the Commissariat of the Navy in 1937.[58] This division of authority lasted until after World War II. In 1946 the two organizations were collapsed into a unified Commissariat for the Armed Forces (later the Ministry of the Armed Forces).[59] In the early 1950s the navy once again enjoyed a brief period of organizational autonomy with the formation of two separate ministries, the Ministry of War and the Ministry of the Navy. By March 1953, however, the two ministries were once again combined into a unified Ministry of Defense, the organizational arrangement that survives today.[60] Given the frequency of previous reorganizations, nearly three decades of a unified MoD is something of a feat of bureaucratic continuity. Centralizing the control and management of all five armed services in one ministry has the advantage of facilitating uniform manpower and training programs. Given the MoD's history of organizational change, however, a future split along service lines into separate military ministries cannot totally be ruled out.

The MoD serves as the executive agency for basic policies forged elsewhere. It is not an autonomous actor in the Soviet policy process. Like other ministries, it is the repository of much of the data and expertise upon which the high-level decisions are based. Ministry of Defense officials are thus conveniently placed to exert a strong influence on Politburo and Defense Council leaders. The MoD's legal mission is to direct armed forces development. It is charged with implementing CPSU military policy and Soviet military doctrine for all services.[61] The MoD's official responsibilities include:[62]

(1) active participation in defense planning, including the formulation of plans for the development of the armed forces, operational plans, and mobilization plans;

(2) direction of military R&D:
    (*a*) improvement of weapons and military equipment, planning the supply of armaments, military equipment, and other materials;
    (*b*) leadership of military science (a respected academic field in the USSR), military research and development, and interservice planning;
    (*c*) organization of scientific–technical information;
    (*d*) ensuring the introduction of technological advances into military R&D;
    (*e*) managing the military attaché system;

(3) direction of military manpower matters:
    (*a*) directing operational, combat, and political training;
    (*b*) maintaining a high level of combat readiness;
    (*c*) direction of premilitary and specialist training;
    (*d*) planning and staffing of military units;
    (*e*) organization of the regular, semi-annual draft.

Note that the Ministry of Defense is charged with compiling "armed forces development plans"—that is, those components of military development that pertain specifically to the military itself. The approval authority for armed forces development plans is probably, as suggested above, reserved by the Defense Council.

Aiding the Defense Minister in preparing armed forces development plans is the MoD Collegium, an advisory committee analogous to those in nonmilitary ministries. The contemporary MoD Collegium is the twentieth-century counterpart of the tsarist Military Council, formed in 1832.[63] The current MoD Collegium is described by the Soviets as "a consultative organ of the Ministry of Defense that works out solutions to problems relating to the development of the armed forces, their combat and mobilization readiness, the status of combat and political training, selection, placement, and indoctrination of military personnel, and other important issues."[64] Collegium membership includes the deputy ministers of defense and the Chief of the Main Political Administration.[65] The three first deputy ministers (Petrov; General Staff Chief Akhromeyev; and Warsaw Pact Commander Kulikov) probably play key roles in Collegium deliberations. The MoD Collegium makes decisions on the basis of the "principle of collegiality" but its decisions are implemented by orders (*prikazy*) of the Minister of Defense, who serves as the chairman.

The MoD Collegium is clearly meant to play a key role in management decisions relating to manpower procurement and personnel issues. Data limitations preclude an assessment of how closely the Collegium in practice fits the theoretical model of collective decisionmaking presented in the Soviet military press. However, information on the role played by collegia in civilian ministries indicates that many of these bodies have evolved from the important, but chiefly advisory, role assigned them in legal statute into real decision-making bodies.[66] If such a trend applies to the MoD Collegium, then it is likely that all important manpower issues, ranging from training programs to the most efficient response to changes in the size of the 18-year-old male draft pool, are placed before it for discussion. Almost every decision that significantly impinges on nonmilitary ministries, however, will be reviewed by higher-level government and party bodies. This is particularly true of manpower procurement issues, which inevitably affect the laborforce as a whole.

Primary responsibility for implementing manning policy falls to the Ministry of Defense.[67] The MoD's manpower-related responsibilities include planning manpower acquisition, directing basic and specialist premilitary training, setting up procedures for military registration, organizing the semi-annual intake of conscripts, and managing the network of officer commissioning schools.[68] To discharge these responsibilities the MoD, like other national-level ministries, has an extensive headquarters component (Figure 1.2). It consists of the command headquarters for each of the five services (strategic rocket forces, ground, air defense, air, and navy), plus a number of functional directorates each specializing in a particular subset of MoD responsibilities. Unlike most civilian ministries, however, the Ministry of Defense has an additional overlay of staff to consolidate and coordinate activities of the directorate—the General Staff.[69] The Soviet General Staff is not directly comparable to its nearest U.S. counterpart, the Joint Chiefs of Staff. It serves rather as an extended personal staff of the Defense Minister, providing a focal

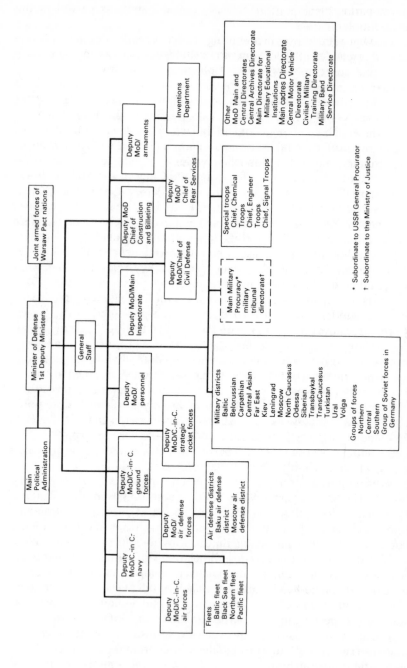

Figure 1.2 *The Ministry of Defense administrative structure.*

Main Political Administration

Minister of Defense 1st Deputy Ministers

Joint armed forces of Warsaw Pact nations

General Staff

Deputy MoD/Main Inspectorate

Deputy MoD Chief of Construction and Billeting

Deputy MoD/ armaments

Inventions Department

Deputy MoD/ personnel

Deputy MoD/Chief of Civil Defense

Deputy MoD/ Chief of Rear Services

Deputy MoD/C.-in-C. strategic rocket forces

Deputy MoD/C.-in-C. ground forces

Deputy MoD/ air defense forces

Deputy MoD/C.-in C.- navy

Deputy MoD/C.-in-C. air forces

Main Military Procuracy*
military tribunal directorate†

Special troops
Chief, Chemical Troops
Chief, Engineer Troops
Chief, Signal Troops

Other
MoD Main and Central Directorates
Central Archives Directorate
Main Directorate for Military Educational Institutions
Main cadres Directorate
Central Motor Vehicle Directorate
Civilian Military Training Directorate
Military Band Service Directorate

Military districts
Baltic
Belorussian
Carpathian
Central Asian
Far East
Kiev
Leningrad
Moscow
North Caucasus
Odessa
Siberian
Transbaykal
TransCaucasus
Turkistan
Ural
Volga

Groups of forces
Northern
Central
Southern
Group of Soviet forces in Germany

Air defense districts
Baku air defense district
Moscow air defense district

Fleets
Baltic fleet
Black Sea fleet
Northern fleet
Pacific fleet

* Subordinate to USSR General Procurator
† Subordinate to the Ministry of Justice

point for the various headquarters, service, and military district organizations involved in implementing Soviet military manning policy.[70] The General Staff's manpower-related responsibilities include directing measures to ensure high levels of combat readiness, managing the military commissariat network, and guiding and overseeing the military mobilization system.[71]

The General Staff provides overall guidance to several key agencies within the MoD's Moscow headquarters that are concerned with personnel. The Civilian Military Training Directorate is responsible for coordinating activities relating to the four major aspects of civilian or paramilitary training (*vnevoyskovaya podgotovka*): initial military training for predraft and draft-age youth, premilitary specialist training, reserve officer training at colleges and specialized secondary schools, and periodic reserve training. For example, the Civilian Military Training Directorate, together with relevant components of other "interested" ministries and offices (for example, the Military Training Directorate of the Ministry of Education), prepares teaching aids and syllabuses for the initial military training program.[72] Cadre matters within the MoD are the responsibility of the Main Cadres Directorate.[73] This organization handles career military personnel only. Its mission includes the analysis of political–moral and practical characteristics of career military personnel; determination of requirements for commissioned officers, warrant officers, and career enlisted personnel; and personnel recruitment and recordkeeping. Officer commissioning schools, however, are managed not by the Main Cadres Directorate, but by the Main Directorate for Military Educational Institutions.[74] This organization provides oversight of the officer commissioning school system, formulates proposals on training and methodological work, and prepares scientific and pedagogical personnel. It does not, however, have direct line management over the nearly 150 officer commissioning schools in the Soviet Union. Service, branch of service, or functional administration chiefs provide direct administrative guidance for schools that serve their component. Officer commissioning schools must also follow the directives of the Ministry of Higher and Specialized Secondary Education for training and methodological matters.[75]

Many aspects of manpower management for both careerists and conscripts are carried out by the Main Political Directorate (MPA), an organization that is part of the Ministry of Defense, but which carries the legal authority of a department of the CPSU Central Committee.[76] The MPA's basic charter is "party political work," but this term carries a far broader meaning than party oversight or control. As detailed in Chapter 5, the MPA is the main organization concerned with personnel issues in the military. It is responsible for directing political socialization, maintaining high morale and discipline, administering cultural and recreational programs, and managing the military's party and Komsomol organizations.

Ministries in the Soviet Union run their "field offices" in one of two ways. Most industrial ministries are organized along "sectoral" lines; that is, the directorate within Moscow headquarters supervising chemical fiber production would monitor five or ten fiber production associations scattered around the

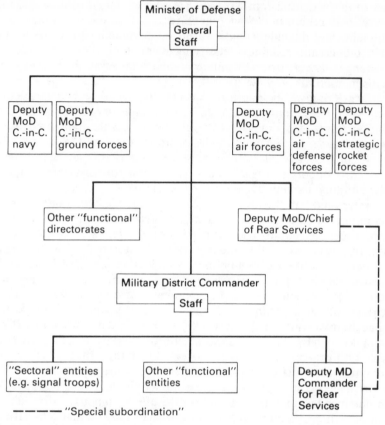

Figure 1.3 *"Special subordination" in the Ministry of Defense.*

Soviet Union. By contrast, the Ministry of Defense and several other ministries (for example, Railways) run most of their "field offices" through a territorial administration. Below the Ministry of Defense headquarters in Moscow troop units and other elements subordinate to the MoD are administered territorially through the military district (MD) system. The rationale for adopting this form of territorial arrangement must be sought in the tsarist past.[77] Until 1862 there were essentially no local military administrative entities in the contemporary sense of the word. Several of the War Ministry's departments had regional representatives; and the individual field units were forced to negotiate with each of them to satisfy their needs for food, clothing, and weapons. In 1862 the War Ministry initiated a reform in military administration designed to reduce the overcentralization at ministry headquarters by creating territorial administrators. The responsibility for troop supply and administrative control of troop units was delegated to a military district administration, with the national-level War Ministry retaining the responsibility of direction and control over MD administration. The powers of the district commander were roughly analogous to those of the War Minister. Like the War Minister, the district commander had a staff and a military district council, which consisted of his deputy, the chief of staff, and the chiefs of the various departments that comprised the district administration (that is, artillery, engineering, medical). The MD council had the right to discuss and prepare draft decisions on all "economic" questions relating to troop life.

The tsarist MDs were abolished in January 1918 but resurrected again in March of that year with the creation of the first Soviet MD in Petrograd.[78] The MD organization, with some modifications of the tsarist model, has existed ever since. Each of the sixteen current military districts (as well as each of the groups of forces operating outside the USSR and the four naval fleets) is organized as a microcosm of the MoD itself, with line entities (troop units and schools) and functional entities (personnel directorate, billeting directorate) directly subordinate to the military district commander but having a "special subordination" relationship with the analogous component at MoD head-quarters in Moscow. For example, the deputy commander of a military district for rear services has an immediate supervisor (the district commander), but for matters pertaining to service and support, he must follow the guidelines and procedures laid down by the Deputy Defense Minister for rear services (see Figure 1.3). This arrangement is a variation on dual subordination—a device used extensively throughout the civilian administration. The main functions served by the military district in regard to military manpower are training (both military and political) and mobilization. The MD staff has an organization–mobilization section, which supervises the mobilization activities of the military commissariats, with overall direction from the Soviet General Staff.[79] The MD's training responsibilities are under the general direction of the MD deputy commander for combat training and deputy commander for military–educational affairs, with political training and cultural and recreational work directed by the MD's MPA representative; the deputy commander for political affairs and his staff.

The contemporary Soviet military district retains two tsarist institutions—the MD staff (which is the MD analogue to the General Staff) and the MD council (which is the MD analogue to the MoD Collegium). Military Council membership includes the MD commander (who serves as council chairman), the MD Chief of Staff, the first deputy commander, the deputy MD commander for political affairs, and the senior regional party official in the area. Nominees for membership in each council are chosen by the MoD and MPA and approved by the CPSU Central Committee.[80] The mission of contemporary MD councils is broader than that of their tsarist counterparts and includes "all important questions" of the life and activities of the MD troops. The councils' mission covers both manpower and materiel.[81] It includes ensuring a high level of combat and mobilization readiness, high-quality combat and political training, strict military discipline, and high morale. The council also oversees matters relating to premilitary training, reserve training, and periodic call-ups of conscripts; and are responsible for introducing new weapons and equipment into the district units, and ensuring materiel technical supply. The military councils are—in practice and in law—decisionmaking, not advisory, bodies. The 1958 resolution states unequivocally: "military councils have the right to examine and decide all important questions of the life and activities of the army and fleet, and are responsible before the Central Committee, government, and MoD for the condition and combat readiness of the troops."[82] Military council decisions are implemented through orders of the MD commander. If a military council member disagrees with a council decision, he has the right to report his opinion to the CC, government, and MoD.

The military district also provides guidance to the military commissariats within its territory.[83] The Soviet military commissariat system occupies an intermediate position between the MoD hierarchy and the local government structure. The commissariat system is based on the existing administrative–territorial divisions, with military commissariats at republic, kray, oblast, autonomous republic, national okrug, city, and rayon levels. Directed by both the General Staff and the relevant military district commander, the military commissariats are responsible for maintaining a manpower registry, administering the semi-annual call-up of draft-age males into active duty service, and executing military mobilization. The military commissariat registers draft-age personnel, manages premilitary training programs, and administers predraft physical examinations. In the event of war or emergency the military commissariat system is responsible for implementing call-up orders for military mobilization. The military commissariat's responsibilities go well beyond that of a draft board and training agency. It is also the local point of contact for recruitment of candidates to officer commissioning schools. Administration of service pensions and allowances, including those of civilian MoD employees, are also handled here. The commissariat network is also responsible for providing assistance to retired officers and to families of servicemen (both conscript and career).

The military district administration also manages the MoD's extensive system of employee services. The Soviet military's high level of involvement in employee services stems in part from the nature of military service itself. Most large employers in the industrialized West are involved to some degree in providing social services to their employees, but military organizations typically carry this involvement much further. The Ministry of Defense's higher level of involvement in employee services also reflects the active role which all Soviet ministries play in providing worker services. Soviet factories build day-care centers and apartment buildings, run cafeterias and stores, and provide a wide range of welfare and recreational services. In the Ministry of Defense this pattern approaches organizational self-sufficiency.

The Ministry of Defense, for example, runs its own commercial establishment. Most state retail stores in the Soviet Union are part of the Ministry of Trade system, but there are also "branch" trade networks—retail systems that are part of other ministries. Ministries that have their own retail network, like the Ministry of Railways and the Ministry of the Coal Industry, maintain these systems to serve employees who live far from large population centers.[84] One of the most extensive of these networks is Voyentorg, the Ministry of Defense's retail trade system. Military personnel can shop in any one of a large number of MoD-run enterprises—laundries, barber shops, shoe repair stores, restaurants, book stores, and department stores.[85] Until 1956 these facilities were administered through the civilian Ministry of Trade, but they are now organic to the military district's Trade Directorate, subordinate to the deputy MD commander for rear services. Although current figures with respect to the trade turnover of this system are not available, historical data pertaining to commodity circulation suggest that the Voyentorg system is extensive. In 1955, for example, retail·commodity circulation was worth 12·5 billion rubles or approximately 2·3 percent of total reported USSR retail trade turnover for that year.[86]

The MoD also has its own food supply system, which includes organizations involved not only in the procurement, storage, distribution, and processing of food commodities, but agricultural production as well. The Central Food Directorate and its corresponding services at MD level produce much of the food required by the military through an extensive network of military agricultural enterprises. The Directorate and many of the food supply departments at military district level (which are subordinate again to the deputy MD commander for rear services) have an undetermined number of subsidiary farms (that is, farms that are attached directly to military units), greenhouses, dairies, warehouses, bakeries, and food processing facilities.[87]

Barracks, classrooms, dining halls, and officer housing are also built and maintained by elements organic to the MoD.[88] At the military district level these facilities are supervised by the deputy MD commander for construction and billeting. The MD construction directorate does the actual construction of military housing, training, and support structures. The billeting and maintenance directorate provides for services, handles upkeep and maintenance, and obtains appropriate sites for military towns, camps, and shooting ranges. These activities probably bring the construction and billeting directorates in close contact with local government authorities, who are responsible for land use.

Cultural and recreational programs for military district servicemen are also provided primarily through internal organizations, specifically by the Main Political Administration (MPA). At MD level cultural and recreational facilities are managed by the cultural instructors of the MD's political directorate. The network of recreational organizations handled by this directorate includes officers' clubs, unit clubs, and military school clubs.[89] The political directorate also operates a variety of on-post facilities (libraries, movie-houses, theatres) for servicemen and family members and MoD civilian personnel. The MoD (through the Central Military Tourism Department) also operates its own travel agency and vacation service. There are over two dozen MoD and military district-managed tourist bases (essentially resort villages) that serve Soviet officers, warrant officers, MoD civilian personnel and family members.[90] During the 1970s over 1·7 million "army and fleet tourists" spent their holidays in such facilities.[91] The MoD also has sports facilities (administered through the Central Army Sports Club), hunting and fishing camps (managed by the All-Army Military Hunting Society), and sanitariums and rest homes (administered by the Central Military–Medical Directorate).[92]

Health care for service personnel is also handled internally. Most Soviet health care facilities—hospitals, clinics, and drugstores—are part of the Ministry of Health network; but there are also "branch" health systems, each administered by the ministry to which it is attached. For example, the Ministry of Railways has its own health care network, so does the Ministry of Civil Aviation.[93] Like many military organizations, the Soviet military also has its own medical system, managed by the Central Military–Medical Directorate, which is again subordinate to the chief of rear services.[94] At military district level medical services are administered through the MD Military Medical Department. Military district facilities include district and garrison military hospitals, polyclinics, sanitariums, and laboratories.

The MoD's involvement in a variety of subsidiary/support activities reinforces the participation of Ministry of Defense officials in the overall policy process. One might argue, of course, that the existence of an organic system of services logically ought to decrease MoD dependence on civilian agencies. In the Soviet context, however, overall policies on civilian activities like agriculture and health care apply as well to the MoD. For example, general policy guidelines affecting agriculture apply to both MoD and Ministry of Agriculture farms. Similarly, national health policies are implemented in the "branch" medical networks as well as the Ministry of Health. The Ministry of Health has regulatory control over the MoD's health care system. In short, the Ministry of Defense's participation in service and support activities requires a close working relationship between defense and nondefense officials.

Defense Policy and Soviet Politics

As noted above, military policy (and all other facets of basic policymaking) is approved by the party leadership and implemented by agencies in the government hierarchy, in particular the Ministry of Defense. The party has four basic institutional mechanisms for controlling agencies in the state administrative hierarchy, including the MoD.[95] First, the CPSU leadership provides formal instructions and directives to the government apparatus. At the national level instructions addressed to an individual ministry, republic, or local government office usually take the form of a CC resolution. Instructions embodying general goals are more often formalized through CPSU congress or plenum resolutions. Key laws formalized through the Supreme Soviet are reviewed first by the party leadership, which issues a resolution recommending submission of the draft law to the Supreme Soviet. This procedure is used to formalize both the five-year and annual state plan.

A second mechanism institutionalizing the party's domination of the state apparatus is the use of joint Party–government resolutions. The most important administrative actions taken to implement party policy are executed by joint CC–Council of Ministers resolutions. Fifteen of the 183 Council of

Ministers resolutions listed in the 1979 collection of such resolutions are joint party–Council of Ministers resolutions.[96] These tend to be primarily of a policy-setting nature. For example, the 12 July 1979 resolution laying out new planning procedures was a joint CC–Council of Ministers resolution. This procedure, through which the party has institutionalized its participation in lawmaking and administration, is replicated throughout the bureaucracy.

The third vehicle for party control of the government is its control of key administrative appointments. The power to hire and fire both military and civilian officials is seen as crucial for ensuring close congruence between party goals and official behavior. Each party committee has its own "nomenklatura," a list of positions over which that committee exercises authority to approve and disapprove personnel appointments. We do not know exactly which posts are within the nomenklatura of which party organizations. It seems clear, however, that all high-level appointments that require formalization through Supreme Soviet decrees or Council of Ministers resolutions are probably reviewed at Politburo/CC Secretariat level. Appointments of military officials are apparently reviewed within the military's Main Political Administration, with the high-level MoD posts almost certainly reserved for CC Secretariat or Politburo approval. A fourth mechanism for party influence over government bodies is the network of party organizations within every government bureaucracy. Because each party organization is held responsible for the compliance of the government organizations under its purview, party elements in both military and civilian organizations have a strong practical incentive to make sure that administrative behavior conforms to party leadership intentions.

This examination of the military policy process has highlighted the extent to which military policymaking and implementation are inextricably linked to the overall Soviet policy process of which it is a part. The handful of Soviets who occupy the apex of the political hierarchy govern a diverse and complex society. They could not possibly oversee all aspects of the policy process, nor do they necessarily desire to be involved to an equal degree in all sectors of government. Some activities are best carried out by local officials, with only the most general guidance from the national-level leadership. On the other hand, some areas are so important as to demand close national-level attention. The Soviet political system is characterized by different degrees of centralization at different levels of administration, a feature which enables the leadership to concentrate attention and resources on areas of greatest interest. National security affairs is one such area. The importance of defense issues to the leadership is reflected in the institutional arrangements supporting military policymaking. One reflection of the high priority of national security is the USSR Defense Council, which provides a mechanism for ensuring that non-military agencies are responsive to military needs. Another is the extent to which top-level decisionmakers become involved in the detail of defense decisions. The military management system inside the MoD itself reflects the most centralized of the Soviet management arrangements. The MoD, as an all-union ministry, operates in a far more centralized fashion than either union–republic or republic ministries. The system of making and implementing military policy, then, is firmly embedded in the overall policy process, but it clearly occupies the more centralized end of the USSR's management continuum.

Like the nonmilitary policy process, the military policy process involves varying levels of centralization, depending on the stage of the decisionmaking process. As in the civilian arena, the number of organizational participants tends to be much greater and the role of professional expertise more significant in the agenda-building, option-forming and implementing stages. The officer corps' dominance of the USSR's community of strategic experts provides career military professionals with important opportunities to influence the process of policy formulation. The professional military is also closely involved in the implementation of defense policies. In sum, the role of the military professional in the defense policy process is an important one, but neither the officer corps nor the MoD itself are autonomous actors in that process.

Another characteristic that the military policy process shares with the overall Soviet policy process is the importance of decisionmaking by committee. Major policy issues at MoD level are discussed in the MoD Collegium. In the MoD's second-tier territorial bodies (the military districts) this collegial decisionmaking function is performed by the district military council. Collegial decisionmaking in both the military and civilian hierarchies represents a check on capricious managers and a way of institutionalizing broad participation by those who will be called upon to carry out policy. Many Western observers of the Soviet scene have drawn attention to the role of consensual decisionmaking and its impact on the outcome of decisions. It is important to remember that this decisionmaking style has been institutionalized and formalized in committee functions at many different levels of the Soviet "super-bureaucracy." It is as much a part of peacetime military management as it is of civilian policy-making.

As with civilian policymaking, national security decisions are formulated and implemented within a dual party–government system in which the government organizations play the role of junior partner. However, the MoD's political arrangements (reflecting its special mission) are somewhat different from those of the civilian ministries. Party organizations in most civilian agencies are subordinate to a territorial party hierarchy that follows the federal system with party bodies paralleling the government structure from rayon to national level. Unlike most civilian government organizations, the MoD's party organizations report up the same command chain as the military hierarchy itself. Moreover, the MoD's party organizations are administered by officials from the Main Political Administration, the military's full-time political workers. These differences, as will be detailed in Chapter 5, mean that party–military relations within the MoD are somewhat different from those of a civilian ministry. However, the relationship between party and nonparty management bodies, either in the MoD or in nonmilitary ministries, appear to be far more harmonious than is often depicted in the West. The political officer and his commander, like the factory party secretary and the plant director, are linked together by a broad network of shared interests and concerns that help to mute institutional antagonisms between them.

This survey of the Soviet military policy process suggests that the decisions the Soviet leaders make in the coming decades (as the military comes into increasing competition with the civilian sector for trained manpower) will not be made exclusively by the military leadership. Rather the policy choices will be reviewed and approved by the highest level of the political leadership. These choices, moreover, will almost certainly be compatible with the kinds of domestic and foreign missions the party leadership has assigned to the armed forces—missions that go far to explain why the Soviet military manning system works as it does and how it will likely be modified to accommodate changes in demographic and economic reality.

Notes: Chapter 1

1 A. A. Grechko, "On draft legislation on universal military service," report to Supreme Soviet, 12 October 1967, in *Zakon SSSR o vseobshchey voinskoy obyazannosti* (Moscow: Voyenizdat, 1967), pp. 31–48; and L. S. Pobezhimov and P. Romanov, "New universal law on military service," *Voyennaya mysl'*, no. 1 (1968).

2 *Yezhegodnik bol'shoy sovetskoy entsiklopedii, 1983* (Moscow: Sovetskaya Entsiklopediya, 1983), pp. 94–5, 100, 104–5, 109–10, 115–16, 121, 125, 130, 134, 162, 167, 171, 177–8, 185.

3 "Gromyko, Andrey Andreyevich," *Sovetskaya voyennaya entsiklopediya* (Moscow: Voyeniz- dat, 1977), Vol. 3, pp. 57–8 (hereafter cited as *SVE*).

4 L. I. Brezhnev, "Report of the Central Committee CPSU and the immediate tasks of the party in the areas of internal and external policy," 24 February 1976, in *Spravochnik partiynogo rabotnika* (Moscow: Politizdat, 1976), Vol. 16, pp. 5–88 (Politburo meetings are discussed on p. 66); and L. I. Brezhnev, "Report of the Central Committee CPSU to the 26th CPSU Congress and immediate tasks in the areas of internal and external policy," in *XXVI s"ezd kommunisticheskoy partii sovetskogo soyuza. Stenograficheskiy otchet* (Moscow: Politizdat, 1983), Vol. 1, pp. 20–99 (Politburo meetings are discussed on p. 88). See also *Kratkiy slovar'-spravochnik agitatora i politinformatora* (Moscow: Politizdat, 1984), p. 50.

5 The meeting reports for 1982 are found in *Pravda*, 11 and 17 December 1982; for 1983, the meeting reports are found in *Pravda*, 1, 15, 21, 29 January; 4, 13, 18, 25 February; 4, 11, 25 March; 2, 9, 15, 22, 30 April; 14, 20, 27 May; 11, 25 June; 1, 9, 16, 30 July; 6, 13, 20, 27 August; 3, 10, 17, 24 September; 1, 8, 15, 22, 29 October; 5, 12, 19, 26 November; 3, 10, 17, 24 December 1983; for 1984, the meeting reports are found in *Pravda*, 7, 14, 21, 28 January; 4, 25 February; 2, 8, 23, 31 March; 6, 20, 27 April; 4, 11, 18, 24 May; 1, 8, 19, 29 June; 6, 13, 20, 29 July 1984. All reports are located on the first page.

6 On the Politburo's role in defense policy see A. A. Yepishev, *KPSS i voyennoye stroitel'stvo* (Moscow: Voyenizdat, 1982), pp. 35–6; B. S. Tel'pukhovskiy, *KPSS vo glave stroitel'stva vooruzhennykh sil SSSR* (Moscow: Voyenizdat, 1983), p. 244; and M. G. Sobolev (ed.), *Partiyno-politicheskaya rabota v sovetskikh vooruzhennykh silakh* (Moscow: Voyenizdat, 1974), p. 103. See also A. A. Yepishev, "Voyennaya politika KPSS," *SVE*, Vol. 2, pp. 191–3; Ye. Nikitin and B. Kanevskiy, "Problems of defense capability and the combat readiness of the Soviet armed forces in CPSU military policy," *Voyenno-istoricheskiy zhurnal* (hereafter cited as *VIZh*), no. 9 (1978), pp. 3–10; P. Yefimov, "The Communist Party—organizer of the defense of the USSR," *VIZh*, no. 11 (1972), pp. 3–11; B. Kanevskiy, "Leninist ideas in CPSU military policy," *Krasnaya zvezda* (hereafter cited as *KZ*), 20 January 1979, pp. 2–3; *SVE*, Vol. 3, p. 225; N. Lomov and S. Alfirov, "To the question of Soviet military doctrine," *VIZh*, no. 7 (1978), pp. 21–30; and G. Sredin, "The bases of Soviet military development," *VIZh*, no. 2 (1978), pp. 3–15.

7 Institutional affiliations of CC members and candidates were compiled in National Foreign Assessment Center, *CPSU Central Committee and Central Auditing Commission. Members Elected at the 26th Party Congress*, CR 81–11349, May 1981.

8 Between the Twenty-fourth and Twenty-fifth Party Congresses the Secretariat is reported to have met 205 times or a little less than once a week. The analogous figure for the period between

the Twenty-fifth and Twenty-sixth Party Congresses was 250. See material cited in n. 4. On the Secretariat's role in preparing issues for Politburo review see "Politbyuro TsK KPSS," *Sovetskiy entsiklopedicheskiy slovar'* (Moscow: Sovetskaya Entsiklopediya, 1983), p. 1026.

9 *Ustav kommunisticheskoy partii sovetskogo soyuza* (Moscow: Politizdat, 1977), p. 65.

10 On Ustinov's defense responsibilities on the CC see "Dmitriy Fedorovich Ustinov," *SVE*, Vol. 8, pp. 227–8. Romanov's involvement in defense and security issues is indicated by his pattern of public activities: *Izvestiya*, 19 February 1984, p. 3; 11 March 1984, p. 4; 7 July 1984, p. 2; *Kazakhstanskaya pravda*, 22 February 1984, p. 3; *Leningradskaya pravda*, 20 April 1984, p. 2; *KZ*, 7 May 1983, p. 5; *Pravda*, 11 July 1984, p. 6, *Izvestiya*, 21 December 1984, p. 3; 12 August 1984, p. 1; 20 January 1985, p. 2; *Pravda* 24 December 1984, p. 1; *Krasnaya Zvezda*, 11 Dec. 1984, p. 3.

11 Jerry F. Hough and Merle Fainsod, *How the Soviet Union Is Governed* (Cambridge Mass.: Harvard University Press, 1979), pp. 411–17.

12 N. A. Petrovichev *et al.*, *Partiynoye stroitel'stvo. Uchebnoy posobiye* (Moscow: Politizdat, 1981), pp. 190–2.

13 "Glavnoye politicheskoye upravleniye," *Voyennyy entsiklopedicheskiy slovar'* (Moscow: Voyenizdat, 1983), p. 195 (hereafter cited as *VES*).

14 See "Dmitriyev, Igor Fedrovich," *Yezhegodnik bol'shoy sovetskoy entsiklopedii 1981* (Moscow: Izdatel'stvo Sovetskaya Entsiklopediya, 1981), p. 575, and "Ustinov, Dmitriy Federovich," ibid., p. 605; and "Ustinov, Dmitriy Fedrovich," *VES*, p. 769.

15 Yu. M. Kozlov *et al.* (eds.), *Upravleniye v oblasti administrativno-politicheskoy deyatel'nosti* (Moscow: Yuridicheskaya Literatura, 1979), pp. 5–16.

16 This analysis of the AOD's role is based on an examination of the public activities of key AOD officials. On AOD association with the justice system see, for example, *Izvestiya*, 9 July 1983, p. 3; *Kazakhstanskaya Pravda*, 20 December 1984, p. 3; and *Pravda*, 20 April 1984, p. 3. On AOD association with the procuracy see *Leningradskaya Pravda*, 30 June 1983, p. 3; *Izvestiya*, 16 July 1983, p. 2, and 6 October 1983, p. 3. On AOD association with DOSAAF see *KZ*, 22 July 1983. On AOD association with the KGB see *KZ*, 28 May 1983; *Kazakhstanskaya Pravda*, 29 January 1985, p. 1; 13 December 1984, p. 2; *Izvestiya*, 16 November 1984, p. 3; *Krasnaya Zvezda*, 30 June 1984, p. 2. On AOD association with the MoD's military forces see *KZ*, 29 July 1983, p. 1, and 20 August 1983, p. 1; and 30 October 1983, p. 1; *Krasnaya Zvezda*, 18 August 1984, p. 1; 25 December 1984, p. 3; 18 January 1985, p. 3; 25 January 1985, p. 3. On AOD association with the MVD see *Pravda*, 11 November 1983, p. 2, and *Izvestiya*, 7 April 1984, p. 2. The AOD also appears to have some monitoring responsibilities over civil aviation: see, for example, *Izvestiya*, 16 July 1983, p. 2.

17 Sergei Zamascikov, *Political Organizations in the Soviet Armed Forces. The Role of the Party and Komsomol*, Delphic Associates monograph series on the Soviet Union (December 1982), p. 23.

18 A. A.Yepishev, "Mighty shield of the socialist fatherland," *KZ*, 1 November 1977, pp. 1, 3; *Konstitutsiya soyuza (osnovnoy zakon) sovetskikh sotsialisticheskikh respublik* (Moscow: Politizdat, 1977), p. 43. See also D. A. Volkogonov (ed.), *Marksistsko-leninskoye ucheniye o voyne i armii* (Moscow: Voyenizdat, 1984), p. 320.

19 A. Kostin and I. Shatilo, "Armed forces of the multinational state," *KZ*, 11 August 1977, pp. 2, 3; I. Shkadov, "Sacred duty," *Kommunist vooruzhennykh sil* (hereafter cited as *KVS*), no. 23 (December 1977), pp. 15–23; and "L. I. Brezhnev," *SVE*, Vol. 1, pp. 586–9. Another source indicates that the Defense Council is an organ for "state direction" over the armed forces; see Kh. M. Akhmetshin, Yu. M. Biryukov, and A. S. Koblikov (eds.), *Voyennoye zakonodatel'stvo i pravovoye vospitaniye voinov* (Moscow: Voyenizdat, 1983), p. 33.

20 *Sovetskoye administrativnoye pravo* (Moscow: Yuridechiskaya Literatura, 1981), p. 375; see also S. A. Tyushkevich, *Sovetskiye vooruzhennyye sily* (Moscow: Voyenizdat, 1978), p. 464.

21 "Brezhnev, Leonid Il'ich," *VES*, p. 100.

22 At this writing, Gorbachev (who was appointed General Secretary on March 11, 1985) has not yet been publicly aknowledged as Defense Council Chairman. His predecessor Chernenko was initially identified as Defense Council chairman by then General Staff chief Ogarkov at a Kremlin reception marking Soviet Armed Forces day in February 1984 (see, for example, *Washington Post*, 27 February 1984, p. A10). Chernenko was subsequently identified in this role by rear services chief Kurkotkin in a radio address honoring Victory Day on 9 May 1984. See also *KZ*, 28 June 1984, pp. 1, 3. On Andropov's chairmanship see Dmitriy Ustinov, "The immortal feat," *Pravda*, 9 May 1983, p. 2.

23 Article 8.1 of the law of 21 November 1967 on Universal Military Service of the Polish People's Republic, as amended. *Dziennik ustaw*, no. 18 (6 August 1979), pp. 245–76, trans. in JPRS 74583, 15 November 1979, pp. 39–117; and *Dziennik ustaw*, no. 61 (22 November 1983), pp. 805–8, translated in JPRS-EPS-84-016, 3 February 1984, pp. 132–44 (hereafter cited as Polish Law on Universal Military Service).

24 The composition of the Romanian Defense Council is based on article 4 of Law No. 5, 1969. *Buletinal oficial al republicii socialiste Romania*, pt. 1, no. 32, pp. 238–9 (hereafter cited as Romanian Defense Council Law). See also *Buletinal oficial republicii socialiste Romania*, pt. 1, no. 118 (11 November 1975), p. 6. A Soviet discussion of the Romanian Defense Council is available in I. I. Yakubovskiy, *Boyevoye sodruzhestvo bratskikh narodov i armiy* (Moscow: Voyenizdat, 1975), pp. 199–200.

25 The inclusion of both party and state officials with responsibilities in the defense product area is also consistent with descriptions of the Soviet Defense Council as an "organ of political, economic and military leadership" which plays "a most important role in mobilizing all means for maintenance of armed forces combat readiness and ensuring that they have all that is necessary"; see B. N. Ponomarev *et al.* (eds.), *Konstitutsiya SSSR. Politiko-pravovoy kommentary* (Moscow: Politizdat, 1982), p. 317.

26 Estimates of Defense Council membership have also been derived from analysis of obituary signatures. The most systematic work in this area is that of Harriet Fast Scott, "Possible members of the Council of Defense derived from obituaries," paper presented at Brookings Institution National Security Policy Seminar, 18 April 1983. Another analysis of Defense Council membership based on obituaries is Tommy L. Whitton, "The Defense Council and military obituaries: a working hypothesis," *Air Force INES Staff Notes*, pp. 83–4. Another Kremlinological approach is that of analyzing attendees at military-related occasions—for example, the October 1982 conference of military leaders; see *KZ*, 28 October 1982, p. 1. Other Western assessments of the Defense Council include: M. P. Gallagher and K. Spielman, *Soviet Decisionmaking for Defense* (New York: Praeger, 1972), pp. 18–19; and D. Garthoff, "The Soviet military and arms control," *Survival*, vol. XIX, no. 6 (November–December 1977), pp. 242–50.

27 S. S. Maksimov, *Osnovy sovetskogo voyennogo zakonodatel'stva* (Moscow: Voyenizdat, 1978), pp. 50–1; and Kozlov, 1979, p. 36. See also M. G. Sobolev and I. S. Mareyev (eds.), *Partiyno-politicheskaya rabota v sovetskoy armii i flote* (Moscow: Voyenizdat, 1979), p. 13.

28 P. I. Romanov and V. G. Belyavskiy, *Konstitutsiya SSSR i zashchita otechestva* (Moscow: Voyenizdat, 1979), pp. 51–2; and "USSR constitution on defense of the socialist motherland," *KVS*, no. 15 (1979), pp. 69–77. See also *Nachal'naya voyennaya podgotovka*, 7th ed. (Moscow: Prosveshcheniye, 1984), p. 16.

29 "Concern of the Communist Party for the security of the socialist motherland," *VIZh*, no. 12 (1981), pp. 5–12; and Tel'pukhovskiy, 1983, p. 244.

30 See, for example, D. Volkogonov, "Actual questions of Soviet military development in light of the decisions of the 24th Party Congress," *KVS*, no. 11 (1972), pp. 10–20; and M. Zakharov, "The Communist Party and the technical rearmament of the army and navy in the years of the pre-war five year plans," *VIZh*, no. 2 (1971), pp. 3–12.

31 Sobolev, 1974, pp. 101–2; and V. I. Osikin, "Voyennoye stroitel'stvo," *SVE*, Vol. 2, p. 219.

32 "O sostoyanii oborony SSSR" (from the Central Committee Resolution of 15 July 1929), excerpted in N. I. Savinkin and K. M. Bogolyubov (eds.), *KPSS o vooruzhennykh silakh sovetskogo soyuza. Dokumenty, 1917–1981* (Moscow: Voyenizdat, 1981), pp. 258–60; Tyushkevich, 1978, pp. 182–5; *KPSS i stroitel'stvo sovetskikh vooruzhennykh sil* (Moscow: Voyenizdat, 1967), pp. 170–2; M. V. Zakharov (ed.), *50 let vooruzhennykh sil SSSR (1918–1968)* (Moscow: Voyenizdat, 1968), p. 196; and Zakharov, 1971.

33 Tyushkevich, 1978, p. 185.

34 A. A. Babakov, "Stroitel'stvo vooruzhennykh sil," *SVE*, Vol. 7, p. 580.

35 Ye. Nikitin, "The CPSU and the development of the Soviet armed forces in the interwar period," *VIZh*, no. 10 (1977), pp. 95–101; and Zakharov, 1971.

36 *KPSS i stroitel'stvo*, pp. 195–7; and *Voyennyy voprosy v dokumentakh KPSS i sovetskogo gosudarstva* (Moscow: Voyenizdat, 1980), pp. 211–12.

37 *KPSS i stroitel'stvo*, pp. 183–4.

38 "Sovet oborony," *VES*, p. 684.

39 Romanian Defense Council Law, article 3. See also article 8, pt. H, "Law Concerning the Organization of the National Defense of the Socialist Republic of Romania," *Scinteia*, 29

December 1972, pp. 4–7. On the GDR case see "Law on the National Defense of the GDR of 13 November 1978," *Neues Deutschland*, 14–15 October 1978, p. 4 (hereafter cited as GDR Defense Law). See also Hoffman's discussion of the law in *Neues Deutschland*, 14–15 October 1978, p. 3.

40 "Law on the State Defense Council," in Jiri Grospic (ed.), *Ceskoslovenska federace, zakony o federativnim u sporadani CSSR* (Prague: Orbis, 1972), pp. 307–13.

41 ibid., section 3, pt. b; Romanian Defense Council Law, article 3, pt. g; GDR Defense Law, section 5, pt. 2; Polish Law on Universal Military Service, article 5.2.

42 Maksimov, 1978, p. 52.

43 G. V. Sredin, "Politicheskiye organy," *SVE*, Vol. 6, pp. 420–2.

44 Romanian Defense Council Law, article 3, pts. B and I; and GDR Defense Law, section 4.

45 The Romanian Defense Council statute specifies that the Defense Council operates in both peace and war (article 1). The Czech State Defense Council regulations include both peacetime and wartime missions (section 3). The Hungarian Defense Law states that the Defense Council's tasks include the effective exploitation of all the country's resources for the defense of the homeland in time of war: Act of Parliament, no. I of 1976 on Defense in *Magyar kozlony*, no. 25 (31 March 1976).

46 On the link between the current Defense Council and the GKO see Yepishev, 1977; on the necessity for a peacetime body to unify the political, economic, and military leadership see V. D. Sokolovskiy, *Voyennaya strategiya* (Moscow: Voyenizdat, 1968), pp. 433–5; on the Leninist Defense Council see "Sovet rabochiy i krest'yanskoy oborony," *SVE*, Vol. 7, pp. 409–10; M. P. Iroshnikov, *Predsedatel' sovnarkoma i soveta oborony* (Leningrad: Nauka, 1980), pass.; and I. F. Pobezhimov, *Pravovoye regulirovaniye stroitel'stva sovetskoy armii i flota* (Moscow: Yuridicheskaya Literatura, 1960), p. 34; and on the GKO see "Gosudarstven-nyy komitet oborony," *SVE*, Vol. 2, pp. 621–2; Pobezhimov, 1960, p. 91; and John Erickson, *The Soviet High Command: A Military–Political History, 1918–1941* (London: Macmillan, 1962), p. 598.

47 *Verkhovnyy sovet SSSR* (Moscow: Izvestiya Sovetov Deputatov Trudyashchikhsya, 1975), p. 27.

48 ibid., pp. 223–45.

49 Maksimov, 1978, p. 51. See also A. G. Gornyy, *Sotsialisticheskaya zakonnost' i voinskiy pravoporyadok* (Moscow: Voyenizdat, 1973), p. 51.

50 *Konstitutsiya*, pp. 42–3; Maksimov, 1978, p. 51; and Romanov and Belyavskiy, 1979, pp. 53–8.

51 *Verkhovnyy sovet SSSR*, p. 86; and Ya. N. Umanskiy, *Sovetskoye gosudarstvennoye pravo* (Moscow: Vysshaya Shkola, 1970), pp. 374–80.

52 M. S. Smirtyutkov, "Sovet ministrov SSSR," *SVE*, Vol. 7, pp. 408–9; "Zakon o sovete ministrov SSSR," *Izvestiya*, 6 July 1978, pp. 1–2; and Maksimov, 1978, pp. 51–2.

53 This conclusion is based on analysis of the resolutions contained in the 1977 and 1979 collection of Council of Ministers decrees, which contain perhaps 20 percent of the resolutions promulgated in a given year. The 1977 collection of Council of Ministers resolutions lists 192 resolutions. Nearly one-half (81) were appointments to government posts. Of the substantive (that is, nonpersonnel) resolutions, over one-half (63) were related to the economy (labor—12; management procedures—9; banking/finance—4; agriculture—3; science—1; transport—6; industry—15; construction—4; establishing educational institutions—9). Fourteen resolutions were on foreign policy; three were on defense issues; seven were on land and water use. Welfare measures accounted for another thirteen (health—1; culture and education—2; trade—2; housing—4; insurance—1): see *Sobraniye postanovleniy SSSR*, 1977.

54 Maksimov, 1978, pp. 51–2.

55 Yu. M. Kozlov, *Administrativnoye pravo* (Moscow: Yuridicheskaya Literatura, 1968), pp. 212–17; P. F. Vasil'yev, *Pravovyye akty organov upravleniya* (Moscow: Izdatel'stvo Moskovskogo Universiteta, 1970), pp. 41–51; A. V. Mitskevich, *Akty vysshikh organov sovetskogo gosudarstva* (Moscow: Yuridicheskaya Literatura, 1967), pp. 117–20; and P. P. Gureyev and P. I. Sedugin, *Zakonodatel'stvo i zakonodatel'naya deyatel'nost' v SSSR* (Moscow: Yuridicheskaya Literatura, 1972), pp. 64–79.

56 "Ministerstvo oborony SSSR," *SVE*, Vol. 5, pp. 294–6.

57 "Narodnyy komissariat po voyennym i morskim delam SSSR," *SVE*, Vol. 5, p. 508.

58 "Narodnyy komissariat oborony SSSR," *SVE*, Vol. 5, p. 508; "Polozheniye o narodnom komissariate oborony soyuza SSR," in *Zakonodatel'stvo ob oborone SSSR* (Moscow: Voyeniz-

National Defense Policymaking 29

dat, 1939), pp. 10–12; and "Ob obrazovanii narodnogo komissariate voyenno-morskogo flota SSSR," ibid., p. 13.

59 "Narodnyy komissariat voyenno-morskogo flota SSSR," *SVE*, Vol. 5, p. 508.

60 "Ministerstvo oborony SSSR," *SVE*, Vol. 5, pp. 294–6.

61 Administrative procedures within the Ministry of Defense are regulated by the MoD's legal charter and the general regulations governing ministerial procedures: see Yu. M. Kozlov (ed.), *Pravovoye polozheniye ministerstv SSSR* (Moscow: Yuridicheskaya Literatura, 1971), *pass*.

62 Yu. M. Kozlov (ed.), *Sovetskoye administrativnoye pravo* (Moscow: Yuridicheskaya Literatura, 1973), pp. 521–3; Maksimov, 1978, p. 53; and A. Ye. Lunev (ed.), *Administrativnoye pravo* (Moscow: Yuridicheskaya Literatura, 1967), p. 458.

63 A. A. Yepishev, "Voyennyy sovet," *SVE*, Vol. 2, pp. 272–4; and A. V. Fedorov, *Russkaya armiya v 50–70 godakh XIX veka. Ocherki* (Leningrad: Izdatel'stvo Leningradskogo Universiteta, 1959), pp. 123–36.

64 "Kollegiya ministerstva oborony SSSR," *SVE*, Vol. 4, pp. 235–6. On nonmilitary counterparts of the MoD Collegium see I. L. Davitnidze, *Kollegii ministerstv* (Moscow: Yuridicheskaya Literatura, 1972), *pass*.

65 *SVE*, Vol. 4, pp. 235–6. See also A. I. Lepeshkin (ed.), *Osnovy sovetskogo voyennogo zakonodatel'stva* (Moscow: Voyenizdat, 1973), p. 91; and Maksimov, 1978, p. 53. The relationship between the Ministry of Defense Collegium and the Main Military Council, another advisory body attached to the MoD, is unclear. The Main Military Council was created in 1938, disbanded at the beginning of the war, then resurrected in 1953 as an advisory committee to the Ministry of War. When the Ministry of War and the Ministry of the Navy were folded together in March 1953, a unified Main Military Council was attached to the new Defense Ministry. It is not clear, however, whether this entity still exists. The two terms may simply be two names for the same body, or the Main Military Council may be a separate body: see A. A. Yepishev, "Voyennyy sovet," *SVE*, Vol. 2, pp. 272–4; "Glavnyy voyennyy sovet," *SVE*, Vol. 2, pp. 566–7; "Polozheniye o voyennom sovete pri narodnom komissariate oborony soyuza SSR," in *Zakonodatel'stvo ob oborone SSSR*, 1939, p. 12; and V. I. Lenin i sovetskiye vooruzhennyy sily, 3d ed. (Moscow: Voyenizdat, 1980), p. 184.

66 Davitnidze, 1972, *pass.*; and Kozlov, 1971, pp. 44–7.

67 Lepeshkin, 1973, p. 91. See also A. G. Gornyy (ed.), *Osnovy sovetskogo voyennogo zakonodatel'stva* (Moscow: Voyenizdat, 1966), pp. 66–8.

68 "Ministerstva oboronys SSR," *SVE*, Vol. 5, pp. 294–6; and Kozlov, 1973, pp. 521–3.

69 V. G. Kulikov, "General'nyy shtab," *SVE*, Vol. 2, pp. 510–13.

70 "Glavnyye i tsentral'nyye upravleniya," *SVE*, Vol. 2, p. 565.

71 This task involves the Staff closely in the formulation of mobilization plans: "Mobilizatsionnyy plan," *SVE*, Vol. 5, pp. 341–2.

72 "Polozheniye o nachal'noy voyennoy podgotovke molodezhi," 17 July 1968, in *Spravochnik po zakonodatel'stvu dlya ofitserov sovetskoy armii i flota* (hereafter cited as *Spravochnik po zakonodatel'stvu*) (Moscow: Voyenizdat, 1970), pp. 43–7; A. M. Popov, "Vnevoyskovaya podgotovka," *SVE*, Vol. 2, pp. 160–1; and "Nachal'naya voyennaya podgotovka," *SVE*, Vol. 5, p. 553.

73 V. Ye. Storozhenkoy, "Kadrovyye organy," *SVE*, Vol. 4, pp. 24–5.

74 "Glavnyye i tsentralnyye upravleniya," *SVE*, Vol. 2, p. 565.

75 K. B. Provorov and A. P. Porokhin, "Voyenno-uchebnyye zavedeniya," *SVE*, Vol. 2, pp. 255–6.

76 On the MPA see Sobolev, 1974, pp. 145–58.

77 Fedorov, 1959, pp. 123–36; and Forrest A. Miller, *Dmitrii Miliutin and the Reform Era in Russia* (Nashville, Tenn.: Vanderbilt University Press, 1968), pp. 26–53.

78 N. T. Konashenko, "Voyennyy okrug," *SVE*, Vol. 2, pp. 270–1; and A. Babakov, "The Soviet military districts: toward a history of their development," *VIZh*, no. 9 (1982), pp. 62–7.

79 P. I. Romanov, "Voyennyy komissariat," *SVE*, Vol. 2, pp. 269–70.

80 F. I. Tatarinov, "Chlen voyennogo soveta," *SVE*, Vol. 8, p. 483.

81 This statement is based on Soviet descriptions of Military Council activities in peacetime. Validation of Soviet descriptions would involve analysis of Council decisions and stenographic reports of each meeting. Unfortunately such data are not available to Western analysts. Soviet military historians do have at least partial access to military district archives, but their reporting is, of course, incomplete and highly selective. For example, the Odessa military district history

mentions fourteen military council meetings between 1945 and the mid-1970s; of these, seven were on military training, four on political training, two on troop living conditions, and one on harvest assistance to local farms: *Odesskiy krasnoznamennyy* (Kishinev: Kartya Moldove-nyaske, 1975), pp. 176–291.

82 "O voyennykh sovetakh sovetskoy armii i voyenno-morskogo flota," 17 April 1958, excerpted in Savinkin and Bogolyubov, 1981, p. 361.

83 Maksimov, 1978, pp. 56–7.

84 *Upravleniye otraslyami narodnogo khozyaystva* (Moscow: Yuridicheskaya Literatura, 1982), pp. 231–3.

85 Ye. Gol'dberg, "Instilling the new, the advanced," *Tyl i snabzheniye* (hereafter cited as *TIS*), no. 7 (1983), pp. 38–42; Ye. Gol'dberg, "60 years of military trade," *TIS*, no. 11 (1978), pp. 41–5; Ye. Gol'dberg, "To improve the material–technical base of military trade," *TIS*, no. 7 (1972), pp. 69–75; and Ye. Gol'dberg, "Voyentorg," *SVE*, Vol. 2, pp. 274–5.

86 V. V. Belov *et al.*, *Sovetskaya voyennaya torgovlya* (Moscow: Voyenizdat, 1968), pp. 65–94; and *Sovetskaya torgovlya* (Moscow: Statistika, 1956), p. 19.

87 N. Ulikhin, "In the nonblack earth zone," *TIS*, no. 7 (1974), pp. 61–4; N. Ulikhin, "On a course of intensification," *Agitator armii i flota*, no. 18 (1981), pp. 23–5; R. Tavadze, "Subsidiary farms," *KZ*, 29 July 1983, p. 4; V. I. Chubukov, "Prodovol'stvennaya sluzhba," *SVE*, Vol. 6, pp. 562–3; and "Polozheniye o prodovol'stvennom snabzhenii sovetskoy armii i voyennomorskogo flota na mirnoye vremya," in *Spravochnik po zakonodatel'stvu*, pp. 262–87.

88 A. Fedorov, "The path providing billeting service," *TIS*, no. 2 (1978), pp. 61–4; N. Shestopalov, "Property of all the people," *KZ*, 3 July 1982, p. 2.

89 Ye. I. Vostokov, "Kul'turno-prosvetitel'naya rabota,'' *SVE*, Vol. 4, pp. 520–4.

90 A. P. Gashchuk and V. S. Vukolov, *Turizm v vooruzhennykh silakh SSSR* (Moscow: Voyenizdat, 1983), *pass.*; *Turistskiye bazy ministerstva oborony SSSR* (Moscow: Voyenizdat, 1977), p. 6, *pass.*; A. Gashchuk, "Development prospects of army tourism," *KZ*, 13 March 1976, p. 4; and N. Garetin, "Army tourism and its further development," *TIS*, no. 4 (1974), pp. 62–5.

91 Gashchuk and Vukolov, 1983, p. 5.

92 Yu. M. Bludov, "Sportvnyye kluby," *SVE*, Vol. 7, pp. 498–9; B. K. Yermashkevich, "Voyenno-okhotnich'i khozyaystvo," *SVE*, Vol. 2, p. 245; B. K. Yermashkevich, "Vsearmeyskoye voyenno-okhotnich'ye obshchestvo," *SVE*, Vol. 2, pp. 394–5; P. V. Pashchenko, *Okhotnikam, rybolovam, turistam VVOO* (Moscow: Voyenizdat, 1973), *pass.*; and V. F. Nazarov *et al.*, *Voyennyye sanitarii i doma otdykha* (Moscow: Voyenizdat, 1984), *pass.*

93 *Upravleniye sotsial'no-kult'urnym stroitel'stvom* (Moscow: Yuridicheskaya Literatura, 1980), pp. 265–6; and V. I. Shabaylov, *Upravleniye zdravookhraneniyem v SSSR* (Moscow: Yuridicheskaya Literatura, 1968), p. 16.

94 "Voyenno-meditsinskaya sluzhba," *SVE*, Vol. 2, pp. 226–8; K. Federov, "In defense of soldiers' health," *TIS*, no. 5 (1978), pp. 15–18; and F. I. Komarev, "Tasks of the military medical service for further improvement of the medical safeguarding of the army and fleet personnel," *Voyenno-meditsinskiy zhurnal*, no. 12 (1977), pp. 3–7.

95 Yu. M. Kozlov (ed.), *Osnovy sovetskogo administrativnogo pravo* (Moscow: Znaniye, 1979), pp. 28–31.

96 *Sobraniye postanovleniy SSSR, 1979.*

2

Soviet Military Manpower Policy

Every society that maintains a military organization faces the common problem of procuring military personnel. The decision to adopt a specific policy of personnel procurement inevitably involves both advantages and disadvantages.[1] The strategy adopted affects the social composition of the military, the scope of military–civilian interaction, patterns of placement and training, and the organization of the military system itself. One of the most basic distinctions between procurement systems is that between a volunteer and a draft army. Each system involves both advantages and disadvantages.

Use of a volunteer system entails development of strong financial incentives to attract and retain a cadre of highly trained military professionals to fill both officer and enlisted ranks. Such financial inducements tend to be expensive; and one of the major economic disadvantages of maintaining a volunteer force of any size is the high price of direct pay and benefits needed to attract volunteers. The financial cost of manpower often involves reliance on a smaller force, which may have direct politico-military consequences: when the military balance is weighed purely in terms of numbers, the smaller (if more professional) force suffers in comparison to the mass army.

There are negative social consequences as well. Reliance on a volunteer system frequently involves a narrow social base, at least for the enlisted ranks, since the military is competing with civilian occupations for its enlisted recruits and will normally draw a disproportionate number of enlistees from regions and socioeconomic groups with less access to high-status civilian occupations.[2] Reliance on volunteers serving long terms may also involve a more rigid civilian–military boundary by decreasing the number of individuals who cycle through the military system.[3] This, in turn, has sometimes been perceived as carrying the threat of political intervention by a small, professional military.[4] Use of volunteers also raises a whole host of personnel problems associated with an increased proportion of soldiers with wives and families: increased pressure on dependent support systems and military housing and increased opportunities for conflict between family and military commitments.

On the other hand, reliance on long-term volunteers holds the promise of higher average skill levels for both enlisted and officer personnel because it facilitates lengthier training periods. The higher skill levels in a volunteer system may allow a cutback in the size of the military, with reliance on a smaller (but more effective and better trained) force. In theory at least, the use of volunteer personnel with longer retention rates should facilitate substantial increases in the technical sophistication of weaponry. Reliance on volunteers may also ameliorate the typical pattern of morale and discipline problems associated with a concentration of young draftees who resent the temporary military intrusion into their private lives.

Reliance on draft personnel involves its own set of advantages and disadvantages. The pattern of costs and benefits, however, depends on the nature of the conscription system itself: what proportion of the military force is procured through conscription? What proportion of the relevant age cohort is actually conscripted, at what ages, and for how long? What functional roles are assigned to conscript v. career personnel and how flexible is this distribution of responsibilities? It should be noted that even in those instances when the draft is used as a supplement to a basically volunteer system, it produces a large number of "draft-motivated" enlistments that significantly modify the character of the military force.

Use of the draft as a procurement mechanism carries with it a number of significant problems. Although direct costs of pay and benefits for draftees is typically much lower than for volunteers, conscript armies involve both manpower opportunity costs and the costs associated with the maintenance of the professional cadres and equipment necessary to train the large influx of draftees. Moreover, those conscription systems that employ a relatively short draft obligation (that is, one to three years) involve not only a tremendous burden on the training system, but frequently very real limitations on strategy and weaponry as well. The two-year conscript, no matter how well educated, cannot absorb the level of training of a long-term military professional; the necessity for relatively short training cycles places a limit on the technological sophistication of those weapons and military equipment designated for conscript-manned units. Moreover, a conscript army that relies on postadolescent males will inevitably reflect the behavioral problems associated with that demographic group.

The primary social cost of conscription is borne by the individual draftee in terms of disruption of personal and professional commitments. Societies that have traditionally placed a high premium on individual freedom are often uncomfortable with the coercive aspect of conscription. This is particularly true in those cases where the draft is highly selective (that is, only a small portion of the relevant age cohort is drafted).[5]

Reliance on conscription involves benefits as well as costs. The primary military benefit is the creation of a large base of reservists who have had recent, intensive, active duty military training. A major social benefit is that of increasing the permeability of boundaries between civilian life and military institutions. The large number of young men cycling through the military system means that there is a consistent flow of large numbers of ex-soldiers returning to civilian life. Obligatory military service provides the state with the opportunity to standardize the health and educational levels of incoming conscripts.[6] Conscription has also been viewed as a hedge against political interventionism; the "citizen soldier" is seen as more closely allied to the civilian world than to that of the professional military.[7]

The costs and benefits of the conscript v. all-volunteer manning systems represent the focal point for what has become in the United States and many West European countries a continuing debate over which system is most compatible with each country's democratic values, international goals, and economic needs.[8] The debate has accompanied a major shift in military organization, generally referred to as the decline of the mass army: transformation of the armed forces from an organization based on conscription and mobilization of extensive reserve forces to a smaller "force in being" recruited from volunteers. This trend has been traced to technological changes in the nature of warfare and a decline in public acceptance of conscription.[9] Britain established an all-volunteer force in 1957, the United States in 1973.[10] Even those states that have retained the draft have reduced the length of compulsory military service and liberalized deferment policies.[11]

The Tsarist and Soviet Heritage

By contrast, in the Soviet Union there has never been any real debate on the conscript v. volunteer issue. Reliance on some form of conscription is one of the strongest military traditions in the Soviet Union—one that predates the Bolshevik Revolution. But the nature of the conscription system has varied substantially during both the tsarist and Soviet periods, variations that reflect internal social, political, and economic constraints as well as external military threats and foreign policy goals.

Use of conscription as a basis for military personnel procurement in the Rusian army dates from the Petrine reforms of the early eighteenth century. Prior to Peter the Great's overhaul of the entire military system, Russia lacked a military in the modern sense of the word. With the exception of few regular regiments, military formations assembled for campaigns and disbanded when the campaign ended. Peter set up a regular army and navy and systematized the personnel procurement system, replacing the earlier patchwork of recruiting procedures with a single procurement system.[12] The officer corps was recruited largely from the nobility, while the burden of recruitment levies fell largely on the peasantry.[13] Obligation to serve was not, however, universal even within the eligible social groups, but rather was based on a quota system that varied with military needs.[14] Only a small portion of the eligible population served. During regular levies five to seven "recruits" were required for every 1,000 "souls." In emergency situations this levy was increased to ten recruits, and during wartime to as many as fifty to seventy recruits per 1,000 souls.[15] Quota requirements were levied on the community, not on the individual.[16] Decisions as to which peasants were subject to the draft were typically made by the village commune, a community assembly also responsible for the distribution of tax obligations.[17]

Those peasants called up for military service were freed from their obligations as a serf.[18] There was no provision for returning the drafted serf to his landlord after military service. Consequently there was strong opposition from serf-owners to any effort to increase the proportion drafted. This meant that the small proportion of the eligible populace which was called up had to serve extraordinarily long tours. During much of the eighteenth century soldiers served a lifetime tour. The basic tour was decreased to twenty-five years in 1793 and twenty years (of which five years was reserve duty) in 1834. Service length was progressively reduced in the late nineteenth century.

The major disadvantage of this selective procurement system was the absence of a trained reserve.[19] The empire lacked a mobilization base. In the late 1700s, for example, only about 3 percent of the male population received military training.[20] In wartime tsarist military officials were forced to call up men with absolutely no military experience or training. Development of a well-trained reserve force could be achieved with shorter service terms and a higher conscription ratio, but such measures met with determined resistance from the tsarist gentry.[21] The emancipation manifesto of 1862 removed one major barrier to a change in the procurement system by freeing the serfs. At the same time, tsarist military officials were becoming increasingly aware of the military force build-up of the other European powers.[22] War Minister Dmitriy Milyutin, urging a complete overhaul of the army, pointed to the massive mobilization base of Russia's potential opponents.[23]

In 1874 Milyutin and other critics of the Petrine system of procurement at last managed to convince Tsar Alexander II to scrap selective recruitment in favor of a universal military obligation. The length of military service was further reduced.[24] Draftees were called up by lot at age 21; and exemptions were provided for health or family hardship. Exemptions were no longer based on social class; the conscription manifesto itself declared bluntly that defense of throne and country was the sacred duty of every Russian subject. Military obligation involved both active duty service and service in the reserves. For example, rank-and-file soldiers in the army spent six years on active duty, followed by nine years in the reserves.[25] During reserve service the soldier could be called up twice each year for reservist training of six weeks' duration.[26]

The "universal" obligation, however, was far from universal in practice. Reduced service terms were provided for educated draft-eligibles. Primary school graduates were required to serve only four years; university graduates only six months. Clergy, physicians, and teachers were totally exempt, as were selected nationalities, including those from Central Asia, Siberia, the far north, and certain Caucasian ethnic groups. Over half of the eligible age group was exempted.[27] Nonetheless, the new procurement system did facilitate a substantial increase both in the size of the standing army and its mobilization base. On the eve of World War I the empire had 3·1 million men under arms with an additional half-million in reserve. This compares with 2·6 million men and 1 million reservists in the German army. The Russian numerical superiority was, however, counterbalanced by the relatively low technical level of her weaponry.[28]

The major motivation for adoption of the new system was the need to create a large mobilization base.[29] The relatively short term of service adopted under the 1874 law allowed a large number of males to "cycle" through army service and be discharged into the reserves. Milyutin and other supporters of the reform found justification for the high financial costs of the measure by pointing to the military threat posed by Germany. Advocates also pointed to the desirability of a more equitable distribution of the responsibility to serve.[30] The military's potential as an agent for social change does not appear to have been a major factor in tsarist calculations.

For the Bolshevik heirs of the tsarist empire, social and political (as well as purely military) factors were important in the choice of a military manpower procurement system. The most immediate problem was dealing with a series of armed threats to Bolshevik power. The Bolshevik seizure of power in Petrograd on 7 November had encountered only token resistance from provisional government forces; extending Bolshevik authority to the Russian hinterlands proved more difficult. The Bolshevik leadership moved quickly to demobilize the old army and negotiate peace with Germany.[31] Simultaneously plans moved forward to create a new socialist army that would be responsive to Bolshevik needs. On 18 January 1918 a decree was passed organizing the new Workers–Peasants Red Army (RKKA).[32] It was to be staffed exclusively by volunteers and limited to workers and poor peasants whose political reliability had been vouched for by a military committee, party organization, or a social organization that endorsed Bolshevik rule.[33] Voluntary procurement was used because many prospective soldiers, newly demobilized from the tsarist army, were interested only in returning home, certainly not in serving the fledgling Bolshevik regime.[34] Moreover, the Bolsheviks lacked the administrative system necessary to procure and process a new mass army. The new Red Army was plagued by insufficient food, arms, and equipment; and it lacked experienced and reliable command cadres.[35]

In February when peace negotiations broke down and Germany launched a new offensive, the German troops advanced virtually unopposed. The Bolsheviks reluctantly signed the Brest-Litovsk peace treaty and turned their attention to repelling anti-Bolshevik forces that were already assembling to launch a civil war that would last three more years. By May 1918 the Red Army stood at perhaps 300,000 men. Arrayed against the disorganized and untrained Red Army troops were an estimated 700,000 anti-Bolshevik troops.[36] Trotsky, now War Commissar, moved quickly to reorganize the tattered remains of the RKKA. This meant the abandonment of the short-lived experiment with a volunteer army and the adoption of a conscription system. On 29 May 1918 the Bolshevik leadership issued a decree making military service obligatory.[37] Mobilization was introduced in the main industrial centers and only gradually extended to the other Bolshevik-controlled areas as the complex military bureaucracy to administer manpower procurement was established. By Sept-

ember 1918 the Red Army numbered 550,000 men. Conscription applied only
to those social classes deemed reliable for military service—the workers and
poor peasantry. At the same time, a system of universal military training for
adult males (*vsevobuch*) was introduced; and by the end of 1920 5 million men
had been through the program, which provided ninety-six hours of military
training on a part-time basis without interruption from work.[38] In March 1919
the party military policy of transition from a volunteer, half-partisan army to a
regular cadre force with strict military discipline was reaffirmed at the Bolsheviks' Eighth Party Congress, over determined opposition from critics who
argued that such measures would alienate the peasantry. Indeed, draft-
dodging by peasants was fairly common; and one of the Red Army's most
pressing problems was large-scale desertions.[39]

In spite of these problems the Red Army that emerged victorious from the
civil war was a very different organization from the small, untrained, and
undisciplined volunteer force of early 1918.[40] Between September 1918 and
December 1920 nearly 5 million men were mobilized. Only 17 percent of the
military personnel were volunteers. Casualties were enormous; more men
were lost from illness and starvation than from battle. Out of the 2·2 million
casualties sustained during this period, fully 1·4 million were due to insufficient
food, clothing, and medical care. Peasants constituted the bulk of the fighting
force at this time. At the end of 1920, 77 percent of the military's 5·5 million
men were peasants, 15 percent were workers, and other groups constituted
8 percent.

As the civil war drew to a close the Bolshevik leadership moved to demobilize the armed forces.[41] By the end of 1924 Red Army strength stood at a
half-million men. It had become clear that the ravaged Soviet economy could
not support a large standing army. In March 1924 the Central Committee
approved a series of proposals that provided the basis for the military reforms
of 1924–5. These reforms inaugurated a fifteen-year period of reliance on a
mixed cadre–territorial militia.

The main motivation for the partial shift to a territorial system was the desire
to expose a large proportion of military-age men to military service.[42] The
territorial militia system (which applied only to rifle and cavalry divisions)
enabled the government to call a larger percentage of the cohort. The new
military service law, introduced in 1925, obligated all citizens to participate in
the defense of the USSR, but limited activities involving weapons to workers.[43]
Obligatory military service involved premilitary training, active duty military
service, and reserve service. Premilitary training for those aged 19–21 consisted
of a one-month training muster each year.[44] This was followed by active duty
service in either a cadre unit or one of the more numerous territorial units.[45]
Males called to service in the territorial units were obligated to a five-year term
and served in units close to their place of residence.[46] Active duty service in the
territorial units consisted of periodic training assemblies once a year, totalling
eight to twelve months over the five years of service, with the soldier going on
extended furlough between musters.[47] The law was designed to avoid lengthy
laborforce interruptions and to expose the largest feasible proportion of the

draft-age cohort to military training with the minimum expense.[48] Technical troops, the navy, and certain units in the frontier military districts were retained as cadre units, staffed by both volunteers and draftees who served a two- to four-year term of full-time service, followed by several years on long-term furlough. Each territorial unit retained a core of cadres to train and socialize the soldiers called for short training musters. Virtually all senior commanders and some mid-level and junior command personnel in such units were full-time, permanent staff.[49] The rank-and-file were part-time soldiers. After completion of the five-year active duty obligation, soldiers were enrolled in the reserve until age 40.[50] Bolshevik leaders, then, were frank about the fact that the militia system was a compromise in the interests of economizing. They recognized the disadvantages of a militia from the standpoint of combat capability, but justified it by pointing to the relatively modest military forces of their European opponents.

By the mid-1930s several factors had prompted a return to a regular, cadre army.[51] First, the military build-up in Europe increased the military threat to the USSR. Second, the increasing technical complexity of military equipment required more training than was available during the brief training musters. Third, the Soviet economy had grown strong enough to support a large regular army. In May 1935 the Politburo approved a series of measures phasing out the territorial units. Within little more than a year the Red Army was transformed from a mixed regular–territorial army with 74 percent of its divisions organized as territorial units to a predominantly cadre force with only 23 percent territorial divisions. The transition involved substantial increases in size. The Red Army grew from less than 900,000 men in 1933 to over 1·5 million at the beginning of 1938.

The phase-out of the militia units was taken one step further by the 1939 law on universal military service.[52] The law removed social class criteria in service assignment, but reaffirmed the obligation of all male citizens to serve. It established two draft ages: for graduates of secondary schools, age 18; for everyone else, age 19. Conscription took place once a year from mid-September to mid-October and the term of service was two to three years for ground forces, four to five years for those assigned to aviation, border troops, and the navy. The provisions of the 1939 law were temporarily suspended by World War II. Normal military tours were suspended for the duration of the war. To expand the mobilization base educational deferments were cut back, and health standards were lowered. Women were drafted.

The current law governing Soviet military manpower procurement—the 1967 law on military service—reflects many of the principles on which the 1939 law was based. The 1967 legislation reaffirmed the Soviet reliance on a regular "cadre" army, in which all adult males are obligated to serve. The historical record of military manning policy in the USSR reveals, then, a strong and continuing commitment to a "citizen," as opposed to a volunteer army. The Soviet system inherited a long-standing tsarist tradition of peacetime military conscription as well as the nineteenth-century tsarist preoccupation with establishing a strong mobilization base by using short-term active duty as a "school for reservists." To these traditions the Bolshevik leadership added its own preoccupation with social engineering. It was only natural that Bolshevik leaders would turn to the military as a convenient way of isolating young soldiers from "traditional" values and instilling approved values and behavioral patterns. The armed forces became, then, not just a "school for reservists," but a "school for life" as well.

Manpower Policy and Armed Forces Functions

Contemporary Soviet manpower policy reflects both the historical heritage of the tsarist army and Marxist ideology. Manpower policy is designed to support the major missions assigned to the armed forces. These missions have been codified in what the Soviets term "CPSU military policy."[53] The basic role of military power in Soviet foreign and domestic policy is to ensure the military security of the USSR. Other military functions are to defend the Warsaw Pact states, to support Soviet foreign policy goals, and to deter aggression.

The army's key role, as defined by CPSU military policy, is to stand ready to fight and win wars.[54] While the Soviets have always been careful to say that they will not start a war,[55] they continue to insist that in the event war does occur the USSR must be prepared to emerge victorious.[56] Military force has consistently functioned as the cornerstone of Soviet national security. Even in the heyday of détente treaty agreements were considered no substitute for military power "because there still exist forces which deviate from the principle of peaceful coexistence." A formulation underlining the military's pivotal role in national security was incorporated into the 1961 CPSU Program and the 1977 USSR Constitution.[57] Soviet concern about being ready for the next war is, in part, a reaction to the devastation suffered in World War II, when the Soviets lost an estimated 20 million people. Vast portions of the Soviet Union came under prolonged German occupation. This experience also helps to explain the Soviet tendency to "hedge their bets" in defense policy, not to rely too heavily on one weapon system or one strategy.

Soviet defense policy is based on the assumption that the armed forces must be ready to fight under a variety of conditions. Because military strategists have concluded that the initial period of war may be decisive, with little time for mobilization or other preparations, fulfillment of the armed forces' primary role (to be ready to fight) requires a large standing army and a high level of combat readiness. On the other hand, they do not rule out a lengthy war, one requiring huge reserves of men and materiel.[58] The Soviet manning system is based on the assumption that it would not be economically feasible to deploy the full array of forces that would be required for war. Active duty military forces serve as a base. Some units are maintained at a high level of combat readiness with essentially complete components of manpower and equipment; other units serve as a peacetime core, around which reservists will be mobilized in time of war and emergency.[59] "Mobilization readiness" is closely linked with combat readiness:[60]

Table 2.1 *Maximum Military Obligations of Reservists*

Category	Age group		
	1	*2*	*3*
Nonofficer reserve	*(to age 35)*	*(35–45)*	*(45–50)*
Category I Reservists with at least 1 year of active duty service or combat experience	Four training courses of up to 3 months each*	One or two training courses of up to 2 months each	One 1-month training course
Category II Reservists with less than 1 year active duty†	Six training courses of up to 3 months each	— Same as above	— Same as above
Officer reserve‡	Once a year for up to 3 months§	Two courses lasting 3 months each	One course lasting 2 months

*Flight personnel may also be called up for up to five flight training courses of 40 days each.
†Reservists in this category who have taken training courses for a total duration of at least 12 months are transferred to the first category of reserves.
‡The total time spent for training courses cannot exceed 30 months.
§Between training courses reserve officers in this age group can be called for 30–60-hour command training courses once every 3 years.
Note: Reservists (both officer and nonofficer) may also be called up for an unspecified number of test courses lasting up to 10 days.
Source: Universal Military Service Law, articles 47–55, 65.

High combat readiness of forces and naval means is unthinkable without well organized mobilization preparations, directed at ensuring a smooth transition from a peacetime to a wartime status. If the aggressor unleashes war, prepared resources of personnel and equipment, earmarked for large units, must reach them in a short time, without delay.

Soviet military mobilization plans involve both fleshing out existing undermanned units and creating new ones. Prerequisites include: a trained manpower reserve; reserve equipment; and a mobilization administration.[61] The primary source of trained manpower reserves (in Soviet terminology "the military-obligated") is the pool of draftees who have served their regular active duty terms and have been discharged into the reserves.[62] The reserve manpower pool is augmented by two other sources: young men who have been deferred but who have been classified fit for military service in wartime; and women with medical or other (unspecified) "specialist" training.[63] Nonofficer personnel in the reserves fall into one of two categories and one of three age classes (as shown in Table 2.1). The career cadre needed to provide leadership and management is drawn from warrant officers (discharged from active duty into the reserves) and reserve officers. The pool of reserve officers is formed from officers who have been discharged into the reserves, from rank-and-file soldiers who pass an examination to receive reserve officer status, from graduates of ROTC programs, from nonofficer reservists with higher or specialized secondary education in a military-related field, from nonofficer reservists who have taken a reserve officer training course, and from warrant officers with at least five years' exerience who receive an officer rank upon transfer to the reserves.[64] As in the tsarist system, reservists can be mobilized for training musters, the number and duration of which are based on their reserve category as described in Table 2.1.

The Soviet manning system also requires a mobilization bureaucracy to maintain records and provide the machinery to call up and assign reservists. The primary component of this system is the military commissariat. Servicemen discharged from active duty service are obligated to report for military registration to the military commissariat in their place of residence within three days. The military commissariats maintain records, with notation of military speciality, of all registered reservists residing within their territory.[65] They also maintain registries of vehicles in local motor pools that have been designated for use in mobilization.[66] Reservists who leave their place of residence (for over six weeks in the case of a temporary change of residence, for over three months for business trips, education, health care, or vacation) must turn in their military service card (*voyenniy bilet*) to the housing administration or military registration desk, so that their names can be removed from the military registration list in that area. They have three days to report for military registration to the housing administration or military registry desk at their new place of residence.[67] These records provide the basis for assignment during mobilization.

Mobilization begins with a declaration of mobilization by the Presidium of the Supreme Soviet, which in all likelihood acts to give legal authority to a decision actually made in the Defense Council.[68] Mobilization is conducted according to a plan that is probably formulated in the General Staff's Organization and Mobilization Directorate and implemented through analogous organization and mobilization departments in each military district staff.[69] Upon declaration of mobilization the service obligation of all persons on active duty would be extended indefinitely and those reservists designated for call-up would receive mobilization instructions, call-up notices, or orders from their military comissariats.[70] Many reservists are permanently or temporarily deferred because of the critical nature of their peacetime jobs.[71] Reservists who are mobilized are required to report to designated mobilization and reserve points for further orders.[72] This system is tested frequently in peacetime through mobilization exercises (which are intended to assess the effectiveness of the mobilization machinery) and through reserve training musters. The mobilization system is also activated in response to real crises: some reservists were mobilized in 1968 when the Soviets invaded Czechoslovakia, and again in 1979 when they invaded Afghanistan.

The reserve base and the mobilization system are critical components of the larger manning system. The commitment to this system stems from a conviction, which the Soviet leadership inherited from its imperial Russian predecessor, that fighting and winning a war requires a mass of trained reservists. Like tsarist military authorities, Soviet military officials see active duty training of conscripts as the most effective way of creating the reserve base they feel they need. Therefore, they must maintain large numbers of trained military reservists and a system to call them up and get them where they are needed in event of war or crisis. The doctrinal requirement for a military force which is both combat ready *and* capable of expanding through mobilization has had a critical influence on Soviet manning policy.

Another aspect of Soviet military doctrine that affects manning policy deals with the type of war that the military may be called upon to fight. Most Soviet military scientists insist that the USSR's military forces must be ready to fight on both the nuclear and the conventional (but nuclear-threatened) battlefield. Until late 1964 Soviet doctrine rejected the possibility of a conventional phase of war, reflecting the party leadership's perception that the next world war would inevitably begin with a nuclear exchange. Conventional forces were acknowledged to have a role to play on the modern battlefield, but leadership attention and resources were focussed on nuclear weaponry. By the end of 1964, however, Soviet doctrinal statements began acknowledging the possibility of a brief conventional phase. In line with this shift the Soviets undertook in the late 1960s a wide-ranging modernization of their conventional forces, which appeared in the 1970s as new weapons. While the nuclear weapon is still considered the decisive factor on the contemporary battlefield, Soviet military scientists concede that offensive and defensive operations may be conducted using only conventional weapons. The Soviet military must be ready to fight effectively in either the nuclear or conventional environment.[73] A strong nuclear force is not viewed as a viable substitute for a large, powerful conventional force. The doctrinal acceptance of the possibility of a conventional phase thus led to increasing stress on the need for a more flexible force structure capable of conducting operations "under a variety of scenarios."[74]

Still another doctrinal tenet that impacts on Soviet manning policy is the officially accepted view on the probable scope of war. Soviet military strategists have concluded that a future world war will most likely be "a decisive struggle between two opposing world socioeconomic systems—socialist and capitalist."[75] Such a war may well involve many different countries. Although the major preoccupation of Soviet strategists is the need to prepare for a world war, the possibility of Soviet involvement in local wars is not ruled out.[76] In official Soviet parlance this means that the Soviet Union is prepared to provide assistance to "wars of national liberation." This assistance may take the form of economic aid, military materiel and advisory teams, or (in the case of Afghanistan, for instance) direct military intervention. (The official Soviet justification for the invasion of Afghanistan is that the "limited contingent" of Soviet troops was provided in accordance with the 1978 Soviet–Afghan Friendship Treaty and in response to an official Afghan request for military aid to repulse counterrevolutionary forces and foreign interventionists.)[77] These considerations mean that the Soviet military must be prepared to dispatch units trained and equipped to fight under varied geographical conditions.

Closely related to Soviet assistance to national liberation wars is the armed forces' role in support for Soviet foreign policy objectives. Soviet theorists view their military power as having foreign policy significance that goes beyond the USSR's ability to intervene militarily in specific situations. "The very fact of the existence of the armed forces of the socialist states" provides an important justification for Soviet claims to superpower status.[78] Military personnel fulfill the armed forces' "international mission" by representing the Soviet government abroad. Ship visits allow the USSR to maintain high visibility in Third World countries.[79]

Military power is also valued for its ability to deter war. Soviet doctrine, articulated here by then General Secretary Brezhnev, has consistently stressed the importance of maintaining a strong military to defend the peace:[80]

> Our efforts are directed so that there will be neither a first strike nor a second strike, that there won't be a nuclear war. Our approach to this question may be formulated as follows: the defense potential of the Soviet Union must be sufficient so that no one will risk disturbing our peacful life.

This position was restated by Brezhnev's successor, Andropov, in his first public statement as General Secretary: "We know well that we cannot beg for peace from the imperialists. It can rest only on the invincible might of the Soviet Armed Forces."[81] The USSR's strategic nuclear forces, therefore, must be maintained at strength and readiness levels necessary to deter a nuclear attack by the West.[82]

The armed forces have also been assigned secondary, but nonetheless significant, nonmilitary functions. Soviet theorists claim that the military no longer performs "domestic" missions, in the sense of quelling widespread internal opposition. The military's role in suppressing internal opponents, said to be a crucial one in the early years of Soviet power, gradually decreased in importance, beginning in the mid-1930s, as the Bolshevik authorities consolidated their power.[83] Soviet theorists concede, however, that the army continues to perform important nonmilitary functions.

One of the most important of these nonmilitary functions is to provide a flexible laborforce to help ease regional and temporary labor shortages. Soviet units routinely supplement civilian labor by assisting in gathering and transporting the annual harvest.[84] Agriculture is considerably more labor-intensive in the Soviet Union than it is in most Western industrialized countries. In some areas local party and government officials arrange for temporary transfers of civilian nonagricultural personnel to assist farmers at harvest-time. This form of assistance, however, places a heavy burden on urban enterprises since it often involves use of highly skilled blue- and white-collar workers in unskilled agricultural labor.[85] Use of the relatively abundant and unskilled labor in military units represents an attractive alternative. Military labor makes an important contribution to the regional economy of those agricultural areas that have only a limited ability to mobilize additional seasonal labor.

A second form of assistance to the civilian economy is provided by the railway troops. Use of military troops for railway construction predates the Bolshevik Revolution. The first military railway units were organized in 1851.[86] Railway troops were used in the Russo-Turkish War to maintain and construct rail lines at the front. They were also employed to build the Vladivostok–Khabarovsk railroad and to complete construction on the Eastern Chinese railroad. Soviet sources estimate that at the end of World War I there were 130,000 railway troops in the Russian army. The Bolshevik government disbanded the railway forces along with the rest of the tsarist army, but were forced almost immediately to resurrect them. During the civil war the railway troops restored some 22,000 kilometers of track, more than 3,160 railway bridges, and more than 220 water supply points; they also repaired and overhauled 16,500 railcars.[87] After the war, railway troops helped to reconstruct railroad and other facilities damaged in the fighting; they also took part in the construction of new lines for both military and general use. During World War II railway troops restored and maintained the railroad in front areas and repaired and rebuilt bridges. By late 1943 the number of railway troops exceeded 250,000. After World War II, the railway troops participated in the reconstruction of damaged railroad and the construction of bridges, new lines, stations, depots, and related storage facilities. Between 1946 and 1975 railway troops built an estimated 27,000 kilometers of railroad and 13,000 buildings. During the 1950s the railway troops helped to construct the Central Siberian mainline; in the 1960s they helped complete the Southern Siberian line.

The most noteworthy of the railway troops' recent projects is the Baykal–Amur mainline (BAM).[88] Railway troops were assigned to work on the eastern division of the BAM.[89] Living and working conditions on the BAM are extremely primitive, as indicated by frequent press reports of the bad weather, housing and food shortages, isolation, and virtual lack of amenities.[90] Assignment of the railway troops to the project spares Soviet authorities the difficulty of attracting civilian construction workers. The use of the railway troops provides a politically acceptable and economically feasible alternative source of labor for a program that has both economic and strategic significance.[91]

A third source of military assistance to the Soviet economy is provided by the construction troops, which are involved in a wide variety of both military and civilian projects.[92] Soviet use of military units for capital construction represents an adaption of tsarist practices.[93] Tsarist authorities used military work battalions in the early nineteenth century on military and defense-related facilities. They disbanded the units in the 1860s, after which military construction projects were contracted out to manufacturers who supplied both workers and materials. During World War I, however, the practice of using military units was reinstituted, and by mid-1917 nearly 400,000 men were working in 287 military work units. Bolshevik authorities adopted the practice during the civil war. After the war, the troops helped rebuild the war-ravaged economy, constructing factories, mines, electric power stations, and border fortifications.[94] The units were reportedly manned by individuals from socioeconomic groups considered unreliable by Bolshevik authorities.[95] By 1940 there were 238,000 military construction workers, many of whom were engaged in building defensive fortifications on the Western front. In the early years of World War II the primary mission of the military construction units was to build defensive lines and obstacles. When the Soviet troops began advancing, the construction troops built roads and bridges for the advancing troops, cleared mines, and rebuilt industrial enterprises and electric stations.[96] After the war, military construction units were involved in the massive postwar reconstruction, building or repairing large-scale military and civilian facilities.

The contemporary construction troops have an ambiguous legal status, and are subject to both military and civilian regulations. Military construction units are part of larger military construction organizations that employ two basic categories of personnel: civilians and military servicemen. The civilians are governed by civil labor codes, while the military come under special statutes.[97] Military construction detachments are manned by draftees conscripted through the regular military commissariat system. Unlike regular draftees, however, they are reportedly paid a salary that goes into a special fund from which charges for room and board are subtracted. The balance is apparently paid to the conscript upon release from service. Conscripts serving in the construction companies are subject to military discipline and are supposed to be given rudimentary military training. According to the 1965 regulations on military construction detachments, two days a month during the winter and one day a month in the summer are to be set aside for "military and specialist training" of the conscript sergeants who command construction platoons. It is not clear whether analogous military training periods have been set aside for rank-and-file draftees assigned to those units.[98] Although these draftees do take the military oath and are given a rank (for example, "military builder-soldier"), the rank-and-file do not appear to be legally categorized as "military servicemen."[99]

The primary mission of the contemporary construction troops is to carry out capital construction projects for the MoD. Construction detachments are used for construction and assembly work, and for the production of construction materials in MoD industrial and wood processing facilities.[100] The troops build military towns, including barracks, officer housing, dining rooms, warehouses, and training facilities. They also build hospitals, sanitariums, rest homes, sport facilities, tourist camps, and stores for the MoD. For example, the construction troops erected a new building for the MoD's Central Polyclinic as well as a twelve-story building for the Military Medical Academy. Many of the facilities of the MoD's extensive agricultural network are built by construction units.[101] The construction troops assist in civilian projects as well, helping to build factories, roads, civilian housing, and telephone lines.[102] For example, seven military construction detachments were assigned to help complete metallurgical enterprises in Kazakhstan.[103] Construction units also helped build facilities for the 1980 Olympic Games held in Moscow.[104] They also provide disaster relief.[105] Units from the Kiev military district participated in relief efforts following the 1966 earthquake in Tashkent.[106] The major economic contribution of the construction troops is that they provide a flexible and inexpensive source of both skilled and unskilled labor for projects that would otherwise require civilian labor. As with projects performed by railway troops, the projects assigned to construction troops are often located in remote and inhospitable areas where retention of a civilian workforce would be very expensive.

The military also serves as a source of vocational and technical training.[107] Not all skills acquired during military service are transferable to civilian life. However, many technical skills—machine operation, diesel engineering, and medical, signal, and electrical work—are much in demand in the civilian economy. One Soviet study revealed that 44 percent of the soldiers discharged into the reserves use the skills acquired while in the military in their civilian jobs.[108] The construction troops, for example, provide a wide variety of specialist training courses in addition to on-the-job training.[109] One-third of all conscripts who have completed such training programs reportedly retain their speciality in their postservice careers.[110]

In addition to these economic functions, the military also serves an important educational role. The political leadership views military service as an important part of the party's overall socialization program. The primary target group for the military's socialization program is, of course, the short-term conscripts, most of whom are drafted at age 18 and discharged at age 20 or 21. Socialization within the armed forces, described in detail in Chapter 6, is accomplished formally by the political training courses required of conscripts and informally by the regimented and physically demanding training program.

Socialization is considered to be especially important in the case of the non-Russian soldier who presents a major challenge to the Soviet socialization system.[111] In many cases the values of the minority ethnic groups are in direct conflict with approved Soviet values. The two- or three-year military experience gives the Soviet political leadership an opportunity to break down nationalist loyalties and to increase political and social assimilation. Minority soldiers are conscripted on the same basis as ethnic Russians, integrated into mixed ethnic units and exposed to the same series of political training programs as their Russian counterparts. The military is also seen as a useful supplement to the school as a teacher of the Russian language for those draftees who enter the service with low levels of fluency in Russian.[112] Draft-age youngsters from Central Asia and the Caucasus have been exposed to Russian classes in elementary and secondary classes, but enter the military with only a halting Russian capability. The Soviet leadership is clearly anxious to utilize the Russian-language environment of the military unit as a means of promoting bilingualism.

As suggested above, the Soviets have developed a manning system that supports the military's national security functions as well as its domestic functions. The armed forces require some form of conscription to carry out

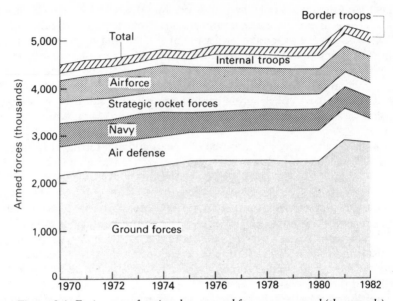

Figure 2.1 *Estimates of active duty armed forces personnel (thousands).*

Source: J. M. Collins, *U.S./Soviet Military Balance. Statistical Trends, 1970–82*, U.S. Congressional Research Service Report No. 93–153S, updated 1 August 1983, pp. 5, 139–43, 149.

both their military and nonmilitary missions. Universal conscription provides large numbers of active duty servicemen to flesh out the core of military professionals in the peacetime army, thus satisfying the military's need for a large standing army. The most recent unclassified data on the active duty force are presented in Figure 2.1. These data include two sizable entities that are not subordinate to the Ministry of Defense: the border guards (which are part of the State Security Committee) and the internal security troops (which are part of the Ministry of Internal Affairs) because the Soviets consider these troops to be part of the "armed forces" and the conscript contingents of these forces are drawn from the same conscription system as those of the regular troops. The active duty service for the draftees also provides future reservists who, in the event of war or crisis, such as Afghanistan, can be mobilized round the professional "core." The large body of trained reservists fulfills the requirement for a vast mobilization base.

A large conscript army also enables the military leadership to accomplish its domestic missions. The two-to-three-year conscript training period exposes the largest possible number of young men to technical training and socialization. The large proportion of draft-age men who are actually conscripted also provides a reservoir of active duty soldiers that can be profitably used to meet spot labor shortages.

The military's dual missions sometimes conflict. Soviet conscription policy, for example, involves drafting as large a proportion of the draft-age cohort as possible. This means that the military routinely conscript many individuals, who because of mental, physical, or language limitations may not be desirable from a purely military standpoint. Military considerations alone might lead to efforts to minimize the number of such draftees to avoid putting undue pressure on the military training system. In terms of socialization and technical training, however, those who are least desirable from a narrowly military perspective are those most in need of the military experience. The military's socialization and educational role, then, argues for drafting such people in spite of their limited contribution to combat capability *per se*. Indeed, the Soviet military minimize the detrimental impact of such individuals on combat capability by assigning them to menial or nonsensitive posts.

This policy of balancing military and domestic needs is never pursued at the cost of reduced combat capability. For example, the political socialization of non-Slavs is enhanced by its practice of assigning them to mixed ethnic units. But the Soviets apparently feel no compulsion to ensure equal representation in every unit. As a result, non-Russians tend to be underrepresented in units requiring high language and communication skills and overrepresented in those positions where such skills are not needed. In this way, the Soviets are attempting to balance goals arising from the military and domestic functions of their armed forces, without sacrificing the primary goal of maintaining a high level of combat capability.

Notes: Chapter 2

1 Morris Janowitz, *Military Conflict—Essays in the Institutional Analysis of War and Peace* (Beverly Hills, Calif.: Sage, 1975), pp. 44–5, 74–8, 121–5, 241–79; Charles C. Moskos, Jr., "The enlisted ranks in the all-volunteer army," in John B. Keeley (ed.), *The All-Volunteer Force and American Society* (Charlottesville, Va.: University Press of Virginia, 1978), pp. 39–63; and Jerald G. Bachman, John D. Blair, and David R. Segal, *The All-Volunteer Force: A Study of Ideology in the Military* (Ann Arbor, Mich.: University of Michigan Press, 1977), pp. 8–18, 119.

2 Morris Janowitz and Charles C. Moskos, Jr., "Five years of the all-volunteer force: 1973–1978," *Armed Forces and Society*, vol. 5, no. 2 (February 1979), pp. 171–218; and Morris Janowitz, "The social demography of the all-volunteer armed force," *Annals of the American Academy of Political and Social Science*, no. 406 (March 1973), pp. 86–93.

3 Morris Janowitz, "The all-volunteer military as a 'sociopolitical' problem," *Social Problems*, vol. 22, no. 3 (February 1975), pp. 432–49.

4 Catherine McArdle Kelleher, "Mass armies in the 1970s: the debate in Western Europe," *Armed Forces and Society*, vol. 5, no. 1 (November 1978), pp. 3–30.

5 D. H. Monroe, "Civil rights and conscription," in Martin Anderson (ed.), *The Military Draft* (Stanford, Calif.: Hoover Institution Press, 1982), pp. 133–51; and Albert A. Blum, "Soldier or worker: a reevaluation of the selective service system," *Midwest Quarterly*, vol. 13, no. 2 (1972), pp. 147–57.

6 Kelleher, 1978.

7 Pierre Dabezies, "French political parties and defense policy: divergence and consensus," *Armed Forces and Society*, vol. 8, no. 2 (Winter 1982), pp. 239–56.

8 Kelleher, 1978. On the U.S. debate on conscription see "The debate on an all-volunteer armed force," in Anderson, 1982, pp. 611–19.

9 Jacques Van Doorn, "The decline of the mass army in the West: general reflections," *Armed Forces and Society*, vol. 1, no. 2 (February 1975), pp. 147–57; and Gwyn Harris-Jenkins

and Jacques Van Doorn, "Armed forces and the social order: a pluralist approach," *Current Sociology*, vol. 22 (1974), pp. 1–33.

10 Conscription in Britain was continued until 1962: Peter J. Dietz and J. F. Stone. "The British all-volunteer army," *Armed Forces and Society*, vol. 1, no. 2 (February 1975), pp. 159–90. See also Thomas A. Fabyanic, "Manpower trends in the British all-volunteer force," *Armed Forces and Society*, vol. 2, no. 4 (August 1976), pp. 553–72.

11 Michel A. Martin, "Conscription and the decline of the mass army in France, 1960–1975," *Armed Forces and Society*, vol. 3, no. 3 (May 1977), pp. 355–406; Philippe Manigart and David Prensky, "Recruitment and retention of volunteers: problems in the Belgian armed forces," *Armed Forces and Society*, vol. 9, no. 1 (Fall 1982), pp. 98–114.

12 The system of selective conscription introduced during the Petrine period is referred to in Soviet sources as "rekrutskaya sistema komplektovaniya": see L. G. Beskrovnyy, *Russkaya armiya i flot v XVIII veke (ocherki)* (Moscow: Voyenizdat, 1958), pp. 22–3. See also M. D. Rabinovich, "Formation of a regular Russian army on the eve of the northern war," *Voprosy voyennoy istorii rossii* (Moscow: Nauka, 1969), pp. 221–3; V. D. Danilov and S. A. Gladysh, "Komplektovaniye vooruzhennykh sil," *SVE*, Vol. 4, pp. 287–90; and N. N. Korol'kov, "Voyennyye reformy petra I." *SVE*, Vol. 2, pp. 264–6.

13 Beskrovnyy, 1958, pp. 22–3, 300–1; and D. V. Pankov, "Russkaya armiya," *SVE*, Vol. 7, pp. 167–75.

14 Beskrovnyy, 1958, pp. 32–3; P. P. Yepifanov, "Rekrutchina," *SVE*, Vol. 7, pp. 103–4; and John Shelton Curtiss, *The Russian Army under Nicholas I, 1825–55* (Durham, N.C.: Duke University Press, 1965), pp. 233–4.

15 Yepifanov, *SVE*, Vol. 7, pp. 103–4; and Beskrovnyy, 1958, pp. 24–36.

16 ibid., p. 301; and P. A. Zayonchkovskiy, *Voyennyye reformy 1860–70 godov v rossii* (Moscow: Izdatel'stvo Moskovskogo Universiteta, 1952), p. 18.

17 Beskrovnyy, 1958, pp. 32–3.

18 Zayonchkovskiy, 1952, pp. 18–19; and Beskrovnyy, 1958, p. 39.

19 A. V. Fedorov, *Russkaya armiya v 50–70 godakh XIX veka. Ocherki* (Leningrad: Izdatel'stvo Leningradskogo Universiteta, 1959), p. 201; Zayonchkovskiy, 1952, pp. 18–19; and L. Bogdanov, "Manning the Russian army on the eve of the motherland war of 1812," *VIZh*, no. 1 (1972), pp. 36–43.

20 Beskrovnyy, 1958, p. 302.

21 ibid., p. 39.

22 Fedorov, 1959, pp. 202–3.

23 Fedorov, 1959, pp. 204–7, 210; and Zayonchkovskiy, 1952, pp. 257–61, 303–5. See also Forrest A. Miller, *Dmitrii Miliutin and the Reform Era in Russia* (Nashville, Tenn.: Vanderbilt University Press, 1968), pp. 182–230.

24 Cossacks were recruited on a different basis and served twenty years. The special treatment of this group reflects the long historical tradition of Cossack military forces in the tsarist empire: UK War Office, Intelligence Division, *Handbook of the Military Forces in Russia* (London: Harrison, 1898), pp. 1–4. A detailed description of the 1874 law is provided in Fedorov, 1959, pp. 248–82. See also Danilov and Gladysh, *SVE*, Vol. 4, pp. 287–90; "Milyutin, Dmitriy Alekseyevich," *SVE*, Vol. 5, pp. 288–9; "Voyennyye reformy Milyutina," *SVE*, Vol. 2, pp. 263–4; and "Voinskaya povinnost'," *SVE*, Vol. 2, pp. 303–4.

25 S. Klyatskin, "On the manning system of the old army," *VIZh*, no. 1 (1966), pp. 107–9; and D. V. Pankov, "The Russian regular army," in *Razvitiye taktiki russkoy armii* (Moscow: Voyenizdat, 1957), pp. 3–30.

26 William Barnes Steveni, *The Russian Army from Within* (New York: Doran, 1914), p. 135.

27 L. G. Syrov, "Kadrovaya sistema," *SVE*, Vol. 4, pp. 23–4; and Fedorov, 1959, p. 251.

28 K. F. Shatsillo, *Rossiya pered pervoy mirovoy voynoy (Vooruzhennyye sily tsarizma v 1905–1914 gg)* (Moscow: Nauka, 1974), pp. 84–5.

29 This assessment is based on the discussions that preceded passage of the 1874 Universal Military Service Law. See Fedorov, 1959, pp. 225–47; and P. A. Zayonchkovskiy, "Preparation of the military reform of 1874," *Istoricheskiye zapiski*, no. 27 (1948), pp. 170–201.

30 Zayonchkovskiy, 1952, p. 263; and Fedorov, 1959, pp. 218, 222–3.

31 For a listing of demobilization decrees see "Letopis' boyevoy slavy," *VIZh*, no. 7 (1966), pp. 111–20, and no. 8 (1966), pp. 106–16. See also John Erickson, *The Soviet High Command: A Military–Political History, 1918–1941* (London: Macmillan, 1962), pp. 3–22.

32 "Dekret ob organizatsii raboche-krest'yanskoy krasnoy armii," 15(28) January 1918, in

Dekrety sovetskoy vlasti (Moscow: Gosudarstvennoye Izdatel'stvo Politicheskoy Literatury, 1957), Vol. 1, pp. 352–7. See also Danilov and Gladysh, *SVE*, Vol. 4, pp. 287–90.

33 F.. A. Khomenok, *Pravovoyye voprosy sluzhby v sovetskikh vooruzhennykh silakh* (Moscow: DOSAAF, 1977), pp. 4–5.

34 *50 let vooruzhennykh sil SSSR* (Moscow: Voyenizdat, 1968), p. 27.

35 S. A. Tyushkevich *et al.* (eds.), *Sovetskiye vooruzhennyye sily. Istoriya stroitel'stva* (Moscow: Voyenizdat, 1978), pp. 19–26, 35.

36 Both figures are Soviet estimates. The data for Red Army strength may be inflated in an effort to demonstrate popular support for the Bolshevik cause: ibid., p.46.

37 "Postanovleniye VTsIK o perekhode k vseobshchey mobilizatsii rabochikh i bedneyshikh krest'yan v raboche-krest'yanskuyu krasnuyu armiyu," 29 May 1918, in *Dekrety sovetskoy vlasti* (Moscow: Gosudarstvennoye Izdatel'stvo Politicheskoy Literatury, 1959), Vol. 2, pp. 334–5; and "Postanovleniye pyatogo vserossiyskogo s"ezda sovetov ob organizatsii krasnoy armii," in ibid., pp. 541–4.

38 *50 let*, p. 43. On the universal military training system see "Dekret VTsIK ob obyazatel'nom obuchenii voyennomu iskusstvu," 22 April 1918, in *Dekrety sovetskoy vlasti*, Vol. 2, pp. 151–3. The system was phased out in 1923 and revived during World War II; see P. N. Dmitriyev, "Vsevobuch," *SVE*, Vol. 2, p. 395.

39 Tyushkevich, 1978, pp. 48–9; and Erickson, 1962, pp. 78–9.

40 *50 let*, p. 158; and Tyushkevich, 1978, pp. 93–4.

41 K. Ye. Voroshilov, "Devyat let," in K. Ye. Voroshilov (ed.), *Stat'i i rechi* (Partizdat TsK VKP(b), 1937), pp. 95–103; I. V. Berkhin, *Voyennaya reforma v SSSR* (1924–5gg) (Moscow: Voyenizdat, 1958), *pass.*; Tyushkevich, 1978, pp. 117–37, 147–51; and *50 let*.

42 Berkhin, 1958, p. 78; and Tyushkevich, 1978, pp. 150–1.

43 *Zakon ob obyazatel'noy voyennoy sluzhby* (Moscow: Izdaniye Voyennoy Tipografii Upravleniya Delami Narkomvoyennom i RVS SSSR, 1927), p. 7.

44 ibid., pp. 11–14.

45 ibid., pp. 8–17.

46 S. A. Gladysh, "Territorial'nyy printsip komplektovaniya," *SVE*, Vol. 8, p. 29.

47 "Peremennyy sostav," *SVE*, Vol. 6, p. 287.

48 V. D. Danilov, "Territorial'no-militsionnaya sistema," *SVE*, Vol. 8, pp. 28–9.

49 V. D. Danilov, "Militsionnaya armiya," *SVE*, Vol. 5, pp. 285–6; "Postoyannyy sostav," *SVE*, Vol. 6, p. 470; and "Kadrovyy sostav," *SVE*, Vol. 4, p. 25.

50 G. N. Kolibaba, "Zakony o voinskoy obyazannosti," *SVE*, Vol. 3, pp. 378–82.

51 L. G. Syrov, "Kadrovaya sistema," *SVE*, Vol. 4, pp. 23–4.

52 Tyushkevich, 1978, pp. 194–207; *50 let*, pp. 197–8; and "Zakon o vseobshey voinskoy obyazannosti," 1 September 1939, in *Sbornik zakonov SSSR i ukazov prezidiuma verkhovnogo soveta SSSR* (Moscow: Izdaniye Vedomostey verkhovnogo soveta SSSR, 1945), pp. 82–95.

53 A. A. Yepishev, "Voyennaya politika KPSS," *SVE*, Vol. 2, pp. 191–3.

54 V. Tretyakov, "The armed forces in the political organization of developed socialism," *Vestnik PVO*, no. 1 (1973), pp. 16–23.

55 See, for example, "Response of L. I. Brezhnev to the question of a *Pravda* correspondent," *KZ*, 22 October 1981, p. 1.

56 "Under the banner of great October. Report of comrade D. F. Ustinov, 6 November 1981," *Pravda*, 7 November 1981, pp. 1, 2, 3.

57 *Programma kommunisticheskoy partii sovetskogo soyuza* (Moscow: Politizdat, 1976), pp. 110–12; and *Konstitutsiya (osnovnoy zakon) soyuza sovetskikh sotsialisticheskikh respublik* (Moscow: Politizdat, 1977), p. 15 (articles 31 and 32).

58 I. Bratishchev, "Contemporary war and manpower resources," *KVS*, no. 22 (1971), pp. 21–9; V. D. Sokolovskiy, *Voyennaya strategiya* (Moscow: Voyenizdat, 1968), pp. 247–8, 250–1, 254–6, 286–7, 370–8, and N. V. Ogarkov, "Strategiya voyennaya," *SVE*, Vol. 7, pp. 555–65.

59 N. V. Ogarkov, *Vsegda v gotovnosti k zashchite otechestva* (Moscow: Voyenizdat, 1982), p. 58.

60 ibid., pp. 58–9.

61 K. V. Chicherin, "Mobilizatsiya," *SVE*, Vol. 5, pp. 342–4; and "Mobilizatsiya," *VES*, p. 452.

62 Ogarkov, 1982, p. 62.

63 "O vseobshchey voinskoy obyazannosti," 12 October 1967, as amended in *Svod zakonov SSSR* (Moscow: Izvestiya, 1982), Vol. 9, pp. 181–202, articles 16, 39–56 (hereafter cited as

Universal Military Service Law). See also I. T. Buslayev, "Zapas vooruzhennykh sil," *SVE*, Vol. 3, pp. 398–9.

64 Universal Military Service Law, article 64.

65 "Voinskiy uchet," *SVE*, Vol. 2, pp. 304–5; and "Voyenno-uchetnaya spetsial'nost (VUS)," ibid., p. 260.

66 P. I. Romanov, "Voyennyy komissariat," *SVE*, Vol. 2, pp. 269–70.

67 Universal Military Service Law, articles 89–93.

68 *Konstitutsiya*, article 121; Universal Military Service Law, article 105, paragraph 16. This assessment of the Defense Council's role in declaring mobilization is based on an examination of East European defense councils.

69 James T. Reitz, Harriet Fast Scott, and Christina F. Shelton, *A Preliminary Net Assessment of the Manpower in the U.S./USSR Enlisted Personnel Accession Systems* (GE TEMPO, GE 76 TMP-54-C, March 1977), pp. 29–30.

70 Universal Military Service Law, article 105.

71 Mitiz Leibst, "Soviet mobilization," in *The Soviet Military District in Peace and War: Manpower, Manning, and Mobilization* (GE TEMPO, GE 79 TMP-30), appendix I, pp. I-1–I-19.

72 Peter Kruschin, "The mobilization process," in *The Soviet Military District in Peace and War*, appendix H. pp. H1–H21.

73 M. M. Kir'yan (ed.), *Voyenno-tekhnicheskiy progress i vooruzhennye sily SSSR* (Moscow: Voyenizdat, 1982), pp. 312, 314.

74 ibid., p. 326.

75 Ogarkov, op. cit., *SVE*, Vol. 7, pp. 555–65.

76 Ye. I. Dolgopolov, "Natsional'no-osvoboditel'naya voyna," *SVE*, Vol. 5, pp. 536–9; and Ogarkov, *SVE*, Vol. 7, pp. 555–65.

77 *Pravda*, 13 January 1980; and *XXVI s"yezd kommunisticheskoy partii sovetskogo soyuza* (23 February–3 March 1981 (Moscow: Politizdat, 1981), Vol. 1, p. 30.

78 K. A. Vorob'yev, *Vooruzhennye sily razvitogo sotsialisticheskogo obshchestva* (Moscow: Voyenizdat, 1980), p. 101.

79 ibid., pp. 111–12.

80 Speech by then General Secretary Brezhnev, *Pravda*, 19 January 1977.

81 Yu. V. Andropov, "Rech na plenume TsK KPSS," in *Izbrannyye rechi i stat'i* (Moscow: Politizdat, 1983), pp. 204–6.

82 D. F. Ustinov, "Struggling for peace and strengthening defense capability," *Pravda*, 19 November 1983, p. 4.

83 Vorob'yev, 1980, pp. 76–88.

84 See, for instance, *Krasnoznamennyy dal'nevostochnyy—istoriya krasnoznamennogo dal'nevostochnogo voyennogo okruga* (Moscow: Voyenizdat, 1971), p. 310; E. L. Kovarskiy et al., *Krasnoznamennyy ural'skiy—istoriya krasnoznamennogo ural'skogo voyennogo okruga* (Moscow: Voyenizdat, 1983), pp. 257–8; F. F. Viktorov et al., *Istoriya ordena lenina leningradskogo voyennogo okruga* (Moscow: Voyenizdat, 1974), p. 535; *KZ*, 15 September 1978, p. 1; 24 September 1980, p. 6; 9 August 1981, p. 1; 25 August 1982, p. 1; 28 August 1983, p. 1; *Krasnoznamennyy severo-kavkazskiy—ocherk istorii krasnoznamennogo severno-kavkazskogo voyennogo okruga* (Rostov: Rostovskoye knizhnoye izdatel'stvo, 1971), pp. 306–8, 353; *Kiyevskiy krasnoznamennyy—istoriya krasnoznamennogo kiyevskogo voyennogo okruga, 1919–1972* (Moscow: Voyenizdat, 1974), pp. 380–1; and *Krasnoznamennyy prikarpatskiy—istoriya krasnoznamennogo prikarpatskogo voyennogo okruga* (Moscow: Voyenizdat, 1982), pp. 234–5.

85 The role of local officials in arranging such transfers is discussed in Jerry F. Hough, *The Soviet Prefects: The Local Party Organs in Industrial Decisionmaking* (Cambridge, Mass.: Harvard University Press, 1969), p. 151. The negative economic consequences of such transfers were criticized by then General Secretary Brezhnev at the 1979 CC plenum: *Spravochnik partiynogo rabotnika. 1980* (Moscow: Politizdat, 1980), p. 19. See also "On further strengthening of labor discipline," in ibid., 13 December 1979, pp. 281–90; and *Sotsialisticheskaya industriya*, 6 September 1983, p. 2.

86 The historical survey of the railway troops is based largely on A. M. Kryukov, "Zheleznodorozhnyye voyska," *SVE*, Vol. 3, pp. 321–3; K. P. Terekhin, A. S. Taralov, and A. A. Tomashevskiy, *Voyny stal'nykh magistraley* (Moscow: Voyenizdat, 1969), pp. 19, 52–86, 148, 268, 290; and M. K. Makartsev, "At war and on the job," *Gudok*, 5 October 1983, p. 3.

87 "Zheleznodorozhnyye voyska," in *Grahdanskaya voyna i voyennaya interventsiya v SSSR. Entsiklopediya* (Moscow: Sovetskaya: Entsiklopediya, 1983), p. 208.
88 A. I. Kupriyanov, "Soldiers' fates,' in *Soldaty BAMa* (Moscow: Voyenizdat, 1977), pp. 79–105; and Ya. Mayorov, "Road, rushing to the future," in *Soldatskiye rel'sy BAMa* (Moscow: Voyenizdat, 1980), pp. 3–17.
89 A. M. Kryukov, "Building of the century," in *Soldaty BAMa*, pp. 3–15; V. Korostelev, "To BAM—skillful specialists," *TIS*, no. 7 (1978), pp. 79–80; Ya. Mayorov, "Soldiers of the steel highways," *Agitator armii i flota*, no. 17 (1978), pp. 20–3; and M. Makartsev, "Soldiers of the steel mainline," *KZ*, 5 October 1983, p. 2.
90 I. N. Krupnitskiy, "By the law of military duty," in *Soldaty BAMa*, pp. 106–39; A. Filimonov, "In order to work better on BAM," *TIS*, no. 5 (1976), p. 52; and V. M. Sergeyev, *Magistral muzhestva* (Moscow: DOSAAF, 1977), pp. 34–7, 103–13.
91 S. A. Kovalev *et al.*, *Baykalo-amurskaya magistral'* (Moscow: Mysl', 1977), pp. 70–80, 98–112; and G. Ya. Berik, "Combat advance guard of youth," in *Soldaty BAMa*, pp. 20–44.
92 N. Shestopalov, "With a feeling of responsibility," *KZ*, 14 August 1983, p. 2.
93 This survey of the construction troops is drawn primarily from A. N. Komarovskiy, "Voyenno-stroitel'nyye chasti," *SVE*, Vol. 2, pp. 251–2.
94 Address by N. F. Shestopalov, "I serve the Soviet Union," Moscow Domestic Television Service, 13 August 1983, transcript translated in *Foreign Broadcast Information Service, USSR National Affairs*, 17 August 1983, pp. v1–v3.
95 Peter Kruzhin, "Construction detachments in the Soviet armed forces," *Radio Liberty Research*, 15 July 1977, RL 145/77, p. 2.
96 A. Tsirlin, "Military builders in the great motherland war," *VIZh*, no. 5 (1968), pp. 107–13.
97 A. I. Romashko (ed.), *Spravochnik voyennogo stroitelya* (Moscow: Voyenizdat, 1978), pp. 317–18.
98 "Polozheniye o voyenno-stroitel'nykh otryadkh ministerstva oborony SSSR," excerpts in *Spravochnik po zakonodatel'stvu dlya ofitserov sovetskoy armii i flota* (Moscow: Voyenizdat, 1970), pp. 167–70.
99 ibid., articles 8 and 17.
100 ibid., article 1.
101 A. Gelovani, "Advances of military builders," *TIS*, no. 8 (1978), pp. 19–23; S. Ul'yanskiy, "To construction—advanced methods," *TIS*, no. 4 (1976), pp. 60–3; and N. F. Shestopalov, "The construction site is life," *Sovetskiy voin*, no. 23 (December 1983), pp. 4–5.
102 Komarovskiy, *SVE*, Vol. 2, pp. 251–2.
103 Ye. Sorokin, "Military builders on construction of metallurgical enterprises in Kazakhstan," *KZ*, 26 September 1981, p. 2.
104 N. F. Shestopalov, "To new advances," *KZ*, 12 August 1979, p. 2; and N. F. Shestopalov, "High duty of military builders," *KZ*, 10 August 1980, p. 2.
105 *Krasnoznamenny turkestanskiy* (Moscow: Voyenizdat, 1976), pp. 362–5.
106 *Kiyevskiy krasnoznamennyy*, p. 380.
107 *Tekhnika i vooruzheniye*, no. 3 (1977), pp. 6–9.
108 O. Kulishev, "A school of patriotism, collectivism, and citizenship," *Zarya vostoka*, 7 August 1980, pp. 2–3; A. Babakov and B. Demidov, "The Leninist principle of the unity of army and people," *Voyennaya mysl'*, no. 11 (1966), pp. 74–89; and V. Vasilev, "Main line to the future," *Tekhnika i vooruzheniye*, no. 11 (1977), pp. 5–7.
109 Komarovskiy, *SVE*, Vol. 2, pp. 251–2.
110 A. Gelovani, "The policy is efficiency," *KZ*, 8 August 1976, p. 2.
111 B. Utkin, "The Soviet army—an army of friendship of the peoples," *VIZh*, no. 2 (1983), pp. 3–11; A. A. Yepishev, "In leadership by the Party," *Armiya bratstva narodov* (Moscow: Voyenizdat, 1972), pp. 27–41; P. Los, "Leninist friendship of the peoples," *KVS*, no. 24 (December 1972), pp. 54–60; and A. Plekhov, "Class and nationalism in Soviet military organizations," *KVS*, no. 23 (December 1972), pp. 14–20.
112 K. S. Grushevoy, "Correctness of Lenin's behests," in *Armiya bratstva narodov*, pp. 280–92.

3

Soviet Conscription Policy: the Citizen Soldier in an Authoritarian State

Military service is an important obligation of citizenship in many Western nation-states.[1] In both the American and French Revolutions the extension of the rights of citizenship (in particular, the right to vote) was closely linked with the responsibility of military service. The linkage between citizenship and mass conscription was most clearly enunciated in France, where conscription was institutionalized early and became widely accepted. In the United States military service has been used as a legitimizing device by groups traditionally excluded from full citizenship. The link between military service and the guarantee of full citizenship was dramatically demonstrated by the extent to which the debate over constitutional recognition of female equality became mired in the more emotional issue of female participation in the military.[2]

Few states, however, have made the linkage between citizenship and military service as explicit as the Soviet Union. The connection between the rights of citizenship and the responsibility to serve is spelled out in the Soviet constitution; article 63 of the 1977 USSR Constitution states that "military service in the ranks of the Armed Forces of the USSR is the sacred obligation of Soviet citizens."[3] This linkage is underlined further in the military oath taken by all soldiers.[4] The principle of universal obligation to serve forms the very basis of Soviet military manpower procurement policy (in Soviet terminology, *komplektovaniye vooruzhennykh sil*).[5] Article 3 of the 1967 law on universal military service states: "All male citizens of the USSR, regardless of origin, social and property status, racial and national affiliation, education, language, attitude toward religion, type and nature of employment and place of residence, must undergo active military service in the USSR Armed Forces."[6] While Soviet conscription policy recognizes that there might be extenuating circumstances in some cases that necessitate deferment or exemption from active duty service, the ultimate goal is "real universality of military service."[7]

Draft Procedures and Deferments

Current procedures governing conscription, deferments, and exemptions from military service are detailed in the 1967 Law on Universal Military Service (as amended). Each year between January and March males who turn 17 during the registration year are registered at the appropriate rayon or city military commissariat, which uses this information to prepare an annual registry of 17-year-old males.[8] The registry provides a basis for evaluating the number and qualifications of the draft-age contingent, and probably is one factor shaping the decision of how many Soviet citizens to draft each year. Military requirements and, to a lesser extent, the needs of the civilian economy are, of course, major factors in this decision, which is legally ratified by the Council of Ministers.[9]

For the draft-age Soviet male, however, it is the local draft board (the induction commission) that determines how his life is to be personally affected by the universal military service law. The induction commission is a committee chaired by the head of the local military commissariat. The commission includes physicians, plus representatives of the local government, party, and Komsomol organizations. Induction commission decisions on whether an individual is to be drafted or granted on exemption or deferment are purportedly based on the individual's desires, health, family status, specialist qualifications, and Komsomol recommendations.[10] Assuming that the available pool of draftees is at least marginally larger than the number actually required in any given region, the induction commission may have considerable latitude in deciding who is drafted and who is deferred and exempted. Most of its decisions, however, are probably based on military commissariat recommendations.

While the Soviet intent to draft as large a proportion of the young male cohort into active duty service is very clear, in practice a small, but undetermined, percentage of young men aged 18–26 avoid active duty service entirely due to a combination of one of the three basic classes of deferments: family hardship, education, and health.[11] Family hardship deferments are provided for those who are the sole support of dependents (parents, children, siblings, wives). Deferments in these cases are necessary because Soviet conscripts are provided with room, board, and pocket money, but not a wage sufficient to support dependents. If the draft-eligible young man is the sole support of his invalid parents or of parents over retirement age, he is temporarily deferred. Family deferments are also granted to individuals who can claim as dependents either (1) two or more children or (2) an invalid wife. Deferments are also granted to individuals who are the sole support of a single, able-bodied mother with two or more children under the age of 8 (who has no other able-bodied children who can support her). Individuals who support either a dependent sibling under the age of 16 or an invalid sibling of any age can get a deferment if they can show that it was not possible to place their dependent siblings in an appropriate institution. These deferments are reviewed periodically, and a change of status (if, for example, the dependent sibling reaches age 16) will result in induction. Young men who reach age 27 without losing their family hardship deferment are exempt from active duty military service and are enrolled in the reserves.

The exact proportion of the 18-year-old pool affected by these provisions is not known. The percentages suggested below are intended to serve only as rough estimates. The number who have managed to acquire two children by age 18 is probably insignificant since less than 4 percent of Soviet males under 20 are married and an even smaller percentage would have acquired the requisite two children.[12] This provision, however, acquires more significance for those who are eligible for educational deferments since young men in their early and mid-twenties who have avoided active duty service through educational deferments are more likely to have acquired a family. The family hardship provision may serve to exempt 3–10 percent of the 18–26-year-old pool from active duty service as conscripts.

A second group of provisions defers active duty military service for individuals attending specified educational institutions.[13] There are three basic types of educational deferments: high school, college, and specialized secondary. The high school deferment is designed to avoid drafting males who for one reason or another have not yet finished high school by age 18. The deferments are granted to all pupils of general education schools (including those in nightschool and correspondence courses) and to pupils of specialized secondary schools who do not already have a high school diploma. This provision is apparently aimed at preventing draft avoidance by youngsters who complete high school in a general education institution, then go back to pick up a specialty diploma at a specialized secondary school. Eligibility for the high school deferment ends after age 20. Youths who take advantage of this deferment are not eligible for the reduced terms of service allowed college graduates. The net impact of the high school deferment is assumed to be very small. Perhaps 1–5 percent of the 18-year-old cohort uses it to postpone service for an average of two years.

A second type of educational deferment is provided for continuing education in full-time day programs of higher educational institutions (VUZy) that are on the list of colleges and universities authorized for such deferments by the Council of Ministers. Students who are granted the college deferment must be continuously enrolled in authorized programs from their first year of study, and the deferment is contingent upon the student maintaining a good standing. The net effect of the college deferment on Soviet conscription rates is not clear. The Soviets publish data on the annual size of the high school graduation classes as well as numbers admitted to full-time college programs, but these data are not broken out by sex, nor do we know what percentage of the entering freshman class came straight from high school with no intervening service or worktime. The data do permit us, however, to place upper limits on the effects of college deferments on conscription rates. In 1982, for example, a year in which 2·4 million young men turned 18, 644,400 students were admitted to higher educational institutions.[14] At this time, females constituted 52 percent of the student body.[15] Applying this ratio to the incoming student body in 1982 results in an estimated male freshman class of 335,088, or 14 percent of the male 18-year-old pool. Clearly, not all of these individuals were recent high school graduates. Because Soviet college admission procedures grant preferential consideration to ex-military servicemen, it is likely that some unknown but significant proportion of male college freshmen are in fact individuals who have already completed their service obligation. Therefore, we may regard 14 percent as the absolute upper limit of young Soviet males who received a college deferment in 1981.

The latest version of the universal military service law limits college deferments to students in institutions approved by the Council of Ministers. The new provision went into effect on 1 January 1982, thereby affecting incoming freshmen for the fall 1982 class.[16] The extent to which this provision limits educational deferment privileges cannot be assessed with precision. Since the Soviets have not published a list of schools affected, we have no way of knowing how many of the 891 higher educational institutions are on the lists of schools for which educational deferments are still granted.[17] Fragmentary data for individual republics, however, suggest that a large proportion of students are excluded from deferment. In Lithuania, for example, only the Lithuanian Agricultural Institute (with 6,800 students) and the Kaunas State Medical Institute (with 27,000 students) are on the list authorized for deferments.[18] Although these institutions represent one-half of Lithuania's student population, the vast majority of the students at the Medical Institute are probably female—meaning that the proportion of male students attending "deferment granting" schools is considerably less than one-half.[19] In other words, the new restriction on college deferments is apparently operating, at least in Lithuania, to cut back substantially on the proportion of young men receiving educational deferments.

A third type of educational deferment covers students of specialized secondary schools that are on the list of authorized institutions and who are enrolled in a reserve officer training program. As with college deferments, deferments are not available for those students who attend one of the unknown proportion of schools not falling on the list of "deferment granting" institutions, nor to students in a "deferment granting" school who are not in an ROTC program. The combined effect of the college and specialized secondary deferment may affect 1–10 percent of the 18–26-year-old males.

Regardless of the actual percentage who receive college or specialized secondary deferments in a given year, not all young men who receive a college or specialized secondary deferment actually escape conscript service. Some are enrolled in a reserve officer training program while in school. Although all such individuals are exempt from conscript service, an undetermined number of them—particularly those in engineering fields—are later called to active duty service as reserve officers for periods ranging from two to three years. Those who are not part of a reserve officer training program will theoretically be eligible for the draft after completion of studies, although their tours of service are reduced to eighteen or twenty-four months. However, repeated educational deferments may serve to postpone eligibility for the draft until the individual is in his twenties, by which time he may have acquired a wife and two children, thus qualifying for a family deferment. Again the marriage patterns for young Soviet males would suggest that this series of circumstances would apply to only a small proportion of males. The proportion affected by the reserve officer training loophole is harder to estimate since we know very little about how many young males are enrolled in ROTC programs. The percentage may range from 10 to 75 percent of the young men who receive college and specialized secondary deferments. Thus the overall estimate of the percentage of young men who manage to avoid conscript service entirely, through use of the educational deferment, ranges from less than 1 to about 9 percent.

Deferments are also granted for health problems.[20] If the problem is a temporary one, the youth will be eligible for call-up after he has received treatment. If not, the youth is granted a deferment and reexamined after three years. If he is still unable to serve on active duty at that time, he will be placed on the reserve roles and be subject to periodic medical reexamination until age 27. The proportion of draft-age males who escape service entirely for medical reasons is not known. Under U.S. medical standards for military service, an estimated 16 percent of the American military-age pool is ineligible for medical reasons.[21] This proportion has sometimes been used as a base from which to calculate the likely Soviet rates for medical rejection. It is probable, however, the U.S. rejection rate significantly exceeds that of the Soviets. First, there is evidence that many young Soviet men with a physical impairment are in fact judged fit for active duty service and drafted. Second, although abuse of health deferments undoubtedly does occur (by bribing physicians to authorize illegal deferments), émigré evidence suggests that such incidents are not common. Standards for medical deferments are established by the Ministry of Defense; doctors and draft board members who are found guilty of illegal rulings for medical exemptions face stiff penalties, and many of these officials (particularly physicians) have outlets for semi-legal activity that are both more lucrative and less risky. In sum, it is likely that the proportion of the draft pool permanently exempted for medical reasons is quite small, probably not exceeding 5 percent. It is also likely that application of the deferment guidelines varies over time as the MoD tightens or loosens requirements to suit conscript demand.

Yet another category of young men exempt from service as conscripts are those who are accepted by one of the nearly 150 officer commissioning schools. Again we do not know what proportion of the male cohort is affected by this provision, nor the extent to which this proportion has varied over time with officer demand or with the size of the available pool. The proportion of draft-age males who avoid conscript service by attending officer commissioning schools could vary from 2 to 10 percent.

These subtractions leave 55–90 percent of the 18-year-old draft pool eligible for conscription. This represents, in effect, the probable upper and lower limit on the conscription rates. Our data suggest that in the late 1970s 65–75 percent of the 18-year-old pool were drafted at age 18 or 19. An additional 5–10 percent were drafted from among 20–26-year-olds whose educational, health, or family

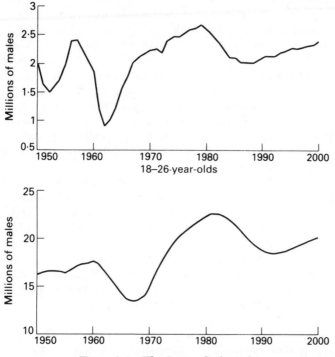

Figure 3.1 *The Soviet draft pool.*

Source: Calculated from unpublished estimates, US Department of Commerce, Bureau of Census Foreign Demographic Analysis Division, June 1972 and May 1982.

deferments expire before age 27. As the draft pool began declining in the late 1970s and early 1980s some of these deferment provisions (particularly those affecting higher education) were tightened, and the percentage drafted at age 18 or 19 may have increased to 75 or 80.

Conscript Supply: Quantity and Quality

The quantity and quality of the 18-year-old male draft pool are important factors determining Soviet military effectiveness. The size of the draft pool has varied substantially, echoing Soviet birth rate trends. Figure 3.1 provides trends in the Soviet draft pool over five decades. The 18-year-old pool increased in the mid and late 1950s, reflecting the relatively advantageous population growth conditions on the eve of World War II. By the late 1950s, however, the smaller cohorts born during the war years were entering their late teens, resulting in a dramatic five-year drop in draft-age males. By 1962 the cohort began to increase again as the postwar Soviet baby-boom reached military age. The 18-year-old pool peaked in 1979 and is now on the decline again. By 1988, according to the most recent estimates by the Bureau of Census Foreign Demographic Division, the 18-year-old male pool will have declined by 25·1 percent from its 1979 peak. In the United States, as a point of comparison, the pool of 18-year-old males is also expected to decline by about one-quarter from its 1975 level.[22] At its lowest point (1988) the Soviet 18-year-old male pool is not expected to fall below 2 million. The supply of 18-year-old Soviet males will begin increasing again in the late 1980s—a reflection of fertility developments eighteen years earlier. In the mid-1960s the Soviet fertility decline began to stabilize. The crude birth rate hit a low of 17 per 1,000 in 1969, then began a modest increase. By 1983 the birth rate was 20·1 per 1,000.[23] The increased fertility of the 1970s and 1980s will produce larger draft pools in the late 1980s and 1990s.

Not all Soviet draftees, of course, are drafted precisely at age 18. Eligibility for the draft extends to the twenty-seventh birthday; and although most young conscripts are drafted at age 18 or 19, a minority are conscripted at slightly older ages. As illustrated in Figure 3.1, the overall 18–26-year-old draft pool follows roughly the same trends as the 18-year-old pool; but the fluctuations are significantly smaller and the peak occurs several years later (in 1981). Soviet military manpower planners are probably using this factor to minimize the detrimental impact of the dramatic ups and downs in the 18-year-old pool, postponing conscription for some 18-year-olds several years to cushion future declines.

Numbers, to be sure, are only one aspect of manpower. Qualitative factors are also an important indicator of potential combat effectiveness. Educational levels have increased rapidly in the last several decades. Figure 3.2 displays the changing educational qualifications of young Soviet males aged 20–30. These data are used as a surrogate for more appropriate age groups (that is, those aged 18–26) because sex-specific data for this latter group are not available. As the data in Figure 3.2 make clear, educational levels in the USSR, even among young males, are well below those in the United States. The low levels of educational attainment relative to the U.S. are understandable in view of the fact that it was not until 1934 that a basic four-year package of obligatory primary education for children of school age was fully implemented. Introduction of the basic seven-year package was completed in 1956, and a basic eight-year package by 1959.[24] In the 1960s the focus shifted to transitioning to a basic ten-year educational package. The guidelines adopted by the Twenty-third Communist Party Congress in April 1966 included the goal of completing the phase in to the ten-year program during the 1966–70 five-year plan.[25] Although the network of schools offering complete secondary education was expanded rapidly in the latter half of the decade, by 1970 only 80 percent of those finishing the eighth grade were continuing their education; and the goal of completing the transition to universal secondary education was reiterated in the ninth five-year plan (1971–5). By the end of the five-year plan in 1975 Soviet planners hoped to expand the proportion of eight-year graduates continuing their education to 90–95 percent.[26]

These goals appear to have been achieved. By the late 1970s virtually all of

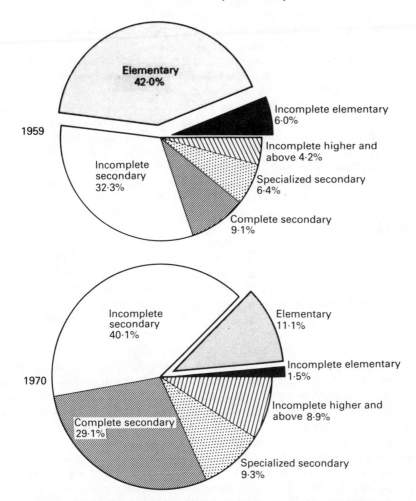

Figure 3.2 *Educational levels among 20–29-year-old males, 1959–70.*

Sources: Itogi, vol. III, 1970, pp. 6–7; *Itogi vsesoyuznoy perepisi naseleniya 1959 godu. SSSR,* Moscow: Gosstatizdat, 1962, pp. 74–5.

those youngsters completing the eighth grade were continuing their schooling in an institution offering a complete (ten-year) secondary education.[27] Education officials claimed that the proportion of youngsters receiving secondary education grew from 86 percent in 1975 to 98 percent in 1978.[28] By 1981, 99·9 percent of those entering the first grade ten to eleven years before were reported to have received a full secondary education.[29] It is not clear, however, whether these data pertain only to pupils in general secondary schools or to the entire school-age cohort (including youngsters in specialized secondary and vocational schools). Full analysis of how well the Soviet school system has implemented the goal of universal secondary education must await the publication of age-specific educational data from the 1979 Census. It seems clear, nonetheless, that a great deal of progress was made during the 1970s in raising educational qualifications of the young age groups.

These trends in overall educational levels were mirrored in educational trends among Soviet conscripts. The conscripts themselves, as opposed to the total 18–26-year-old pool of young people, represent a group with somewhat lower educational qualifications since that portion of the age cohort with the strongest educational background has been selected out (either through college deferments or the reserve officer loophole or through entry to a military commissioning school). One would expect, therefore, that conscript educational qualifications would fall somewhat below those of all 18–26-year-olds. Even so, conscript educational attainments (as reported in the Soviet military press) rose steadily in the 1960s and 1970s.[30] In short, the military has benefited richly from civilian educational programs designed to enhance general educational attainments.

The most recent phase in the program to extend educational opportunity includes a plan to begin regular schooling at age 6. Soviet children begin elementary classes at age 7. While many preschool youngsters (an estimated 52 percent of the 3–6-year-olds in 1978) are enrolled in some sort of child care facility,[31] the primary purpose is to provide baby-sitting services to working Soviet mothers. In the mid and late 1960s Soviet educators began experimenting with preparatory classes for 6-year-olds. These programs were endorsed by the leadership at the Twenty-sixth Party Congress in 1981. The five-year plan directives for 1981 called for efforts "to create the basis for the gradual transition to teaching six year olds in preparatory classes of general education schools."[32] The integration of 6-year-olds into the regular school system was part of a broader overhaul of the educational system endorsed in April 1984. The program calls for the development of a standard curriculum in 1984–5 and a gradual phase-in of schooling for 6-year-olds throughout the country over 1986–90. The new system means that the "basic" educational package will be increased from ten to eleven years.[33] The program has most significance for non-Russian areas. Soviet educators have found that the preschool ages are the time when absorption of a new language is easiest. Beginning the school program one year earlier will have the highest pay-off in non-Russian republics where minority 6-year-olds can begin learning Russian sooner.

Length of schooling, of course, is only one factor in assessing the educational qualifications of the draft-age cohort. Educational quality and curriculum are also important determinants of draftee quality. With relatively few exceptions, Soviet youngsters attend basic, "nontracked" general schools to the end of grade eight; with the implementation of the 1984 school reform, this portion of schooling will begin one year earlier, ending with grade nine (Figure 3.3). The exceptions are a few schools for gifted children and a larger number of special schools for mentally and physically disabled children, plus those with behavioral problems. Elementary schooling, with emphasis on basic reading, writing, and math, now lasts only three years. Adoption of the new reforms will increase this phase of schooling to four years. Over the past several decades

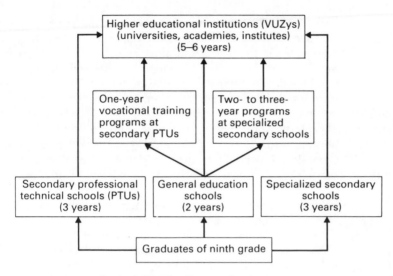

Figure 3.3   *The Soviet school system.*

Soviet planners have been phasing out the smaller elementary and eight-year schools and centralizing all grades in basic ten-year dayschools[34]—a trend Soviet educators view as improving the quality of education. Soviet educators, like their American counterparts, have also been moving to upgrade the educational qualifications of the teaching staff. The proportion of Soviet teachers with college degrees increased from 42 percent in the 1965–6 school year to 75 percent in the 1982–3 school year, while those with only secondary "pedagogical" training declined from 34 to 17 percent.[35]

The curriculum at Soviet general educational schools is academic with strong emphasis on science and math.[36] Classroom routines are more authoritarian than in the United States, with greater stress on rote learning, heavy homework assignments, and frequent assessment. Elective courses are relatively limited; five or six hours of math per week is required in all grades. Biology begins in the fifth grade, physics in the sixth, and chemistry in the seventh. Foreign-language training is mandatory beginning in grade five.

To counterbalance the heavy emphasis on college preparatory courses the curriculum also includes mandatory vocational courses. In the late 1970s these courses were expanded from two to four hours weekly in the last two years of high school.[37] These courses prepare pupils for blue-collar occupations such as tractor repair, metalworking, and machine operation. Schools have been encouraged to affiliate with nearby factories and farms, which provide on-site training for senior pupils.[38] In the next five years the time devoted to vocational training in general secondary schools will be significantly increased, as the changes mandated by the 1984 school reform are put into effect.[39] The new program includes expansion of both "labor training" (that is, classroom coursework in blue-collar skills such as woodworking and draftsmanship) and "socially productive labor" (that is, hours devoted to actually performing blue-collar labor). The time allocated for these purposes in the new program is three hours in the second through fourth grade, four hours in the fifth through seventh grade, six hours in the eighth and ninth grade and eight hours in the tenth and eleventh grade. In addition, beginning in the fifth grade, school-children will be obliged to participate in a "labor practice" session of ten to twenty days' duration during summer vacation. In theory, this expansion of vocational programs in general educational schools should produce an increase in the technical skills of the draft pool. Although many vocational courses are of limited applicability to the type of technical qualifications needed in the military, the expanded class hours devoted to "labor training" will probably produce at least marginal improvements in the technical skills of incoming draftees.

Of greater relevance for draftee quality are Soviet efforts to expand voca-tional and specialized secondary education. Both types of schooling represent a larger effort to "track" graduates of incomplete secondary school into blue-collar and low-level white-collar specialties, including many low-prestige tech-nical occupations in perennially short supply. Vocational–technical schools (professional'no-tekhnikcheskiye uchilishcha, or PTUs) are an alternative to on-the-job training or apprentice programs for skilled and semi-skilled blue-collar workers. The PTU graduates specialize in one of over 1,400 occupations, ranging from skilled blue-collar jobs in carpentry, metalworking, electrical, tractor driving, mechanics, welding, weaving, lathe operation, and typesetting to occupations in the service sector (for example, cook, checkout cashier, barmaid, and waiter) and low-level white-collar jobs (for instance, stenogra-pher, clerk-typist, secretary).[40]

Until 1984 there were several types of PTU: secondary PTUs with a three- to four-year program of study; PTUs with one- to two-year programs designed for students who concurrently or subsequently attend general secondary schools at night; technical schools with a one- to one-and-a-half year program for high school graduates who need a vocational specialty; and evening PTUs.[41] The 1984 school reform includes a provision that will transform all PTUs into secondary PTUs, with separate shorter programs for secondary school grad-uates.[42] The network of PTUs is to be greatly expanded; and the number of admissions of incomplete secondary graduates is to be gradually increased, with the long-term goal of doubling such admissions.

These goals represent a continuation of trends in vocational schooling over the past several decades. Although consistent data broken out by sex are not available, the overall trend (Figure 3.4) is one of expanding access to PTU training within the relevant age cohort.[43] These data suggest that a growing proportion of draft-age males has received technical training that should facilitate related training within the military.[44]

Like the PTUs, specialized secondary schools (or tekhnikums) accept both eight- and ten-year graduates, with shorter programs for high school graduates. By 1982 two-thirds of the students enrolling in day, evening, and correspon-dence programs were ten-year graduates.[45] Graduates of specialized second-

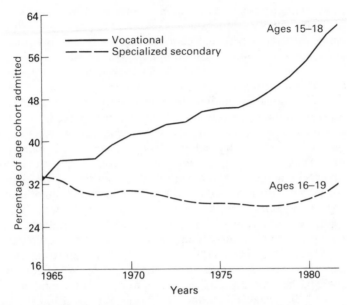

Figure 3.4 *Trends in school admission rates: vocational and specialized secondary.*

ary programs are qualified for a wide variety of mid-level technical jobs in geology, mining, metallurgy, machinebuilding, radio technology, communications, chemical technology, food processing, transport, construction, and agriculture. Mid-level "specialist" jobs in the planning, administrative, and supply bureaucracies are also filled by tekhnikum graduates, who take such posts as bookkeeper, credit inspector, and finance specialist. Mid-level medical personnel (nurses, dentists, and pharmacists) and 'cultural' workers (primary and nursery schoolteachers, library technicians) are also trained in the specialized secondary programs.[46] The expansion of this program occurred in the 1950s and 1960s, and has now leveled off. The slight decline (Figure 3.4) in admissions to specialized secondary schools (relative to the 16–19-year-old cohort) is more than offset by the concurrent expansion in the PTU program.

In sum, the educational qualifications of both the overall Soviet population and of draft-age males have improved dramatically in the last two decades. These trends should facilitate the training of conscripts—a factor of growing importance since the integration of advanced weaponry into the Soviet military is placing greater technical demands on the Soviet soldier.

Predraft Military Training

Of more immediate interest to the Ministry of Defense are the organized programs for predraft military training. When service terms were reduced in 1967, the universal military service law also made mandatory a program of

initial or basic military training (*nachalnaya voyennaya podgotovka*, or NVP)
prior to call-up. The NVP program was intended to partly offset the reduced
training-time associated with the shortened tours.[47] The program has two
purposes: socialization, and military training. As a socialization program, the
NVP course is designed to reinforce earlier lessons in Soviet patriotism and
respect for the armed forces.[48] As a military training program, the NVP course
is intended to instill enough military technical information to allow draftees to
quickly absorb a military specialty once they are conscripted.[49]

The NVP courses are offered in four types of institution: general education
schools; specialized secondary schools; PTUs; and training points at civilian
enterprises. Those attending school take a two-hour-per-week course of
instruction in NVP in the ninth and tenth grades. Youths who are already out of
school and in the laborforce take the NVP course (beginning at age 16) at
enterprise training points designated by the local government.

Implementation of the NVP program, which began in 1968, was a task
of immense proportions. Curriculum, training aids, and equipment had to
be developed and disseminated throughout the country; instructors had to be
hired and trained; and access to firing ranges and other facilities had to be
arranged for. In the 1968–9 school year there were 41,314 secondary (ten-year)
schools and 4,129 specialized secondary schools, plus over 4,000 PTUs.[50] To
complicate matters further these schools are subordinate to many separate
ministries. While most of the general education schools are part of the Ministry
of Education, tekhnikums and PTUs (while coming under the general guidance
of the Ministry of Higher and Specialized Secondary Education and the State
Committee for Vocational–Technical Education, respectively) are subordinated to dozens of specialized, economic ministries. Tekhnikums, for
example, are subordinated to over 100 ministries and other agencies.[51] Even
within the school system, then, the task of integrating the new NVP course
nationwide was by no means a simple one.

Extending the program to boys who had left school to join the laborforce
before completing secondary education was an even more complex problem.
In 1968 there were nearly 50,000 industrial enterprises and about the same
number of farms, plus thousands of stores, construction agencies, and other
places of employment.[52] Incorporating the basic military training course in all
enterprises with youngsters of predraft age proved to be a very difficult task. To
simplify the problem somewhat, small firms with relatively few eligible employees sent their predraft trainees to centralized training points at nearby enterprises.[53] Still, many enterprise officials, preoccupied with the more pressing
problem of meeting plan indicators, viewed their responsibility to provide the
NVP courses with little enthusiasm; and in some cases courses were never set
up or classes met only sporadically.[54] Many young men who left school at the
end of eight years were drafted without having taken the NVP course.

Implementation of the program went much more smoothly in the school
system. By the 1971–2 school year the course had been introduced in the
majority of both general and specialized secondary schools. By the following
year virtually all general education schools had begun the program.[55] By the

mid-1970s less than 1 percent of the secondary general education schools had failed to set up an NVP course.[56] The difficulties of integrating the NVP program were considerably eased by the shift from eight- to ten-year mandatory schooling. The extended schooling program meant that most youngsters could be channeled into military classes within the school system. Virtually all youngsters cycling through the senior years of high school from about the late 1970s on have been through the military course.

The shift in emphasis to the formal educational system did not immediately solve the problems of integrating the new course throughout the country. The most immediate problem was recruitment of instructors (*voyennyy rukovoditel*, or *voyenruk*). The military instructor is part of the school staff. Although directly subordinate to the school director, the *voyenruk* is chosen jointly by the military commissariat and the educational agency in the region. The ideal *voyenruk* is a reserve officer with higher or secondary military education as well as teaching skill.[57] In practice, many military instructors fall far short of the ideal. In the late 1970s the chief of the Ministry of Education's Department of Initial Training complained that rural schools in Moldavia, Kazakhstan, and some of the Siberian and far eastern regions of the RSFSR had particular difficulty in finding qualified instructors. One-third of the military instructors in these areas were reserve sergeants and soldiers (as opposed to reserve officers); and some had only a high school diploma and two years of military service as a conscript, with no military or pedagogical education whatsoever. To alleviate the shortage of qualified instructors Tadzhikstan's Ministry of Education, together with the republic military commissariat, began a program of recruiting reserve sergeants, sending them to a three-month training session in nearby military units, and commissioning them as reserve officers to serve as military instructors in the school system.[58] Other republics set up short-term courses for military instructors in institutes for advanced teacher training.[59]

The long-term solution to the problem of qualified staff, however, is the expansion of special training programs at teacher training institutes. In the late 1970s four-year programs for military instructors were set up in conjunction with the physical education division of several teacher training institutes. The program, which was developed jointly by the Ministry of Defense and the Ministry of Education, includes instruction in pedagogy, military science, and physical education, plus basic military training methods and the fundamentals of military and patriotic socialization. Most of the students in these programs (who are chosen by the military units and military commissariats in conjunction with the education agencies) are ex-servicemen. Graduates are commissioned as reserve officers with the rank of lieutenant and are qualified to teach both military training and physical education. The dual specialty is provided because many rural schools, particularly in the RSFSR, do not have enough pupils to warrant a full-time military instructor.[60] Expansion of these programs should result in significant improvement in instructor quality in the 1980s and 1990s.

Another major problem in implementing the basic military training program within the school system was that of setting up and equipping the necessary training facilities. Guidelines for establishing such facilities were approved by

Red Army and Society

Table 3.1   *Typical NVP Course Plan*

Subject	Number of hours devoted to subject			
	grade 9		grade 10	
	boys	girls	boys	girls
Introduction	1	1	—	—
The Soviet armed forces in defense of the motherland	4	4	7	7
Armed forces regulations	3	3	7	—
Weapon training	20	13	6	6
Tactical training	4	4	6	—
Drill training	7	—	4	—
Military topography	—	—	2	—
Military medical training	2	—	—	—
Civil defence	29	29	—	—
Military technical training	—	—	35	35
First aid	—	16	—	19
Examination	—	—	3	3
Total	70	70	70	70

Source: Adapted from *Uchebno-metodicheskoye posobiye po nachal'noy voyennoyrpodgotovke,* Moscow: Prosveshcheniye, 1981, pp. 227–8.

the MoD's Directorate of External Military Training in 1977. The ideal NVP training complex includes a military office (where classroom lessons are given), a room to store weapons; a firing range, drill field, obstacle course, sentry post, and antiradiation shelter.[61] In practice, of course, many schools fall far short of the ideal. Although virtually all schools had set up facilities for classroom instruction and weapons storage, by 1982 only one-quarter of the schools had a complete training complex, and over one-half lacked a firing range.[62] Substandard facilities in some schools have a serious impact on the quality of training. Although many schools that do not have their own firing range were able to make arrangements to use those of other schools or of nearby military units, the time consumed in transporting students to these facilities eats into class-time, cutting down on opportunities for live-fire target practice.[63]

In spite of these problems in staffing and facilities, the quality of training at NVP courses has undoubtedly improved substantially over the last fifteen years. Curriculum has been developed and refined; textbooks and training aids have been produced and disseminated. The current 140-hour NVP program (Table 3.1) provides basic information on armed forces missions and structure, military regulations, map-reading, and civil defense. Weapon training, tactical field exercises, and drill are also covered. A typical lesson plan is provided in Table 3.2. The course incorporates a five-day field exercise held in the summer between the ninth and tenth grades. Military instructors are urged to site the summer field exercises on the training field of nearby military units whenever possible, in order to approximate service conditions as closely as possible.[64] Other schools use nearby military sports camps.[65]

Assessing the military utility of the NVP course is difficult because of

Table 3.2 *Basic Military Training Course Content*

Theme	*Topics covered*
Soviet armed forces in defense of the motherland	
1 Defense of the motherland and service in the Soviet armed forces—the high and sacred duty of the Soviet citizen	Nature of the Soviet armed forces; military traditions, citizenship, and military service
2 The armed forces in the contemporary state	Principles of armed forces development; influence of the scientific–technical revolution on the armed forces, services, and branches of troops
3 The CPSU on the missions of the armed forces during the period of building communism	The nature of war; the character of a future nuclear war; CPSU policy on further strengthening of defense
4 Command, political, and engineer cadres of Soviet armed forces	Role of cadres in combat, training, and socialization; one-man command, political organs, and party and Komsomol organizations in the armed forces
5 The military oath	Content and significance of oath; the unit military banner
6 Soviet military legislation on service in the armed forces	Role of Soviet law in armed forces development; the universal military service law; legislation on privileges of servicemen and their families
Armed forces regulations	
1 Internal service regulations	Military servicemen and relationships between them; procedures for giving and fulfilling orders, daily detail of the company, internal order in training camps
2 Disciplinary regulations	Military discipline, incentives, and disciplinary punishments
3 Regulations for garrison and sentry duty in armed forces	Sentry duty; changing of the guard
Weapons training	
1 Small-caliber rifle	Mission and combat characteristics; dismantling, assembling, cleaning, lubrication, preparation for fire
2 Firing basics	Processes occurring in the gun barrel during firing, flight of the bullet
3 Methods and rules of fire and fire from small-caliber rifle	Preparing for fire in prone position; qualifying for GTO (ready for labor and defense) norms
4 Kalashnikov rifle	Combat characteristics and structure of AKM; the purpose and structure of parts and mechanism, rules of handling, care and upkeep; RPK v. AKM

Theme	*Topics covered*
5 Methods and rules of fire for stationary targets	Safety measures; preparing to fire from prone position, sitting position, and standing position; target practice
6 Handgrenades and methods of throwing	Structure and combat characteristics of handgrenades; parts and mechanism of grenade, care, handling, and maintenance

Tactical training

1 Basics of combat action and organization and staff structure of the motorized rifle squad, platoon, and company	The essence of tactics, fire, and maneuver in battle, march; precombat and combat formation; interaction in battle; fire control
2 Command and control signals	
3 (Not provided)	
4 Activities of soldiers in battle	Movement of soldiers into battle; overcoming obstacles; choice of place to fire; observers; the soldier in the offense; the soldier in the defense
5 The squad in the offense	Actions of the squad in the offense
6 The squad in the defense	Actions of the squad in the defense
7 Reconnaissance	Basic regulations on military reconnaissance; activities of recce patrols
8 March and march protection	Basic regulations on organization and executing a march; the platoon in protection on the march
9 Location on the ground and outposts	Basic regulations on location on the ground and sentries; the platoon at outposts

Drill training

1 Drill and drill control; commands and obligations of soldiers in drill	Drill and obligations of soldiers in drill
2 Methods of drill and movement without weapons	Drill commands; turning in place; movement at march pace; movement at ceremonial pace; turning left and right; turning around; saluting; leaving formation; approaching commander
3 Methods of drill and movement with weapons	Drilling with weapons
4 Actions of personnel with machines	Drill methods with machines
5 Drilling the squad	Drill preparations within the squad

Military topography

1 Orienting in a location without a map	Basics of orienteering; practice session
2 Movement by azimuth	Understanding azimuth; practice
3 Topographic maps	Measuring distance on topographical maps; representing relief on topographical maps

Theme	Topics covered
Civil defense	Role of civil defense in defense of the
1 Civil defense of economic facilities	motherland; organization and nonmilitarized formations
2 Characteristics of weapons of mass destruction of imperialist governments	Nuclear blasts; zones of radioactive activity; chemical and biological weapons
3 Defense against weapons of mass destruction	Collective means; individual means; evacuation and dispersal of urban population; rules for activity after radioactive, chemical, and biological burst; detoxification
4 Instruments of radiological and chemical reconnaissance	Tactical–technical data; radioactive and chemical measuring instruments; practice session
5 Reconnaissance of burst center	
6 Clean-up work	

Source: As Table 3.1 (*pass.*).

probable variations in the way the course is implemented. It seems clear, nonetheless, that the 140-hour course provides only the most rudimentary introduction to military skills. Nearly one-half of the coursetime, even for the recommended program, is spent in classroom instruction.[66] For example, the recommended program allows each student up to twenty-four shots for live-fire practice using the small-caliber rifle and nine on the Kalshnikov.[67] Few pupils achieve proficiency in the use of these weapons with such limited opportunities for live-fire practice. Similarly, two forty-five-minute lessons are allowed to cover handgrenades. Both lessons are conducted in the classroom (using a mock-up grenade). Pupils have no chance to practice the techniques they are being taught in lecture and text.[68] In short, the NVP course provides no more than a superficial introduction to military skills; and in fact this is precisely what Soviet military educators have designed it to do. The course was never intended to replace the training year lost when service terms were shortened in 1967, but rather to partly offset the shortened terms by instilling enough military–technical knowledge to facilitate absorption of a military specialty once the conscript is actually drafted.

The other plank in the predraft training program is specialist training.[69] Specialist training is provided through DOSAAF training organizations and the vocational–technical education system. Attendance is mandatory for young men aged 17 assigned to such courses. In the city training takes place after a reduced workday. Those attending have special-leave periods of seven to fifteen days to prepare for examinations. Students in rural areas are given leave from work (at half-pay) to attend the specialist schools in the fall and winter. The number of military specialists trained annually through DOSAAF and vocational–technical schools is not known. The DOSAAF schools train specialists for both the military and the civilian economy, and disentangling the two types of training in the general DOSAAF statistics provided by Soviet officials is difficult.[70] The DOSAAF officials claim that one-third of all draftees entering the military have received one of over forty military or related specialties in the DOSAAF schools.[71] The DOSAAF schools provide driver training, naval, radio–technical, and other military specialties. Driver training courses appear to be the most numerous.[72] Naval DOSAAF schools turn out ships' electricians, divers, radio-telegraph operators, mechanics, specialists for ships' engineering departments, and signalmen–helmsmen. Aviation schools train parachutists and other aviation specialists.[73]

The military, then, has certainly profited from the rapid expansion in both general and technical education that took place during the 1960s and 1970s. It is questionable, however, whether these trends, even when coupled with increases in the quantity and quality of the predraft military training programs, have offset the loss of a full year of active duty training when service tenures were shortened in 1967. The new conscript arriving at his military commissariat in response to a call-up notice is certainly better prepared—both intellectually and emotionally—for military service than the average American high school graduate, but he is still a long way from being a soldier.

The Conscript's Role in the Soviet Military

Young men who report to their military commissariats are taken to assembly centers, then dispatched (generally by train and under close supervision) to their military assignment. The length of time they serve will vary depending on the draftee's educational level and on which component of the armed forces he is assigned. The basic term of service for draftees assigned to the army (ground, SRF, PVO, and air) and to the shore and aviation units of the navy, border guards, and internal troops is two years; it is eighteen months for college graduates. Sailors on ships or in combat-support shore units in the navy and naval units of the border guards serve a basic three-year term with reduced tours of two years for conscripts with higher education.[74] The nature of work and training during these service tours varies with the component to which the draftee is assigned.

The five services constitute the primary fighting force of the Soviet military. The youngest of the services, the Strategic Rocket Forces (SRF), was formed in January 1960; and designed to fulfill strategic missions in nuclear war.[75] Conscripts assigned to the SRF serve in a variety of posts. Some conscript positions (for example, radio operator, electrician) are essentially low-level technician jobs requiring some specialist training. Other SRF conscripts serve as drivers or clerks, while others perform menial labor, as sentries, warehouse and supply personnel, mess hall workers, and clerks. The relatively high proportion of jobs requiring technical ability or specialist training means that educational requirements for SRF conscripts are relatively high. The sensitive nature of some SRF assignments means that the standard of reliability are also tighter than for most other conscript posts.

Largest in terms of manpower of the five services are the ground forces. The ground forces consist of five branches of troops (*roda voysk*): the motorized rifle troops, tank troops, airborne troops, rocket and artillery, and air defense.[76] These components are organized into combined arms units which are designated by the name of the predominant branch. The motorized rifle component of the ground forces is the contemporary Soviet version of the infantry.[77] The basic tactical unit of the motorized rifle troops is the squad. The typical squad has an assault strength of eight men, all conscripts, serving a basic two-year term. The squad leader is generally a draftee with the rank of sergeant and a minimum of six months of active duty training. In addition, there are two machine-gunners, one antitank grenadier, and four riflemen.[78] The motorized rifle squad is the basic building-block that absorbs a large proportion of Soviet conscripts drafted into the ground forces. Tank troops are the other basic building-block of combined arms units.[79] The primary building-block for a tank unit is the tank crew, which normally consists of four conscript soldiers: crew commander, gunner, driver-mechanic, and loader. Because crew members are responsible for rudimentary repairs and routine maintenance of their vehicle and equipment,[80] technical and skill requirements for conscripts who serve in tank crews are somewhat higher than for those who are part of a rifle squad. Many former tank crewmen are said to put the maintenance skills they developed in the army to good use in civilian life as mechanics, drivers, and tractor operators.[81] The rocket troops and artillery forces represent the primary fire power of the ground forces.[82] Conscripts assigned to these units serve as squad leaders, drivers and mechanics and in low-level technical jobs (for example, radio-teletype operator, missilemen, cannoneers). Conscripts assigned to air defense units in the ground forces serve as artillerymen, drivers, and maintenance crewmen.[83]

The third service, PVO (Troops of Antiair Defense), is the successor to the now-defunct PVO Strany. Conscripts assigned to the PVO serve in one of several branches: antiaircraft rocket troops, antiaircraft artillery, PVO aviation (fighter aircraft), or radio-technical troops.[84] Many conscripts assigned to PVO units have some specialist training. Some of these serve as drivers and driver-mechanics in motor transport units, communication specialists, or weapons or radar crewmen. There are also a large number of menial positions involving no specialist training (for example, guards, mess hall and warehouse personnel).[85] Conscripts in the airforce also serve two-year terms in one of several branches: long-range aviation, frontal aviation, and military transport aviation.[86] Conscripts assigned to airforce units serve as equipment maintenance personnel, as drivers, and in other support capacities.

Fifth in terms of official Soviet protocol is the Soviet navy. Conscripts assigned to the Soviet navy serve in one of several components: surface ships, submarines, naval aviation, shore rocket-artillery troops, or marines.[87] Draftees in selected posts in shore and aviation units serve a two-year term; the remainder serve a basic three-year term. As with the SRF, PVO, and air forces, the conscript–careerist ratio in the navy is considerably lower than in the ground forces; and technical qualifications are higher.[88]

Combat support for all five services is provided by special troops such as engineer troops, communications troops, chemical troops, and radio-technical and topographic troops.[89] These units are integrated into combined arms formations. Draftees are used in virtually all of the types of special troop units, although the nature of service and the technical qualifications varies widely depending on unit of assignment and position. For example, the communications platoon of a motorized rifle battalion includes several conscript radio operators most of whom will have completed a specialist course. The engineer battalion of a tank division, by contrast, includes many unskilled conscript posts.[90]

Special troops also comprise the mainstay of the Soviet rear services (*Tyl*). Rear services include units designated to maintain transport lines and to provide food, clothing and other supplies, health care, financial support, housing and communal services. In effect, rear services represent a link between the armed forces and the civilian economy.[91] Rear services units support all five services and are integral components of combined arms units. The nature of conscript jobs in rear services components varies. Some posts (for example, ambulance driver in a medical unit, mechanic in a vehicle repair unit) require specialist qualifications, while others involve only unskilled manual labor.

Conscripts may also be assigned to civil defense units,[92] and to two components outside the MoD: the border guards and the internal troops.[93] The border guards, who patrol ground and coastal borders, are subordinate to the Committee for State Security (KGB). They are administered through border districts which are part of the KGB's Main Administration of Border Guards.[94] Conscripts who serve in the border guards are procured through the regular military commissariat system. Most serve a regular two-year term; those in border units that patrol coasts and rivers serve a basic three-year term. Draftees assigned to border guards units must meet particularly high standards of political reliability. The internal troops are subordinate to the Main Directorate of Internal Troops of the Ministry of Internal Affairs (MVD).[95] The internal troops' mission is to provide guard service for key government installations and to maintain militarized formations to help maintain internal order and to quell domestic uprisings. Combat training within the internal troops is governed by the regular armed services regulations; and conscripts assigned to the internal troops generally must meet fairly rigid political reliability standards.

Regardless of the component of the armed forces to which they are assigned, conscripts serve in one of two basic capacities: as rank-and-file soldiers or junior commanders/specialists. Rank-and-file soldiers are assigned directly to their unit upon conscription. There they undergo a "program for young soldiers," a basic training course that lasts about a month. The program is a more intensive version of the NVP course, with heavy emphasis on drill and basic military procedures. During this period the daily routines are even more regimented than those during the balance of the service obligation.[96] By regulation there are no pass privileges until the completion of the program, when the young conscript takes the military oath.[97]

The "program for young soldiers," plus the high school NVP course, represents the sum total of preliminary training received by the rank-and-file soldier. Such conscripts hold the rank of private (*ryadovoy*) or private first class (*yefreytor*). The latter rank, which is awarded for good performance, designates soldiers authorized to fill in for their squad leaders.[98] Rank-and-file soldiers with no specialized training normally serve as riflemen in motorized rifle squads or loaders in a tank crew.[99]

Conscript specialists who have completed a DOSAAF specialist course prior to conscription may also be assigned directly to their unit. Others, however, receive specialist training after conscription, prior to arrival in their regular unit. Until the early 1960s this training was accomplished through division and regiment schools. Division schools, designed to produce both junior commanders (that is, squad and tank crew leaders) and junior specialists (that is, drivers and mechanics) had three- to twelve-month programs.[100] Regimental schools with three- to ten-month programs filled a similar purpose. In 1959 the Soviets introduced a new system of training units; and both the division and regimental schools were phased out.[101] The current system encompasses several types of specialist training. The list of specialties and length of the program is approved at MoD/GS level, while the course content is worked out jointly by training officials at MoD and service level. Junior commanders (conscript sergeants who serve as squad leader or crew chief) are prepared in training units.[102] Specialists are now trained in "junior specialist schools." These programs produce tank gunners, tank driver-mechanics, and antitank guided missile operators for the ground forces, aviation mechanics and radar operators for the air forces, and weapons specialists and repairmen for the navy.[103] Students are recruited from draftees with complete secondary or vocational–technical education. After completion of the three- to six-month program, they are assigned to serve out their regular service obligation in "soldier-specialists" slots in a regular unit.

Reliance on conscript sergeants to serve as tank crew and squad leaders introduces a difficult control problem. The young sergeant is placed in a supervisory relationship over young men who are of the same age and, in many cases, of a more "senior" service tenure. Many sergeants find it virtually impossible to exert any authority over their subordinates; and are pressured into colluding with rank-and-file soldiers to cover up disciplinary offenses.[104]

A major mission of all conscripts—both rank-and-file and junior commanders—is to absorb the military skills necessary to become part of the trained reserve base. The twice-yearly cycle of demobilization of 'senior' soldiers and their replacement by a new batch of freshly drafted conscripts is a tremendously disruptive process for those military units affected. Dealing with this influx of postadolescent males—turning boys into men and civilians into soldiers—absorbs a large portion of the time and energy of the Soviet career force: the professional 'core' in the Soviet citizen army.

Notes: Chapter 3

1 M. Janowitz, *Military Conflict—Essays in the Institutional Analysis of War and Peace* (Beverly Hills, Calif.: Sage, 1975), pp. 74–86.

2 M. D. Feld, "Arms and the woman: some general considerations," *Armed Forces and Society*, vol. 4, no. 4 (August 1978), pp. 557–68.

3 *Konstitutsiya (osnovnoy zakon) soyuza sovetskikh sotsialisticheskikh respublik* (Moscow: Politizdat, 1977), p. 25.

4 "Voyennaya prisyaga," in P. A. Gusak and A. M. Rogachev, *Nachal'naya voyennaya podgotovka: Spravochnoye posobiye* (Moscow: Prosveshcheniye, 1981), pp. 258–9.

5 V. D. Danilov and S. A. Gladysh, "Komplektovaniye vooruzhennykh sil," *SVE*, Vol. 4, pp. 287–90.

6 "O vseobshchey voinskoy obyazannosti," 12 October 1967, as amended in *Svod zakonov* (Moscow: Izvestiya, 1982), Vol. 9, pp. 181–202, article 3 (hereafter cited as Universal Military Service Law).

7 Yu. M. Kozlov *et al.* (eds.), *Upravleniye v oblasti administrativno-politicheskoy deyatel'nosti* (Moscow: Yuridicheskaya Literatura, 1979), pp. 58–9.

8 On induction procedures see "Under combat colors," *KZ*, 28 September 1975, p. 1.; M. Morozov, "For high level of work by the military commissariat," *KVS*, no. 8 (April 1975), pp. 63–70; and V. Kovalev, "Good reinforcements," *KZ*, 29 April 1981, p. 1. The procedures are summarized in V. M. Manokhin (ed.), *Administrativnoye pravo* (Moscow: Yuridicheskaya Literatura, 1977), pp. 440–5; Yu. M. Kozlov, *Administrativnoye pravo* (Moscow: Yuridicheskaya Literatura, 1968), pp. 513–18; and Kozlov *et al.*, 1979, pp. 55–60.

9 Manokhin, 1977, p. 76.

10 Ya. Malyy, "Into the army with a specialty," *Sovetskyy patriot*, 11 June 1975, p. 2; and V. Yanelis, "Reception center of the army," *Smena*, no. 21 (1973), pp. 16–19.

11 Universal Military Service Law, articles 34–8.

12 *Itogi vsesoyuznoy perepisi naseleniya 1970 goda* (Moscow: Statistika, 1972), Vol. II, p. 263.

13 Universal Military Service Law, article 35.

14 *Narodnoye khozyaystvo SSSR v 1982 g* (Moscow: Finansy i Statistika, 1983), p. 468.

15 ibid., p. 473.

16 "On certain questions stemming from the ukase of the Presidium of the Supreme Soviet 'On making amendments and supplements to the USSR law governing universal military service'" 17 December 1980, *Vedomosti verkhovnogo soveta soyuza sovetskikh sotsialisticheskikh respublik*, no. 52 (24 December 1980), p. 1142.

17 *Narodnoye khozyaystvo SSSR v 1982 g.*, p. 462.

18 V. Mitskevichus, "On certain changes in the USSR law on universal military service," *Sovetskaya litva*, 20 March 1982, p. 2. Enrollment data were found in *Sovetskiy entsiklopedicheskiy slovar'* (Moscow: Izdatel'stvo Sovetskaya Entsiklopediya, 1980), pp. 566, 726.

19 In 1977 Lithuania's twelve higher educational institutions had 66,500 students: *Narodnoye khozyaystvo SSSR v 1977 g.* (Moscow: Statistika, 1978), p. 499.

20 Universal Military Service Law, article 36.

21 John M. Collins, *American and Soviet Military Trends* (Washington, D.C.: Center for Strategic and International Studies, 1978), p. 49.

22 Bureau of the Census, "Projections of the Population of the U.S.: 1977–2050," *Current Population Reports*, series D-25, no. 704 (Washington, D.C.: U.S. Department of Commerce, July 1977).

23 *Naseleniye SSSR. 1973. Statisticheskiy sbornik* (Moscow: Statistika, 1975), p. 69; and *SSSR v tsifrakh 1983. Kratkiy statisticheskiy sbornik* (Moscow: Finansy i Statistika, 1984), p. 16.

24 "Vseobshcheye obucheniye," *Sovetskiy entsiklopedicheskiy slovar'*, p. 256.

25 "Direktivy XXIII s''yezda po pyatiletnemu planu razvitiya narodnogo khozyaystva SSSR na 1966–1970 gg," 8 April 1966, in *Resheniya partii i pravitel'stva po khozyaystvennym voprosam* (Moscow: Politizdat, 1968), Vol. 6, pp. 48–103; educational goals are summarized on pp. 82–3.

26 *Gosudarstvennyy pyatiletniy plan razvitiya narodnogo khozyaystva SSSR na 1971–1975 gody* (Moscow: Politizdat, 1972), pp. 308–11. These goals were underlined by a 20 June 1972 Central Committee/Council of Ministers resolution "O zavershenii perekhoda ko vseobshchemu srednemu obrazovaniyu molodezhi i dal'neyshem razvitii obshcheobrazovatel'noy shkoly," in *Resheniya partii i pravitel'stva po khozyaystvennym voprosam* (Moscow: Politizdat, 1974), Vol. 9, pp. 111–18.

27 See, for instance, Ye. Kozhevnikov, "The Soviet teacher—an active, creative force," *Narodnoye obrazovaniye* (hereafter cited as *NO*), no. 10 (1980), pp. 2–7; and "Go further, achieve more," *NO*, no. 12 (1980), pp. 2–6.

28 Ye. Kozhevnikov, "Further improvement of party direction of the general school," *NO*, no. 5 (1979), pp. 2–9.

29 K. Nozhko, "To better compile plans, to better fulfill them," *Uchitel'skaya gazeta*, 24 June 1982, p. 2.

30 The share of conscripts with higher and secondary education increased from 25 percent of those called up in 1959, to 31 percent in 1964, to 72 percent in 1976, and to 87 percent in 1982–3: M. M. Lisenkov, *Kul'turnaya revolyutsiya v SSSR i armiya* (Moscow: Voyenizdat, 1977), pp. 110–11; B. Sapunov, "Our spiritual wealth," *KVS*, no. 12 (1978), pp. 18–27; and *KZ*, 30 March 1983, p. 1. The final source refers to the "present draft"—apparently the spring 1983 contingent.

31 Figures were computed from enrollment data for the end of 1977 provided in *Narodnoye khozyaystvo SSSR v 1977 g* (Moscow: Statistika, 1978), p. 437; and age data for January 1978 provided by the Foreign Demographic Analysis Division, U.S. Bureau of the Census (March 1977).

32 *Pravda*, 14 March 1981, p. 3; and "Osnovnyye napravleniye ekonomicheskogo i sotsialnogo razvitiye SSSR na 1981–1985 gody i na period do 1990 goda," in *Materialy XXVI s''yezda KPSS* (Moscow: Politizdat, 1981), p. 181. The preparatory classes are based on a five-day, twenty-hour-week lesson plan: see "Ob utverzhdenii vremennogo polozheniya o podgotovitel-'nykh klassakh obshcheobrazovatel'nykh shkol," 10 August 1981, excerpted in *Byulleten' normativnykh aktov ministerstva prosveshcheniya SSSR*, no. 12 (1981), pp. 28–30.

33 On the school reform program, as approved by the CC plenum on 10 April 1984 and by the Supreme Soviet on 12 April 1984, see "Basic guidelines for the reform of general educational and vocational school," *Pravda*, 14 April 1984, pp. 3–4. See also the various implementing resolutions relating to the additional school year, "On further improvement of general secondary education of youth and improvement of conditions of work of the general educational school," *Pravda*, 29 April 1984, pp. 1, 3; and "On further improvement of preschool social upbringing and preparing children for study in school," *Kazakhstanskaya pravda*, 19 May 1984, p. 1.

34 The proportion of youngsters in grades 1–3 attending elementary schools declined from 25 percent in 1965–6 to 4 percent in 1982–3. During the same period the proportion of youngsters enrolled in general education day classes (grades 1–10) who were attending ten-year schools increased from 52 percent to 83 percent; computed from data in *Narodnoye khozyaystvo SSSR v 1982 g*, pp. 454–5.

35 ibid., p. 459; and *Narodnoye khozyaystvo SSSR, 1922–1982* (Moscow: Finansy i Statistika, 1982), p. 503. Data on trends in the educational qualifications of American teachers in public schools are available in U.S. Department of Commerce, Bureau of the Census, *Statistical Abstract of the United States, 1981* (Washington, D.C.: U.S. Government Printing Office, 1981), p. 151.

36 Joseph I. Zajda, *Education in the USSR* (Oxford: Pergamon, 1980), pp. 70–83.

37 "O dal'neyshem sovershenstvovanii obucheniya, vospitaniya uchashchikhsya obshcheobrazo-vatel'nykh shkol i podgotovki ikh k trudu," Central Committee/Council of Ministers resolution of 22 December 1977, in *Resheniya partii i pravitel'stva po khozyayastvennym voprosam (1977–1979 gg)* (Moscow: Politizdat, 1979), Vol. 12, pp. 179–90.

38 L. Shilo, "An important link in the system of work training," *NO*, no. 10 (1979), pp. 70–4; A. Plekhov, "Work begins at school," *NO*, no. 9 (1980), pp. 76–9; and *Byulleten' normativ-nykh aktov ministerstv i vedomstv SSSR*, no. 7 (1979), pp. 3–5.

39 "Basic guidelines for the reform of general and vocational education," *Pravda*, 14 April 1984, pp. 3–4. See also subsequent implementing resolutions, "On further improvement of general secondary education of youth and improvement of the conditions of work of the general educational school," *Pravda*, 29 April 1984, pp. 1, 3; and "On improving the labor education, training, and vocational orientation of schoolchildren and organizing their socially beneficial productive labor," *Pravda*, 4 May 1984, p. 1.

40 See, for example, Ye. D. Katul'skiy, V. G. Nikulin, and V. A. Sidorov, "Preparation of young replacements for the working class in the vocational–technical education system," *Sotsiologicheskiye issledovaniye* (hereafter cited as *SI*), no. 4 (1978), pp. 87–93; *Professional'no-tekhnicheskiye i tekhnicheskiye uchilishcha leningrada i leningradskoy oblasti. 1980* (Leningrad: Lenizdat, 1980), *pass.*; *Kommunist tadzhikistana*, 30 May 1980, p. 4; and P. Selivanov, "Professional technical education on the paths of growth and improvement," *NO*, no. 3 (1979), pp. 9–12.

41 "Polozheniye o professional'no-tekhnicheskikh uchebnykh zavedeniyakh SSSR," 11 April 1980, *Sobraniye postanovleniy pravitel'stva soyuza sovetskikh sotsialisticheskikh respublik*, no. 11 (1980), pp. 251–70.

42 "On the further development of the system of vocational and technical education and the enhancement of its role in the training of skilled worker cadres," *Pravda*, 11 May 1984, pp. 1, 3.

43 It should be noted that many students admitted to both vocational-technical and specialized secondary programs have already graduated from general secondary programs. The vocational-technical schools and specialized secondary schools draw their students from graduates of incomplete secondary programs (8/9 years) and graduates of complete secondary programs (10/11 years), as well as young people from the labor force. Data computed from *Narodnoye khozyaystvo SSSR v 1982 g*, pp. 373, 468; *Narodnoye khozyaystvo SSSR 1922–1982*, pp. 410, 512; *Narodnoye obrazovaniye, nauka i kul'tura v SSSR. Statisticheskiy sbornik* (Moscow: Statistika, 1971), p. 187; *Narodnoye obrazovaniye, nauka i kul'tura v SSSR. Statisticheskiy sbornik* (Moscow: Statistika, 1977), p. 174; *Narodnoye khozyaystvo v 1980 g* (Moscow: Finansy i Statistika, 1981), p. 468; and *Narodnoye khozyaystvo v 1974 g* (Moscow: Statistika, 1975), pp. 567, 693. Age data provided by U.S. Department of Commerce, Bureau of the Census.

44 Although the vast majority of PTU entrants are 18 or under (suggesting that most young males enter before rather than after service), an unknown proportion of the male PTU entrants are service veterans. Age breakdowns of PTU students provided in A. A. Bulgakov, *Professional'no-tekhnicheskoye obrazovaniye SSSR na sovremennom etape* (Moscow: Vysshaya Shkola, 1977), p. 107.

45 *Narodnoye khozyaystvo SSSR v 1982 g*, p. 468. See also A. S. Shuruyev, "Development of specialized secondary education in the present state," *Sredneye spetsial'noye obrazovaniye*, no. 6 (June 1982), pp. 6–11.

46 B. A. Kuz'min, *Tekhnikumy i uchilishcha SSSR* (Moscow: Vysshaya Shkola, 1974), pp. 87–111.

47 Provision for initial military training (NVP) is established by article 17 of the Universal Military Service Law.

48 A. Getman, "Military knowledge for the people," *Voyennaya mysl'*, no. 4 (1968).

49 "Polozheniye o nachal'noy voyennoy podgotovke molodezhi," article 1 in *Spravochnik po zakonodatel'stvu dlya ofitserov sovetskoy armii i flota* (Moscow: Voyenizdat, 1970), pp. 43–7; and "Nachal'naya voyennaya podgotovka," *SVE*, Vol. 5, p. 553.

50 *Narodnoye obrazovaniye, nauka i kul'tura v SSSR*, 1971, pp. 44, 151, 221.

51 *Upravleniye sotsial'no-kul'turnym stroitel'stvom* (Moscow: Yuridicheskaya Literatura, 1981), p. 116.

52 *Narodnoye khozyaystvo SSSR v 1969 g* (Moscow: Statistika, 1970), p. 144, 285.

53 M. Sokolov, "The daily routine—military," in S. F. Fel'dman (ed.), *Gotovyatsya parni k voyennoy sluzhbe. Sbornik statey* (Moscow: DOSAAF, 1975), pp. 13–19; and *Sovetskaya estoniya*, 3 March 1970, p. 1.

54 G. Belykh, "Training … without drills," *Sovetskiy patriot*, 4 February 1976, p. 2.

55 G. A. Karpov, "On basic military training of pupils," *Sredneye spetsial'noye obrazovaniye*, no. 4 (1972), p. 13; and I. Averin, "To the results of the All-Union Scientific Practical Conference on Basic Military Training," in *Nachal'naya voyennaya podgotovka v obshcheobrazovatel'noy shkole* (Moscow: Prosveshcheniye, 1973), pp. 3–9.

56 F. Shtykalo, "The high duty of the school," *Sovetskiy patriot*, 22 August 1976, p. 2.

57 P. I. Bykov, "Voyennyy rukovoditel'," *SVE*, Vol. 2, p. 272.

58 A. Averin, "Basic military training: experience and tasks," *NO*, no. 5 (1979), pp. 33–6.

59 A. Kanimetov, "An important task for the school," *Voyennyye znaniya*, no. 6 (1976), pp. 30–1. Advanced teacher training institutes provide refresher courses for teaching staff and other educational workers. In 1977 there were 182 such institutes: "Instituty usovershenstvovaniya uchiteley," *Sovetskiy entsiklopedicheskiy slovar'*, p. 500.

60 *Uchitel'skaya gazeta*, 25 November 1982, p. 3; Yu. Kovalev, "A faculty prepares military instructors," *Voyennyye znaniya*, no. 9 (1981), p. 38; and A. Utkin, "An institute prepares military instructors," *Voyennyye znaniya*, no. 12 (1983), pp. 26–7.

61 F. Ye. Shtykalo and A. I. Averin (eds.), *Uchebno-metodicheskoye posobiye po nachal'noy voyennoy podgotovke (v pomoshch' voyennomu rukovoditelyu)* (Moscow: Prosveshcheniye, 1981), p. 15.

62 F. Shtykalo, "Reserves for improvement," *Voyennyye znaniya*, no. 9 (1982), pp. 36–7; and *KZ*, 25 September 1982, p. 2.
63 *KZ*, 30 May 1981, p. 1; 11 November 1983, p. 2; 23 November 1983, p. 2.
64 N. Yendovitskiy, "Soldier in battle," *Voyennyye znaniya*, no. 5 (1977), pp. 35–6.
65 *KZ*, 29 August 1980, p. 4.
66 Computed from time estimates for each lesson provided in Shtykalo and Averin, 1981, *pass*.
67 ibid., pp. 90–108.
68 ibid., pp 109–11.
69 Universal Military Service Law, article 18.
70 *Kryl'ya Rodiny*, no. 2 (1983), p. 9; and S. I. Grachev, *DOSAAF—Stupeni rosta, 1966–1975* (Moscow: DOSAAF, 1976), p. 124.
71 *KZ*, 31 July 1982, p. 1; A. Odintsov, "The victorious stride of communism," *Voyennyye znaniya*, no. 2 (1976), pp. 2–3; and S. Konobeyev, "Improve the technical means," *Voyennyye znaniya*, no. 9 (1976), p. 38.
72 *Za rulem*, no. 7 (1976), pp. 2–3; K. Shestopalov, "All advanced things in training practice," *Sovetskiy patriot*, 30 May 1976, p. 2; *KZ*, 11 January 1981, p. 1; V. Mel'nichenko, "Not only a specialty," *Voyennyye znaniya*, no. 6 (1982), p. 24; and *Sovetskiy patriot*, 23 August 1978, p. 2; 28 September 1978, p. 3.
73 P. Grishchuk, "On a level with new tasks," *Voyennyye znaniya*, no. 10 (1981), pp. 22–3; A. Pokryshkin, "School of patriotism," *Izvestiya*, 21 January 1981, p. 3; *KZ*, 29 September 1979, p. 4; V. Sinev and A. Stepanenko, "Our experience at preparing specialists for the fleet," *Morskoy sbornik*, no. 12 (1976), pp. 23–5; N. Stepanishchev, "Steps to the sea," *Sovetskiy patriot*, 18 January 1976, p. 1; P. Grishchuk, "Outstanding specialists for the navy," *Voyennyye znaniya*, no. 10 (1976), pp. 38–9; and A. Pokrishkin, "Defense society—50 years," *Morskoy sbornik*, no. 12 (1976), pp. 10–15; and *KZ*, 15 February 1976, p. 1.
74 Universal Military Service Law, article 13.
75 V. F. Tolubko, "Raketnyye voyska strategicheskogo naznacheniya," *SVE*, Vol. 7, pp. 51–3. See also Richard T. Ackley, "Strategic rocket force (SRF)," in David R. Jones (ed.), *Soviet Armed Forces Review Annual* (Gulf Breeze, Fla.: Academic International Press, 1982), Vol. 6, pp. 105–13.
76 A. I. Kvirchishvili and V. K. Zhdanov, *Obshchevoyskovaya podgotovka* (Tbilisi: Izdatel'stvo Tbilisskogo Universiteta, 1969), pp. 48–67.
77 M. P. Shmelev and A. F. Goloborodov, "Motostrelkovyye voyska," *SVE*, Vol. 5, pp. 435–7; and I. G. Pavlovskiy, *Sukhoputnyye voyska* (Moscow: Znaniye, 1977), pp. 37–8.
78 Defense Intelligence Agency, *The Soviet Motorized Rifle Company*, DDI-1100-77-76, pp. 43–4, and *The Soviet Motorized Rifle Battalion*, DDB-1100-197-78.
79 V. Z. Yakushin, "Tankovyye voyska," *SVE*, Vol. 7, pp. 669–72. See also Defense Intelligence Agency, *The Soviet Tank Division*, DDB-1120-19-82, *pass*.
80 Defense Intelligence Agency, *Soviet Tank Company Tactics*, DDI-1120-129-76, May 1976, pp. 3, 9, 11.
81 Pavlovskiy, 1977, pp. 39–40.
82 ibid., 1977, pp. 40–2; G. Ye. Peredel'skiy, "Raketnyye voyska sukhoputnykh voysk," *SVE*, Vol. 7, pp. 53–4; and F. M. Bondarenko, "Artilleriya," *SVE*, Vol. 1, pp. 272–90.
83 Kvirchishvili and Zhdanov, 1969, pp. 60–1; and P. G. Levchenko, "Voyska protivovozdushnoy oborony sukhoputnykh voysk," *SVE*, Vol. 2, pp. 321–3.
84 Well-documented analyses of the PVO are available in David R. Jones, "National air defense force," in Jones (ed.), *Soviet Armed Forces Review Annual* (1979), Vol. 3, pp. 24–44; and David R. Jones, "Air defense forces," *Soviet Armed Forces Review Annual* (1982), Vol. 6, pp. 132–95. See also "Voyska protivovozdushnoy oborony," *VES*, p. 154; and S. Bobylev, "People and traditions," *KZ*, 10 April 1983, p. 2.
85 "In defense of the skies of the motherland," *KVS*, no. 5 (1980), pp. 41–6.
86 "Voyenno-vozdushnyye sily," *VES*, pp. 138–9; and P. S. Kutakhov, "Voyenno-vozdushnyye sily," *SVE*, Vol. 2, pp. 201–8. See also Alfred L. Monks, "Air forces (VVS)," in Jones (ed.), *Soviet Armed Forces Review Annual* (1982), Vol. 6, pp. 196–210.
87 "Voyenno-morskoy flot," *VES*, pp. 142–3; and S. G. Gorshkov, "Voyenno-morskoy flot," *SVE*, Vol. 2, pp. 235–43. On the Soviet marines, see Peter Hertel Rasmussen, "Naval infantry," in Jones (ed.), *Soviet Armed Forces Review Annual* (1982), Vol. 6, pp. 231–4.
88 N. Smirnov, "Ocean shield of the motherland," *KZ*, 31 July 1983, p. 2.
89 "Spetsial'nyye voyska," *SVE*, Vol. 7, pp. 493–4.

90 *The Soviet Tank Division*, p. 11.
91 S. K. Kurkotkin, "Tyl vooruzhennykh sil," *SVE*, Vol. 8, pp. 152–6; and I. M. Golushko, "Tylovoye obespecheniye," *SVE*, Vol. 8, pp. 156–8.
92 A carefully researched analysis of the role of civil defense troops is provided in David E. Murphy, "Military management of Soviet civil defense," in *The Soviet Military District in Peace and War: Manpower, Manning, and Mobilization* (GE TEMPO, GE 79 TMP-30), appendix J, pp. J1–J34.
93 An excellent treatment of non-MoD troops is James T. Reitz, "The Soviet security troops—the Kremlin's other armies," in Jones (ed.), *Soviet Armed Forces Review Annual* (1982), Vol. 6, pp. 279–327.
94 Kozlov *et al.*, 1979, pp. 86–7, 91. See also V. A. Matrosov and V. K. Gaponenko, "Pogranich-nyye voyska," *SVE*, Vol. 6, pp. 365–8; and V. A. Matrosov, *Pogranichnyye voyska* (Moscow: Znaniye, 1979), pp. 24–33.
95 I. K. Yakolev, "Vnutrenniye voyska," *SVE*, Vol. 2, pp. 164–5.
96 "Polozheniye o poryadke prinyatiya voyennoy prisyagi," 30 July 1975, in *Svod zakonov SSSR* (Moscow: Izvestiya, 1982), Vol. 9, pp. 321–2; and V. N. Khropanyuk, "Prisyaga voyennaya," *SVE*, Vol. 6, pp. 546–7.
97 "Uvol'neniye iz raspolozheniya chasti," *SVE*, Vol. 8, p. 165.
98 The corresponding ranks of the navy are *matros* (seaman) and *starshiy matros* (senior seaman): see "Zvaniya voinskiye," *VES*, pp. 272–3; A. A. Ilin, A. D. Kuleshov, and V. K. Marchenkov, "Zvaniya voinskiye," *SVE*, Vol. 3, pp. 433–8: and "Yefreytor," *SVE*, Vol. 3, p. 317.
99 *The Soviet Motorized Rifle Company*, pp. 31–44; and *Soviet Tank Company Tactics*, p. 11.
100 "Divizionnyye shkoly," *SVE*, Vol. 3, pp. 179–80.
101 "Polkovaya shkola," *SVE*, Vol. 6, pp. 426–7.
102 "Uchebnaya chast'," *SVE*, Vol. 8, pp. 233–4; and *VES*, p. 770.
103 *The Soviet Motorized Rifle Company*, p. 31; *Soviet Tank Company Tactics*, p. 11; "Shkoly mladshikh spetsialistov," *SVE*, Vol. 8, p. 521; and *VES*, p. 818.
104 P. Slepukhin, "The role of interrelationships in the system of military indoctrination," *Voyennaya mysl'*, no. 10 (1973). See, for example, Ye. Filatov, "Moral force of competition," *Znamenosets*, no. 12 (1981), p. 9.

4

The Professional Soldier: Career Military in a Conscript Army

Career military personnel represent the professional core of the Soviet armed forces. Initial Bolshevik policies toward military "cadres" (the Soviet term for careerists) were dominated by their deep distrust for military professionals.[1] Many officers from the tsarist army numbered among the staunchest opponents of Lenin's revolution. Because there were few qualified military professionals among the Bolsheviks or their supporters, the new regime was soon forced to turn to former officers of the tsarist army. The deep Bolshevik distrust of these military specialists led to two developments: first, the introduction of a "watchdog" in the form of the military–political commissar; and second, the rapid establishment and then expansion of a military educational system to train politically reliable "Red commanders." The graduates of the first command courses organized under the auspices of this system were trained only in the very loosest sense of the word. After the civil war, the courses were converted to military schools with two- and three-year programs. While these efforts resulted in improvements in the educational level of military cadres, the educational level of the Red Army's leadership still remained very low. By the late 1920s only 6·3 percent of the command staff could boast a higher degree; nearly one-fifth had only elementary education (Table 4.1).

The need to remedy the low educational and technical qualifications of the Red Army's cadres became more pressing in the late 1920s and early 1930s, when Stalin launched the entire country on a breakneck industrialization program designed in part to create the industrial base necessary to support a modern military system. But efforts to train the military in the technical and educational skills needed to master the new military technology were interrupted by the short-lived "cultural revolution"—a campaign begun in 1928 that was intended to increase the proportion of politically trustworthy workers and Communists in both the military and civilian educational systems. The "cultural revolution" produced chaos in both systems and was repudiated in 1931 with a return to stricter standards in selection and grading.[2] This latter policy, coupled

Table 4.1   *Educational Level of Red Army Commanders and Other Personnel,*
1926 (Excluding Navy)

Commanders	Higher	Secondary	Lower	None
Junior	0·1	5·6	84·2	10·0
Middle	0·7	77·3	21·7	0·3
Senior	15·3	69·1	15·4	0·2
Higher	64·1	29·6	5·8	0·5
Total for commanders	6·3	73·6	19·8	0·3
Others				
Administrative	9·2	41·4	48·4	0·6
Political	5·0	44·3	50·0	0·7
Medical	52·9	31·2	15·8	0·1
Veterinary	47·7	28·2	28·7	0·4
Total for all personnel	7·4	51·1	40·6	0·9

Note: No subtotal available for "other" personnel.
Source: Adapted from Ye. Ioseliani, "Party membership and education level of ground forces servicemen," *Statisticheskoye obozreniye*, no. 11, 1928, pp. 99–103.

with a revamping and expansion of military educational institutions, produced significant improvements in the military and educational qualifications of the career force in the 1930s.

The upgrading of military and educational qualifications was part of a larger trend that eventually led to the emergence of a professional Soviet officer corps in the true sense of the word. Moreover, traditional military ranks—which the Bolshevik leadership had abolished in December 1917—were partially reestablished in 1935. This important step toward the development of a corporate identity was reinforced by other policies intended to enhance the authority of an officer. These improvements in status and educational levels were overshadowed by the heavy toll of the Stalinist purges on military cadres. Between 1936 and 1938 many key military commanders were executed, including some of the top officers in the Defense Commissariat.[3] The military cadres that survived the purges were ill-equipped to provide sound leadership on the battlefields of World War II. Many of the early losses sustained by the Soviets were due, in part, to ineffective command.

To meet the pressing need for command personnel the Soviets expanded their military educational system and introduced accelerated training programs. Under the wartime system command programs lasted only one year; engineering specialty programs lasted two years. These programs produced an estimated 400,000 to 500,000 graduates each year during the war. Other steps were taken to legitimize the officer corps. In 1942 line commanders were given more authority when the military commissar (who had the right to countersign the commander's orders) was replaced by a deputy commander for political affairs. In the next year a unified rank structure was adopted. Top officers and the officer corps as an institution were given wide publicity and military hierarchy and discipline were more widely emphasized.

After the war, the Soviets renewed their efforts to modernize the military cadres—taking up, in effect, where they left off when interrupted by the purges and the war. The pressures toward expanded military education programs were increased by the "revolution in military affairs" begun in the early 1950s, which involved the incorporation of nuclear technology into the armed forces. This factor prompted a radical revamping of the officer training system. At this time the standard programs offered in officer commissioning schools were three-year programs in secondary military educational institutions.[4] These schools accepted males up to the age of 23 who had completed secondary education. Applicants were also required to pass an entrance examination. Students who completed the three-year program and passed the state examinations received a government diploma and were commissioned as lieutenants. A smaller number of schools offered four-year programs, leading to a military commission plus a college degree.[5]

Beginning in the 1950s, however, many of the secondary three-year programs were transformed into four- or five-year higher military programs.[6] In addition, new schools offering the longer program were established.[7] This process of upgrading and expanding spanned several decades.[8] Currently, with the exception of a few technical schools, the approximately 140 commissioning schools cited in the Soviet media offer a four- or five-year program. Specifically SRF and navy command schools, as well as the higher military engineering schools, are five years in length.[9] The postwar shift from secondary- to college-level officer commissioning programs has had a major impact on the educational profile of the officer corps.[10] On the eve of World War II only 7 percent of the officer corps had higher military education. Over one-third lacked even a secondary military diploma. The educational attainments of officers changed rapidly in the 1950s and 1960s (Table 4.2). By the mid-1970s Soviet sources were claiming that "over half" of the officer corps had either higher military or military–specialist education. Officer educational levels apparently vary by service; in 1974, for example, over 60 percent of the SRF officers had higher education. By 1984 over 70 percent of the officer corps as a whole was said to have higher military or specialist education.

Keyed to this upgrade in the credentials of the officer corps were a series of modifications in the other components of the career force. Junior officers in the Soviet Union have traditionally filled low-level positions that in many Western countries would be handled by noncommissioned officers. As the Soviet officer corps became better educated and more technologically sophisticated there was an increasing discrepancy between qualifications and duties for many junior officers in lower command posts. It began to make increasing sense from the standpoint of efficiency to staff such posts with career personnel who have qualifications similar to those of noncommissioned officers in other armies. But the noncommissioned officer corps had been virtually abolished with the demise of the tsarist army in 1917 and had never been resurrected. In the early 1970s with the introduction of the warrant officer program, the Soviet military

Table 4.2   *Changing Educational Qualifications of Soviet Officer Corps*

	In typical air forces unit		In typical ground forces unit	
Education type	1951	1966	1946	1966
General education				
Higher	5·0	9·9	7·0	14·0
Secondary	41·0	84·4	31·0	83·0
Incomplete Secondary	54·0	5·7	59·0	3·0
Lower	—	—	3·0	—
Military education				
Higher	5·5	9·8	3·0	11·0
Secondary	70·0	85·9	22·0	84·5
Remedial	21·0	2·8	65·0	4·0
No military education	3·5	1·5	10·0	0·5

Source: M. M. Lisenkov, *Kul'turnaya revolyutsiya v SSSR i armiya*, Moscow, Voyenizdat, 1977, p. 121.

leadership took the first step in the direction of creating a Soviet NCO corps. The Soviet warrant officer program is still in its infancy and it is difficult to predict precisely what effect it will have on the nature of the officer corps and on the character of the career force as a whole. Three other components of the MoD career force—long-term re-enlistees, women, and civilian employees, also examined below—continue to play a relatively minor role in the manpower system. The Soviet officer corps remains, however, in both a quantitative and qualitative sense, the mainstay of the military career force.

Recruiting Soviet Officers

The emergence of an officer corps in the real sense of the word involved an enhancement of the political, economic, and social status of the Soviet officer. Available data suggest that a career as a Soviet officer enjoys fairly high prestige in the USSR. Published studies of Soviet youth attitudes toward various careers abound, but relatively few include data on officer careers—apparently because of the sensitivity of such data. One study that does provide relevant information was conducted between 1968 and 1970; it examines the lifeplans of rural schoolchildren from Amur, Leningrad, Moscow, and Rostov oblasts. Subjects were asked to evaluate fifteen professions on a five-point scale; military careers ranked second highest in Amur oblast (with an average evaluation of 4·32); third in Moscow and Rostov oblasts (with average evaluations of 4·33 and 4·37 respectively); and fourth in Leningrad oblast (with an average score 4·19).[11] A series of early 1970s studies of career orientation among secondary school graduates in Kiev found that a career as a military officer ranked in sixth to eighth place among forty occupations.[12] A 1966 study of career prestige among secondary schoolteachers in Nizhniy Tagil rated "military officer" eleventh of thirty occupations for boys.[13] Other studies reveal that the proportion of young people indicating an intention to enter military commissioning school is considerably greater than actual admissions opportunities. A late 1970s study of career choice that surveyed respondents in sixteen large industrial centers found that 17 percent of the young men in the sample intended to choose a military specialty.[14] A 1973 study of the plans of tenth-graders in Orel found that 8 percent of those surveyed (which apparently included both sexes) intended to enter a military school. Only 3 percent in fact were selected.[15] Another study of career plans of Siberian young people provided data broken out by sex, region, and nationality. These data indicate that Russian boys were more likely to plan on attending a military or aviation higher school than members of native Siberian nationalities. As with many other specialties requiring a higher degree, considerably fewer young men actually realized their intention of attending such institutions.[16]

The explanation for these findings lies partly in the fact that military officers enjoy relatively favored treatment in terms of pay, perquisites, and status. Officer salaries consist of basic rank pay (adjusted for length of service) and position pay. The base pay is supplemented by a variety of bonuses for hardship conditions (for time spent in harsh climatic zones, on field maneuvers, and long voyages) or for specialist qualifications.[17] While the Soviets do not publish military pay scales, there seems to be a common perception among former Soviets that members of the officer corps are relatively well paid. In the mid-1970s military salaries reportedly averaged 150 rubles per month for lieutenants, 160 per month for captains, 220–230 per month for majors, and 250 per month for lieutenant colonels.[18] During this time the average salary for white- and blue-collar workers was 145·8 rubles—a figure that considerably overstates Soviet salaries as a whole since the calculation excludes collective farmers, whose pay is significantly lower.[19] Military pay is somewhat less attractive when compared to salary levels for jobs that are comparable in education. In 1975 engineering and technical workers in industry averaged 199 rubles per month; those in construction averaged 207 rubles per month.[20] Moreover, since average salaries for male employees within a single economic sector are considerably higher than those for females, we may safely assume that the average *male* engineer or technician in industry or construction earned substantially more than 200 rubles per month in 1975.[21] When these factors are considered, reported military salaries appear far less generous. Still, compared to living standards for many segments of society (particularly agricultural workers on collective farms), military officers must surely be perceived as members of the privileged class.

Aside from real income, employee benefits for Soviet officers are relatively generous compared to most of their civilian counterparts. All Soviet employees, as noted in Chapter 1, are dependent on their place of employment for a wide variety of services. The quality of these services varies with the status of the ministry. For example, the quality of medical care for career personnel within the MoD's health network is said to be higher than at analogous civilian facilities. The assortment of goods in Voyentorg stores are reported to be better than those available on the open market. Officer vacation benefits are also relatively generous. The regular paid vacation for officers with up to twenty-five years of service is thirty days, plus travel time; those with more than twenty-five years of service, as well as pilots and submariners, get forty-five days, plus travel time.[22] The minimum civilian vacation is fifteen working-days, with increments for longevity. In 1977 the average annual vacation for adult blue- and white-collar workers was 21·6 working-days.[23] Unlike most civilians, officers are also entitled to sick leave based on the decision of a military medical commission. The only limitation is that officers who are ill longer than four months are examined for fitness to serve and may be released from service on this basis.[24] Civilian employees, by contrast, do not have sick leave. Instead they are entitled to sickness benefits—a percentage of regular wages, the size of which is keyed to years of uninterrupted employment.[25] State employees who are union members and who have three uninterrupted years of employment receive 50 percent of their wages; those with eight or more years receive the full wage. Collective farmers and nonunion employees receive significantly lower sickness benefits.

Pension benefits for military officers are also considerably more generous than those for civilian employees. The military pension system is particularly advantageous for officers on the higher end of the salary scale. Civilians (with the exception of certain categories of workers such as pilots, ship captains, health and educational workers) receive old-age pensions. Career military service personnel, on the other hand, are awarded pensions based on length of service.[26] In other words, an officer can retire after twenty-five years' service regardless of his age. His civilian male counterpart (who must also have twenty-five years' service) cannot retire until age 60. For civilians, the size of the monthly pension check is calculated on a sliding scale, from 100 percent of salary for those making 35 rubles per month to 50 percent of salary for those making 100 rubles or more. The top civilian pension is 120 rubles per month. Military pensions are keyed to length of service. The basic benefit for those with twenty-five years' service is 50 percent of total salary (rank plus position pay), with an additional 3 percent for each year of service over twenty-five, up to a maximum of 75 percent of salary. (Those retired because of unfitness for service or because they reached the mandatory age limit receive a basic package of 60 percent of salary.) Unlike the civilian pensioners, however, there is no 120-ruble ceiling. This provision, of course, is of greatest benefit to senior officers.

In sum, the contemporary Soviet officer corps has benefited from a relatively generous package of pay and perquisites. The living standards of the typical Soviet officer, although spartan by contrast to those in the United States, compare favorably to those of other white-collar "specialists" in the USSR. Still, the relative economic benefits of an officer career should be balanced against the disadvantages. For junior officers especially, the hours are often long and the working conditions poor (particularly during field training exercises). Military assignments frequently involve moving to an isolated military town where amenities are few and employment opportunities for the young officer's spouse virtually nonexistent. The material advantages of a career as a military officer, then, do not fully explain the relatively high social status of a career as a military professional.

An additional explanation is the fact that Soviet schoolchildren and their parents continue to place high value on careers requiring a higher degree.[27] In spite of Soviet efforts to instill in citizens respect for manual labor, and in spite of relatively generous wages for some skilled jobs, blue-collar occupations are still rated low on the scale of occupational prestige.[28] Other studies of factors that contribute to high occupational prestige indicate that the variety, complexity, and challenge of a job are important factors in career rankings. A career in the officer corps is apparently seen as offering these qualities. One study that rated each of seventy-five occupations on several dimensions found that a career as a military officer was similar to those of design engineer and school director in the amount of complexity and variation that characterize job responsibilities.[29] Careers in the officer corps are prized partly because they provide the type of responsibilities to which young people aspire.

Perhaps more important, however, are the efforts made to popularize both the armed forces as an institution and the military officer himself. As a result, the military professional receives wide and favorable publicity across all organs of Soviet mass communications, particularly television. A 1970 study of levels of coverage for fifty-four professions by various types of mass communication indicated that "line officer" ranked tenth. For national-level television coverage it ranked second after scientific work.[30] The military profession, then, seems to have benefited from the generally favorable treatment the armed forces receive in the mass media. These considerations suggest that the officer recruitment system can expect a ready supply of prospective candidates.

Soviet officers are currently procured through one of three separate channels: the officer commissioning school system; reserve officers called to active duty service; and direct commissions of nonofficer personnel.[31] The most important source of new officers at present is the officer commissioning school system—a network of approximately 140 schools similar to, but much more specialized than, the U.S. service academies such as West Point and Annapolis. Each of these commissioning schools prepares officers in one of three general categories: command, political, and engineering/technical.[32] While each school offers its own specialization, certain core subjects are included in all curricula. Programs common to all three categories include: social sciences (that is, Marxism–Leninism, political economy, CPSU history); general disciplines (for instance, math and physics); and certain military disciplines such as operational art, tactics, the history of war and military art, and armed forces regulations. The inclusion of these core courses in the curriculum is designed to produce "specialists with a broad profile."[33]

Programs designed to produce military commanders stress tactics, management, the history of war and military art (including intensive study of World War II and exercise data), and command skills (including military pedagogy and psychology).[34] Programs designed to produce military–political workers place heavier emphasis on the social sciences, particularly party history and the role of party organizations in the military, but the curricula also include heavy

doses of military and military–technical subjects. This is a reflection of the
recent efforts to upgrade military qualifications of Soviet political officers.[35]
Similarly, while the emphasis in engineering–technical programs is naturally on
the repair, maintenance, and the use of arms and equipment, engineering
cadets must also take courses designed to develop their organizational and
pedagogical skills.[36]

Beyond the general core curriculum, the program of study is fairly specialized. Each school produces junior officers for a specific service and branch of
the armed forces.[37] For example, there are twenty-seven schools with an
"aviation" profile, two of which—one in Chelyabinsk and one in Voroshi-
lovgrad—produce graduates specifically intended to fill navigation specialties.
The PVO navigators attend a school for PVO pilots and navigators in Stavro-
pol. There are separate schools for chemical defense, naval radio electronics,
transportation, physical culture, and so on. This sort of specialization reflects
the pattern of Soviet higher education. Soviet civilian institutions of higher
education, particularly those run by the noneducational ministries (for
example, an agricultural institute subordinate to the Ministry of Agriculture)
tend to produce graduates specialized to fill a particular range of jobs.[38]

Admission to the officer commissioning school program is through a series of
competitive entrance examinations. The individual applies to a single school.
The initial application procedure requires information on education, work
experience, and basic biographic data, plus a party or Komsomol reference.[39]
The applications are screened by a selection committee. Those who clear this
hurdle are allowed to take a series of entrance examinations keyed to the
specialty offered by each school.[40] Entrance examinations generally include
mathematics, physics, and Russian language and literature. Applicants to
political schools, however, take examinations in geography and Soviet history
rather than physics.[41] Applicants to one of the three chemical defense schools
take an examination in chemistry as well.[42] Civilian candidates must be male,
single, and under the age of 21. Their applications are handled through the
local military commissariat. Long-term servicemen are also eligible up to the
age of 23, as are warrant officers under the age of 25 who have served three
years. Certain categories of applicants receive a preference in the selection
process. For example, draftees and long-term servicemen who have been
designated as "outstanding" are admitted in a separate selection process, after
completing the entrance examination with an acceptable grade.[43] Tutoring
and/or special preparatory courses for the admission examinations are apparently common. This practice reflects the extreme competitiveness of most
Soviet higher educational programs. Preparatory courses for active duty
servicemen are provided free of charge by the Ministry of Defense; and soldiers
selected to take the entrance examinations are given time off regular duties to
attend the thirty-day course.[44]

Graduates of military secondary schools represent a special source of
recruits for the officer commissioning schools.[45] The military secondary
schools were organized during World War II and originally served children
orphaned by the war. They later evolved into a farm league for the officer

commissioning schools.[46] There are currently eight Suvorov schools and a Nakhimov naval school, plus a secondary school for military musicians.[47] The Suvorov and Nakhimov schools, subordinate to the Ministry of Defense, are explicitly designed to prepare candidates for the officer commissioning school. They accept graduates of eight-year general schools who wish to become officers; graduates of the two-year program are assigned to a specific officer commissioning school, where they are admitted without entrance examinations.[48]

Acceptance by an officer commissioning school marks the beginning of what is reportedly a fairly exhaustive program.[49] Cadets are subject to harsh disciplinary standards and regimented life styles. Those cadets who fail to meet academic standards or who run foul of disciplinary regulations are dropped from the program. If they have entered commissioning school without having completed their conscript service obligation, they are sent to a military unit to serve out their time as a conscript.[50]

Ministry of Defense regulations have also made provision for "direct" commissioning of warrant officers and soldiers. Warrant officers with college or secondary education who successfully complete an external examination covering material in a secondary military training program are commissioned as officers. Such personnel can also enter the officer corps by completing a higher or specialized secondary civilian institution with a concentration similar to one of the military specialties. In addition, soldiers with higher or secondary education can be commissioned after they have completed a junior officer preparatory program and have passed external examinations covering material in a secondary military training program.[51]

The number of Soviet officers who entered the officer corps through this route is not known. One-third of the Soviet officer corps in the early 1970s were reported to be former conscripts or career enlisted men. However, there is no indication what proportion of these men achieved officer status through the various direct commissioning programs as opposed to attendance of a regular officer commissioning school, which grants preferential admission to ex-servicemen.[52] Because direct commissions were an important source of new officers in the past, it seems reasonable to conclude that most of those officers who entered the officer corps through this provision did so a decade or more ago. The frequent references in the Soviet military press to the officer commissioning school system as the major source of officers would suggest that other sources play a much more limited role, particularly for younger officers.

The third source of Soviet officers is the reserve officer corps. Reserve officers are procured from six different sources.[53] It includes, first of all, those officers discharged from active duty service and enrolled in the reserves. Reserve officers are also drawn from among those ex-soldiers with higher or secondary education who receive a reserve commission after passing an examination. In addition, reserve commissions are granted to those soldiers and career enlisted personnel who have completed higher or specialized secondary schools with a military specialty. Such individuals may also receive a commission after a training muster and an examination. Warrant officers with at least five years' experience as a warrant officer can also apply for a reserve officer's commission. The largest source of reserve officers, however, is represented by individuals attending higher or specialized secondary civilian educational institutions who complete the military training program offered through their college's military *kafedra*. All male students attending the day program at civilian institutions that have a military program are apparently required to enroll. The military program generally lasts three years and begins in the third semester of study at four-year courses and in the fifth semester of five-year courses. The programs are specialized and vary depending on the faculty in which the student is enrolled. The quality and quantity of military training received through these programs varies; in some faculties up to one day of instruction per week is devoted to military subjects and there are two monthly field training sessions that are conducted in uniform. Most programs apparently involve a two-month field training exercise after the final year of study.

The distribution of the contemporary Soviet officer corps between the three basic sources of officers—commissioning school graduates, direct commissions, and reserve officers—is not known. The proportion of commissioning school graduates is probably higher among younger officers. The vast majority of new admissions to the Soviet officer corps are products of the officer commissioning school system.[54] A much smaller component (perhaps 5–10 percent of the overall officer corps) consists of reserve officers, mainly those who are serving a two- to three-year tour after having completed reserve officer training programs in civilian colleges and universities.[55] Finally, a very small proportion of the new admissions to the officer corps are "direct commissions."[56]

Officer Career Patterns

The relative stability of the last two decades has meant a regularization of the system of officer promotions and assignments.[57] Cadets who complete officer commissioning school are awarded the rank of lieutenant. They are then assigned to one of a series of lower-level officer posts such as tank platoon commander (in the ground forces) or pilot (in the air forces). Lieutenants generally spend two or three years in rank. Promotion to the next rank (senior lieutenant) is dependent on both assignment and efficiency rating. First, the officer must be appointed to a post that qualifies him for promotion; appointment is based on the recommendation contained in the formal efficiency report (*attestatsiya*).[58] The efficiency report contains narrative descriptions of the officer's political and professional characteristics.[59] There are several types of efficiency reports: regular reports that are issued after the officer has served a specific period of time in his position; those that are prepared when he is reassigned or discharged into the reserves; and those issued for candidates receiving their first officer rank.[60]

The efficiency report is normally prepared by the officer's immediate supervisor, taking into account the opinions of the political office and party or

Komsomol organization. It should include an assessment of the officer's military skills, attitude toward service, relationships with peers and subordinates, and leadership ability.[61] The efficiency report also contains recommendations for the next assignment, or a notation that the officer is unqualified for his present assignment. The report is reviewed by an "attestation commission," consisting of the immediate supervisors of those undergoing attestation, the chief of the political office, the secretary of the party or Komsomol committee, and the chief of the personnel office. In cases where an officer's rating recommends removal from post or includes significant shortcomings the individual being rated must be invited to the attestation commission meeting considering his case. The efficiency reports are approved by the unit commander at a higher echelon.[62] If recommended for a more responsible position (that is, one authorized for a higher rank), the officer should be assigned to the next appropriate post that opens up. After service in this position, the officer can be recommended for promotion in rank. While no minimum set time in post is required before an officer can be recommended for the next rank, simultaneous promotion in position and rank is only supposed to occur in an emergency.

The qualities an officer is rated on are compatible with those used in rating civilian managers. As with civilian rating systems, an officer is evaluated for both his political and professional characteristics. Both the ideal Soviet officer and the ideal civilian bureaucrat are strongly patriotic, hardworking, and display high moral qualities; both are good organizers and enthusiastic leaders who show initiative and creativity.[63] The major difference between the civilian and military manager is the military's greater emphasis on discipline and teaching ability.

As with all rating systems, the Soviet officer efficiency report system is not without problems. Because there are no time limitations on how long an officer can fill a particular position, commanders who are happy with a subordinate's performance often downgrade him on efficiency reports in order to retain his services for as long as possible. Conversely, officers who perform poorly may be enthusiastically recommended for promotion in order to get rid of them. Even when a good officer is recommended for advancement in his efficiency report, he may languish for years in his old job because his superiors, who must recommend him for promotion to a higher-level job, are loathe to give him up.[64]

The Soviet career progression system, then, links rank to position, with promotion to the next-higher rank being dependent on assignment to a position authorized for that rank. This means that upwardly mobile senior lieutenants are frequently assigned to command companies, even though the company commander post is, by "position category," a captain's slot.[65] Table 4.3 provides position categories for ground, PVO, airborne and naval infantry. The career progression implied by this categorization reflects the Soviet version of what is known in the U.S. military as "ticket-punching"—a term to describe the pattern of career assignments that are most conducive to promotion in rank. The "ticket-punching" process in the U.S. military is an informal one, in the sense that no comprehensive regulations exist requiring officers to fill certain posts as a

Table 4.3   *Officer Position Categories in the Ground Forces, PVO, Airborne and Naval Infantry*

Position	Military rank (corresponding to position)
Platoon commander	Junior Lieutenant, Lieutenant, Senior Lieutenant
Deputy company commander	Senior Lieutenant
Company commander	Captain
Deputy commander of battalion	Major
Battalion commander	Lieutenant Colonel
Deputy commander of regiment; regimental chief of staff	Lieutenant Colonel
Regimental commander	Colonel
Deputy division commander; division chief of staff; chief of division political department; assistant division commander	Colonel
Division commander	General Major
Deputy corps commander; corps chief of staff; commander of artillery corps	General Major
Chief of political department/deputy corps commander for political affairs	General Major
Corps commander	General Lieutenant
Assistant commander of army; chief of the rear of army; chief of the engineering troops of the army; chief of the operational department of the army staff; chief of the department of combat training of the army	General Major
Member of military council/chief of politcal department of army; army chief of staff	General Lieutenant
Army commander	General Colonel
Military district commander	General Colonel, Army General, Marshal

Source: 'Polozheniye o prokhozdenii voinskoy sluzhby ofitserami, generalami i admiralami sovetskoy armii i voyenno-morskikh sil,' in *Spravochnik po zakonodatel'stvu dlya ofitserov sovetskoy armii i flota*, Moscow, Voyenizdat, 1970, pp. 171–89.

prerequisite for promotion; in the Soviet military the process is much more formalized and systematized.

Upward mobility also depends to some extent, as it does in the U.S. military, on advanced training. There are two basic forms of advanced training: advanced courses, and military academy programs. Advanced courses, with an instruction program up to one year in duration, are generally taken where the officer is a captain, major, or lieutenant colonel. Junior courses prepare officers for assignment as battalion commander or assistant regimental chief of staff; senior courses qualify officers for assignment as regimental commander or regimental chief of staff.[66] There do not appear to be entrance examinations for these courses. Priority is given to officers who have been recommended for further training in their efficiency reports and those requiring retraining due to reorganization.[67]

The most prestigious (and career-enhancing) form of advanced training is attendance at a military academy. The academies train officers for command and staff positions from regiment to army level. Competition for academy programs is keen. Candidates (usually captains, majors, and lieutenant colonels) generally have to be graduates of an officer commissioning school.[68] Candidates must compete through a series of examinations roughly analogous to those required for entrance to the officer commissioning schools. The pinnacle of the advanced training program is the General Staff Academy, which prepares graduates for assignment to command, staff, and political positions at military district level, at the General Staff itself, or at other MoD headquarters components. Students at the General Staff Academy are colonels and generals (or equivalent ranks) in all five services who have already attended one of the sixteen service/branch academies.[69] The regular program is two years in duration; but the Academy also offers "higher academic courses" of ten to twelve months' duration.[70]

The service military academies and the General Staff Academy represent the essential educational "tickets" for officers who aspire to the top echelons of the military hierarchy. An analysis of military district and groups of force commanders serving in their posts from 1964 to 1981 revealed that 96 percent of those for whom data were available had attended a service academy. Of those, 70 percent attended Frunze Academy, which is the most prestigious of the ground force academies, and 95 percent had attended either the regular or higher academic course at the General Staff Academy.[71]

Career progression in the Soviet officer corps, as in the U.S. counterpart, is linked to position, education, and efficiency reports. In both systems upwardly mobile officers in regular "line" career paths tend to follow a rather rigid progression of command and staff assignments designed to facilitate promotion. The Soviet system, however, seems to be more effective in providing for the nonline officer—the professional specialist (finance officer, administrative officer) for whom the regular "line" career pattern makes little sense.[72] Moreover, while both the U.S. and Soviet upward-bound officers must rotate through a series of career-enhancing posts, tour lengths in the Soviet system are considerably longer. The 1955 officer service regulations specified a normal tour of four years for a company commander. In the late 1970s, as a point of comparison, the optimum length of command tours for U.S. army company grade officers was eighteen months (with a minimum of twelve months).[73] While the 1971 version of the Soviet officer service regulations does not specify length of tours for specific posts, the USSR's personnel management system still operates on the assumption that "a frequent change of officers, particularly in basic command slots, is extremely undesirable."[74] The Soviet treatment of mandatory retirement also differs from U.S. practice. The U.S. 'up or out' policy links retention to promotion (for example, a lieutenant will normally be terminated after being twice considered and twice rejected for promotion).[75] The Soviet system links retention directly to age.

Until 1967 Soviet lieutenants were not allowed to serve after age 30; the 1967 service law raised the maximum age for lieutenants to 40. Majors can now serve until age 45 (as against 40 under the old law); colonels to age 50 (as against 45).[76] Officers who have reached the maximum age are transferred to reserve status and can be retained on active duty for an additional five years (ten years in cases of particular need). The effect of this policy is to dilute the "up or out" principle and to increase the social heterogeneity and age range of each rank.

Corporate Identity of the Soviet Officer Corps

These trends have direct implications for the development of a strong corporate identity among Soviet officers. The historical development of the Soviet career force, as described above, meant that development of a corporate identity was delayed for many decades. The relative stability of the last two decades has provided a more auspicious base for the development of such an identity. This trend has been facilitated by the increased status of the officer professionals during the Brezhnev and post-Brezhnev periods, as well as the increasing emphasis on militarization within civilian society. Another factor facilitating the growth of a corporate identity is an increasing social homogeneity. The Soviet officer corps, like other sectors of the Soviet elite, has historically been recruited from a broad base. The Red Army's earliest commanders represented an uneasy alliance of former tsarist officers, red commanders, and virtually illiterate and undertrained blue-collar workers and peasants. Large World War II losses and rapid recruitment of replacements also operated to maximize social and regional heterogeneity. A sample of general-level officers in 1970 revealed that 54 percent were peasants by social origin—a pattern that probably reflected the social composition of the officer corps in the late 1940s and early 1950s. By contrast, only 18 percent of the junior officers (lieutenants and captains) came from collective farm families—a suggestion of how postwar shifts in social composition are affecting the officer corps.[77] Moreover, postwar trends in officer education mean that an increasing proportion of officers are products of a four- to five-year commissioning school. These graduates can be expected to have a far more favorable attitude toward the armed forces in general, and the officer corps in particular, than either "direct commissions" or reserve officers. This is likely to result in increasing homogeneity of attitudes and values. In addition, Soviet officers like representatives of other segments of the Soviet elite are increasingly passing their own preference for a military career onto their sons and grandsons. Young men from educated, white-collar families are in a more advantageous position to gain admittance to higher education in general; those whose fathers have chosen a military career are more likely to make the same choice. One late 1970s study of parental preferences in careers revealed that 19 percent of the military servicemen wanted their child to attend an officer commissioning school. Only 8 percent of the blue-collar males, 3 percent of the male mid-level specialists, and 1 percent of the male college-educated specialists favored this choice. Similar findings were reported in a

study of attitudes toward military service and officer careers. This factor is likely
to result in a narrowing of the social base of the Soviet officer corps and an
increase in the officer corps' professional identity.[78]

There are, however, several key factors that operate in the opposite direction. One factor that has often been viewed as a prerequisite for the development of a strong corporate identity has been a degree of insulation from the
civilian community. The retention of conscription as a basis for manpower
procurement has ensured a continuing flow of young civilians in uniform
through the military system. This factor has contributed to the permeability of
boundaries between the military and civilian world. A second element that
works against the development of a strong sense of identity is the congruence of
approved values in the military and civilian economy. The ideal Soviet officer,
as detailed above, is a variation on the ideal Soviet civilian manager. The Soviet
system of career appraisal and advancement means that the officers who
flourish are trusted party members whose values are consistent with those of
nonmilitary elites. The conflict between the professional military and the
civilian value system that helps to contribute to a feeling of distinctiveness in
other systems is much less present in the USSR.

Finally, the development of a strong sense of professional identity among
Soviet officers, as among military professionals in other national settings, is
hindered by the existence of competing loyalties. One factor that undermines
officer corps' identity in many Western societies is the existence of competing
service loyalties. This factor, I would argue, is considerably less important in
the USSR. The Soviet Ministry of Defense is more centralized and less
civilianized than the U.S. Defense Department; and the service commands
have less autonomy. The high degree of centralization means there is a relative
abundance of joint commands (staffed by representatives of more than one
military service). These factors have eroded service identity among Soviet
officers, with the possible exception of Soviet naval officers. There are, of
course, other cleavages within the officer corps. One is the distinction between
the "regular" officer and the political officer, which is examined at length in
Chapter 5. Another is the dichotomy between the officer as traditional
commander and the officer as technical specialist. While we do not have precise
figures, it is clear that the proportion of officers with engineering and technical
training is increasing in parallel with the increasing educational profile of the
officer corps. In 1940 only 16 percent of the officer corps was classed as
engineers or technicians. In 1945 this had increased to 28 percent; and by 1971
to 45 percent.[79] By the mid-1970s about 50 percent of the officers in the armed
forces were engineering–technical specialists; over 70 percent of the Air
Defense officers fell into this category.[80] In the SRF alone, by the late 1970s,
over 80 percent of the officer corps consisted of engineers and technicians.[81] At
the same time officers with engineering backgrounds are gradually moving into
command positions. In 1965, in the rocket troops, less than 10 percent of the
unit commanders were engineering officers; about 30 percent of the subunit
commanders were also trained engineers. By the early 1970s over one-half of
the subunit commanders and almost all the unit commanders had higher

military engineering educations.[82] Moreover, the "technocratization" of the officer corps, which is closely linked to the advancing technology of weapons systems, has more recently been accompanied by the increased visibility of technically oriented officers in the MoD decisionmaking hierarchy—a trend personified by former General Staff chief Marshal Ogarkov, an officer with an engineering-specialist background who served as Chief of the General Staff from 1977 to 1984.[83]

Another source of diversity in the Soviet officer corps stems from the long-term practice of assigning active duty officers to selected posts in civilian ministries, generally those involved in defense work. Although such officers are paid by the ministry to which they are assigned, they maintain the legal status, privileges, and obligations of active duty officers and control over their service tours remains with the Defense Ministry's Main Cadres Directorate.[84] Vitaliy Shabanov, now Deputy Defense Minister for Armaments, was apparently part of this program during his 1974–8 tour as Deputy Minister of the Radio-Technical Industry.[85] Aksel' Berg, who was Deputy Defense Minister from 1953 to 1957, may have been assigned under this program both before and after his MoD assignment.[86] Career patterns like Shabanov's and Berg's point up the diversity of experience represented in the officer corps elite. Such officers must surely bring a different set of values and expectations than, say, a Viktor Kulikov—the current Warsaw Pact commander who worked his way up through the regular "line" officer career pattern.

Another source of divergent values within the military hierarchy is the polarity between the large majority of officers who entered the military in the postwar period and the smaller, older group of World War II veterans who dominate the higher echelons of the Ministry of Defense. Soviet scholars writing in 1960 claimed that 60–90 percent of the commanders from company to division level were World War II veterans; in 1957 70 percent of the officers graduating from military academies had participated in World War II.[87] While the wartime generation still dominates the top of the military hierarchy (from deputy military district commander up), as one moves lower in the military hierarchy the proportion of World War II veterans must surely decrease dramatically.[88] Until the late 1970s entry to the very pinnacle of the military elite was very difficult for the younger generation of officers who, although better educated, lacked battle experience. The Soviet invasion of Afghanistan has modified the equation by providing combat experience to a younger generation of upwardly mobile officers. It is too soon to tell how this factor will influence the officer corps' professional identity. On the one hand, the emergence into the top military elite of a younger generation of officers with both sound educational qualifications and combat experience might invigorate the "old guard" of World War II veterans who now dominate the upper echelons of the Ministry of Defense. On the other hand, the existence of these "combat-tempered" cadres may further polarize the top officer elite between men in their sixties and seventies, whose combat experience was in a European war that ended forty years ago, and men in their forties, whose military outlook has been shaped by their contemporary experience in Afghanistan.

Career Enlisted Men and Warrant Officers

The development of the nonofficer career force is inextricably tied with trends affecting the Soviet officer corps. As the general educational and military credentials of the officer corps improved, there was a growing contradiction between the qualifications and the missions assigned to junior officers. The very lowest levels of the "command" hierarchy (that is, squad leaders) have traditionally been occupied by conscript sergeants. Other posts for which neither officers nor conscripts were appropriate have been filled by nonofficer career personnel. Until the early 1970s only one type of serviceman fell in this category: the long-term serviceman. The Russian designation for this category of service, *sverkhsrochnaya voennaya sluzhba* ("above-the-short-term military service"), accurately depicts the only authorized source of such personnel: they are recruited from conscripts serving regular tours. Applicants for the program must have at least eight years of schooling and be 35 or younger; they sign up for periods of two, four, or six years. They are eligible for active duty until age 50.[89] Most long-term servicemen served in one of the four sergeants' ranks or the analogous ranks in the navy. The low educational requirements, generally low pay and status, and the absence of opportunity for career advancement meant that many of the enlistees were of low quality.

The difficulty in attracting and retaining an effective career enlistee force became more acute with the decrease in conscript service terms from three to two years in 1967.[90] The shorter conscript tours created additional difficulties for the conscript sergeant. After the usual six-month training program, the typical drafted sergeant is at his post for only eighteen months—scarcely long enough to gain the experience and expertise necessary to fulfill singlehandedly the control and training mission assigned to the lower-level leadership.

One obvious solution was to beef up the career force. To do this the Soviets introduced a new category of career personnel—the warrant officer.[91] When the warrant officer program was established in 1971, it was clear that the Soviet intent was to phase out the category of long-term servicemen in favor of the better trained and, it was hoped, more effective warrant officers. Indeed, the category of long-term servicemen was temporarily abolished at the same time as the warrant program was instituted. Two years later the Soviets resurrected the program, apparently because the warrant officer program had not grown as rapidly as hoped.[92] Nonetheless, it seems clear that this form of career enlistment is slated for eventual demise. The proportion of long-term enlistees among the current force is quite small. These men are currently assigned to a limited number of relatively menial positions such as drivers or clerks.

The Soviets have now had over a decade of experience with the warrant officer program.[93] The program was introduced by an 18 November 1971 *ukaz* of the Presidium of the Supreme Soviet.[94] This legislation, which came into effect in January 1972, marked the reintroduction of a rank that had been abolished in 1917. Applicants to the program become *praporshchiky* (in the ground, air, PVO, and SRF forces) and *michmany* (in the navy). Applicants must be under 35 with secondary education.[95] Warrant officers are recruited from several sources. One of the main sources is conscripts who have success-fully completed their regular term of obligatory military service and who, under sponsorship of their unit or local draft board, enroll in a specialty warrant officer course. Individuals sponsored by a military unit generally return to that unit to fulfill their five-year service contract. Those sponsored by a local voyenkomat generally attend school within the MD and are assigned to one of the MD's units. Such individuals can also become warrant officers by completing a technical course as part of a specialized secondary program. Conscripts or reserve soldiers with higher and specialized secondary education and a concentration similar to military specialties, who have spent at least one year of active duty service in a conscript capacity, may also apply for warrant status. Active duty warrants are also recruited from among reserve warrant officers. A final source of warrant officers are reserve soldiers who have already completed conscript service, plus a special warrant officer course. Warrant officers sign up for an initial tour of five years and can extend by agreeing to serve additional tours of at least three years, until age 45.

The warrant officer schools are set up in military districts and fleets as either training units or military–educational establishments.[96] The length of the program and curriculum varies, depending on the specialty.[97] When the schools were first established in the early 1970s the curricula were not sufficiently speci-alized and it was, therefore, necessary to set up supplemental lessons—for example, in military administration for future company first sergeants and in vehicle services for future tank and truck-driving instructors.[98] By the early 1980s there were special programs to train platoon commanders in construction units. The training programs for the most responsible posts (like those of platoon commander and senior company technician) generally last longer than those for less technical posts.[99] Warrant officers may also apply to one of several night and correspondence educational programs in military-related fields.[100]

Warrant officers are routinely described in the Soviet military press as "the officer's closest assistant," occupying posts similar to those traditionally occu-pied by junior lieutenants and often working directly with the conscript troops. Warrant officers fill four basic types of position: command, political, technical, and administrative support.[101] Typical command assignments include command of a tank or motorized rifle platoon.[102] In this capacity warrant officers fill a gap between the draftees and the increasingly well-educated career officers. Warrant officers are also assigned to administrative duties at tank company headquarters such as chief of supply.[103] One of the most typical warrant assignments is that of *starshina* or company first sergeant. The *starshina* is responsible for directing morning inspection, distributing duty assignments, making sure uniform regulations are followed, and so on.[104] At battalion headquarters warrant officers are assigned as supply platoon leaders, working closely with the battalion chief of staff.[105] Warrant officers also fill a wide variety of technical positions such as senior company technician or radar station chief.[106] Warrant officers in the navy may serve as sonar team chiefs on ASW ships.[107] Typical warrant assignments in rear services include chief of a dining room, tailor shop, warehouse, depot, or pharmacy. Warrant officers also serve as medical assistants and in posts involving the care of uniforms, housing, and training equipment.[108]

Both salaries and status are higher for warrant officers than for long-term enlistees. As with the regular officer corps, warrant offices are paid a combination of basic rank pay, keyed to length of service, and position pay.[109] The highest position pay is apparently reserved for warrant officers serving in posts (such as platoon leader) to which junior officers can be assigned. Warrant officers also receive a rations allowance and bonuses for first enlistment and uninterrupted service.[110] Vacation benefits are on a par with those of officers: thirty days' leave plus travel time for those on active duty up to twenty-five years; and forty-five days' leave plus travel time for those with more than twenty-five years' service.[111] Additional vacation time is granted for hardship service, that is, on extended submarine duty or in remote areas.[112] Pension benefits are relatively generous and, like those for officers, calculated on years of service.[113]

The program of enhanced pay, status, and perquisites for the warrant officer was clearly more successful in attracting and retaining skilled cadres than the reenlistee system. However, the extent to which the program generated an adequate supply of warrant officers is open to question. Opportunity for advancement within the warrant system was still relatively limited; and this undoubtedly had a detrimental effect on retention. To remedy this problem the Soviets introduced (beginning 1 January 1981) the rank of senior warrant officer.[114] The new rank is awarded to warrant officers with at least five years' service in the warrant program and at least one year's experience in positions authorized for senior warrants or officers.[115] Senior warrant officers typically occupy such posts as platoon commander and company first sergeant in the ground forces and commander of a frogman subunit in the navy.[116] Steps are also being taken to upgrade training. Some of the higher military schools have set up three-year programs for warrant officers leading to a specialized secondary diploma.[117] Warrant officers can also receive specialized secondary training at MoD technikums.[118] The broadening of warrant educational programs is evidently designed to fill the need for low-level technical specialists.[119]

The educational upgrading and expansion of positions open to warrant officers, and the introduction of the senior warrant officer rank, have improved potential for career development. Warrant officers can now improve their military standing through increases in rank or transfer to a more highly rated position. Career progression for warrants, as for officers, is closely linked to the efficiency report (*attestatsiy*).[120] For warrant officers, the report is prepared once every five years by the immediate supervisor. The reports consist of narrative descriptions of the individual being rated, demographic data, the conclusions of the previous efficiency report, the level of training and ability of the warrant officer, and individual shortcomings. The conclusion of the report contains an assessment as to whether the individual is suited for his present job; future posts that he may be qualified for; and the training needed to improve his skill levels. Reports must reflect the opinion of the party or Komsomol secretary and the relevant MPA entity on the individual's political, military, and personal qualities. The efficiency reports are reviewed by the permanent boards set up in units to review applications for the warrant officer program and approved by the direct supervisor of the rater. While warrant officers who do not agree with their rating can submit a complaint to the approving officer, there are no provisions for appeal if the complaint is turned down. Warrant officers in Komsomol staff posts are not rated, but given performance appraisals by the relevant Komsomol committees or bureaus. Such appraisals are approved by the appropriate MPA element.

The net effect of recent Soviet policies relating to the career enlisted contingent is to move the Soviet armed forces somewhat closer to the U.S. pattern. The Soviet warrant officer corps, however, is still in its infancy. The armed forces are competing with the civilian economy for a commodity that is in growing demand: skilled low- and middle-level technicians. In several Western armies this same problem has contributed to a growing reliance on female soldiers—an option that so far the Soviets have avoided.

Women in Uniform

Perhaps no other aspect of manpower policy provides a better mirror of social values than the roles assigned to females in the armed forces. In most industrialized societies military service has been viewed as a quintessentially male activity. With few exceptions, female participation—even in times of urgent need during war—has been largely limited to noncombat and auxiliary roles; the USSR is such an exception. Women were used in relatively large numbers and in a wide variety of both combat and noncombat roles during World War II. Yet paradoxically the peacetime role of women in uniform is quite limited. The rapid increase in females in the peacetime military that occurred in the United States during the 1970s has yet to occur in the USSR.

The virtual exclusion of females from a role in the peacetime military predates the Bolshevik Revolution. Traditional Russian peasant society mirrored its counterparts in Western Europe in its virtually complete reliance on males as a source of military manpower. Female participation in the prerevolutionary military was minimal. The first female officer was Nadezhda Durova, a writer who in 1806 dressed in men's clothing to join a cavalry regiment and later became a heroine of the war of 1812.[121] Women served in more traditional roles as nurses in the Crimean War (1853–6) and in World War I.[122] In 1917, in the final months of World War I, nearly 2,000 female volunteers in Petrograd were organized into a "Woman's Battalion of Death."[123] Despite this dramatic exception, female participation in the Russian military was generally marginal and confined largely to traditional nursing and support functions.

Military roles under the Bolsheviks continued to be assigned almost exclusively to males. During the Civil War, to be sure, a handful of women served as commanders or political workers. Individual women were also active as partisans in Siberia, the Ukraine, Belorussia, and the Caucasus.[124] On the whole, however, female participation in the military during the civil war was limited to traditional roles in nursing and communications. The 1918 decree establishing universal military service extended the obligation to serve to males only. Women had the right to enter the armed forces on a volunteer basis.[125] By the end of the civil war, according to Soviet data, 66,000 women served in the Red Army (2 percent of all military personnel).[126] Nearly all served in traditional female roles as medical workers, administrative personnel, and communications specialists. Nearly 60 percent of all servicewomen during the civil war did administrative work, while 40 percent were involved in medical work. Women also served the military as communications workers.[127] It seems fair to conclude, then, that the utilization of women in the early Soviet military mirrored that in Britain and the United States in World War I—women served primarily in an auxiliary capacity.[128] The Soviet civil war experience, however, does contrast sharply with imperial Germany's refusal to use women in military roles. Female civilians were employed by the German military, but German women were never allowed to become soldiers.[129]

Female participation in the Soviet armed forces remained at a minimal level until World War II. The 1925 and 1939 universal military service laws limited regular conscription to males, although both laws allowed mobilization of women with special skills, such as physicians and veterinarians, during wartime. During World War II, however, women served in the military as both volunteers and draftees. According to Soviet sources, over 800,000 women (an estimated 8 percent of the total number of military personnel) saw service in a variety of posts.[130] In quantitative terms the Soviet use of females in uniform was significantly larger than that of the United States, where women comprised only 2·2 percent of the military force, and a slightly lesser role than in wartime Britain, where women constituted about 9 percent of the armed forces.[131]

As in the United States and Britain, a large number of Soviet servicewomen served in a support capacity; female participation was particularly important in the medical service. Women constituted 41 percent of the physicians serving at the front, and 43 percent of the military surgeons. Virtually all nurses in the military medical service were female, as were 43 percent of the feldshers, and 40 percent of the medical orderlies and attendants.[132] Women also played a major role among traffic controllers; by 1942 more than one-half of the personnel assigned to the military-transport road network were female.[133] Women served as intelligence personnel and communications specialists. Up to 80 percent of the soldiers in some communications units were women.[134] Females served as interrogators for German prisoners of war.[135] While these and other rear service posts filled by females are properly categorized as "support," the nature of much of the fighting in Soviet territory meant that many women assigned to such positions in the Soviet military, unlike their counterparts in the United States and Britain, worked directly at the front, frequently coming under enemy fire.

The most telling contrast between the wartime use of servicewomen in the USSR and that in the United States and Britain is the extensive use of Soviet women in combat roles. Soviet servicewomen served in combat units, many in special female combat formations, others in mixed units. The former included several bomber regiments. In the ground forces Soviet women served as snipers, machine-gunners, and tank crew members.[136] Women were especially prominent in the PVO forces which they began entering on a large scale in the spring of 1942, when the State Defense Committee promulgated two resolutions directing that combat-capable males in the PVO be transferred to regular units.[137] In June 1943, for example, 37 percent of the PVO forces were female.[138] Women served as pilots and air observers, and as antiaircraft and artillery personnel.[139] The widespread presence of females in the PVO forces apparently led to abuses of authority by male officers. One of the concerns of political workers and party organizations in the PVO was to promote correct "relationships" between officers and servicewomen.[140] Soviet women were also active as political workers and as partisans behind enemy lines in the resistance movement.[141]

The Soviet willingness to employ female soldiers in combat contrasts sharply with the extreme reluctance of U.S. and British authorities to allow females in a combat environment, even in auxiliary or support roles. Part of the explanation for this contrast is due to the fact that the USSR was in a far more desperate military situation, facing a foreign invader who occupied vast portions of Soviet territory. While many Soviet males were clearly uncomfortable (at least initially) working in close proximity with military women, the emotional issue "of whether society was ready for women in combat"—an issue that has intensified the debate on the role of women in the U.S. military[142]—was in the Soviet Union preempted by military necessity.

Another factor that helps explain the Soviet willingness to involve women in combat during World War II is the nature of social values governing women's roles. In the United States the traditional role assigned to women is that of full-time wife and mother; in the USSR the cultural ideal is that of a dual commitment to job and family. Middle-class American ideals of womanhood link feminity with physical weakness and helplessness; the predominant female image in the USSR is that of a woman who is capable and strong as well as warm and nurturing.[143] While these differences are to some degree a function of Bolshevik ideology, they also reflect the traditional social values of prerevolutionary peasant society.[144] The focal point for economic and social relationships in the Russian empire before the revolution was the peasant household, invariably headed by a male family member. Although women could not function as head of the household or represent it in the commune (the second major social institution in peasant society), female labor played an important role in family economic activities. The subordinate status of Russian women in the traditional peasant society, then, did not exclude them from an important mission in the agricultural laborforce. The Bolshevik Revolution involved a major transformation in female roles. For both ideological and pragmatic reasons, the new Bolshevik government championed women's legal and social equality. Marxist theory linked women's exploitation with the bourgeois family and the capitalist economic system. The solution to the "woman question" was part of the larger remedy for other forms of oppression—a socialist revolution.[145] The pragmatic reasons for early Soviet support for legal equality were more straightforward. The modernization program sponsored by the

Soviet leadership could not be accomplished without female participation. By 1926 females constituted 47 percent of the employed populace; and although female access to jobs in the modern sector of the economy were considerably more restricted, women comprised 28 percent of the blue-collar industrial laborforce.[146] Changes in gender roles were also spreading—although at a much slower pace—to the Russian countryside.

While many of the changes introduced by the Soviet government were alien to traditional Russian peasant culture (the acceptance of women as full-fledged citizens, for example), the Soviet reliance on females for harsh, physically demanding labor was not at all new. The continuity between the roles assigned to women in Russian peasant society and the heavy Soviet reliance on female labor helps to explain the relative ease with which Russian women moved into industrial occupations that in the West, until recently at least, have remained a virtual male monopoly. The same social values that allowed the use of Soviet women in hard, menial labor probably facilitated their participation in combat during World War II.

Extensive use of servicewomen ended, however, with the close of the war. As in the United States and Great Britain, most servicewomen were demobilized after the end of the war. Those female officers remaining in the service were used as physicians, political officers, interpreters, censors, and staff officers, while enlisted women served mainly in medical, communications, and administrative capacities. In the early 1960s as the supply of young males hit a low point the Soviets accelerated their recruitment of women in certain specialties, including electronics technicians, telephone and radio operators, medical and supply personnel, clerks, and cooks.[147]

The role of women in the contemporary Soviet military is extremely limited. Their virtual exclusion from most military roles contrasts sharply, both with Communist ideals of equality and with the wide female participation in most civilian occupational fields. Perhaps 10,000 servicewomen serve in the Soviet armed forces. They are enlisted under article 16 of the 1967 military service law. This provision states that women aged 19–40 with medical and other specialized training can be (1) registered in military records in peacetime, (2) enlisted for training courses, and (3) admitted as volunteers for active duty service.[148] The legal provisions for female service in the enlisted rank allows physically fit women aged 19–40 to volunteer for duty as soldiers, sailors, sergeants, and starshiny if they are unmarried and childless and have at least eight years of education.[149] Women who meet these qualifications can volunteer for periods of two, four, and six years. Female enlisted personnel appear to serve mainly as radio and telegraph specialists, switchboard operators, nurses, and clerks, and as secretaries on unit staffs.[150]

Women up to age 30 may also volunteer as warrant officers. They must have a higher or specialized secondary education, with a specialization related to one of the military fields for which women are recruited. The military prefer to recruit women who have had some practical experience in their specialties rather than those fresh out of school. Women must accept an initial enlistment obligation of five years; they may reenlist for minimum periods of three years and remain eligible for active duty up to age 45. Female warrant officers serve in rear service specialties associated with communications equipment maintenance, materiel storage and accounting, clerical work, and medical care.[151]

Opportunities for females in the officer corps are extremely limited. Female college graduates (up to age 30) may volunteer as officers. Most women recruited under this provision are graduates of civilian higher educational institutions who have received training in the military departments of those schools.[152] Women are not eligible to attend any of the USSR's officer commissioning schools. Most female officers apparently serve as medical officers after graduating from a medical school ROTC program, others as engineers in communications specialties.[153]

Women serving as enlisted personnel, warrant officers, and officers are recruited through the military commissariat system based on quotas and job specialties designated by the military district headquarters. Lists of occupational specialties open to women are maintained by the General Staff. Female recruits are assigned to their duty stations by military district headquarters. As with the male military personnel, women must take a military oath, but they are not subject to the rigorous physical training of male conscripts. Female enlisted personnel have the same pension, allowance, entitlement and privilege rights as male long-term enlistees. Female officers and warrant officers enjoy the same service benefits (that is, housing assignments, allowances and pension rights) as their male counterparts. All female personnel are subject to disciplinary regulations, although there are separate provisions covering incentives and punishments for servicewomen.[154] All female service personnel are integrated into the military establishment; there is no separate organization for women analogous to, for example, the British Women's Royal Army Corps or the now-defunct Women's Army Corps in the United States. The absence of a separate military hierarchy for women means that Soviet servicewomen have not enjoyed the kind of command experience afforded military women in those countries with parallel male and female service structures.[155]

As in the early 1960s (when demographic trends created a shortage of conscript-aged males) the Soviet military establishment appears to have responded to the demographic downturn of the 1980s by a stepped-up recruitment of women. Opportunities for females in the armed forces have been more widely publicized; and one major drawback for young women considering a military career—a provision mandating that pregnant women be discharged into the reserves—has been remedied. According to a resolution approved in 1981, pregnant servicewomen can request early discharge. They may also be discharged by decision of their command if the pregnancy interferes substantially with their service duties. Those who remain on active duty are provided the same paid leave and maternity-benefit package (liberal by United States standards) as their civilian counterparts.[156] These trends are part of a larger program to upgrade the core of career enlisted personnel both male and female. The range of positions available to servicewomen, however, is far more limited than that open to males; and there are no indications that the General Staff intends to make significant changes in this practice. Restricted job mobility is likely to continue as a major impediment to recruitment of servicewomen.

The relatively modest Soviet efforts to expand the use of females in the peacetime military contrasts sharply with the rapid changes in female military pàrticipation rates in the United States and the slower, but still significant, expansion of female roles in the French and British armed forces.[157] The most dramatic changes have occurred in the American military. Faced with a shortage of male enlistees, the U.S. military rapidly expanded the role of servicewomen. The proportion of females in the U.S. military increased from less than 2 percent in 1971 to 8·5 percent at the end of 1980; and the number of job specialties open to female recruits rose dramatically. In 1976 females gained entry to U.S. service academies for the first time. Only combat specialties remain closed to them.[158] These trends—and the analogous, if less dramatic, changes in women's roles in the British and French militaries—contrast sharply with the continued exclusion of Soviet females from the peacetime military in the USSR. The minimal role of Soviet servicewomen is still more surprising when viewed against the background of their extensive use during World War II.

Part of the explanation lies in differing personnel needs. While both the U.S. and the USSR face similar demographic trends, the USSR's continued reliance on conscription ensures a far larger supply of personnel replacements. The American decision to opt for an all-volunteer force created far more pressing demands for expanded female military participation.[159] Moreover, the salient shifts in women's roles in the American military were part of a larger transformation in gender roles that has no counterpart in the USSR. In the Soviet Union legal equality of the sexes has always been linked to a constitutional recognition of very different male and female roles.

Another explanation for the continued exclusion of Soviet females from the military is the role played in the USSR by military service as a rite-of-passage for adolescent males. The predominance of women in the Soviet school system and the active participation of Soviet highschool girls in school leadership means that the typical Soviet male is socialized in an environment dominated, qualitatively and quantitatively, by females. The conscript tour is generally the first sustained contact of young men with an all-male environment; and Soviet officials stress its importance in providing male role models and instilling masculinity. From this perspective Soviet officials may feel that use of servicewomen on a large scale would undermine the all-male environment of the service experience, and weaken a key aspect of the armed forces' socialization role.

Civilians in the Ministry of Defense

Like servicewomen, civilians play a relatively limited role in the Ministry of Defense. In a quantitative sense the use of civilian labor by the MoD represents an important supplement to uniformed personnel. Figure 4.1 presents estimates of civilian employment within the MoD by military service. As reflected

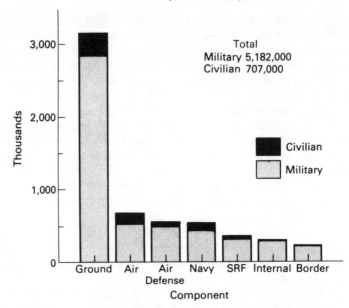

Figure 4.1 *Civilian manning in the Ministry of Defense, 1982.*

Source: J. M. Collins, *US/Soviet Military Balance. Statistical Trends, 1970–1982*, US Congressional Research Service Report No. 93-153S, updated 1 August 1983, pp. 5, 9, 139–43.

by these estimates, the MoD's use of civilian employees is widespread. Civilians, however, tend to be concentrated in the lower and less skilled positions.[160] The use of civilian employees, for example, is common in MoD service organizations such as those administered by Voyentorg and the Clothing Supply Directorate.[161] The agricultural workers on most military farms appear to be predominantly civilian, although some of the enterprise directors and other management personnel at such enterprises may be active duty military officers.[162] Personnel at military schools and academies also include both civilian instructors and military officers, with the civilians probably concentrated in language posts or as librarians.[163] The MoD also employs some civilian technicians such as those employed by *Krasnaya zvezda*'s printing facilities as well as research workers in an undetermined capacity.[164] The scope of civilian assignments in the MoD's support organizations appears to be quite broad. A 1968 Ministry of Defense order lists 117 civilian technical and white-collar occupations in the MoD that have been exempted from rules governing the normal working-day; the list includes a variety of occupations such as administrator, artist and economist. Civilians can also be assigned to military representative teams which provide quality control in factories producing military equipment and goods. Other MoD agencies which employ civilians include medical facilities, military commissariats, sports facilities, MoD-subordinate factories, and housing and supply organizations.[165]

The bulk of the MoD's civilian employment, however, appears to be nonprofessional; even the MoD's civilian white-collar workers appear to be limited to nonpolicy positions. Data limitations preclude more definitive statements on the nature of civilian employment. Some MoD entities fulfilling sensitive missions are so rarely treated in the Soviet military press that any analysis of their staffing practices must be considered very tentative. However, analysis of individuals associated with a variety of command, management, and high-level staff posts suggests that the U.S. practice of integrating civilian staffers in some of the top defense decisionmaking organizations has no direct counterpart in the USSR. Those civilians who are assigned to top positions in the MoD—such as former Defense Minister Dmitry Ustinov—are given military rank commensurate with their position and wear a military uniform.

The Military Professional and the Citizen Soldier

The Soviet career military share many of the missions of their counterparts in other countries. Like virtually all career forces, Soviet military professionals are partly concerned with the here and now effectiveness of the military machine (fighting a war like that in Afghanistan), and partly with training men for a future war. It is the career force that keeps running what is after all a massive bureaucracy—the equipment maintained, the barracks heated, and the paperwork flowing. These missions demand specialization and differentiation. In many military settings these needs have resulted in a high level of specialization in posts assigned the two major strata of military careerists: the officer corps and the noncommissioned officers/career enlisted. In the Soviet Union the absence of a strong NCO corps has created additional burdens on the officer corps, with officers assigned many of the missions that would in other armies be allocated to NCOs. As the Soviet armed forces moved along the same modernization path as their Western counterparts the absence of a well-developed NCO corps became more problematic, and the Soviets have taken steps to remedy the problem through the creation and strengthening of the warrant officer program. To the degree these efforts succeed, allocation of labor within the Soviet career force will become more efficient.

The missions of the Soviet career force, however, go beyond that of keeping running a complex military machine. The career force is also preoccupied with preparing human resources for the next war. This latter mission has been magnified by Soviet reliance on active duty service as a form of both reservist training and socialization. The army that is both "a school for the reserves" and "a school for life" has a great demand for teachers, reflected in the heavy stress laid on pedagogical skills in Soviet military press treatments of the ideal officer. Because the career force must not only teach specific military skills, but also create the regimented, martial environment thought to be most conducive for "making a man" out of the average Soviet draftee, the participation of women in the peacetime military has been significantly limited. Much of the officer corps' attention and energy has been directed toward controlling and socializing the citizen soldiers who make up the majority of the USSR's uniformed military personnel. This preoccupation with control is the natural result of a manning system that relies on short-term draftees and that employs relatively few filtration devices to select out those least fit for service. The officer corps' responsibility for dealing with the predictable pattern of manpower problems of the citizen soldier has gradually devolved on the political officer—the contemporary representative of an institution which began as a political control force but which gradually evolved into one specializing in the manpower problems of a conscript army.

Notes: Chapter 4

1 This description of historical trends affecting officer corps development is based on D. A. Voropayev and A. M. Iovlev, *Bor'ba KPSS za sozdaniye voyennykh kadrov*, 2d ed. (Moscow: Voyenizdat, 1960), pp. 11–225; P. Spirin, "V. I. Lenin and the creation of Soviet command cadres," *VIZh*, no. 4 (1965), pp. 3–16; V. Domnikov, "V. I. Lenin on military cadres of the army of a new type," *VIZh*, no. 4 (1970), pp. 24–32; V. Domnikov, "Great October and the creation of Soviet military cadres," *VIZh*, no. 11 (1967), pp. 14–25; I. I. Vlasov, *V. I. Lenin i stroitel'stvo sovetskoy armii* (Moscow: Voyenizdat, 1958), pp. 130–43; V. V. Britov, *Rozhdeniye krasnoy armii* (Moscow: Gosudarstvennoye Uchebno-pedagogicheskoye Izdatel'stvo Ministerstva Prosveshcheniya RSFSR, 1961), pp. 165–208; A. Cheremynkh, "Development of military schools during the prewar period (1937–1941)," *VIZh*, no. 8 (1982), pp. 75–80; P. Smirnov, "Activity of the CPSU in preparation of military cadres during World War II," *VIZh*, no. 6 (1981), pp. 62–4; and V. Yelyutin, "The higher school during the Great Motherland War," *VIZh*, no. 5 (1975), pp. 61–9.

2 An excellent survey of how the cultural revolution affected the civilian school system is available in Sheila Fitzpatrick, *Education and Social Mobility in the Soviet Union, 1921–1934* (Cambridge: Cambridge University Press, 1979), pp. 113–205.

3 On the Red Army purges see John Erickson, *The Soviet High Command: A Military–Political History, 1918–1941* (New York: St. Martins, 1962), pp. 449–509; and David R. Jones, "Motives and consequences of the Red Army purges, 1937–1938," in Jones (ed.), *Soviet Armed Forces Review Annual* (Gulf Breeze, Fla.: Academic International Press, 1979), Vol. 3, pp. 256–64.

4 K. V. Provorov and A. P. Porokhin, "Voyenno-uchebnyye zavedeniya," *SVE*, Vol. 2, pp. 255–6; and "Uchilishcha voyennyye," *SVE*, Vol. 8, pp. 240–1.

5 A. G. Gorniy (ed.), *Osnovy sovetskogo voyennogo zakσnodatel'stva* (Moscow: Voyenizdat, 1966), pp. 94–6.

6 A. Sinitsa and I. Vakurov, "For further development in training of military cadres," *Voyennaya mysl'*, no. 8 (1966).

7 Ye. Ye. Mal'tsev (ed.), *KPSS—Organizator zashchity sotsialisticheskogo otechestva*, 2d ed. (Moscow: Voyenizdat, 1977), pp. 370–5.

8 *Ordena lenina moskovskiy voyennyy okrug*, 2d ed. (Moscow: Voyenizdat, 1977), pp. 368–9.

9 Data compiled from information provided in Defense Intelligence Agency, *Soviet Military Schools*, DDB-2680-52-78. See also *KZ*, 17 April 1981, p. 4; and *Noorte Haal*, 21 April 1984, p. 3, trans. in JPRS-UMA-84-047, 9 July 1984, pp. 79–87.

10 Voropayev and Iovlev, 1960, p. 193; M. M. Lisenkov, *Kul'turnaya revolyutsiya v SSSR i armiya* (Moscow: Voyenizdat, 1977), p. 120; *KVS*, no. 21 (1974), pp. 28–33; V. Zotov, "CPSU leadership—the source of strength of the army and fleet," *KVS*, no. 10 (1983), pp. 49–58; I. Shkadov, "The officer corps," *Izvestiya*, 8 August 1984, p. 3.

11 A. F. Tarasov *et al.*, "Professional orientation of rural school-age youth," in *Opyt sotsial'no-ekonomicheskogo izucheniya professional'noy orientatsii sel'skoy molodezhi* (Rostov-Na-Donu: Gosudarstvennyy Pedagogicheskiy Institut, 1974), pp. 25–81.

12 V. F. Chernovolenko *et al.*, *Prestizh professiy i problemy sotsial'no-professional'noy orientatsii molodezhi. Opyt sotsiologicheskogo issledovaniya* (Kiev: Naukova Dumka, 1979), pp. 203–4.

13 M. N. Rutkevich and F. R. Filippov, *Sotsial'nyye peremeshcheniya* (Moscow: Mysl', 1970), pp. 233–6.

14 Ye. V. Belkin, "Professional technical education in the life plans of youth," *SI*, no. 2 (1981), pp. 105–9.
15 L. I. Shishkina, "Some data on the orientation of Orel students toward work and education," in *Sotsiologicheskiye issledovaniya professional'noy orientatsii molodezhi* (Moscow: Institute for Sociological Research, 1975), pp. 78–83.
16 V. G. Kostyuk, M. M. Traskunova, and D. L. Konstantinovskiy, *Molodezh' sibiri. Obrazovaniye i vybor professii* (Novosibirsk: Nauka, 1980), pp. 52, 154–7, 188–91. See also M. A. Men'shchikova, "Interests and life intentions of school youth," *Voprosy psikhologii*, no. 6 (1979), pp. 135–41.
17 "Denezhnoye dovol'stviye voyenno-sluzhashchikh," *SVE*, Vol. 3, p. 147.
18 Harriet Fast Scott, "The military profession in the USSR," *Air Force* (March 1976), pp. 76–81.
19 *Narodnoye khozyaystvo SSSR. 1922–1982* (Moscow: Finansy i Statistika, 1982), p. 405.
20 ibid., pp. 405–6.
21 Alastair McAuley, *Women's Work and Wages in the Soviet Union* (London: Allen & Unwin, 1981), pp. 11–31.
22 "Polozheniye o prokhozhdenii voinskoy sluzhby ofitserami, generalami i admiralami sovetskoy armii i voyenno-morskikh sil," 25 April 1955, in *Spravochnik po zakonodatel'stvu dlya ofitserov sovetskoy armii i flota* (Moscow: Voyenizdat, 1970), pp. 171–89; M. Ya. Parshin, *L'goty voyennosluzhashchim i ikh sem'yam. Spravochnik* (Moscow: Voyenizdat, 1976), pp. 184–7; V. G. Belyavskiy, "Otpusk voyennosluzhashchikh," *SVE*, Vol. 6, p. 162; and *KZ*, 25 May 1977, p. 4.
23 *Sbornik zakonodatel'nykh aktov o trude* (Moscow: Yuridicheskaya Literatura, 1977), p. 267; and *Narodnoye khozyaystvo SSSR v 1980 g* (Moscow: Finansy i Statistika, 1981), p. 367.
24 Parshin, 1976, pp. 187–8.
25 "Polozheniye o poryadke naznacheniya i vyplaty posobiy po gosudarstvennomu sotsial'nomu strakhovaniyu," 5 February 1955, as amended, *Spravochnik normativnykh dokumentov po sotsial'nomu obespecheniyu* (Moscow: Finansy i Statistika, 1982), pp. 276–304.
26 The regulations governing old-age pensions for civilians are summarized in A. D. Zaykin (ed.), *Sovetskoye pravo sotsial'nogo obespecheniya* (Moscow: Izdatel'stvo Moskovskovo Universiteta, 1982), pp. 136–56. The relevant statutes may be found in *Spravochnik normativnykh dokumentov*, pp. 9–72. On military pension provisions see A. I. Kotlyar and S. G. Bochenkov, *Spravochnik po pensiyam dlya voyennosluzhashchikh* 2d ed. (Moscow: Voyenizdat, 1980), *pass.*; and Zaykin, 1982, pp. 189–202.
27 See, for example, V. V. Nikitenko and V. L. Ossovskiy, "Education and professional orientation of youth. The case of the Ukraine," in E. K. Vasil'eva (ed.), *Sovetskaya molodezh''. Demograficheskiy aspekt* (Moscow: Finansy i Statistika, 1981), pp. 32–43.
28 M. Kh. Titma, *Vybor professii kak sotsial'naya problema* (Moscow: Mysl', 1975), p. 128; and M. Titma, *Sotsial'no-professional'naya orientatsiya molodezhi* (Tallin: Izdatel'stvo Eesti raamat, 1982), Vol. 2, p. 35.
29 O. I. Shkaratan and V. O. Rukavishnikov, "Social strata in the class structure of socialist society," *SI*, no. 2 (1977), pp. 62–73.
30 A. V. Korbut, "The treatment of professions in mass communications," in *Sotsiologicheskiye problemy obshchestvennogo mneniya sredstv massovoy informatsii* (Moscow: Institute for Sociological Research, 1975), pp. 138–47, 201.
31 S. S. Maksimov (ed.), *Osnovy sovetskogo voyennogo zakonodatel'stva* (Moscow: Voyenizdat, 1978), pp. 74–5.
32 I. N. Shkadov (ed.), *Voprosy obucheniya i vospitaniya v voyenno-uchebnykh zavedeniyakh* (Moscow: Voyenizdat, 1976), pp. 117–19.
33 ibid., p. 118.
34 ibid., pp. 119–23.
35 ibid., pp. 123–7. See also M. A. Shapovalov, "Politicheskiy sostav," *SVE*, Vol. 6, p. 422; and G. V. Sredin, "Partiyno-politicheskaya rabota," *SVE*, Vol. 6, pp. 240–2.
36 Shkadov, 1976, pp. 128–32.
37 "For those who wish to become officers," *KZ*, 17 January 1981, p. 4.
38 *Spravochnik dlya postupayushchikh v vysshiye uchebnyye zavedeniya SSSR v 1984 godu* (Moscow: Vysshaya Shkola, 1984), *pass.*
39 "Officer is a heroic professional," *Sovetskaya molodezh'*, 23 April 1983, p. 4.
40 "Pravila priyema v vysshiye voyenno-uchebnyye zavedeniya ministerstva oborony SSSR," 30 October 1969, in *Spravochnik po zakonodatel' stvu*, pp. 190–210; and *KZ*, 30 April 1981, p. 4.

41 *V pomoshch' postupayushchemu v vyssheye voyenno-politicheskoye uchilishche* (Moscow: Voyenizdat, 1977), pp. 28–9.
42 *KZ*, 17 January 1981, p. 4, and 31 January 1984, p. 4.
43 *Sovetskiy voin*, no. 6 (1983), p. 47.
44 V. Makarov, "For those entering military educational institutions," *Znamenosets*, no. 9 (1976), p. 36.
45 *Sovetskiy voin*, no. 8 (1981), p. 41; P. A. Buchenkov and V. F. Kashev, "Suvorovskiye voyennyye uchilishcha," *SVE*, Vol. 7, pp. 588–9; and "Nakhimovskiye voyenno-morskiye uchilishcha," *SVE*, Vol. 5, pp. 532–3.
46 P. A. Buchenkov, *Suvorovskoye voyennoye* (Moscow: Voyenizdat, 1981), pp. 5–31; and Kh. Ambaryan, "Suvorov schools—40 years," *Voyennyy vestnik*, no. 8 (1983), pp. 33–6.
47 "O suvorovskikh voyennykh, nakhimovskikh voyenno-morskikh i voyenno-muzykal'nykh uchilishchakh," *Sobraniye postanovleniy pravitel'stva SSSR*, no. 23 (1980), pp. 579–81.
48 "Polozheniye o suvorovskikh voyennykh uchilishchakh," 4 August 1969, in *Spravochnik po zakonodatel'stvu*, pp. 233–7, and "Polozheniye o Leningradskom nakhimovskom voyenno-morskom uchilishche," ibid., pp. 237–41.
49 Viktor Suvorov, *My Life in the Soviet Army* (New York: Norton, 1981), pp. 1–58.
50 "Polozheniye o prokhozhdenii deystvitel'noy srochnoy voyennoy sluzhby v sovetskoy armii i voyenno-morskom flote," 23 May 1968, article 46, in *Spravochnik po zakonodatel'stvu*, pp. 132–45.
51 Maksimov, 1978, pp. 74–5.
52 V. Konoplev and V. Konavlev, "On the role of the armed forces in contemporary society," *KVS*, no. 4 (1971), pp. 27–34.
53 Maksimov, 1978, pp. 74–5; and N. G. Lebedev, "Ofitserskiy sostav," *SVE*, Vol. 6, pp. 175–6.
54 Lebedev, *SVE*, Vol. 6, pp. 175–6.
55 Yu. M. Kozlov et al. (eds.), *Upravleniye v oblasti administrativno-politicheskoy deyatel'nosti* (Moscow: Yuridicheskaya Literatura, 1979), p. 60.
56 Gorniy, 1966, pp. 93–5.
57 For the text of the 1955 regulations on conditions of service for Soviet officers, as amended to 1970, see "Polozheniye o prokhozhdenii voinskoy sluzhby ofitserami, generalami i admiralami sovetskoy armii i voyenno-morskikh sil," 25 April 1955, in *Spravochnik po zakonodatel'stvu*, pp. 171–89. These regulations were modified in 1971; the text of the 1971 version of the regulations is not available, but the changes it introduced are discussed in K. Chernov, "Some questions of work with officer cadres," *Voyennaya mysl'*, no. 3 (1972).
58 "Attestatsiya," *VES*, p. 54.
59 "Attestatsiya," *SVE*, Vol. 1, p. 323. Selected categories of civilian employees, including scientific, pedagogical, and medical workers, are also evaluated through a similar efficiency reporting system: L. Samel and L. A. Sergiyenko, "Terms of state service," *Apparat upravleniya sotsialisticheskogo gosudarstva* (Moscow: Yuridicheskaya Literatura, 1977), Vol. 2, pp. 204–17.
60 A. Polunin, "Officer efficiency reports," *Aviatsiya i kosmonavtika*, no. 10 (1981), pp. 8–9.
61 G. Lazarev, "Efficiency report: appraisal, incentive, perspective," *Morskoy sbornik*, no. 9 (1981), pp. 31–6.
62 I. Shkadov, "Regular efficiency reports," *KZ*, 11 June 1981, p. 2; and I. Shkadov, "After the efficiency report," *KZ*, 16 February 1980, p. 2.
63 Ideal civilian management qualities are described in V. I. Remnev, "Formation of cadres for the state management apparatus," in *Apparat upravleniya*, Vol. 2, pp. 175–87; and Yu. A. Rozenbaum, *Formirovaniye upravlencheskikh kadrov* (Moscow: Nauka, 1982), pp. 85–92. Ideal political attitudes of military officers are described in D. Volkogonov, "Personality of the Soviet officer," *KZ*, 29 October 1981, pp. 2–3; A. Volkov, "The power of example," *KZ*, 25 October 1977, p. 2; D. Yazov, "A commander's development: official zeal," *KZ*, 2 April 1978, p. 2; and I. Shkadov, "Professional qualities of the officer: from a position of high demands," *KZ*, 20 August 1982, p. 2.
64 Ye. Aleksandrov, "Conclusions in efficiency reports," *KZ*, 4 March 1983, p. 2; N. Bezdenezhnykh, "Certified for promotion," *KZ*, 13 May 1977, p. 2; and Yu. Voronov, "Results of efficiency reports—in life," *Morskoy sbornik*, no. 6 (1983), pp. 36–40.
65 "Dolzhnostnaya kategoriya," *SVE*, Vol. 3, p. 232.
66 "Kursy usovershenstvovaniya," *SVE*, Vol. 4, pp. 540–1; "Vystrel," *SVE*, Vol. 2, pp. 432–3; and *Soviet Military Schools*, pp. 20–1.

67 "Polozheniye ob ofitserskikh kursakh vooruzhennykh sil SSSR," *Spravochnik po zakonodatel-'stvu*, pp. 230–1.
68 "Akademii voyennyye," *SVE*, Vol. 1, pp. 130.
69 I. Ye. Shavrov, "Voyennaya akademiya generalnogo shtaba," *SVE*, Vol. 2, pp. 172–4.
70 V. G. Kulikov (ed.), *Akademiya generalnogo shtaba* (Moscow: Voyenizdat, 1976), pp. 201–2.
71 *Patterns in Career Development of Soviet Military Officers, 1964–1981*, DDE-2200-125-81, pp. 2–3.
72 On the U.S. system see *Selective Service System Plans Officer Personnel Management*. Hearing before the Subcommittee on Manpower and Personnel of the Committee on Armed Services, U.S. Senate, 17 July 1979 (Washington, D.C.: U.S. Government Printing Office, 1979), pp. 17–31.
73 "Polozheniye o prokhozhdenii voinskoy sluzhby ofitserami," article 36; and *Selective Service System*, p. 55.
74 Chernov, 1972.
75 *Selective Service System*, p. 81.
76 "O vseobshchey voinskoy obyazannosti," 12 October 1967, as amended in *Svod zakonov SSSR* (Moscow: Izvestiya, 1982), Vol. 9, pp. 181–202, article 62 (hereafter cited as Universal Military Service Law). On the rationale for these changes see A. A. Grechko, "On the draft law on universal military service," *Zakon SSSR o vseobshchey voinskoy obyazannosti* (Moscow: Voyenizdat, 1967), pp. 31–48.
77 Timothy J. Colton, *Commissars, Commanders, and Civilian Authority: The Structure of Soviet Military Politics* (Cambridge, Mass.: Harvard University Press, 1979), p. 269; and B. S. Tel'pukhovskiy, *KPSS vo glave stroitel'stva vooruzhennykh sil SSSR* (Moscow: Politizdat, 1983), p. 239.
78 N. N. Yefimov and Yu. I. Deryugin, "Ways to increase effectiveness of military–patriotic socialization of youth," *SI*, no. 1 (1980), pp. 60–6; and Ye. Ye. Levanov, "Family socialization: status and problems," *SI*, no. 1 (1979), pp. 115–18. On social origins of higher education admissions see Richard B. Dobson and Michael Swafford, "The educational process in the Soviet Union: a case study," *Comparative Education Review*, vol. 24, no. 2 (June 1980), pp. 252–69.
79 A. M. Iovlev, *Deyatel'nost' KPSS po podgotovke voyennykh kadrov* (Moscow: Voyenizdat, 1976), pp. 217–18.
80 "Inzhenerno-tekhnicheskiy sostav," *SVE*, Vol. 3, pp. 543–4.
81 M. P. Shendrik (ed.), *Sovetskiy voyennyy inzhener—sotsiologicheskiy ocherk* (Moscow: Voyenizdat, 1977), p. 4.
82 ibid., p. 37.
83 "Ogarkov, Nikolay Vasil'yevich," *SVE*, Vol. 6, pp. 7–8.
84 "Polozheniye o prokhozhdenii voinskoy sluzhby ofitserami," articles 32 and 33.
85 *KZ*, 28 June 1981, pp. 2, 3; and "Shabanov, Vitaliy M.," *SVE*, Vol. 8, p. 488.
86 "Berg, Aksel' Ivanovich," *SVE*, Vol. 1, p. 444. Other defense industrial officials with military rank include Zhosef Kotin, who served as Deputy Minister of the Defense Industry from 1968 to 1979, and Georgiy Beriyev, a top aviation designer, *SVE*, Vol. 1, p. 453, and Vol. 4, pp. 409–10; and *Tekhnika i vooruzheniye*, no. 2 (1983), p. 25, and no. 3 (1983), p. 7.
87 Voropayev and Iovlev, 1960, p. 237.
88 Jerry F. Hough, *Soviet Leadership in Transition* (Washington, D.C.: Brookings Institution, 1980), pp. 79–108.
89 "Sverkhsrochnaya voyennaya sluzhba," *VES*, p. 658; "Sverkhsrochnaya voyennaya sluzhba," *SVE*, Vol. 7, p. 262; and Maksimov, 1978, pp. 72–3.
90 John Erickson, "New warrant officers for the Soviet armed forces," *Military Review* (December 1973), pp. 70–7.
91 "Praporshchik," *VES*, p. 584.
92 "O voyennosluzhashchikh sverkhsrochnoy sluzhby," 25 April 1973, in *Svod zakonov SSSR* (hereafter cited as *SZ*), Vol. 9, p. 494.
93 "Michman," *SVE*, Vol. 5, p. 332; and "Praporshchik," *SVE*, Vol. 6, p. 498.
94 "O praporshchikakh i michmanakh vooruzhennykh sil SSSR," *SZ*, Vol. 9, pp. 543–4; and A. Maksimenko, "On the procedure for military service of *praporshchiky* and *michmany*," *KVS*, no. 1 (1972), pp. 84–6.
95 "Polozheniye o prokhozhdenii voinskoy sluzhby praporshchikami i michmanami vooruzhen-

110   Red Army and Society

nykh sil SSSR," *SZ*, Vol. 9, pp. 496–507, articles 8–15; "Soldier and the law," *KVS*, no. 4 (1979), p. 41; "We want to become warrant officers," *KZ*, 17 May 1977, p. 4; "Soldier and the law," *Znamenosets*, no. 22 (1980), p. 27; and "We answer your questions," *Znamenosets*, no. 2 (1983), p. 30.
96 "I want to be a warrant officer," *KZ*, 28 June 1983, p. 2.
97 "Shkoly praporshchikov i michmanov," *VES*, p. 818.
98 B. Osmakov, "They will be warrant officers," *Znamenosets*, no. 6 (1974), pp. 8–10.
99 *KZ*, 28 June 1983, p. 2; 18 February 1982, p. 2.
100 "On evening and correspondence study in civilian educational institutions," *Znamenosets*, no. 5 (1976), pp. 36–7.
101 "How to become a warrant officer," *Znamenosets*, no. 2 (1982), p. 30. On warrants in officer billets see *Znamenosets*, no. 5 (1974), pp. 36–7, and no. 5, 1976, p. 29.
102 V. Filatov, "Comrade *praporshchik*," *KZ*, 29 August 1981, p. 2; and Defense Intelligence Agency, Department of Defense, *Soviet Tank Battalion Tactics*, DDI-1120-10-77, pp. 3–4.
103 loc. cit.
104 Yu. Grigorak, "Your military uniform," *Znamenosets*, no. 3 (1982), p. 19; *KZ*, 8 July 1982, p. 2; A. Tyurinn, "Company *starshina*," *KZ*, 15 October 1983, p. 2; "Starshina," *SVE*, Vol. 7, p. 532; and "Starshina," *VES*, p. 706.
105 Defense Intelligence Agency, Department of Defense, *The Soviet Motorized Rifle Battalion*, DDB-1100-197-78, p. 31.
106 *Znamenosets* no. 8 (1976), p. 13; A. Klyuyev, "Following Leninist precepts," *Znamenosets* no. 1 (January 1978), pp. 4–5.
107 *KVS*, no. 14 (July 1981), pp. 31–7; *KZ*, 10 February 1977, p. 2.
108 *TIS*, no. 2 (1972), pp. 32–5; and A. Voronkov, "With care for people," *Znamenosets*, no. 2 (1984), p. 15.
109 "Denezhnoye dovol'stviye voyennosluzhashchikh," *SVE*, Vol. 3, p. 147; and "Denezhnoye dovol'stviye voyennosluzhashchikh," *VES*, p. 228.
110 "Payek," *SVE*, Vol. 6, p. 189; *Znamenosets*, no. 6 (1976), p. 37, and no. 11 (1980), p. 28.
111 "Polozheniye o prokhozhdenii voinskoy sluzhby praporshchikami," article 28; and *Znamenosets*, no. 10 (1975), p. 35.
112 *Znamenosets*, no. 4 (1982), p. 30.
113 *KZ*, 17 March 1981, p. 1; "Concern about the defenders of the motherland," *Znamenosets*, no. 12 (1980), p. 30; and A. Kotyar, "Pension security," *Znamenosets*, no. 3 (1978), p. 37.
114 *KZ*, 8 February 1981, p. 2.
115 "O vnesenii nekotorykh izmeneniy i dopolneniy v zakonodatel'nyye akty SSSR o praporshchikakh i michmanakh vooruzhennykh sil SSSR," 24 December 1980, *Vedomosti verkhovnogo soveta soyuza sovetskhikh sotsialisticheskikh respublik*, no. 52 (24 December 1980), pp. 1145–7; and *KZ*, 17 March, 1981, p. 1.
116 *Znamenosets*, no. 12 (1981), pp. 5–7; and I. Alikov, "Increase the role and authority of warrants," *KVS*, no. 14 (1981), pp. 31–7.
117 *KZ*, 23 July 1981, p. 2.
118 "Preparation of specialists," *KZ*, 12 October 1983, p. 2.
119 I. Shkadov, "*Praporshchiky* and *Michmany*," *KZ*, 6 January 1982, p. 2.
120 "Attestation," *Znamenosets*, no. 1 (January 1978), pp. 36–7, and "In the interests of service," no. 5 (1977), p. 38.
121 A short, popularized biography of Durova is A. I. Os'kin, *Nadezhda Durova—Geroinya otechestvennoy voyny 1812 goda* (Moscow: Gosudarstvennoye Uchebno-pedagogicheskoye Izdatel'stvo, 1962). Much of this material is drawn from Durova's memoirs: *Kavelerist-devitsy* (Moscow: Sovetskaya Rossiya, 1962). See also "Durova, Nadezhda Andreyevna," *SVE*, Vol. 3, p. 272.
122 G. N. Kolibaba, "Zhenshchiny na voyennoy sluzhby," *SVE*, Vol. 3, pp. 332.
123 Ye. V. Kabanov, "Zhenskiy batal'on smerti," *SVE*, Vol. 3, pp. 331–2. See also Richard Stites, *The Women's Liberation Movement in Russia: Feminism, Nihilism, and Bolshevism, 1860–1930* (Princeton, N.J.: Princeton University Press, 1978), pp. 295–300.
124 Larisa Reysner, for example, was a commissar in the naval General Staff from 1918 to 1919, and later served aboard ships in the Volga–Caspian military flotilla. Ol'ga Ovchinnikova participated in the Bolshevik uprising in Moscow, then became a company commander in the Red Army: see "Reysner, Larisa Mikhaylova," in *Grazhdanskaya voyna i voyennaya interventsiya v SSSR. Entsiklopediya* (Moscow: Sovetskaya Entsiklopedia, 1983), p. 500, and "Ovchin-

nikova, Ol'ga Mitrofanovich," in ibid., p. 409. Other female civil war commanders and political workers listed in the encyclopedia include: Lyudmila Mokiyerskaya-Zubok (pp. 353–4), Rozaliya Zemlachka (p. 219), Glafira Okulova (p. 412), and Aleksandra Yanysheva (pp. 680–1). On partisans see "Zhenskoye dvizheniye," ibid., p. 209.

125 P. M. Chirkov, "Women in the Red Army in years of civil war and imperialist intervention, 1918–1920," *Istoriya SSSR*, no. 6 (1975), pp. 104–13.
126 Chirkov, 1975. A slightly higher figure is quoted in Stites, 1978, pp. 317–22. See also Anne Elliot Griesse and Richard Stites, "Russia: ...volution and war," in Nancy Loring Goldman (ed.), *Female Soldiers—Combatants or Noncombatants? Historical and Contemporary Perspectives* (Westport, Conn.: Greenwood Press, 1982), pp. 61–84.
127 "Zhenskoye dvizheniye," *Grazhdanskaya voyna i voyennaya interventsiya v SSSR. Entsiklopediya*, p. 209.
128 See, for example, George H. Quester, "American dilemmas and options: the problem," in Goldman, 1982, pp. 217–35.
129 Jeff M. Tuten, "Germany and the world wars," in ibid., pp. 47–60; see also Tuten, "Women in military service," *Armed Forces and Society*, vol. 8, no. 1 (Fall 1981), pp. 160–2.
130 A detailed treatment of female roles during World War II, which relies mainly on Soviet primary sources, is Anne Elliot Griesse, "Soviet women and World War Two: mobilization and combat policies," MA thesis, Georgetown University, August 1980. See also G. N. Kolibaba, "Zhenshchiny na voyennoy sluzhba," *SVE*, Vol. 3, p. 332; and G. I. Litvinova and N. V. Popova, "The historical experience of resolving the woman question in the USSR," *Voprosy istorii*, no. 11 (1975), pp. 3–18.
131 Nancy Loring Goldman and Richard Stites, "Great Britain and the world wars," in Goldman, 1982, pp. 21–45; and Mady Wechsler Segal and David R. Segal, "Social change and the participation of women in the American military," in Louis Kreisberg (ed.), *Research in Social Movements, Conflicts and Change: A Research Annual*, vol. 5 (1983), pp. 235–58.
132 V. S. Murmantseva, *Sovetskiye zhenshchiny v velikoy otechestvennoy voyne, 1941–1945*, 2d ed. (Moscow: Mysl', 1979), pp. 147–8. See also "Self-denial and heroism of female military medics," *Voyenno-meditsinskiy zhurnal*, no. 3 (1975), pp. 10–13; *Voyenno-meditsinskiy zhurnal*, no. 5 (1980), pp. 19–20; and A. I. Strel'tsova, "Nurse," *Izvestiya*, 7 June 1983, p. 3.
133 Murmantseva, 1979, p. 141.
134 ibid., pp. 143–4.
135 "Soviet procedure for interrogating prisoners of war in World War II," PW Project, study no. 2, ms. no. P-018b, p. 26; located in the National Archives, Washington, D.C.
136 K. Jean Cottam, "Soviet women in combat in World War II: the ground forces and the navy," *International Journal of Women's Studies*, vol. 3, no. 4 (1980), pp. 345–57. See also "Daughter of the motherland," *Sovetskiy voin*, no. 17 (1978), pp. 16–17; N. Lobkovskaya, "A living memory," *Znamenosets*, no. 23 (1977), pp. 30–1; and O. Mukhin, "A step to immortality," *Kazakhstanskaya pravda*, 15 October 1983, p. 3.
137 Murmantseva, 1979, pp. 138–9.
138 N. A. Kirsanov and V. F. Cheremisov, "Women in PVO troops during the years of the Great Motherland War," *Istoriya SSSR*, no. 3 (1975), pp. 63–75. See also V. Murmantseva, "Soviet women in the battle for Moscow," *VIZh*, no. 11 (1971), pp. 81–96.
139 Murmantseva, 1979, pp. 138–41. See also V. Murmantseva, "Soviet women in the Great Motherland War, 1941–1945," *VIZh*, no. 2 (1968), pp. 47–53.
140 V. Grushkin, "Party-political work among women soldiers of the PVO troops," *VIZh*, no. 3 (1977), pp. 80–4.
141 K. Jean Cottam, "Soviet women in combat in World War II: the rear services, resistance behind enemy lines and military political workers," *International Journal of Women's Studies*, vol. 5, no. 4 (1982), pp. 363–78. On female political workers see Murmantseva, 1979, pp. 150–9; on females in the partisan movement see ibid., pp. 198–238.
142 Cecile S. Landrum, "The role of women in today's military," in John B. Keeley, *The All-Volunteer Force and American Society* (Charlottesville, Va.: University Press of Virginia, 1978), pp. 150–65.
143 On male/female images in American primary school readers see *Dick and Jane as Victims: Sex Stereotyping in Children's Readers* (Princeton, N.J.: Carolingian, 1972), *pass*. An analogous study of Soviet readers is available in Mollie Schwartz Rosenhan, "Images of male and female in children's readers," in Dorothy Atkinson, Allexander Dallin, and Gail Lapidus (eds.), *Women in Russia* (Stanford, Calif.: Stanford University Press, 1977), pp. 293–305.

144 On community and family life in prerevolutionary Russia see *Narody yevropeyskoy chasti SSSR* (Moscow: Nauka, 1964), Vol. 1, pp. 406–26, 462–78, 685–93, 702–14. Stephen P. Dunn and Ethel Dunn, *The Peasants of Central Russia* (New York: Holt, Rinehart & Winston, 1967), pp. 8–13; Dorothy Atkinson, "Society and the sexes in the Russian past," in Atkinson *et al.*, 1977, pp. 3–38; Rose L. Glickman, "The Russian factory woman, 1880–1914," in ibid., pp. 63–83; Ethel Dunn, "Russian rural women," in ibid., pp. 167–87; and Teodor Shanin, *The Awkward Class: The Political Sociology of Peasantry in a Developing Society—Russia, 1910–1925* (Oxford: Clarendon, 1972), *pass.*

145 Discussions of Marxist-Leninist theory relating to gender roles can be found in Gail Warshofsky Lapidus, *Women in Soviet Society: Equality, Development, and Social Change* (Berkeley, Calif.: University of California Press, 1978), pp. 40–53; Alfred G. Meyer, "Marxism and the women's movement," in Atkinson *et al.*, 1977, pp. 85–112; and Alastair McAuley, *Women's Work and Wages in the Soviet Union* (London: Allen & Unwin, 1981), pp. 3–9.

146 The latter statistic refers to "large industry" only. Female laborforce participation rates (females as a percentage of the blue-collar workforce) was highest in textiles (60 percent), and lowest in mining and metalworking (7·3 and 9·2 percent respectively): *Sotsialisticheskoye stroitel'stvo SSSR. Statisticheskiy yezhegodnik* (Moscow: Soyuzorguchet, 1934), pp. 346–7. The overall laborforce data are from *Zhenshchiny v SSSR. Statisticheskiy sbornik* (Moscow: Statistika, 1975), p. 27.

147 See Mitzi D. Leibst, *Women in the Soviet Armed Forces*, Defense Intelligence Agency, Department of Defense, DDI-1100-109-76, pp. 3–4.

148 Universal Military Service Law, article 16.

149 "Polozheniye o prokhozhdenii voyennom sluzhby zhenshchinami, prinyatymi na dobrovol'nykh nachalkh na voyennuyu sluchbu v sovetskuyu armiyu i voyenno-morskoy flot na dolzhnosti soldat, matrosov, serzhantov i starshin," 9 October 1962, in *Spravochnik po zakonodatel'stvu*, pp. 163–6; and *Sovetskiy voin*, no. 5 (1983), p. 35.

150 *Morskoy sbornik*, no. 3 (1982), pp. 76–7; *KZ*, 8 March 1981, p. 1; 18 September 1981, p. 2; 22 September 1981, p. 2; *Sovetskiy voin*, no. 20 (1982), pp. 39–42; *Sovetskiy voin*, no. 5 (1980), p. 40; *Znamenosets*, no. 10 (1976), p. 40, and no. 3, 1977, p. 32, no. 3, 1981, p. 27, and no. 3, 1982, p. 31.

151 See article 8 of "Polozheniye o prokhozhdenii voinskoy sluzhby praporshchikami i michmanami vooruzhennykh sil SSSR," *SZ*, Vol. 9, pp. 496–507; V. Storozhenko, "Warrant officers—women," *Znamenosets*, no. 3 (1983), p. 30, and no. 10 (1982), p. 31, and no. 3 (1984), p. 30; and A. Shadrin, "Together with men," *Sovetskiy voin*, no. 5 (1983), pp. 31–5.

152 *Sovetskiy voin*, no. 5 (1983), p. 35; and *KZ*, 17 February 1984, p. 2.

153 *KZ*, 25 February 1983, p. 4; and *Voyennyy vestnik*, no. 3 (1984), p. 32a.

154 Universal Military Service Law, article 16; and "Distsiplinarnyy ustav vooruzhennykh sil SSSR," in *SZ*, Vol. 9, pp. 463–94. The relevant articles on servicewomen are 23 and 51.

155 Goldman and Stites, 1982, pp. 21–45.

156 "Polozheniye o prokhozhdenii voinskoy sluzhby zhenshchinami," in *Spravochnik po zakonodatel'stvu*, article 30; and Parshin, 1976, pp. 36–8. The new provision is contained in "O komplektovanii dolzhnostey ofitserskogo sostava, praporshchikov, michmanov, serzhantov, starshin, soldat i matrosov zhenshchinami, prinyatymi v dobrovol'nom poryadke na deystvitel'nuyu voyennuyu sluzhbu," 18 December 1981, *SZ*, Vol. 9, pp. 508–9.

157 Michel L. Martin, "From periphery to center: women in the French military," *Armed Forces and Society*, vol. 8, no. 2 (Winter 1982), pp. 303–33; and Martin Binkin and Shirley J. Bach, *Women and the Military* (Washington, D.C.: Brookings Institution, 1977), *pass.*

158 Segal and Segal, 1983, pp. 235–55.

159 Nancy Goldman, "The utilization of women in the armed forces of industrialized nations," *Sociological Symposium*, vol. 18 (Spring 1977), pp. 1–23.

160 A brief summary of the legal status of MoD civilian employees is available in D. N. Artamonov, "Rabochiye i sluzhashchiye sovetskoy armii i voyenno-morskogo flota SSSR," *SVE*, Vol. 6, p. 660. See also A. I. Lepeshkin (ed.), *Osnovy sovetskogo voyennogo zakonodatel'stva* (Moscow: Voyenizdat, 1973), pp. 141–54.

161 On civilian employees in commercial and service organizations see V. Rogovoy, "Fleet trade and life of the military sailors," *Morskoy sbornik*, no. 12 (1978), pp. 72–4; G. Kovalenko, "In order that books find readers," *TIS*, no. 12 (1977), pp. 62–5; Zh. Vakhmyanina, "Welcome to the tea room," *TIS*, no. 10 (1978), pp. 60–3. On civilian employees in clothing supply organs see *TIS*, no. 2 (1977), pp. 16–17.

162 "Military agricultural enterprises," *KZ*, 24 August 1982, p. 1; and N. Ulikhin and M. Samarina, "Experience of the participants of VDNh SSSR," *TIS*, no. 1 (1977), pp. 69–73.
163 V. G. Kulikov (ed.), *Akademiya generalnogo shtaba* (Moscow: Voyenizdat, 1976), *pass.*
164 G. A. Makayev, *Profsoyuznye organizatsii v sovetskoy armii* (Moscow: Voyenizdat, 1977), *pass.*; see also *Tekhnika i vooruzheniye*, no. 8 (1978), pp. 40–1; and *Tekhnika i vooruzheniye*, no. 2 (1978), pp. 38–40.
165 *Spravochnik po zakonodatel'stvu*, pp. 775–9; A. Tishin, "New conditions of payment of blue-collar workers and white-collar employees," *TIS*, no. 9 (1977), pp. 75–7; and S. Lagodskiy, "The concerns of a collective, in our military enterprises," *KZ*, 7 June 1983, p. 2.

5

The Soviet Political Officer

All large military organizations need institutions and mechanisms to handle manpower issues such as the maintenance of morale and discipline. In the Soviet military, as in other communist military organizations, a key role in these areas is played by the political officer. While the political officer (zampolit) fulfills many missions common to Western military systems, the institution he represents is unique. Alongside the more traditional manpower-related duties, the zampolit discharges political responsibilities that have no direct counterpart in most non-Communist militaries; these include the management of the army's party and Komsomol (Youth League) organizations and political oversight of the military. The contemporary Soviet political officer is part-personnel officer, part-educational or orientation officer, part-socializing agent, and part-chaplain.

The Main Political Administration

The contemporary zampolit is part of an organizational hierarchy—the Main Political Administration (MPA)—that has a curious legal status; it is both a part of the Ministry of Defense and a part of the Communist Party hierarchy. The primary link between the MPA and the party hierarchy is at the top. The MPA is described in Soviet sources as having "the right of a department of the Central Committee":[1] "The Main Political Administration is accountable for its activities to the Central Committee of the CPSU and the Defense Council, and reports to the MoD on troop conditions and political work in the Army and Navy."[2] The primary missions of MPA headquarters are to direct the military's political organs, party organizations, and Komsomol organizations; to ensure "party influence" on all aspects of troop life; and to improve combat readiness and military discipline. The MPA's most important responsibility is to organize what the Soviets call "ideological work," a term that is more accurately translated as "political socialization"—instilling military personnel with approved values and attitudes. The headquarters structure of the MPA, as shown in Figure 5.1, reflects these missions. Like analogous components of the armed forces (and most civilian agencies as well), MPA headquarters is broken down into administrations (*upravleniya*) and departments (*otdely*). Several of

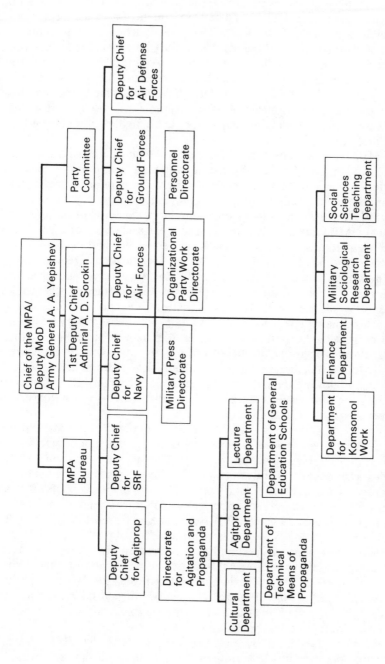

Figure 5.1 *Main political administration of the Soviet Army and Navy.*

the MPA's subcomponents perform basic housekeeping functions common to all Soviet organizations. The Finance Department, for example, handles the financial aspects of MPA activities. The other functional components are an institutional embodiment of the MPA's primary missions. The Directorate for Agitation and Propaganda plays a key role in dispensing the MPA's political socialization functions. The MPA's responsibility for directing internal party affairs is discharged by the Organizational–Party Work Directorate. The Department for Komsomol Work is the focal point for the MPA's responsibility for providing guidance over the activities of the armed forces Komsomol organizations.

The MPA is headed by a chief (*nachal'nik*) who operates basically as the fourth First Deputy Minister of Defense, although he does not officially hold that title. The current chief, Yepishev, had extensive experience in the regional party apparatus and in diplomatic work before his assignment to head the MPA hierarchy. At age 77 and a living embodiment of "stability of cadres," he has headed the MPA for over two decades and has served under three Defense Ministers and four party leaders.[3] He is assisted by an advisory committee, the MPA Bureau—the MPA analogue of the MoD Collegium. Created in August 1960, the MPA Bureau consists of the MPA chief (who serves as chairman), his deputies, the chiefs of the service political administrations, the chiefs of selected subcomponents at MPA headquarters, the chief editor of the military's central newspaper (*Krasnaya zvezda*), and the secretary of the MPA Party Commission.[4] Like most collegial entities in one-man-command organizations, Bureau decisions are based on majority vote and are implemented through MoD–MPA directives (*direktivy*) or orders (*ukazaniya*) of the head of the MPA.[5] Following the pattern of other collegial bodies, Bureau members who disagree with Bureau decisions have the right to communicate their disagreement to the Central Committee.[6]

Very little information is available on the operations of the MPA Bureau. There are virtually no clues, for example, as to the frequency of meetings, and very little data on Bureau meeting agendas. The fullest information on Bureau activities is from the early and mid-1960s. During this period it was common for the Bureau to hear reports on party political issues from the chiefs of political administrations at military district, groups of forces, and fleet level. For example, in February 1963 the MPA Bureau heard a report of the chief of the political administration of the southern group of forces on the state of ideological work among troops assigned to that command. In May the Bureau heard a report by the chief of the Kiev MD political administration on the status of political socialization work with the top military professionals in the district. In January and again in April 1962 the Bureau heard reports on the training of military–political cadres. In August 1966 the Bureau heard a presentation on the preparation of mid-level political officers.[7]

Fragmentary data from Bureau meeting reports in the 1970s and 1980s suggest that the current MPA Bureau operates in much the same way as its MoD analogue. For instance, in an April 1972 meeting the Bureau examined the status of social sciences training in military political schools. Reports on the

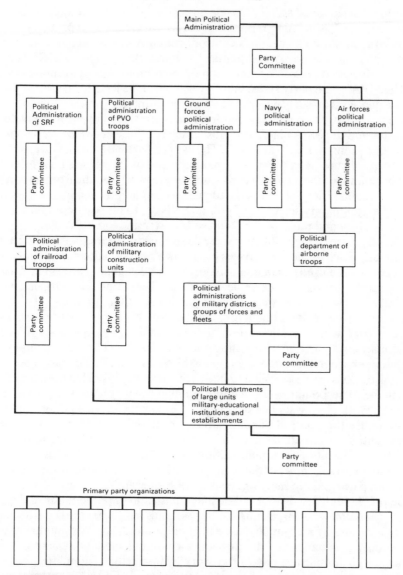

Figure 5.2 *Structure of political organs in the Soviet Armed Forces.*

Source: L. A. Bublik *et al.*, *Partiyno-politicheskaya rabota v sovetskoy armii i voyenno-morskom flote*, Moscow: Voyendizdat, 1982, p. 52.

subject were provided by the chief of the Novosibirsk Higher Military–Political Combined Armed School; a deputy chief of the MPA; the chief of the PVO's political administration; and the chief of the MPA's Department for the Teaching of Social Sciences.[8] The Bureau also discusses issues relating to the internal party affairs. In October 1980 the Soviet press reported on a Bureau meeting that surveyed accounting–election meetings in the ground forces party organizations.[9] A meeting reported in July 1981 focussed on problems in the work of the military's "people's control" committees (inspection committees that are administered by the political hierarchy). A January 1983 Bureau meeting focussed on MPA supervision of the military's party commissions.[10]

The MPA's dual party/state status is reflected in the legal form used to promulgate decisions on party political work within the military. According to Soviet sources, directives on military-political issues are signed by both the Defense Minister and the MPA chief. The most crucial of these decisions are said to be subject to preliminary CC approval. The MPA chief himself issues directives on day-to-day issues only.[11] Another manifestation of the MPA's dual role is its responsibility for the choice of personnel with regard to political officers on the CC nomenklatura. The MPA headquarters apparently maintains files and makes a preliminary selection of political officers to fill posts on both the CC nomenklatura and those of the Defense Minister and the MPA chief.[12]

The structure of the MPA hierarchy below headquarters level is depicted in Figure 5.2. Each of the five services has its own political administration. These entities are organized in a manner analogous to MPA headquarters itself. Each of the service entities, for example, has its own Department for Organization–Party Work (which works closely with the MPA's Organization–Party Work Directorate) and a Department for Agitation and Propaganda (which works in close accord with the Directorate for Agitation and Propaganda at MPA headquarters).[13] The service political administration chiefs are members of both the service military councils and the MPA Bureau.[14] The service political administrations are responsible to both agencies; they report to both the MPA and to the corresponding service military council on the status of the troops and political work among service personnel.[15] Below the service political administration are the political administrations of the military districts and fleets. These entities again are structured as microcosms of MPA headquarters. As with the service political administrations, the head of the MD political administration is also a member of the military district's military council and, as noted above, a participant in meetings of the MPA Bureau.

Below the military district political administration are the political departments (*politotdely*) of large units, military schools, and other MoD institutions. At division level, for example, the head of the politotdel, who is simultaneously the deputy commander of the division for political matters, is assisted by a deputy, who administers day-to-day work by instructors, formulates the politotdel workplan, and directs activities of the people's control groups and other "social" organizations; and by the Party Commission Secretary, who is a full-time political officer.[16] The primary missions of the division politotdel— management of party and Komsomol organizations, political socialization, and cultural/recreational issues—are dispensed by four subcomponents: the senior instructor for party political work, the assistant chief for Komsomol work, the politotdel propagandist, and the senior instructor for cultural/mass work.[17] The senior inspector for organization–party work (generally, at division level, a major) supervises internal party affairs within the division. The assistant chief for Komsomol work generally holds the rank of captain and has one or two instructors (sergeants or privates) subordinate to him. The Komsomol assistant is responsible for Komsomol activities within the division: meetings, recruitment of Komsomol members, and training of secretaries for primary Komsomol organizations. Political socialization work in the division (management of the activities of unit propagandists, methodological guidance to leaders of Marxist–Leninist training groups for officers and political classes for conscripts, and direction of ideological work in general) is the job of the politotdel propagandist. Direct administration of cultural and recreational activities within the division falls to the senior instructor for cultural/mass work. He directs the activities of the unit club chiefs and libraries. There is also a party school chief, who organizes the work of party schools within the division and assists party organizations in the selection and training of the party and Komsomol *aktiv* (party and Komsomol members fulfilling political assignments outside their regular jobs). The final member of the division politotdel is an instructor who maintains party and Komsomol documents for the division.

Below division level there are no political departments *per se*, but both the regimental and battalion zampolits do have full-time staff. At regimental level there are at least two full-time staff members (*shtatniy rabotniky*): the regimental propagandist and the head of the regimental club.[18] The regimental zampolit is also assisted by the secretary of the party committee and the secretary of the Komsomol committee. In full-strength units these individuals may be freed from other duties and are then said to be staff workers. The zampolit himself generally runs one of the Marxist–Leninist training groups for officers. He also helps to organize political training classes for conscript personnel, and directs the selection and training of class leaders. Direct responsibility for political socialization falls to the regimental propagandist. He runs one of the Marxist–Leninist groups for officers and directs political training classes for conscripts. The other full-time staffer runs the regimental club and organization's cultural, recreational, and sports activities.

At battalion level the zampolit is assisted only by the party and Komsomol secretaries.[19] In less than full-strength units these posts may be filled on a "social" basis, meaning that their occupants are fulfilling these duties in addition to a regular assignment. The lowest level of the MPA hierarchy—the zampolit at company level—was added in 1967. The company and equivalent units have about 100 men; and the zampolit works alone, unassisted by other full-time staffers. One of the main occupations of the company zampolit is that of running the political training classes for conscript personnel. The zampolit personally conducts one of the training groups and directs the leaders of the remaining groups.

As suggested by the material presented above, a large portion of the day-to-day party political work in any given unit is performed by individuals (usually officers) working on a "social" basis; that is, in addition to their regular assignment. Many of the political training classes are led by such individuals, and much of the attention of the full-time political staffer is devoted to recruiting, training, and overseeing the activities of these individuals. Much, then, of the grassroots labor that makes the MPA programs run is "volunteer." This characteristic has the effect of involving the nonpolitical officer corps closely with the MPA's missions—a factor that has contributed to a blurring of the boundary lines between the military and political command.

The Evolution of Zampolit Functions

The contemporary zampolit is a descendant of the civil war military commissar. The zampolit's current political control mission evolved from the commissar's role as a political watchdog over former tsarist military officers, who were used in great numbers during the Civil War.[20] Many of these men were actively hostile to the new regime, and the commissar's primary role was to counter potential sabotage.[21] The commissar system was one of joint command and authority. At operational levels orders by the military commander were not binding unless also signed by the political commissar. The commissar system grew out of the need to rely on individuals who were professionally qualified, but politically suspect. The Bolsheviks faced a similar problem in the civilian arena; and in both cases a variety of mechanisms was established requiring that command or management decisions by nonpolitical specialists be reviewed by trusted political cadres.

In the armed forces, however, Bolshevik suspicion of military specialists led to more energetic efforts to replace them much sooner with "Red" commanders than was the case in the civilian economy. The phase-out of military specialists began well before the civil war. The proportion of ex-tsarist military officials, who had accounted for 75 percent of military commanders in 1918, dropped by about two-thirds by the close of the war. By 1929 such individuals made up less than 11 percent of the command personnel.[22] By contrast, in the civilian economy reliance on bourgeois specialists continued long after the end of the civil war. A 1929 study of specialists at selected major industrial and research facilities revealed that nearly one-third of all specialists in the sample (31 percent) had begun work in a specialist capacity before the revolution. This trend was even more pronounced at higher levels of the civilian apparatus, where 62 percent of the leading staff and specialists had begun work in a specialist capacity before the revolution.[23] On the civilian side, then, bourgeois specialists remained an important element in Soviet industrial management throughout the 1930s.[24]

The greater Bolshevik stress on replacing military specialists with politically reliable cadres is reflected in comparative data on the social and party composition of the military and civilian leadership cadres. The proportion of party members and individuals of "desirable" social classes was consistently higher in the military during the 1920s and 1930s. Figure 5.3 depicts trends in levels of party membership among command personnel in the 1920s and early 1930s. Levels of party membership among command personnel, which grew rapidly if unevenly in the 1920s, were considerably higher than among civilian specialists. For example, in 1930, 53 percent of the military command personnel, compared to 13 percent of civilian specialists, were party members or candi-

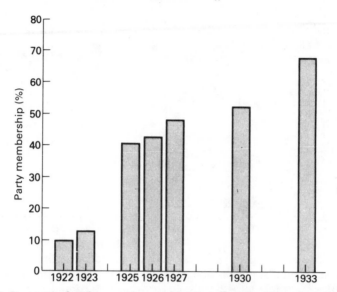

Figure 5.3 *Party membership trends among military command personnel, 1922–33.*

Sources: D. A. Voropayev and A. M. Iovlev, *Bor'ba KPSS za sozdaniye voyennykh kadrov*, Moscow: Voyenizdat, 1960, pp. 145–6; Politicheskoye Upravleniye RKKA, *X let krasnoy armii. Albom diagram*, Moscow: Izdatel'stvo Voyennyy Vestnik, 1928, p. 35.

dates.[25] In 1933 when 68 percent of the military command were party members or candidates, only 29 percent of the specialists and leading personnel in the civilian economy fell into this category.[26] A similar contrast can be found in comparative data on the social composition of military and civilian cadres. The blue-collar component among command personnel increased rapidly in the 1920s from 17 percent in 1920 to 21 percent in 1925, and to 28 percent in 1928.[27] In 1930 31 percent of the military command cadres, but only 24 percent of the civilian specialists, were of blue-collar origin.[28] By 1933 42 percent of the military's command cadre came from blue-collar backgrounds compared to 31 percent of the specialists and leading personnel in the civilian economy.[29]

The rapid proletization of the military cadres in the 1920s and 1930s was due, in part, to stricter admissions criteria for the military schools. Figure 5.4 provides trend data from 1918 to 1927 on the social and political credentials of military school graduates. As these data make clear, the increasing blue-collar component of the military cadres in the late 1920s was due, in part, to substantial declines in the proportion of graduates whose social credentials were less desirable from the party's standpoint (that is, those who were neither blue-collar workers nor poor peasants). Similarly, the increasing party saturation of the military cadres in the late 1920s can be traced to a sharp decline in the nonparty members graduating from military schools. Comparative data for 1931 suggest that the proportion of blue-collar workers and party members in the military schools was considerably higher than that in civilian schools; 44 percent of students in military schools were party members or candidates, while

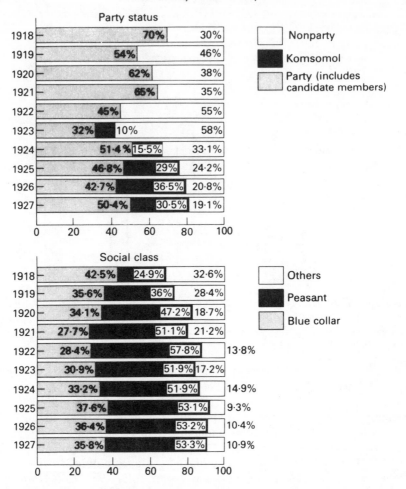

Figure 5.4 *Party and social composition of commanders graduating from military educational establishments (excludes air and naval institutions), 1918–27.*

Source: Politicheskoye Upravleniye RKKA, *X let krasnoy armii. Albom diagram*, Moscow: Izdatel'stvo Voyennyy Vestnik, 1928, p. 40.

an additional 39 percent were Komsomol members. This compares with 13 percent Communists and 33 percent Komsomols in civilian higher educational institutions and tekhnikums. A similar pattern pertains to social composition; 59 percent of the students at military schools v. 44 percent of those in civilian VUZ and tekhnikums were reported to be of blue-collar background.[30]

In spite of the consistently more acceptable social and political credentials of military cadres, the political control mechanisms applied to the military sphere was considerably more rigid than those used in the civilian economy. One explanation is that military reliability was absolutely crucial to Bolshevik survival. The stricter political controls and more rigorous political and social standards required of military cadres were necessary precisely because the con-, sequences of dissent in an insurgent military unit were so much higher than they were in an analogous civilian enterprise. Moreover, while the vast majority of the technical intelligentsia were not pro-Bolshevik and many supported the early boycott of Bolshevik-controlled offices, only a small proportion of the civilian intelligentsia were active participants in the anti-Bolshevik movement. Once the passive resistance to Bolshevik rule ended, many "bourgeois specialists" entered into an active collaboration and cooperation with the Bolshevik authorities.[31] Former tsarist military officials, by contrast, were far more vehemently anti-Bolshevik than their civilian counterparts. The instances of actual subversion when ex-tsarist officers led their units to defect to the anti-Bolshevik forces were numerous enough to create a deep-seated and long-lasting Bolshevik mistrust of the professional military. This mistrust was reflected in a need for more rigid political controls over the military.

The more rigorous social and political standards applied to military professionals led, in turn, to the creation of a military cadre with political qualifications that differed little from those of the political officers. This factor had effectively preempted the MPA's role as political watchdog by the mid-1930s. Political control, in the sense of ensuring the loyalty of military professionals, was gradually relegated to a relatively minor role in the MPA's portfolio of missions. This process was accelerated by the existence of another control mechanism within the military—the network of "special departments" in military, MVD, and border guard units.[32] The contemporary "special departments" have their origin in the network of Cheka organs set up in 1918 to run counterintelligence operations against enemy agents and monitor and control counterrevolution and treason within the Red Army. Special departments, which are subordinate to the KGB's Third Directorate, currently exist at military district, army, and division level. In addition, several KGB case officers are assigned to each unit of regimental level. The KGB officials who man the special departments gather personal information on the servicemen in their unit through a network of informers. Potential anti-Soviet elements within military units can be identified and reassigned or dismissed. This system is designed to limit the potential for dissent within a military unit; and it—not the MPA—represents the most important source of political surveillance of the military and (from the standpoint of the party leadership) the primary backup to the military's regular chain of command.

If political control ceased very early to be the main mission of the military's political hierarchy, other functions quickly grew in importance. Chief among these was political socialization—instilling the Soviet serviceman with a sense of loyalty to the Soviet Union and the Communist Party. The contemporary arrangement, in which direct responsibility for virtually all facets of political socialization and culture is concentrated in the MPA, is by no means the only organizational option. A proposal embodying an alternative approach—to assign these responsibilities to the civilian education and publishing agencies—had been advanced and then rejected in the spring of 1920. The idea was revived after the civil war. In March 1921 responsibility for administering the military's socialization efforts were transferred to the Main Committee for Political Enlightenment, a civilian agency created in 1920 to centralize all cultural and social activities for adults under one administrative umbrella.[33] This agency was simultaneously a part of the People's Commissariat for Enlightenment and an organ of the Bolshevik Central Committee. Incorporated into it were the political–socialization agencies of the Komsomol Central Committee and the cultural agencies of the trade unions.[34] As an institutional link between the military's political hierarchy and the civilian agency the chief of the Red Army Political Administration was given the rights of a deputy chairman of the Main Committee for Political Enlightenment.[35] While the military's political hierarchy retained the mission of directing political socialization work in units at the front, even there the political organs were subject to committee regulations on political socialization matters. The overlap in functions resulted in confusion and institutional conflict. The Tenth Party Congress resolution included the proviso that the CC organize a conference of responsible workers from the army's political apparatus and from the civilian Enlightenment Committee to come up with a mechanism to promote smooth working relations. The uneasy partnership between civilian and military officials involved in ideological work in the army is reflected in various decrees regulating the Political Administration's activity.[36] In 1922 steps were taken to solidify the civilian agency's control of political socialization work in the armed forces.[37] The October 1922 regulations on the functions and structure of the national-level Political Administration stated clearly that "direction of all political socialization work in the Red Army and Fleet is the responsibility of Main Committee for Political Enlightenment [working] through PUR" (the Red Army Political Administration); PUR's Agitation–Propaganda Department functioned as the committee's Military Section.[38]

Military officials, however, were already lobbying to regain control over what they saw as one of the Political Administration's primary missions. A conference of military delegates to the Eleventh Party Congress in April 1922 noted that Glavpolitprosvet's local agencies were not capable of directing political socialization work among the troops. They tended to ignore the specific problems of working in a military environment. In response, a special commission was set up to draft a CC decision specifying how political–socialization work in the military should be managed. The commission recommended that responsibility for political socialization be returned to the military's political organs. At the end of 1922 the CC formally transferred the function back to the military political organs from whence it had originally come. The military section of the Main Committee for Political Enlightenment was reorganized into an Agitation–Propaganda Department of the Political Administration, and corresponding changes were made in the structure of the military district political administrations. Thus ended the brief experiment with managing the armed forces socialization program through a civilian agency. The experiment was never repeated, although in the years that followed the Main Committee for Political Enlightenment worked closely with the army's political organs, particularly in the area of socialization of predraft youth.[39] The function of political socialization has been retained within the military's political hierarchy ever since.

The MPA's involvement in all facets of political socialization represents an institutional concentration that contrasts sharply with the fragmented institutional arrangements outside the military. In the civilian environment responsibility for political socialization is dispersed among officials from the territorial party apparatus (who run voluntary party and political training classes for civilians as well as much of the press); the Ministry of Culture (which handles "fine arts," libraries, and museums); the State Committee for Cinematography (which manages the cinema); and the various entities that direct the civilian school system. Within the military these missions are concentrated in a single structure. The MPA-managed political socialization program represents an important supplement to the larger civilian program and is discussed in detail in Chapter 6.

Political socialization, of course, is by no means the MPA's sole political mission. A large proportion of the attention of the military's political officers is devoted to managing the armed forces' party and Komsomol organizations. These are important missions because the vast majority of the uniformed force belongs to one of these organizations. Again the contemporary arrangement— one in which the army's party and Komsomol organizations are managed by a hierarchy of full-time political workers integrated into the military chain of command—is by no means the only organizational option. Several alternative approaches were tried in the early years of Bolshevik rule. During the civil war there was a great deal of local initiative in this matter.[40] At first, overall guidance for the military's party organizations was provided by local party organs. But military units, unlike factories, moved from place to place in the course of combat, frequently losing contact with their parent committee. The result was chaos. In some cases individual armies took matters in their own hands and set up their own party committees to direct the activities of party organizations, while socialization work among the troops continued to be managed by political departments (politotdel). The confusion resulting from this duplication of effort led several armies to experiment with organizational arrangements that combined the party function previously performed by the party committee with the political–administrative mission of the politotdel. The success of these experiments led the CC to abolish the army and division party committees in October 1918. A statute defining the missions of the political departments came in the following month. To rationalize the division of labor between the commander, commissar, political department, and party organization formal instructions were issued in early 1919 forbidding the party organizations from interfering with the commanders and commissars and reaffirming the right of the politotdel to direct the activities of party organizations.

The decision to subordinate party organizations within the military to the military's political hierarchy (as opposed to the territorial party apparatus) was reaffirmed after the civil war. During the Tenth Party Congress in March 1921 proposals to shift direction of the army party bodies to the territorial party

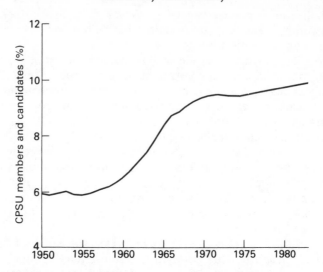

Figure 5.5 *Communists in the adult population, 1950–83.*

Sources: Party data from *Partiniya zhizn*, no. 15, 1983, pp. 14–15; population data (aged 20 and over) from FDAD unpublished estimates.

apparatus were rejected.[41] The military's political apparatus remained essentially independent of the civilian party apparatus at regional level. The primary institutional link between the military's party political hierarchy and the civilian party hierarchy is at the Central Committee level: the MPA's legal status is that of a department of the national-level Central Committee.

Management of both Komsomol and party activities remains one of the MPA's primary functions. The Komsomol is the CPSU's "farm league" for teenagers and young adults. It is open to individuals aged 14–28.[42] Unlike the CPSU which includes less than 10 percent of the eligible population, the Komsomol is truly a "mass" organization. In 1979 54 percent of the eligible population belonged; the corresponding figures for 1980 and 1983 were 56 and 60 percent respectively.[43] The level of Komsomol membership, however, is even higher in the armed forces. Over 60 percent of the uniformed force were members in 1974.[44] Considering that a large minority of the military force are career personnel who are beyond the age-limit for Komsomol membership, this represents well over 60 percent of the eligible servicemen. Indeed, in some units Komsomol membership among the eligible contingent approaches 100 percent; and the percentage of Komsomol members among draftees increased from 72 for those drafted in 1961 to over 80 in 1965. Komsomol membership is limited largely to conscript personnel. Relatively few Soviet officers are Komsomol members because many have reached the age and stage of career where party membership is considered highly desirable. In 1966 only 8 percent of the military Komsomols were officers or officer candidates.[45] Most of these appear to be junior officers.

Soviet sources do not provide precise data on levels of CP membership

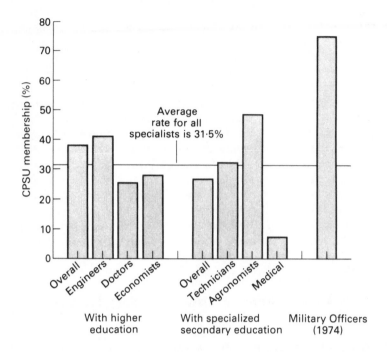

Figure 5.6 *CPSU representation among military and civilian specialists, 1977.*

among Soviet officers. One 1974 source indicates that 75 percent of the officer corps is in the party (with an additional 15 percent in the Komsomol). A 1981 source claimed that the 'Party group among officers has reached 80 percent.'[46] This extraordinarily high level of CP membership contrasts sharply with that in the civilian sector. Party membership among Soviet adults has not exceeded 10 percent, at least in the postwar period (Figure 5.5). The high levels of party representation among armed forces professionals can be traced to several factors. First, populations with higher levels of education tend to have higher party membership rates. In 1983 30 percent of the college-educated adults were party members compared to 9 percent of those with secondary education, and 6 percent of those with incomplete secondary education.[47] Relative to the general adult population, the Soviet officer corps is well educated. As noted in Chapter 4, 70 percent of the officer corps had higher education in 1983, compared to 8 percent of the overall population over age 10, and 11·3 percent of the employed population.[48] To some degree, then, the high party membership rates of the officer corps are due to the corps' high educational qualifications. A second explanation is the tendency throughout the Soviet Union for white-collar professionals to have higher CP levels than their blue-collar counterparts. Among "specialists" (a Soviet term that includes all employed individuals with college or specialized secondary diplomas), the level of CP membership (about 31 percent in 1981) is over three times that of the general adult population.[49] The CP membership rates are particularly high in some professions such as engineering (Figure 5.6). The level of CP membership climbs rapidly as one goes up the managerial ladder. Virtually all key management posts in Moscow-level ministry headquarters are manned by party members. This is also true of plant managers and chief engineers. The same trend is apparent in the military hierarchy.[50] Closely related to these two factors is the fact that the officer corps is an almost exclusively male institution; and historically males have had much higher levels of CP membership than females. In 1983 16 percent of adult males compared to less than 5 percent of adult females were party members.[51] An additional explanation of the high levels of party membership in the officer corps, then, is the virtual exclusion of women from the professional military.

Still, reported membership levels among military officers vastly exceed those of virtually all other groups other than top-level Moscow officials. This is a continuation of the trend discussed above in which more stringent political requirements were placed on military officers than on their civilian counterparts.

The Political Officer's Military Missions: Military Training and Discipline

The political officer also performs a variety of military functions. These functions have steadily grown in importance as the MPA's political control mission declined. Much of the zampolit's efforts are now devoted to promoting the military effectiveness of his unit. The basic mission of every combat unit is to be ready to fight, and ultimate personal responsibility for the level of combat readiness falls to the unit commander. The political officer, however, has been assigned an important supporting role. His task in this regard is primarily motivational—instilling servicemen with a sense of the importance of the military mission and inspiring them with the requisite determination to carry it out. The major weapons in the political officer's arsenal—the formal political classes, evening lectures, group discussions, and so on—are used not just to produce better Soviet citizens, but to motivate service personnel to become better soldiers. Because mastery of weapons and military equipment is essential to combat readiness, part of the zampolit's efforts are devoted to motivating servicemen to improve their technical skills.[52] For instance, the zampolit helps the deputy commander for technical affairs to organize weapons demonstrations and other forms of "military technical propaganda," including lectures, conferences, and exhibits. Portions of the formal political classes are devoted to convincing personnel of the importance of technical mastery.

Another focus of the zampolit's efforts to support combat readiness is a series of programs designed to enhance the authority of the command personnel.[53] To help officers and warrant officers within the unit improve their pedagogic and leadership skills the political officer arranges seminars and conferences. At the same time, portions of conscript political classes and supplementing propaganda materials are devoted to instilling respect for the commander. The goal of all of these activities is to facilitate military training.

One of the political officer's most important motivational techniques for stimulating better performance by service personnel is the "socialist competition" campaign.[54] The campaigns are used throughout the Soviet system to encourage workers to perform more effectively. In the military socialist competitions are arranged between individual soldiers, squads, crews, platoons, companies, and higher-level units. Ground forces units, for example, compete to improve their speed at march. Units also compete against each other to maximize the proportion of soldiers awarded a class specialty. The process is designed, of course, to harness the servicemen's competitive spirit to the task of completing the military missions of their unit. It is the zampolit's job to assist the unit commander in organizing the competition, making sure that service personnel are informed of its results and publicizing the winners.

Another major preoccupation of the zampolit is supporting the commander in efforts to improve military discipline. This function is, of course, common to all military organizations. All face the problem of maintaining order: seeing that military procedures and rules are followed, prosecuting criminals, rewarding exemplary behavior. Maintaining high levels of discipline in military units means minimizing a wide range of deviant behavior from misconduct specific to the military environment (such as wearing an improper uniform, leaving barracks without authorization, failure to salute, sleeping on guard duty, and leaving post without a pass) to "common" crimes (such as assault, theft, and murder).[55] While the level of compliance with disciplinary regulations and laws varies widely within the Soviet military, disciplinary standards are (in comparison to the West) extremely strict. This was also true of disciplinary practices in the tsarist army. One British observer who was a special correspondent in Russia noted, "I should say that the discipline in the Russian army is more severe than in any other European force."[56] In 1918 the Soviets experimented briefly with a more relaxed system. The resulting chaos led quickly to a hasty reimposition of the harsh disciplinary standards inherited from the tsarist army.[57]

The Soviet military currently employs a two-tier system for maintaining order and discipline within military units. One is the official network of institutions and officials charged with this mission. Within this network the zampolit plays a key role. While ultimate responsibility for maintaining discipline rests with the unit's commanding officer, in the division of labor that characterizes Soviet military management many of the activities involved in maintaining good order and discipline are carried out by the zampolit, who is seen as the unit's "engineer of human spirit"—a specialist in understanding and manipulating soldiers' behavior.[58] By regulation the zampolit is responsible for providing the commander with periodic reports on the political/moral climate in the unit, determining the source of disciplinary violations and organizing training, discussion, and lecture sessions with disciplinary and military–legal themes.[59] Both the commander and the zampolit are jointly liable for disciplinary infractions and crimes committed by unit personnel.[60] (The zampolit is not, however, responsible for the actual policing of military bases and garrison areas. This mission falls to the garrison service, which also administers the base guardhouse, handles firefighting, and provides honor guards.[61])

The zampolit must also be alert to problems which are potentially detrimental to good morale and discipline, including poor living and working conditions.[62] The state of unit discipline is seen as closely linked to troop life styles. The MPA officials warn that soldiers must feel that their command hierarchy is concerned about their welfare. Maximizing military performance means creating living conditions that conform to the requirements of regulations—that is, heated barracks in winter, hot meals, available medical care, reliable mail service, and access to stores and laundry facilities. All of these services, of course, are the job of *tyl* (rear services), but the human dimension of troop living conditions is part of the zampolit's mission. He monitors all aspects of the living conditions of service personnel, including the quality of food, housing facilities, medical and laundry services, and clothing supplies. He is charged with isolating deficiencies in living and training conditions that might lead to low morale among the soldiers, and of alerting the commander of the need for prompt remedies. The political officer is also responsible for instilling rear services personnel with a sense of the close relationship between *byt* (everyday life) and the military mission, and mobilizing them to ameliorate deficiencies in facilities and services.

Neither the zampolit nor the company commanding officer are in constant contact with the troops. They depend on the lower-level leadership—the company *starshina* or first sergeant (generally a warrant officer), platoon commanders (warrant officers or junior lieutenants), and squad leaders (conscript sergeants). Because the squad leaders are themselves draftees, and the products of a six-month training program and usually the same age as their troops, they frequently encounter a great deal of difficulty in exerting their authority over other conscripts. In practice, therefore, discipline within troop units is maintained primarily by the noncommissioned officer contingent.[63]

Control is also maintained through an informal and unauthorized seniority or "caste" system among conscripts.[64] Because soldiers are drafted at six-month intervals, a typical ground force unit will have _four_ classes of conscripts: new soldiers (freshly arrived conscripts), soldiers with six to twelve months' previous service, those with twelve to eighteen months' service, and senior conscripts with less than six months' service remaining before demobilization. While informal customs regarding responsibilities and privileges of each "class" vary from unit to unit, the senior soldiers enjoy a far higher status than their newly arrived counterparts, who must endure a six-month period of hazing by conscripts with longer time in service. The system is widely accepted by both conscripts and the career force. Conscripts accept the hazing they receive in the first six months in return for the privileges they receive upon achieving "senior" status. The career force accepts the system because it simplifies the problems of maintaining control of large groups of postadolescent males. The control exerted through the caste system represents the second, unauthorized, tier of the military's system of maintaining control and good order.

Breaches of military discipline are handled, as in the United States, either nonjudicially (that is, outside the court system) or judicially, depending on the seriousness of the offense. Nonjudicial procedures are handled by the military command (generally on the basis of recommendations by the unit political officer), judicial procedures by the military–legal system. The latter consists of two separate hierarchies: the military procuracy and the military tribunal (courts-martial) system.[65] The military procuracy is responsible for prosecution of all crimes committed by uniformed personnel. Although staffed by military personnel and organized parallel to the armed forces hierarchy, it is part of the USSR Procuracy-General, not the MoD. Cases involving military personnel are tried not in the regular court system, but in the military tribunal system—a hierarchy of courts roughly analogous to the U.S. courts-martial. Like the military prosecutor's office, the military tribunals mirror the military hierarchy itself with tribunals at military district, garrison, and large-unit level. Although the tribunals are composed of military personnel and the administrative support system is staffed by uniformed military, like the military procuracy, the tribunals are not legally part of the MoD. They are administered by the USSR Ministry of Justice through the Military Tribunals Directorate. The MoD and the Ministry of Justice are jointly responsible for organizing and staffing the tribunals.

Soviet procedures make a clear distinction between military crimes and disciplinary infractions.[66] Disciplinary infractions are relatively minor forms of misconduct. For example, soldiers who leave the unit area to go to some other part of the post without proper authorization are guilty of a disciplinary infraction. So are service personnel whose uniforms do not comply with regulations. Given the rigid nature of Soviet military regulations and the many restrictions imposed on uniformed personnel (particularly conscripts), disciplinary infractions are common in virtually all units. The severity of the violations, however, varies widely from unit to unit.

There are two avenues available to the military command to minimize the frequency of disciplinary infractions: rewards (incentives) for good behavior and punishments for misconduct. Guidelines for both are contained in the Disciplinary Regulations.[67] Authorized incentives vary, depending on the service status of the individual involved. For conscripts, authorized incentives include extra passes to leave the unit area, money, promotion to the next higher rank, and a ten-day leave. This last incentive is a particularly attractive reward since conscripts are not automatically given leave during their two- to three-year term. "Moral" incentives for conscripts include commendations, certificates, chest emblems, inclusion in the unit "honor book," publicizing the serviceman's accomplishments in his home town, and photographs of the serviceman taken in front of the unit banner. Authorization for all incentives is keyed to position, not rank. For example, a squad commander (who is generally a conscript sergeant) can make a commendation to a soldier in his squad, but only a regimental or division commander can grant a ten-day leave.[68] In practice, the unit political officer plays a key role in recommendations for incentive awards.

The other side of the coin is punishment. There are three ways of dealing with offenses committed by uniformed personnel: public censure, disciplinary

Table 5.1   *Offenses and Punishments in the Military Crime Code*

Offense	Punishment	
	Peacetime	War or combat conditions
1 Insubordination (open refusal to obey orders)	1–5 years' confinement	Death or 5–10 years' confinement
2 Nonfulfillment of orders*	3 months to 3 years	3–10 years
3 Opposition to superior or compelling him to breach service obligations	1–5 years	Death or 5–10 years
4 Threatening one's superior*	3 months to 3 years	3–10 years
5 Forcible action in relation to superior (i.e. bodily harm)	2–10 years	Death or 5–10 years
6 Insults of a superior by his subordinate or vice versa*	6 months to 5 years	
7 Assault by one service person on another in the absence of any subordinate relations between them*	Up to 2 years (up to 12 years in some cases)	
8 Voluntary absence (more than 1 but less than 3 days)*	3 months to 2 years in disciplinary battalion	2–10 years
9 Voluntary absence (more than 3 days, but not more than 1 month)†	1–5 years (3–7 years if more than 1 month)	5–10 years
10 Desertion†	3–7 years	Death or 5–10 years
11 Voluntary absence of any duration under combat conditions		Death or 3–10 years
12 Avoidance of military service by self-inflicted wounds or simulating illness	3–10 years	Death or 5–10 years
13 Wasting or losing military property*	3 months to 1 year in disciplinary battalion	1–5 years‡
14 Intentional destruction or damage to military property	1–5 years	Death or 5–10 years
15 Infraction of rules for driving or using combat or transport machinery	2–10 years	
16 Violation of regulations governing the handling of weapons and dangerous substances	Up to 3 years (up to 15 years if grave consequences)	
17 Infraction of flight rules or rules of flight preparation causing accident	3–10 years	
18 Infraction of navigation rules causing accident	3–10 years	

Table 5.1 (*continued*)

Offense	Punishment	
	Peacetime	War or combat conditions
19　Violation of service regulations on guard duty*	6 months to 3 years[§]	2–7 years[§]
20　Infraction of rules for border service*	Up to 3 years[§]	
21　Infraction of rules for carrying out watch duty*	1–5 years[§]	Death or 5–15 years
22　Infraction of internal service regulations by duty personnel other than guard duty*	3–6 months[§]	1–5 years
23　Divulging military secrets or loss of documents containing military secrets*	Punishment varies by type of information revealed	
24　Abuse of authority, exceeding one's authority, or not using one's authority	Up to 5 years[§]	Death or 5–15 years
25　Negligent relation to service*	Up to 3 years[§]	3–10 years
26　Giving the enemy the means to conduct war		Death or 3–10 years
27　Abandoning a military ship before fulfilling service obligation	5–10 years	Death or 10–15 years
28　Voluntarily leaving the field of fire or refusal to fire weapons		Death or 15 years
29　Voluntarily being taken prisoner		Death or 15 years
30　Criminal offenses committed by service personnel while being held prisoner		Punishment varies
31　Pillaging		Death or 3–10 years
32　Violence against population in area of combat activity		Death or 3–10 years
33　Ill-treatment of military prisoners		Punishment varies
34　Illegal use of Red Cross symbol		3 months to 1 year

*Offense which, if committed under extenuating circumstances, is not treated in the criminal system but as a disciplinary infraction.
[†]Applies to conscripts; there are separate provisions and schedules of punishment for cadres.
[‡]Stricter penalties if the military property is combat-related such as weapons.
[§]Stricter punishments if the offense has harmful consequences.
Sources: "Zakon ob ugolovnoy otvetstvennosti za voinskiye prestupleniya, 25 December 1958," as amended in A. G. Gorniy (ed.), *Komandiru o voyenno-ugolovnom zakonodatel'stve*, Moscow, Voyenizdat, 1983, pp. 167–74, and "O vnesenii izmeneniy i dopolneniy v nekotoryye akty ugolovnogo zakonodatel'stva SSSR," *Vedomosti verkhovnogo soveta SSSR*, no. 51, 21 December 1983, pp. 817–20; for details of how and when the provisions apply as well as examples see Gorniy (ed.), *Kommentariy zakona ob ugolovnoy otvetstvennosti za voinskiye prestupleniya*, Moscow, Yuridicheskaya Literatura, 1981, *pass*.

(that is, nonjudicial) punishment, and criminal prosecution. Minor misconduct by conscripts can be publicized and the offender chastised at company and battalion meetings. Misdeeds of cadre personnel are publicly censured at comrades' courts of honor. While these measures have no direct counterpart in the U.S. military's disciplinary system, they are typical of broader Soviet reliance on peer-group pressure to enforce correct behavior. In addition, the comrades' courts can also petition the culprit's commander to take much more stringent measures: removal from post, decrease in rank, or discharge from active duty.[69]

More serious offenses are dealt with by disciplinary (nonjudicial) punishment, ranging from admonition to reduction in rank, arrest, and confinement. As with incentives, the list of authorized nonjudicial punishments varies with service status and rank. The Soviet system of nonjudicial punishment is very different from that used in the U.S. military. In the United States the commanding officer can elect to apply either nonpunitive disciplinary measures (that is, corrective admonishments and reprimands) or (for more serious offenses) nonjudicial punishment levied in accordance with article 15 of the Uniform Code of Military Justice (UCMJ).[70] In the USSR there is a single array of disciplinary punishments that apply to both disciplinary infractions and to relatively minor crimes committed under extenuating circumstances. (Crimes that can be processed under the disciplinary regulations are designated as such in Table 5.1.) In the U.S. case only company and field-grade commanding officers can impose nonjudicial punishment; in the USSR disciplinary punishments can be imposed by all commanders beginning at squad level. As in the United States, the severity of punishment in the Soviet Union depends on the level of command, with division commanders and above exercising authority to impose the most onerous punishments. In general, the nonjudicial punishments available to Soviet commanders are far more severe than those in the United States. Moreover, in the U.S. individuals accused of infractions handled through article 15 enjoy several rights (that is, to remain silent, to consult counsel) and can demand trial by court-martial.[71] There are no such provisions in the Soviet case. Moreover, a U.S. serviceman cannot be punished under article 15 for an offense that falls under the jurisdiction of a civil court. In the USSR, by contrast, a serviceman who has been given a nonjudicial punishment can be tried for the same offense in the military court system: "a serviceman subjected to disciplinary (nonjudicial) punishment for a crime he committed is not relieved of criminal liability."[72]

The range of punishments available to the Soviet commander includes extra duty and reduction in rank. Soviet conscripts, however, are not required to forfeit pay as part of a disciplinary punishment since they do not receive a salary. One of the most common punishments is arrest and confinement to the guardhouse; the maximum confinement is currently ten days. This provision reflects a general easing of the severity of punishment for disciplinary infractions. The 1946 regulations allowed a twenty-day confinement; and the 1960 regulations, which superseded them, fifteen days.[73] Soviet émigrés suggest that confinement to the guardhouse is the usual punishment for unauthorized absence from post and for disorderly conduct. Physical punishments, while not authorized in the regulations, are still relatively common in the Soviet military. Like their tsarist counterparts, the career enlisted men and warrant officers in particular are prone to a quick blow when more approved methods fail. The use of physical force appears to have declined in the last few decades or so as the Soviet military tried to shift their socialization methods away from coercion and toward persuasion.[74]

Soldiers guilty of more serious misconduct are prosecuted under the criminal code. Military personnel may be prosecuted either for offenses that are covered by the general criminal code or for military crimes. In either case military personnel are prosecuted by the military procuracy and tried in military tribunals. There is no separation between the jurisdiction of the civil court system and that of the courts-martial system as there is in the United States. In the United States service personnel accused of assaulting a civilian off-post while out of uniform, under circumstances having nothing to do with the military, would probably be prosecuted by local civil authorities. In the USSR such an individual would be prosecuted within the military judicial system.

The Soviet analogue to the U.S. Uniform Code of Military Justice is the Law on Criminal Liability for Military Crimes.[75] This portion of the Soviet criminal code applies only to service personnel and includes offenses relevant to military duties.[76] Many of the offenses spelled out in the military crime code overlap with disciplinary infractions, and many instances of misconduct that formally fall within the definition of a crime—if such actions were committed under extenuating circumstances and do not represent "a significant danger" to military order—can be dealt with as disciplinary infractions. Although the offenses to which this proviso applies are spelled out in the legal code, the commander still has a great deal of latitude in interpreting the statutes and, in practice, many relatively minor crimes are handled as disciplinary infractions. This is partly because disciplinary action provides the military hierarchy with far more flexibility than criminal procedures (for example, they need not prove in a court-martial that the accused committed the offense), and partly because both the commander and the political officer will be blamed if a large number of criminal offenses occur within their unit. Both, then, have a strong incentive to handle as many incidents as possible "administratively," within disciplinary channels. As a result, those charges that are brought to trial tend to be of a more serious nature (for example, rape or murder which, by law, cannot be handled through disciplinary channels) or those in which the evidence against the accused is particularly strong.

As with Soviet criminal legislation, all crimes described in the code are associated with a particular range of punishments (for example, one to two years' confinement). Punishments differ for many offenses depending on whether they occur during peace or war, and for some offenses the severity of the punishment is linked to service status, with cadre personnel subject to more stringent sentences than their conscript counterparts. The punishments specified in the military crime codes range from three months' to fifteen years' confinement as well as the death sentence. For certain offenses (as specified in the military crime codes), Soviet servicemen, like their tsarist counterparts, are sentenced to serve this confinement in a disciplinary unit, rather than a civilian corrective labor colony or prison.[77] Offenders confined to a disciplinary unit are under armed guard and the sentence does not count toward their basic service obligation. They do, however, enjoy several of the same rights as regular soldiers—that is, their families continue to be eligible for the same privileges granted to service families. The purpose of the disciplinary unit is to rehabilitate through corrective labor. In this sense punishment of military personnel in a disciplinary unit reflects the stress on rehabilitation through labor that forms the basis of the entire Soviet penal system.[78]

How effective are these procedures in maintaining high levels of discipline? A review of the Soviet military press and the comments of former Soviet servicemen suggest that the most common forms of misconduct in the Soviet armed forces include: disobedience of orders, unauthorized absences, alcohol use and abuse, theft of military property, and fights between draftees.

Disobedience of orders is apparently one of the most frequent types of misconduct. It seems to be most common among newly arrived conscripts, who may be having difficulty adjusting to the strict regimen of military life. Most common are violations of regulations on the proper wearing of uniforms. Other frequent offenses include being late for formations, unsatisfactory maintenance of lockers, and failing to salute properly. Studies by Soviet military sociologists show that over 60 percent of the offenses committed by soldiers in their first months of service fall into this category.[79] These kinds of relatively minor misconduct are also very common among "senior" soldiers, about to be demobilized.[80] It is not uncommon, for example, for "senior" soldiers to skip morning calisthenics, or to fail to go to bed promptly at lights out. The frequency of minor violations among senior soldiers is due, in part, to the absence of meaningful rewards and punishments. Many squad and platoon leaders traditionally ignore such offenses when committed by soldiers about to be demobilized. Soldiers who have been awarded a ten-day leave for good behavior or performance know they can't expect another leave and may no longer have any incentive to maintain earlier efforts to be model soldiers.[81] Also common are cases in which a soldier neglects to carry out an order from his superior or protests an order. Strictly speaking, failure to execute an order is a crime (covered by article 2 of the Law on Criminal Liability for Military Crimes). In practice, however, some low-level commanders ignore offenses of this nature or treat them as disciplinary infractions.[82] This is particularly true in cases when conscript soldiers fail to carry out orders of conscript sergeants and is symptomatic of the problems inherent in the conscript sergeant system.

Another very common offense among conscripts is unauthorized absence from either the immediate unit area or from unit activities. Both are considered to be minor breaches of military discipline and are generally punishable by extra duty. More serious are unauthorized absences from post. For conscripts, this means any absence from post not covered by a pass (provided for outstanding performance of duties).[83] The frequency of such misconduct varies widely from unit to unit, depending on the accessibility of the nearest town, the nature of pass policy, and to some extent the leniency of lower-level commanders. Conscripts from units located in remote areas are less likely to go on unauthorized absence than those from units located adjacent to towns or villages. Units with a very limited pass policy have more unauthorized absences. This misconduct also varies with the nature of the duty assignment. For example, conscripts assigned to transportation units whose duties frequently take them off-post can more easily go joy-riding during the day. Those conscripts who drill, train, and perform work details under more supervised conditions simply have less opportunity to evade military authorities during the day. The most common form of unauthorized absence occurs at night, after evening inspection and lights out, or on Sunday during periods of free time.

Most unauthorized absences by conscripts are treated as disciplinary infractions and are punished by several days in the guardhouse.[84] Absences of more than twenty-four hours, but less than three days, are technically a violation of military law, although a first offense may be dealt with as a disciplinary infraction if there are "extenuating circumstances." Repeated absences, even those of less than twenty-four hours, are also classified as a military crime. A conscript charged under this provision of the military law code can be tried in a military tribunal and, if convicted, be sentenced to three months to two years in a disciplinary battalion.[85] Absences of over three days are considered a more serious offense. Soldiers convicted of this crime are sentenced to deprivation of freedom from one to five years if the duration of absence is less than a month. Soldiers absent for over a month are subject to three to seven years' confinement.[86] Desertion in the Soviet military, as in the U.S., is defined not by length of absence, but by intention. A deserter is one who stays away from his unit or place of assignment with the goal of avoiding military service. The penalties are corespondingly harsher: a soldier convicted of desertion is sentenced to three to seven years' confinement.[87]

The incidence of prolonged absence and desertion is relatively rare. Most unauthorized absences last only a few hours. More prolonged absence (short of desertion) is much less frequent and is apparently prosecuted as such even less frequently. The command and political hierarchy prefers to handle all but the most flagrant absences within the military discipline system, as opposed to the military tribunal system. Cases of desertion are even more rare.

Another common offense is alcohol abuse. Use of alcohol by conscripts is prohibited. It is not allowed in the barracks and restrictive pass policies in many units severely limit opportunities to acquire alcohol off-post. Despite these restrictions, drinking is a common problem in many units. Alcoholic beverages are frequently smuggled in by soldiers returning from leave, by civilians working on the base, or by career enlisted personnel (who are not ordinarily confined to barracks in their off-duty hours). Conscripts whose work detail takes them off-post and out of direct military supervision often capitalize on the opportunity by buying alcohol for themselves and their friends. Free time on pass privileges is often used for getting drunk.[88] Obtaining alcohol is a common motive for going off post without a pass. Draftees determined to drink reportedly resort to drinking cologne, alcohol intended for cleaning purposes, or various home brews concocted from shoe polish or strong tea.

Since alcohol use by conscripts has been defined as a breach of discipline, Soviet authorities treat it as a disciplinary issue and often link drinking and disciplinary problems.[89] How serious is alcohol abuse in the Soviet military? Émigré reporting suggests that in most units alcohol consumption by both conscripts and career personnel occurs largely during off-duty hours.[90] Drinking during duty hours or appearing drunk for duty is much less common, although driving while intoxicated is a major cause of accidents involving military vehicles.[91]

Alcohol abuse in the Soviet armed forces mirrors the pervasiveness of the problem in civilian life. Hard drinking, often inebriation, is a cultural tradition throughout many of the Slavic regions.[92] The "struggle with drunkenness" long predates the Bolsheviks. During World War I the tsarist government initiated a series of measures curtailing the production and distribution of alcoholic beverages. Sir Alfred Knox, an English military attaché, tells how one group of Russian soldiers, ordered to destroy the alcohol reserves of a Polish land-owner, could not bring themselves to complete their mission without first drinking to the point of stupor.[93]

Alcohol abuse remains a serious problem in the contemporary Soviet civilian world. Available data do not permit a direct comparison between current levels of alcohol abuse or alcoholism in the USSR as compared to other industrial societies. It seems clear, nonetheless, that alcohol abuse is a serious social problem and has been recognized as such by Soviet authorities.[94] Western estimates (derived in part from Soviet data) rank the Soviet Union seventh or eighth among nations in alcohol consumption, fourth in the consumption of strong alcoholic beverages (vodka, as opposed to beer or wine). Such data also point to high growth rates in per capita alcohol consumption in the USSR.[95] Excessive drinking has been blamed for a number of social problems ranging from family difficulties (alcohol abuse by husbands is a frequent cause for divorce) to increased mortality among middle-aged males.[96] Soviet data suggest that most problem drinkers began drinking in childhood or ado-lescence.[97] This suggests that newly assigned draftees bring the problem with them to their units. One study of drinking patterns among schoolchildren in Perm found that 31 percent of the children in first through third grade had tried alcoholic beverages.[98] Because draftees are male—and Soviet research shows that both drinking and drinking problems are much more common among males of all ages[99]—the potential problems of alcohol abuse are magnified in the armed forces. Given these factors, it is not surprising that those conscripts who get access to alcohol drink to excess in response to the stress, boredom, and isolation of military life.

Fighting and physical assaults by service personnel represent a fourth type of disciplinary problem. Most physical assaults occur between military personnel, usually conscript soldiers. In some units "fighting in the ranks" is a common occurrence and is frequently covered up by the conscript sergeants.[100] The most common form such violations take is an assault by a senior soldier on a new conscript. Indeed, a large proportion of interpersonal conflicts in most units is due to the hazing system.[101] Fights that grow out of ethnic tensions between soldiers of different nationalities (that is, between a Georgian and a Ukrainian or between a Russian and an Uzbek) also occur, although with much lower frequency. Overt ethnic conflict is held in check partly by the general intolerance of such incidents within the command hierarchy, and partly by the existence of the seniority system. Interpersonal ties based on seniority generally cut across groupings based on common ethnic and/or regional background.

Abuses of the seniority system, then, appear to be the most common cause of interpersonal friction within most units. Former Soviet soldiers recount incidents in which the young soldier is forced to relinquish his new uniform, plus watches and other personal items, to soldiers about to be demobilized. The new recruits are frequently coerced into shining boots, making beds, and cleaning weapons for the "oldtimers." The young soldiers within a given squad are often forced to perform the lion's share of any unpleasant duties assigned to the squad.[102] A new recruit who resists exploitation by senior servicemen may be assaulted or beaten by the oldtimers in his unit.[103] Indeed, abuse of the seniority system is recognized by Soviet military authorities as a serious disciplinary problem.[104] One of the major difficulties in controlling such problems is that the victims are seldom willing to report the abuse to their superiors because of peer-group pressure and for fear of reprisals.[105]

Many disciplinary infractions among conscripts grow out of adjustment problems. The new conscript, who may be accustomed to arguing with a teacher at school or a supervisor at work, finds it difficult to accept the fact that a military order is not open to discussion.[106] In one group of young draftees who were interviewed about their attitudes toward military life 45 percent admitted they disliked the strict discipline. Many interpreted their superior's demands as an effort to belittle them.[107] Others find it hard to comply with certain military requirements—for example, making a bed according to regulation—which may be perceived as unnecessary.[108] Some lack maturity and self-control.[109] In other units boredom appears to be the major cause of discipline problems. Soldiers from units with a high frequency of unauthorized absences and drunkenness complain that there was simply nothing better to do with their free time;[110] and Soviet authorities, who advocate better-organized recreational activities as an antidote to alcohol abuse and other disciplinary problems, implicitly agree with them.[111]

Discipline problems are rarely isolated; that is, a unit experiencing one form of disciplinary infraction generally has a wide range of behavioral problems. Units with a high frequency of unauthorized leave often have many problems with alcohol and abuse of the hazing system as well. This is partly due to the demographic composition of specific units, and partly to weaknesses of unit leadership. In some low-priority units, such as the construction troops, a relatively large proportion of the draftees are young men with prior behavioral problems. These tendencies are exacerbated because the least-able career enlisted men and officers tend to be assigned to such units. Not surprisingly, these units have more than their share of disciplinary problems. Conversely, in high-status or high-priority units, which have a larger proportion of the best-educated and most conscientious soldiers, disciplinary problems are virtually nonexistent. This wide variation in disciplinary rates helps to explain why some ex-Soviet soldiers claim to have served in exemplary units, while others describe their unit as undisciplined and disorderly.

One factor that contributes to the concentration of disciplinary infractions in "problem" units is the tendency by lower-level commanders to conceal problems from their superiors. In one case that was aired in the pages of *Red Star* the company commander failed to report a soldier on unauthorized absence. The soldier returned to his unit, but the incident was discovered because he had committed a crime. The officers involved in the cover-up defended their actions by noting that officers who reported fairly and honestly about their units were often penalized for their honesty. In one case a major who reported a disciplinary infraction through channels as required by regulation was given a reprimand and his political deputy a severe reprimand.[112] Not surprisingly, many Soviet officers learn quickly to conceal offenses by their subordinates, making it impossible to employ legitimate punishments and this, in turn, may undermine discipline still further. In order to maintain control some inventive officers devise "nonofficial" punishments, such as scheduling night training in bad weather, as a substitute for the official system which may be used only sparingly.[113]

The disciplinary system is also used to deliver reprisals against "whistle-blowers." One case investigated by *Red Star* involved a warrant officer who publicized wrongdoing by his battalion commander. After the commander was penalized for his transgressions, he almost immediately took revenge on his accuser by a series of disciplinary actions and later turned him over to the warrant officers "comrades court" with a recommendation that he be dismissed from the service.[114] A similar fate befell another warrant officer involved in a people's control inspection of irregularities in the unit's food service.[115]

In theory, the political hierarchy is intended to prevent these abuses by serving as an independent source of information on personnel problems. In practice, the political officer frequently colludes with his commander in covering up offenses and in exploiting disciplinary punishments to deter whistle-blowers. This problem points to the commonality of interests between the zampolit and commander. Both are jointly liable for disciplinary problems in their unit. In one case reported by *Red Star* equipment and personnel from an air defense unit were being illicitly hired out to civilian enterprises. Both the unit commander and his political deputy were reprimanded. In another incident a submarine commander had apparently used the proceeds from a similar operation to purchase three Zhiguli cars. When the situation came to light, both the submarine commander and his political deputy (who had covered up the illicit activities with placating reports to his superiors at the next highest political department) were severely punished.[116] While instances of a political officer standing up to his commander and dutifully reporting irregularities to his superiors in the political hierarchy are not unknown, the way such instances are handled in the military press suggests that these incidents are exceptions and not the rule.[117] Most political officers, it seems, find it easier to cooperate with their commanders in dealing with personnel problems, even if that cooperation means concealing disciplinary violations from their superiors in both the command and political hierarchies.

The Political Officer's Role in the Soviet Military

The political officer and the commander are also linked by other shared goals that go beyond a mutual concern for discipline and good order. Both the commander and political officer are responsible for ensuring that regulations regarding personnel sevices are followed. When irregularities in the food service for a unit in the Pacific fleet were discovered, the warrant officer directly in charge was given a strict reprimand, and so too were the unit commander and his political officer.[118] When needed repairs on several residential buildings in Kaliningrad were not made, both the deputy commander for construction of the Baltic fleet and his political deputy came in for official criticism.[119]

In general, whenever there are problems in fulfillment of unit or agency mission, both the commander and his political officer are held responsible. In one case publicized in the Soviet press, officials at a city military commissariat were found guilty of ignoring the needs of a World War II veteran. The city military commissar was fired. His superior (the oblast military commissar) and the chief of the Political Directorate at the oblast military commissariat were given disciplinary punishment.[120]

Joint responsibility also extends to other military missions. Although the quality of combat training is the primary responsibility of the commander, both commanders and their political deputies may be punished for training deficiencies. One incident reported in the military press involved deficiencies in combat training on one of the ships of the Pacific Ocean fleet. Both the ship's captain and political officer received severe reprimands.[121] Similarly, Soviet commanders are usually liable for deficiencies in political work within their units. Inadequate socialization work in one unit resulted in a disciplinary action against both the political officer and his commander.[122] In sum, both the political officer and his commander are measured by the same standard— fulfillment of the unit mission. They function far more as partners than as adversaries. To be sure, the idealized image presented in the Soviet press of the zampolit as political and military educator, and faithful supporter of the unit commander, may tend to understate potential areas of conflict between them. For example, the professional military officer, intent on harnessing the educational capability of the political officer for purely military training, may find himself at odds with the political officer, who must balance these activities with ones that relate to the inculcation of political values. The same may be said, of course, for other staff officers. There is, however, a basic commonality of interests that link the zampolit with the military commander and the rest of his staff. The two hierarchies (military command and MPA) are so thoroughly interconnected that the MPA's role as an autonomous source of information and control has gradually atrophied.

The common goals that unite the commander and his political officer are not dissimilar from those that link the enterprise director with the enterprise party secretary. In both cases the relationship between the two officials, which has often been viewed by Western observers as an adversarial relationship, is more one of partnership. Just as the Soviet enterprise director and enterprise party secretary must work cooperatively to achieve common goals and fulfill the enterprise's plan indicators, the military commander and his zampolit have important professional incentives to maintain a fairly harmonious working relationship.

What distinguishes political arrangements within the MoD from those in the civilian world is the nature of the party chain of command at intermediate and higher levels. Civilian party committees report to a network of regional party agencies at rayon, city, oblast, and republic levels. By contrast, the enterprise director reports up his ministry chain of command rather than the government's territorial apparatus. The director of a large factory complex, for example, may report directly to a ministry agency in Moscow, while his party secretary reports to the local party committee. These two entities, the ministry agency in Moscow and the local party committee, have different sets of interests. The local party committee, for instance, may be more concerned with the factory's attention to its employees' housing needs than the ministry agency in Moscow. The divergence between the ministerial chain of command and the party's territorial hierarchy has thus tended to preserve the autonomy of the party network as a control mechanism and as an alternate source of information. By contrast, in the MoD the military's political chain of command parallels the military chain. This factor has effectively undermined the MPA's value as an independent source of control and oversight over the military.

These comments suggest that MPA activities within the armed forces are basically irrelevant to the issue of civil-military conflict. The relationship between the political officer and the commander cannot be used as a barometer of party–military relations. Calls to enhance the role of the zampolit have been interpreted as a reflection of party determination to gain a firmer hold on the military leadership. An alternate (and much more plausible) explanation is that they are part of a continuing effort to maximize the zampolit's efficiency in discharging a variety of both political and military duties. Political control, in the sense of ensuring the political reliability of military professionals, is only one of the broad array of MPA responsibilities; and it is currently one of the least significant of the MPA's missions. Much more important are the MPA's responsibilities in directing the political socialization of armed forces personnel—an issue taken up in Chapter 6.

Notes: Chapter 5

1 N. A. Petrovichev *et al.*, *Partiynoye stroitel'stvo. Uchebnoy posobiye* (Moscow: Politizdat, 1981), p. 225.
2 G. V. Sredin, "Politicheskiye organy," *SVE*, Vol. 6, pp. 420–2.
3 "Yepishev, Aleksey Alekseyevich" *SVE*, Vol. 3, pp. 311–12; *Deputaty verkhovnogo soveta*

SSSR. Desyatyy sozyv (Moscow: Izvestiya, 1979), p. 153; and *Istoriya gorodov i sel ukrainskoy SSR. Odesskaya oblast* (Kiev: Glavnaya Redaktsiya Ukrainskoy Sovetskoy Entsiklopedii, 1978), p. 96.

4 "Glavnoye politicheskoye upravleniye," *SVE*, Vol. 2, pp. 562–4.

5 ibid., p. 563. See also A. A. Yepishev (ed.), *KPSS i voyennoye stroitel'stvo* (Moscow: Voyenizdat, 1982), p. 185.

6 Yu. P. Petrov, *Stroitel'stvo politorganov partiynykh i komosomol'skikh organizatsiy armii i flota. 1918–1968* (Moscow: Voyenizdat, 1968). p. 441.

7 ibid., pp. 487–8, 514–15.

8 *KVS*, no. 10 (1972), pp. 3–4.

9 *KZ*, 25 October 1980, p. 2.

10 *KZ*, 26 July 1981, p. 2; and 9 December 1983, p. 2; and 5 June 1977, p. 2. See also *KZ*, 30 August 1981, p. 2.

11 L. A. Bublik *et al.* (eds), *Partiyno-politicheskaya rabota v sovetskoy armii i voyenno-morskom flote* (Moscow: Voyenizdat, 1982), p. 53.

12 Petrovichev *et al.*, 1978, p. 225.

13 See *KZ*, 21 August 1981, p. 2; and *KVS*, no. 6 (1982), p. 47.

14 Yepishev, 1982, pp. 155–6. See, for example, the biography of "member of the Military Council—chief of the *politupravleniye* of the ground forces," Semen Petrovichev Vasyagin, *SVE*, Vol. 2, p. 29.

15 Petrovichev *et al.*, 1978, p. 227.

16 Sergei Zamascikov, *Political Organizations in the Soviet Armed Forces: The Role of the Party and Komsomol*, Delphic Associates monograph series on the Soviet Union, December 1982, pp. 34, 93.

17 M. G. Sobolev *et al.* (eds.), *Partiyno-politicheskaya rabota v sovetskikh vooruzhennykh silakh* (Moscow: Voyenizdat, 1974), pp. 156–60; and Zamascikov, 1982, pp. 28–34, 45–6.

18 Sobolev, 1974, pp. 160–4.

19 Zamascikov, 1982, pp. 93–4; Sobolev, 1974, pp. 164–71; and A. A. Yepishev (ed.), *Ideologicheskaya rabota v vooruzhennykh silakh SSSR. Istoriko-teoreticheskiy ocherk* (Moscow: Voyenizdat, 1983), p. 272.

20 V. G. Kolychev, "Voyennyy komissar," *SVE*, Vol. 2, pp. 268–9; A. Chilyants, "V. I. Lenin and the creation of the political organs and party political apparatus in the Soviet armed forces," *VIZh*, no. 2 (1983), pp. 12–17; V. Soshnev, "From the history of the development of Party organizations in the Soviet armed forces," *VIZh*, no. 6 (1973), pp. 3–12; M. Rudakov, I. Kolesnichenko, and V. Lunin, "Several problems of the work of political organs in the years of foreign military intervention and Civil War," *VIZh*, no. 8 (1962), pp. 3–12.

21 *SVE*, Vol. 2, p. 268; and *VES*, p. 146.

22 P. Spirin, "V. I. Lenin and the creation of Soviet command cadres," *VIZh*, no. 4 (1965), pp. 3–16; D. A. Voropayev and A. M. Iovlev, *Bor'ba KPSS za sozdaniye voyennykh kadrov* (Moscow: Voyenizdat, 1960), p. 41; "Voyenspets," *SVE*, Vol. 2, p. 274; Timothy J. Colton, *Commissars, Commanders, and Civilian Authority: The Structure of Soviet Military Politics* (Cambridge, Mass.: Harvard University Press, 1979), p. 48; and "Voyennyye spetsialisty," *Grazhdanskaya voyna i voyennaya interventsiya v SSSR* (Moscow: Sovetskaya Entsiklopediya, 1983), p. 106.

23 Russia (1923—U.S.S.R.), Tsentral'noye upravleniye narodno-khozyaystvennogo ucheta gosplana SSSR, Otdel ucheta truda, *Sostav rukovodyashchikh rabotnikov i spetsialistov soyuza SSR* (Moscow: Soyuzorguchet, 1936), pp. 5–6.

24 Jeremy R. Azrael, *Managerial Power and Soviet Politics* (Cambridge, Mass.: Harvard University Press, 1966), pp. 56–8.

25 The civilian party data are from May 1930 and were derived from *Narodnoye khozyaystvo SSSR. Statisticheskiy spravochnik, 1932* (Leningrad and Moscow: Gosudarstvennoye sotsial'no-ekonomicheskoye Izdatel'stvo, 1932), pp. 494–5.

26 The civilian party data are from *Sostav*, table 5, pp. 12–13.

27 K. Ye. Voroshilov, "On the results of the first five year plan," in K. Ye. Voroshilov, *Stat'i i rechi* (Moscow: Politizdat TsK VKP(b), 1937), pp. 481–524; and *X let krasnoy armii. Albom diagramm* (Moscow: Izdatel'stvo Voyennyy vestnik, 1928), p. 34.

28 Voropayev and Iovlev, 1960, pp. 145–6; and *NK SSSR, 1932*, pp. 488–9.

29 loc. cit., and *Sostav*, table 5, pp. 12–13.

30 The military data are from Voropayev and Iovlev, 1960, p. 133. The civilian data were

computed from *Sotsialisticheskoye stroitel'stvo SSSR. Statisticheskiy yezhegodnik* (Moscow: Soyuzorguchet, 1936), pp. 574–6. See also K. Ye. Voroshilov, "Against slander in the Red Army," in Voroshilov, 1937, pp. 149–58.

31 Azrael, 1966, pp. 28–30.

32 Amy W. Knight, "The KGB's special departments in the Soviet armed forces," *Orbis*, vol. 28, no. 2 (Summer 1984), pp. 257–80. See also "Osobyye otdely," *SVE*, Vol. 6, pp. 142–3; and *VES*, pp. 525–6.

33 Soviet sources differ on the date at which the transfer of responsibility took place. Petrov dates it to the Tenth Party Congress in March 1921. The Soviet Military Encyclopedia's survey of cultural-socialization work gives the date as 1920: see Petrov, 1968, pp. 123–4. Extracts from the Tenth Party Congress resolution on the issue are provided in N. I. Savinkin and K. M. Bogolyubov (eds.), *KPSS o vooruzhennykh silakh sovetskogo soyuza. Dokumenty 1918–1981* (Moscow: Voyenizdat, 1981), pp. 154–5. See also Ye. I. Vostokov, "Kul'turno-prosvetitel'naya rabota v vooruzhennykh silakh SSSR," *SVE*, Vol. 4, pp. 520–4; Chilyants, 1983; and A. Geronimus, *Partiya i krasnaya armiya. Istoricheskiy ocherk* (Moscow: Gosudarstvennoye Izdatel'stvo, 1928), pp. 130–1.

34 "Glavpolitprosvet," in *Grazhdanskaya voyna i voyennaya interventsiya v SSSR. Entsiklopediya*, p. 152.

35 Petrov, 1968, pp. 123–4.

36 "Iz polozheniya o politicheskom upravlenii voyennogo okruga (armii i flota)," 18 July 1921, in *Partiyno-politicheskaya rabota v krasnoy armii. Dokumenty, 1921–1929 gg* (Moscow: Voyenizdat, 1981), pp. 25–7; and "Iz polozheniya o politicheskom otdele divizii (flotilii)," in ibid., pp. 27–8.

37 "Polozheniye ob organizatsii bibliotechnoy raboty v Krasnoy armii i flote," 17 October 1922, in ibid., pp. 101–6.

38 "Polozheniye o politicheskom upravlenii revolyutsionnogo voyennogo soveta respubliki," 18 October 1922, in ibid., pp. 106–12.

39 ibid., no. 6, p. 521; and Petrov, 1968, p. 125.

40 Chilyants, 1983; and Soshnev, 1973.

41 S. A. Tyushkevich *et al.*, *Sovetskiye vooruzhennyye sily. Istoriya stroitel'stva* (Moscow: Voyenizdat, 1978), p. 143.

42 "Vsesoyuznyy Leninskiy Kommunisticheskiy Soyuz Molodezhi (VLKSM)," *VES*, p. 167.

43 Komsomol membership data are provided in *Yezhegodnik bol'shoy sovetskoy entsiklopedii, 1979* (Moscow: Izdatel'stvo Sovetskaya Entsiklopediya, 1979), p. 17, and *1980*, p. 21, and *1983*, p. 17. The age data used to standardize these data were derived from estimates and projections provided by the Bureau of the Census, Foreign Demographic Analysis Division (May 1982).

44 I. G. Bezuglov *et al.* (eds.), *Komsomol'skaya rabota v sovetskoy armii i flote* (Moscow: Voyenizdat, 1974), p. 21.

45 A. V. Barabanshchikov, *Voyennaya pedagogika* (Moscow: Voyenizdat, 1966), pp. 54–5; and Petrov, 1968, p. 510.

46 V. Khrobostrov, "Political organs and party and Komsomol organizations in the Soviet armed forces," *KVS*, no. 4 (1974), pp. 69–76; and V. Izmalov, "The 26th CPSU Congress on strengthening the nation's defense might," *KVS*, no. 8 (1981), pp. 77–84. See also Bublik, 1982, pp. 70–1.

47 Calculated from party data in *Partiynaya zhizn*, no. 15 (1983), p. 22; and educational data in *Narodnoye khozyaystvo SSSR v 1982 g* (Moscow: Finansy i Statistika, 1983), p. 26.

48 ibid.

49 Calculated from data in *Partiynaya zhizn*, no. 15 (1983), p. 22; and *Narodnoye khozyaystvo SSSR, 1922–1982* (Moscow: Finansy i Statistika, 1982), p. 407. The data shown in Figure 5.6 were calculated from "KPSS v tsifrakh," *Partiynaya zhizn*, no. 21 (1977), pp. 20–43; and *Narodnoye khozyaystvo SSSR v 1977 g* (Moscow: Statistika, 1978), p. 393.

50 T. H. Rigby, *Communist Party Membership in the USSR, 1917–1967* (Princeton, N.J.: Princeton University Press, 1968), pp. 432–3; and Colton, 1979, p. 48.

51 Calculated from *Partiynaya zhizn*, no. 15 (1983), pp. 14–15, 24. Age and sex data computed from estimates and projections provided by the Bureau of the Census Foreign Demographic Analysis Division (May 1982).

52 Bublik, 1982, pp. 168–74; A. I. Sorokin (ed.), *Partiyno-politicheskaya rabota v sovetskikh vooruzhennykh silakh* (Moscow: Voyenizdat, 1979), pp. 305–14. See also Sobolev, 1974,

pp. 372–86; and I. Repin, "Improve military technical propaganda," *Tekhnika i vooruzheniye*, no. 1 (1978), pp. 2–4.

53 F. S. Stepanov *et al.* (eds.), *Zamestitel' komandira polka (korablya) po politicheskoy chasti* (Moscow: Voyenizdat, 1975), pp. 61–76; and Bublik, 1982, pp. 161–3.

54 Bublik, 1982, pp. 163–5; Sorokin, 1979, pp. 248–68; V. K. Luzherenko, "Sotsialisticheskoye sovernovaniye," *SVE*, Vol. 7, p. 458; and N. I. Smorigo and P. F. Isakov, *Zamestitel' komandira roty (baterei) po politchasti*, 2d ed. (Moscow: Voyenizdat, 1982), pp. 95–101.

55 N. N. Arisov and V. G. Belyavskiy, "Distsiplina voinskaya," *SVE*, Vol. 3, pp. 197–9.

56 William Barnes Steveni, *The Russian Army from Within* (New York: Doran, 1914), p. 143.

57 The restoration of strict discipline was codified in the 1919 Disciplinary Regulations. I. Kolesnichenko, "Action of the Communist Party to strengthen military discipline in the period of formation of the Soviet armed forces," *VIZh*, no. 9 (1963), pp. 3–11; A. Pozdnyakov, "First Soviet laws and military regulations on discipline in the army and navy," *VIZh*, no. 12 (1965), pp. 15–25; and A. Gorniy and A. Pozdnyakov, "From the history of Soviet military legislation in the area of strengthening military discipline," *VIZh*, no. 6 (1968), pp. 29–36.

58 A. I. Kitov (ed.), *Sovremennaya armiya i distsiplina* (Moscow: Voyenizdat, 1976), p. 258.

59 "Ustav vnutrenney sluzhby vooruzhennykh sil SSSR," 30 July 1975, in *Svod zakonov SSSR* (Moscow: Izvestiya, 1982), Vol. 9, pp. 218–346 (hereafter cited as Internal Service Regulations). Regulations on the responsibilities of regimental commanders are on pp. 232–4; on regimental zampolit see pp. 235–6. Analogous data on the battalion command and zampolit are on pp. 254–5, 256–7; on the company commander and zampolit see pp. 259–61, 261–73. See also Stepanov, 1975, pp. 242–59; Smorigo and Isakov, 1982, pp. 125–48; and Sorokin, 1979, pp. 212–26.

60 See, for example, V. Levitskiy, "Commander and the law: behind a convenient wording," *KZ*, 1 August 1976, p. 2.

61 "Ustav garizonnoy i karaulnoy sluzhb vooruzhennykh sil SSSR," in *Svod zakonov*, Vol. 9, pp. 347–462.

62 Stepanov, 1975, pp. 285–300; and I. Repin, "Everyday life and military discipline," *Tyl i snabzheniye*, no. 2 (1983), pp. 43–7.

63 See, for example, V. Panov, "Infraction or crime?" *Znamenosets*, no. 1 (1979), p. 27; V. Boyarshinov, "Not from fear, but from conscience," *Znamenosets*, no. 12 (1981), p. 8. On squad leaders' problems with maintaining discipline see *Serzhanty i distsiplina* (Moscow: Voyenizdat, 1977), *pass.*

64 N. Chistyakov and V. Maslov, "Persuasion and compulsion in the struggle against legal violations in the army and navy," *Voyennaya mysl'*, no. 5 (1973).

65 "Polozheniye o voyennoy prokurature," in *Sbornik zakonov SSSR i ukazov prezidiuma verkhovnogo soveta SSSR, 1938–1975* (Moscow: Izvestiya, 1976), pp. 106–13; and "Polozheniye o voyennykh tribunalakh," approved 25 December 1958, as amended, in ibid., pp. 23–31. Secondary materials are available in A. G. Gorniy (ed.), *Osnovy sovetskogo voyennogo zakonodatel'stva* (Moscow: Voyenizdat, 1966), pp. 358–66; A. I. Lepeshkin *et al.* (eds.), *Osnovy sovetskogo voyennogo zakonodatel'stva* (Moscow: Voyenizdat, 1973), pp. 213–25; S. S. Maksimov (ed.), *Osnovy sovetskogo voyennogo zakonodatel'stva* (Moscow: Voyenizdat, 1978), pp. 250–63; A. G. Gorniy, "Prokuratura voyennaya," *SVE*, Vol. 6, pp. 566–7; A. S. Koblikov, "Pravosudiye v vooruzhennykh silakh SSSR," *SVE*, Vol. 6, pp. 493–4; and N. F. Chistyakov, "Tribunal voyennyy," *SVE*, Vol. 8, pp. 107–8.

66 A. G. Gorniy (ed.), *Komandiru o voyenno-ugolovnom zakonodatel'stve* (Moscow: Voyenizdat, 1983), pp. 18–21.

67 "Distsiplinarnyy ustav vooruzhennykh sil SSSR," 30 July 1975, in *SZ*, Vol. 9, pp. 463–94 (hereafter cited as Disciplinary Regulations).

68 Leave may be granted only once to two-year conscripts, no more than twice to three-year conscripts.

69 "Polozheniye o tovarishcheskikh sudakh chesti ofitserov v vooruzhennykh silakh SSSR," in *SZ*, Vol. 9, pp. 515–22. There are separate comrades' courts of honor for officers, warrant officers, and extended service personnel. See "Polozheniye o tovarishchekikh sudakh chesti praporshchikov, michmanov i voyennosluzhashchikh sverkhsrochnoy sluzhby v vooruzhennykh silakh SSSR," *SZ*, Vol. 9, pp. 523–30; and V. Bobkov, "To educate the collective," *Znamenosets*, no. 11 (1977), p. 37.

70 "Uniform Code of Military Justice," 5 May 1950, as amended, in *Manual for Courts Martial, United States 1969* (rev.) (5 April 1983), appendix 2, pp. A2-1 to A2-37.

71 H.Q. Department of the Army, *Legal Guide for Commanders. A Guide to the Administration of Military Justice and Administrative Law at the Company Level*, FM 27-1 (Washington, D.C.: 18 May 1981), pp. 3-1–3-7 and 8-1–8-8.
72 Disciplinary Regulations, article 46.
73 *Distsiplinarnyy ustav vooruzhennykh sil soyuza SSR*, 1 June 1946, (Moscow: Voyenizdat, 1948), articles 23–5; and *Distsiplinarnyy ustav vooruzhennykh sil soyuza SSR*, 23 August 1960 (Moscow: Voyenizdat, 1969), article 36.
74 S. Ilin, "Methods of educating Soviet soldiers," *Voyennaya mysl'*, no. 5 (1968); and P. Slepukhin, "The role of interrelationships in the system of military indoctrination," *Voyennaya mysl'*, no. 10 (1973). On tsarist use of physical coercion see Steveni, 1914, p. 52.
75 "Zakon ob ugolovnoy otvetstvennosti za voinskiye prestupleniya," 25 December 1958, as amended, in Gorniy, 1983, pp. 167–74.
76 "Service personnel" to whom military crime codes apply are those serving on active duty in the army, navy, border, or internal troops (including cadets) as well as reservists on training musters and service personnel and officers in the organs of the KGB: A. G. Gorniy (ed), *Kommentariy zakona ob ugolovnoy otvetstvennosti za voinskiye prestupleniya* (Moscow: Yuridicheskaya Literatura, 1981), pp. 14–20.
77 Ye. V. Prokopovich, "Distsiplinarnaya chast'," *SVE*, Vol. 3, pp. 200–1.
78 W. E. Butler, *Soviet Law* (London: Butterworths, 1983), pp. 279–89; see also V. A. Kirin, *Zakonodatel'stvo o bor'be s prestupnost'yu* (Moscow: Yuridicheskaya Literatura, 1978), pp. 246–62.
79 A. M. Danchenko and I. F. Vydrin, *Voyennaya pedagogika* (Moscow: Voyenizdat, 1973), trans. by U.S. air force as *Military Pedagogy: A Soviet View*, p. 103 (hereafter cited as *Military Pedagogy*). See also S. Morozov, "Outside the unit area," *Znamenosets*, no. 11 (1978), p. 37; and "Unpardonable violations," *KZ*, 28 June 1981, p. 2.
80 N. Onufriychuk, "Fulcrum," *KZ*, 16 September 1981, p. 2.
81 I. Volkov, D. Prilepskiy, and L. Cherkasov, "Theoretical questions of military discipline," *Voyennaya mysl'*, no. 3 (1968).
82 See, for example, N. Bukharin, "Unconditionally and on time," *KZ*, 6 February 1977, p. 2; and A. Milyukov, "The first commandment," *Znamenosets*, no. 2 (February 1983), pp. 18–19.
83 Disciplinary Regulations, article 22.
84 Technically soldiers held in the guardhouse for disciplinary infractions are under arrest: "Gauptvakhta," *VES*, p. 181.
85 "Zakon ob ugolovnoy otvetstvennosti za voinskiye prestupleniya," article 9.
86 ibid., article 10.
87 ibid., article 11.
88 Morozov, 1978.
89 D. Volkogonov, "Moral conflict," *Sovetskiy voin*, no. 12 (1976), pp. 32–3; and V. M. Grishanov, "An important party matter," *Morskoy sbornik*, no. 11 (1972), pp. 3–7.
90 See for example, P. Reynis, "On the state of affairs in the Soviet army," *Posev*, no. 6 (June 1982), p. 62.
91 L. Petukhov, "Alcohol—a precondition of traffic accidents," *TIS*, no. 2 (1972), pp. 83–5; and V. Koblyanskiy, "Alcohol—the reason for many traffic accidents," *TIS*, no. 1 (1978), pp. 77–9.
92 David E. Powell, "Alcohol abuse: the pattern of official response," in Karl W. Ryavec (ed.), *Soviet Society and the Communist Party* (Amherst, Mass.: University of Massachusetts Press, 1978), pp. 134–52; Boris M. Segal, "Drinking and alcoholism in Russia," *Psychiatric Opinion*, vol. 12, no. 9 (1975), pp. 21–9; and Walter D. Connor, *Deviance in Soviet Society: Crime, Delinquincy, and Alcoholism* (New York: Columbia University Press, 1972), pp. 39–42.
93 Sir Alfred Knox, *With the Russian Army, 1914–1917* (New York: Dutton, 1921), Vol. 1, p. 307; see also Steveni, 1914, pp. 31, 42.
94 A recent Soviet source that summarizes much of the available Soviet data on alcohol use and abuse is Yu. P. Lisitsyn and N. Ya. Kopyt, *Alkogolizm. Sotsial'no-gigienicheskiye aspeky*, 2d ed. (Moscow: Meditsina, 1983).
95 Vladimir G. Treml, *Alcohol in the USSR: A Statistical Study* (Durham, N.C.: Duke University Press Policy Studies, 1982), pp. 67–70.
96 Ye. V. Boldyrev, *Alkogolizm—put' k prestupleniyu* (Moscow: Yuridicheskaya Literatura, 1966), *pass.*; B. Levin, "A social portrait of the alcoholic," in *Mneniye neravnodushnykh* (Moscow: Politicheskoy Literatury, 1972), pp. 63–133; N. Ya. Kopyt and V. V. Gudzha-

bidze, "Influence of alcohol abuse on several indicators of the health of the population," *Zdravookhraneniye rossiyskoy federatsii*, no. 6 (1977), pp. 25–8.

97 A. V. Fedotov, "Social problems of the struggle against alcoholism," *SI*, no. 4 (1976), pp. 195–201; and Ye. S. Skvortsova, "On anti-alcoholic propaganda in the school," *Zdravookhraneniye rossiyskoy federatsii*, no. 5 (1978), pp. 26–9.

98 Z. Balayan, "An evil which gives rise to an evil," *Literaturnaya gazeta*, no. 36 (8 September 1982), pp. 12–13.

99 A study of secondary students in two northern cities revealed that 62 percent of the 14–15-year-old boys, compared to 43 percent of the girls in this age group, had experimented with alcoholic beverages; the analogous figures for the 16–17-year-olds were 84 percent and 60 percent: Yu. R. Tedder and P. I. Sidorov, "Influence of the family on the children's attitudes toward alcohol use," *Zdravookhraneniye rossiyskoy federatsii*, no. 7 (1976), pp. 10–12.

100 A. Milyukov, "The first commandment," *Znamenosets*, no. 2 (1983), pp. 18–19.

101 A. Gornyy, "Strengthening regulation order," *KZ*, 17 August 1983, p. 2.

102 See, for example, Viktor Suvorov, *Inside the Soviet Army* (New York: Macmillan, 1982), pp. 222–3.

103 P. Reynis, "On the state of affairs in the Soviet army," *Posev*, no. 6 (1982), p. 62; and Kiril Podrabinek, "In the barracks of Turkmenistan," *Posev*, no. 5 (1978), pp. 40–9.

104 See, for example, V. Frolov and A. Khalin, "Legal knowledge," *Znamenosets*, no. 9 (1977), pp. 34–5; D. Volkogonov, "Your friend," *Znamenosets*, no. 13 (1977), pp. 34–5; and A. V. Barabanshchikov, "My mother, my father, my master sergeant and I," *Komsomolskaya pravda*, 21 January 1976, p. 4.

105 Volkogonov, 1976.

106 Volkov, Prilepskiy, and Cherkassov, 1968.

107 *Komsomolskaya pravda*, 4 July 1975, p. 4.

108 *Military Pedagogy*, pp. 102–3.

109 Yu. Deryugin, "Discipline—a political and moral category," *KZ*, 8 June 1982, pp. 2–3.

110 V. V. Shelyagin, A. D. Glotochkin, and K. K. Platonov (eds.), *Voyennaya psikhologiya* (Moscow: Voyenizdat, 1972), trans. by the U.S. air force as *Military Psychology: A Soviet View*, pp. 348–52 (hereafter cited as *Military Psychology*).

111 A. Voropay, "Alcohol—enemy of labor and health," *TIS*, no. 8 (1972), pp. 66–8.

112 V. Levitskiy, "Behind a convenient wording," *KZ*, 1 August 1976, p. 2. See also B. Supey, "An incident occurred," *KZ*, 11 March 1981, p. 2; and L. Golovnev, "Look truth in the eye," *KZ*, 5 July 1981, pp. 2–3.

113 See, for example, Suvorov, 1982, pp. 255–6.

114 V. Bogdanovskiy and V. Zhitarenko, "In retaliation for criticism," *KZ*, 31 October 1980, p. 2.

115 A. Zlydnev, "Preconception," *KZ*, 21 April 1981, p. 2.

116 *KZ*, 17 January 1984, p. 2; and 6 September 1983, p. 2. See also *KZ*, 26 August 1983, p. 2; 24 January 1984, p. 2; A. Buylov, "Political organs: style of work; attitude toward shortcomings," *KZ*, 6 September 1983, p. 2; and B. Pokholenchuk and A. Yurkin, "A souvenir for the inspector," *KZ*, 14 July 1983, p. 2.

117 See, for example, *KZ*, 1 June 1983, p. 2; and 25 August 1983, p. 2.

118 *KZ*, 18 April 1981, p. 2.

119 *KZ*, 8 December 1983, p. 2.

120 *Komsomolskaya pravda*, 30 March 1984, p. 2.

121 *KZ*, 5 February 1984, p. 2.

122 *KZ*, 13 May 1981, p. 2; see also *KZ*, 10 April 1981, p. 2.

6

The Military as an Agent for Political Socialization

In the ongoing debate on the pros and cons of a manpower system based on conscription, one of the most frequently used arguments in favor of the draft in Western democracies is the utility of military service as a socializing experience. In the United States, for example, military service has been depicted as a vehicle for "inculcating spiritual and moral ideals in support of American democracy."[1] The Israeli defense forces have been regarded since their inception as "the workshop of the new Israeli culture,' instilling civic spirit and patriotism.[2] In West Germany conscript service in the Bundeswehr is seen as an opportunity to develop democratic ideals among young 'citizens in uniform."[3] The assumption implicit in this line of reasoning is that the experience of service has a measurable impact on social and political attitudes.

Soviet leaders, it seems, share the belief of many of their Western counterparts that military service is beneficial to draftees. They depict the military as a training-ground for discipline and patriotism, molding young men with little "life experience" into responsible, upright citizens.[4] In the USSR, however, the army is only one component in a larger, well-coordinated socialization program. This program is designed to produce law-abiding and hard-working citizens with political beliefs supportive of the Soviet system.

The Soviet use of their armed forces as a socialization agent differs in many respects from most Western systems. One crucial difference is that government control of the major socialization agents is very limited in Western democracies. Citizens in open societies are exposed to a wide variety of conflicting values and contradictory messages. By contrast, in the USSR the state controls most socialization agencies, and only one message—that approved by the political leadership—is communicated. The political values transmitted through the mass media, the workplace, the school system, and through organized youth groups are virtually identical. This is not to say that Soviet educators do not recognize the significance of informal family and peer groups in transmitting contradictory messages. Soviet methods, however, are explicitly intended to minimize this conflict. The highly regimented environment of a military unit provides them with a unique opportunity to do so.

A second difference is the Soviet emphasis on adult socialization. Until recently Western socialization research has stressed the importance of the early years in the formation of attitudes and values. Soviet socialization specialists, by contrast, emphasize continuing socialization during the adult years as a means of modifying negative attitudes and reinforcing approved ones. In part, this focus stems from the Soviet system's origin in political revolution. In the early years of Soviet rule, opposition to the nascent Soviet regime was widespread. In dealing with popular resistance to their policies, Soviet leaders relied heavily on coercion to neutralize opposition. The second tactic was socialization. This involved a series of programs targeted at the adult population. It also involved programs targeted at the younger generation, to encourage them to reject the anti-Soviet political values and beliefs of their parents. In effect, the early Soviet socialization program was designed to counteract the family's role as a primary agent of socialization.

As the Soviet regime matured, its attitude toward the family changed. Individuals who had been born after the revolution grew up and began raising their own families. In cases where the parents supported the Soviet regime and its policies, parental efforts to transmit these values were naturally encouraged by the Soviet authorities. The initial hostility of the Bolshevik regime toward the family was gradually supplanted by a program designed to harness the family's socialization potential and to direct it into channels consistent with Soviet-approved values. However, the emphasis on adult socialization and on resocialization to eradicate anti-Soviet attitudes instilled by the family remains a strong theme.[5] This helps to explain the significance the Soviets attach to the role of military experience in the socialization of young adult males.

A related issue is the USSR's explicit use of the political socialization process to promote and support socioeconomic change. Most Western research on political socialization has approached the process from the standpoint of system maintenance and stability of political beliefs.[6] The Soviet system, by contrast, is closely identified with rapid economic modernization; and the USSR's socialization process is designed to promote political values and behaviors consistent with an industrializing and urbanizing society. The desired Soviet citizen is one who (among other things) adapts smoothly to a changing socioeconomic environment. The military experience is of particular value in this adaptation process because it involves a radical change in physical and social environment, a change that, the Soviets feel, is conducive to a modification of values and behavior. The special environment offered by military service, then, is particularly relevant for the party's social-engineering efforts.[7]

This chapter is an analysis of how the Soviets have taken advantage of that environment. It examines the extent to which the USSR derives an important nonmilitary benefit from the investment in a large conscript army. The characteristics of the primary target group, the young draftees, are surveyed as well as the content and methods of the military's socialization program itself. Finally, the effectiveness of the military as an agent of political socialization is evaluated.

The Primary Target Group: Soviet Conscripts

Soviet conscripts are the primary target group of the military's socialization program. The Soviet conscript is male, young (in his late teens or early twenties) and (as detailed in Chapter 3) relatively well educated compared to the general population. The draft pool is predominantly urban. In 1959 51 percent of the 15–24-year-old males lived in urban areas. The analogous figure for 1970 was 65 percent, and the urban share of the draft pool has almost certainly risen further since then.[8] Like the Soviet population itself, the draft-age cohort (as detailed in Chapter 7) is ethnically heterogeneous.

It is this group that the army's socializers must mold into the New Socialist Man. The New Socialist Man—the ideal toward which the Soviet socialization process strives—is strongly patriotic, hard-working, and morally upright. He takes an active role in civic activities, is well informed, supports the Communist system, and hates his enemies, scorning both bourgeois ideology and national chauvinism.[9] The recipe for the ideal Soviet soldier would also add a readiness to defend the USSR and a willingness to fulfill the military service obligation. In addition, the ideal soldier respects his commander, likes his comrades, loves his unit, and keeps military secrets.[10]

How does the average Soviet soldier compare to this ideal? The 18-year-old draftee who arrives at his unit is the product of an integrated socialization program that begins from birth. Because the key socialization agent in early childhood is the family, Soviet educators have devoted a great deal of attention to the problem of teaching parents what values to transmit and how to transmit them. In fact, rearing the child "in the spirit of the moral code of a builder of communism" is a legal obligation. Failure to fulfill this obligation is legal grounds for removing the child from parental custody.[11] Soviet child care handbooks describe in detail the techniques for instilling obedience to authority, self-discipline, and morality (collectivism and Soviet patriotism).[12] The family, as described in Soviet child-care literature, is the child's first collective—a place to develop a sense of responsibility and respect for others that will, it is hoped, be transferred to the classroom and later to the workplace and community.[13]

One indication that not all Soviet parents are able or willing to fill the socialization role assigned to them in law and pedagogical theory is the existence of organized "parenting" courses provided by the kindergarten or school.[14] Typical course material provides basic information on the physical and intellectual development of children at various ages as well as on the timing and techniques of socialization. Children in the preschool years, for example, should be introduced to the concept of collectivism and taught to love the motherland and V. I. Lenin. In the middle preschool ages they should be assigned simple household chores as a way of instilling responsibility and respect for work. Parents of children of aged 5–6 are instructed on the proper techniques to prepare their children to begin school.[15]

The extent to which such programs achieve the goal of coordinating family socialization with the more systematic teaching of values within the school system cannot be determined with precision. Families are clearly more effective in instilling some values than others. One study of 6-year-olds revealed, for example, that virtually all were looking forward to starting school. Most children also appear to have internalized the need to submit to authority. Western journalists and scholars frequently comment on the docility of Soviet children in this age group.[16] Soviet educators are far less satisfied, however, with the family's success in instilling love of work. Many preschool-age children are not assigned household chores and show few signs of developing a proper work ethic.[17]

Those preschool children who attend day care or kindergarten (about one-half of the 3–6-year-olds) are exposed to a much more systematic form of socialization. The preschool curriculum applies the same teaching pattern recommended to families. By law, the goals of preschool upbringing are to instill love of work, respect for elders, and love of the socialist motherland and the child's native region.[18] Children of ages 3–4, for example, should be assigned regular classroom chores as a way of promoting good work attitudes.[19] While not all Soviet preschool institutions follow the rigid curriculum prescribed in Soviet handbooks, it is clear that Soviet authorities have a far greater degree of control over the socialization process in a school environment than in the home.

The main formal agent of socialization programs in the USSR, as in other national settings, is the school system. The Soviet school is responsible for both intellectual and moral development. In addition to basic knowledge, the school curriculum is designed to instill a Marxist–Leninist world view, socialist internationalism, Communist morality, Soviet patriotism, and a readiness to defend the socialist motherland.[20] Of particular importance for military socializers are the school's efforts at "military–patriotic" socialization—inculcating a high level of respect for military institutions and an acceptance of military service.[21] These themes are stressed in both formal lessons and organized extracurricular activities. History courses, for example, place heavy emphasis on the suffering associated with the Nazi invasion and occupation in World War II. Reading materials in language and literature classes are designed to present the military as a revered institution. Soviet primary school readers devote a separate section to "Our native army," with stories highlighting the romance and glamour of military life and presenting the Soviet soldier as a heroic protector of Soviet children.[22] These themes are repeated in the children's periodical press. Stories glorifying the military's exploits in World War II depict the war not as an interlude in the remote past, but as a recent and significant event. Readiness to defend the homeland is portrayed as a fundamental aspect of citizenship; and the armed forces are depicted as a much-respected institution.[23]

These themes are prominent in extracurricular activities too. The school system, as well as the Pioneer and Komsomol network (party-supported youth organizations for those aged 8–14 and 15–28 respectively) and DOSAAF, organize a wide variety of activities to promote patriotism. These include a series of military sports games ("Zarnitsa" for Pioneer-age children; "Orlenok" for older teens) intended to instill patriotism while providing military training and physical conditioning.[24] Another technique is to familiarize schoolchildren with the wartime activities that took place in their own region. To this end, many excursions to war memorials, cemeteries, and battlefields are organized. Groups of schoolchildren are often assigned projects involving maintenance and clean-up tasks at such locations, or installing memorial plaques at new sites.[25] Many schools, often in cooperation with Pioneer and Komsomol organizations, have organized "museums of combat glory". Pupils are assigned projects to establish the names of Soviet soldiers and partisans associated with their locality, to correspond with the commanders of military units that liberated their region from the Germans, and to decorate soldiers' graves. All of these activities are designed to perpetuate the memory of the war as well as to instill respect for the armed forces.[26]

The effectiveness of all of these programs in instilling patriotism depends on how that quality is measured. The task of keeping alive the memory of wartime in children whose parents were born long after the war's end grows more complicated each year. Soviet researchers were horrified to find in a 1977 study of youth of draft age (drawn from the RSFSR, Lithuania, Belorussia, and Uzbekistan) that many respondents knew very little about specific events or heroes of the civil war and World War II.[27] Still, Western visitors to the USSR are struck by the depth of undiluted patriotism they find in many Soviet citizens—old and young alike.[28] The repeated emphasis on patriotic themes in the school and mass media apparently has a cumulative impact on Soviet youth.

The heavy emphasis on patriotic duty that forms a staple theme for virtually all socialization agents also helps to explain the degree to which most Soviet youth accept the draft as an inescapable fact of life.[29] Data providing insight into public opinion regarding the draft are limited and consist of occasional Soviet public opinion surveys, nonquantitative Soviet discussions of youth attitudes toward military service (usually in conjunction with discussions of military–patriotic education), and the testimony of former Soviet citizens. The available information, however, suggests strongly that the Soviet leadership has succeeded to a large degree in instilling in its draft-age males a sense of inevitability about military service, which fosters at least a resigned acceptance of the two- to three-year service obligation.

A survey, for example, of draftees in Moscow, Moscow oblast, Moscow State University, and the Baltic military district revealed that most youths recognized the importance of military service.[30] Attitudes toward personal service in the army varied with age; 58 percent of the younger (18–19-year-old) respondents said they regarded military service with "great interest," compared with only one-quarter of those over 21 (Table 6.1). Thirty-four percent of the younger men indicated that while they did not have a personal desire to serve, they recognized "the social significance, necessity, and importance of military service"; while 52 percent of those over 21 chose this response. The survey suggests at least a grudging acceptance of the universal military service obligation. This finding is echoed by reports from former Soviet citizens.

Table 6.1   *Attitudes of Draftees toward Military Service by Age (Percent)*

	Age group		
	18–19 (%)	*20–21* (%)	*over 21* (%)
Response			
I am serving in the army with great interest, having aspired to this while still in my school years	58·0	34·0	25·0
Personally, I do not have a special interest in studying military affairs; however, I under-stand the social significance, necessity, and importance of military service	34·2	56·0	52·3
I am not attracted to the study of military affairs at all	4·3	8·0	12·7
No response	3·5	2·0	10·0

Source: N. N. Yefimov and Yu. I. Deryugin, "Ways to increase the effectiveness of military–patriotic socialization of youth," *SI*, no. 1, 1980, pp. 60–6.

Soviet socialization programs, then, appear to have been at least partly successful in producing a draft-age cohort that accepts military service as an unavoidable, if unpleasant, interval in their lives. The negative side of the picture, from the standpoint of the Soviet military socializers, is that many of the 18-year-old conscripts arriving at their units are immature, undisciplined, lazy, and spoiled.[31] Many conscripts from highly urbanized European areas are reared in small families of one or two children in what Soviet writers frequently refer to as "hothouse" conditions. The parents, particularly the mothers (who dominate childrearing), are overprotective and excessively permissive. The child is showered with too much attention and material goods, but deprived of both discipline and opportunities to develop independence and self-reliance. Such an environment, Soviet educators warn, produces teenagers who are self-centered and lazy, unwilling to fulfill their obligations to society and so used to immediate gratification of all desires that they find it very difficult to adjust to military life.[32] Soviet educators are particularly concerned about the effects of such an environment on the development of young boys. Children, they warn, need a strong male hand.[33] But Soviet fathers play only a secondary role in child care, and the classroom environment is dominated by female teachers and pupils.[34] Many Soviet parents apparently see the army as a needed maturing experience that will "make a man" out of their recalcitrant sons.[35] Soviet military socializers concur, depicting military service as a healthy counterbalance to the feminizing effects of an overprotective home life on young Soviet boys: "the soldier's life is a strong antidote against the infantilism and 'feminization' of men."[36]

Another social trend that has generated increasing concern among both civilian and military leaders is the rise of consumerism among Soviet teenagers. Soviet authorities are particularly concerned over what they portray as an increasing preoccupation with Western-style clothing and music.[37] Some appear convinced that listening to Western music is itself dangerous, portraying "Americanized jazz" as a "narcotic" which has the function of "diverting the masses from the pressing problems of life and destroying faith in noble ideals," and Western rock music as a weapon in the "offensive" aimed at "emasculating national identity."[38] Soviet educators blame the younger generation's interest in Western life styles partly on alien ideas imported from the West, and partly on higher living standards that have produced more demanding consumers in the Soviet Union.[39]

The interest in Western consumer items is linked to what is described as an upsurge of pacifism and "political naivety" among Soviet youth.[40] The younger generation, Soviet authorities complain, did not live through the trying years of World War II; they take peace for granted and underrate the dangers of war:[41]

> Nearly forty years have passed since the end of World War II. During this time, two generations of Soviets have grown up not knowing of their own experience what war is like and not experiencing the difficulties of wartime. Peace for them is the usual status of society. Some think that its continuation and strengthening demand nothing of them personally.

Soviet military commentators link these trends with "individual instances of an insufficiently responsible attitude by citizens toward the fulfillment of their constitutional duty to defend the socialist fatherland."[42] To be sure, Soviet authorities claim that such attitudes are found only in a minority of Soviet teenagers, and the survey data on attitudes toward the draft cited above suggest that this claim may be valid. The high-level concern over youth pacifism, however, is suggestive of a trend that many Soviet officials find extremely disturbing: as World War II recedes further into the past, efforts to invoke the patriotism associated with it become more and more difficult, and this can have a negative effect on youth acceptance of the military service obligation.

Many of the negative characteristics noted above are more common among draftees from urbanized, European areas. Conscripts from rural areas pose a different set of problems. Rural residents in general tend to be less completely socialized than their urban counterparts. Soviet data suggest that individuals from rural areas have less access to the major vehicles of socialization such as the mass media.[43] Conscripts from non-Slavic areas may have language difficulties that interfere with military training and their social integration in unit life. Such soldiers pose a special challenge to the military's socialization program because they bring with them values and ethnic loyalties that conflict with approved Soviet values. This is especially true for minority draftees from rural areas. On the other hand, soldiers from rural areas appear to have an easier time adjusting to the physical rigors and low living standards in the army, and the greater social controls characteristic of many rural communities may facilitate adjustment to the strict discipline of military life.

Soviet authorities are also concerned about soldiers who display religious beliefs. The "overwhelming majority" of contemporary draftees, according to the Soviet military press, are convinced atheists. The proportion of "religious believers" is highest among draftees from Central Asia, the Baltic, and the western Ukraine. Many religious believers join construction units, and most are said to fulfill their military service obligation conscientiously. Some, however, use religious belief to try to avoid service.[44] Baptists who are drafted sometimes refuse to take the military oath.[45] Other draftees from Christian evangelical sects refuse to carry weapons.[46] Celebration of religious holidays, often accompanied by heavy drinking, is said to disrupt the conscripts' training program.[47] Military service is seen as an excellent opportunity to convert "believers" into atheists, because the draftee has been removed from family and community and is insulated from the supportive network of other believers.[48]

The inductees, then, are a heterogeneous group of young males whose childhood and adolescent years have exposed them to political values approved by the party leadership. Soviet educators see the draftee's military experience as an important opportunity to further the individual's approximation of the ideal Soviet citizen, occurring as it does at an important stage in the individual's development, the transition from youth to adulthood.[49] For those conscripts who are already well socialized, the concentrated political training received during military service represents a reinforcement of values instilled at an earlier period of life. For others, whose rural and/or ethnic backgrounds have effectively isolated them from the mainstream of Soviet (that is, Russian and urban) life, the political training may represent an unlearning of earlier values (that is, religious beliefs instilled by parents, ethnic loyalties) in a setting designed to maximize receptivity to the message.

The Socialization Program

Political socialization in the Soviet armed forces is carried out by a wide variety of military officials: the commander, party and Komsomol leaders, and unit activists.[50] The primary agent of political socialization in the Soviet military, however, is the political officer (zampolit), the unit-level representative of the Main Political Administration (MPA). As noted in Chapter 5, one of the zampolit's primary duties is to conduct comprehensive political training programs for all categories of military servicemen. This responsibility involves, first of all, organizing the formal political courses.[51] The zampolit must also provide guidance for all forms of unit propaganda and agitation activities, which form an adjunct to the formal programs. In addition, the zampolit runs the unit's cultural and recreational programs, and serves as military point of contact for the local nonmilitary party organizations, arranging visits and joint activities between the troops and local factories, farms, and schools. The zampolit also bears primary responsibility for maintaining cohesiveness and strong morale and discipline within the unit, manipulating peer group pressure to control "undersocialized" soldiers. Finally, the zampolit organizes political training, social, and recreational activities for the wives and families of officers and enlisted military professionals.[52] The zampolit's duties, then, involve him in virtually every aspect of political socialization that would (in the USSR's civilian sector) be handled by several different ministerial hierarchies. This concentration of responsibility for all phases of political socialization under one organizational umbrella facilitates consistency in message.

The main goal of the military's socialization program is to generate support for the Communist Party, its leadership, goals, and policies.[53] The importance assigned to the program can be roughly gauged by the amount of time devoted to it. Soviet surveys indicate that 90–100 minutes of a serviceman's working-day is devoted to political work. On days off these activities consume two-and-a-half to four hours.[54] The core of this program is a series of formal political study courses. There are separate programs for different categories of service personnel.[55] The formal political classes for officers, comprising fifty hours of service time per year, are called "Marxist–Leninist training" programs. The course covers Marxist theory, party military policy, military theory, armed forces development, and practical personnel management issues.[56] Warrants get a modified version of the officers' course (the warrant course is 100 hours long) which emphasizes Marxist theory, Soviet domestic and foreign policy, and political and military socialization issues.[57] Servicemen who are CPSU or Komsomol members can elect to take more demanding courses in the party educational network in place of the required formal classroom political training.[58]

Most draftees, however, do not elect to take the more demanding party course, so for the vast majority the core of the political socialization program is the formalized political study classes. The classes are part of a very centralized program, organized by the zampolit on the basis of detailed MPA guidelines. Classes are conducted as part of the regular training program.[59] Classes are usually held twice weekly for two hours each, and are obligatory for all draftees.[60] The training plan is developed by the MPA, which also provides textbooks, visual aids, and lesson plans.[61] To assist the group leaders detailed lesson-guides are regularly published in the MPA's journal, *Kommunist vooruzhennykh sil.* A typical lesson plan might include six hours of instruction with two hours each devoted to classroom lecture, independent study, and organized discussion. Lesson plans are quite specific and include a detailed description of the points to be covered in each lecture, a list of reading assignments for the students, and questions to be included during the discussion period. Students are reportedly tested and graded on their command of the assigned material.

The content of the political classes—consistent with the larger goal of the military's socialization program—is a mixture of political and military material designed to instill "a scientific world view and high moral–political and combat qualities."[62] The recommended program varies from year to year, often using a major event such as the Twenty-sixth Party Congress as a unifying device.[63] There are, however, several common themes. There is usually a series of five two-hour lessons designed for new draftees during their period of "basic" training before the beginning of each training-year. These lessons are designed to initiate draftees to their new responsibilities as servicemen.[64] The five-lesson sequence represents a review of some of the material provided in the NVP course given in high school. It generally begins with a lesson on "why we serve," underlining the universality of the military service obligation, followed by a lesson on the military oath. The third lesson usually covers military regulations and the obligations they impose on draftees; this is followed by a lecture on conditions of service (that is, length of service, rights and obligations of soldiers). The final lesson in the sequence is on combat traditions of the soldier's unit and military district; it includes a brief history of the district (invoking heroic deeds of district soldiers during World War II) and the unit. Impressed on young draftees is the obligation they bear to uphold the honor of the military district and the unit.

In the beginning of the regular training-year there are generally lessons on the military's educational and socializing role and the need for combat readiness and teamwork (often including a thinly veiled reference on the dangers of abusing the hazing system). There is also a section on the achievements of Soviet society and the CPSU intended to dramatize the beneficial effects of party policy on the life style of the Soviet citizen. An additional segment of the training program is devoted to international affairs; this series of lessons highlights the differences between socialism and capitalism and provides the conscript with the "correct" framework for evaluating party military and foreign policy. The content of the lessons on world affairs reflects the broader framework of Soviet foreign policy. In the 1970s the anti-NATO and anti-U.S. rhetoric was deliberately played down in the political lessons, as it was in the Soviet media in general. By the early 1980s this trend had reversed and renewed attention was being devoted to the "adventurist" foreign policies of the Western democracies.

A large portion of classroom time in the conscript political training program is earmarked for Soviet military history, which is usually covered in a four- to six-lesson sequence of about thirty classroom hours, supplemented by ten hours of self-study. This training segment has generally begun with a brief review of the armed forces development during the revolution and civil war, followed by a lesson on the interwar armed forces, a more detailed treatment of the Soviet military during World War II, and a lesson on postwar military developments. An innovation in 1983 was the insertion of a twelve-hour segment on prerevolutionary military history, beginning with the "liberation struggle of the Russian people" against the Tartars in the thirteenth and fourteenth centuries. The inclusion of prerevolutionary material is explicitly designed to depict the contemporary Soviet soldier as the heir of military traditions that span many centuries.[65] Such material reflects the increasing willingness of Soviet authorities to acknowledge their prerevolutionary antecedents.

The obligatory political classes provide the core of the formal political training program for draftees. Much of the other political work aimed at the conscripts is intended to reinforce material presented in these classes. Another important component of the program is the series of political information sessions, held twice a week for thirty minutes. All conscripts are required to attend. The political information sessions are intended to clarify decisions of the CPSU and Soviet government, current events, and military tasks of the unit. Again it is the unit zampolit who plans and organizes these sessions, making sure they conform to the guidelines furnished by the MPA and MoD and are consistent with the messages imparted by the formal political training classes.[66]

The conscripts are also exposed to a wide variety of agitation and propaganda activities designed to fill up the soldier's free time with politically approved messages:[67] Lenin readings, discussions, general assemblies, lectures, and question-and-answer sessions.[68] These activities are coordinated by the political officer, who is also responsible for ensuring that every draftee reads the newspaper regularly and, more important, interprets the news correctly. All units of regiment level have their own wall newspaper that publicizes the successes of outstanding soldiers and subjects the shortcomings of others to public criticism.[69] The soldier is also exposed to a broad range of "visual agitation" coordinated by the zampolit: displays, wall posters, and banners.[70]

Soviet military educators also stress the importance of well-organized cultural and recreational activities in the serviceman's political education.[71] The consistency of the political message implicit in these activities is ensured by overall coordination through the MPA hierarchy.[72] At regiment level cultural and recreational activities for draftees are coordinated by the club chief, who is directly subordinate to the zampolit.[73] The club chief, as chairman of the club council, is directly involved in long-term and current planning of cultural measures; he also supervises the club library. The more important activities are integrated into the unit plan for party political work and as such are designed to supplement and enrich the formalized political training. The center of cultural work below regiment level is the Lenin Room, supervised by the battalion or company zampolit.[74] The company Lenin Room provides an area for the soldiers to relax, read the newspaper, write letters, and play chess.[75] During troop maneuvers the Lenin Room takes to the field as a "mobile Lenin Room," equipped with political posters and pamphlets.

The recreational activities provided to the draftees through the network of clubs and Lenin Rooms include films, radio, television, lectures, reports, discussions, thematic evenings, and excursions to local schools, enterprises, exhibits, and war memorials. During all of these activities the conscripts are closely supervised and their contacts with elements outside the unit are controlled as carefully as possible. Film-showings, for example, are often preceded and followed by organized discussions of the film's theme.[76] This procedure is explicitly designed to ensure that the conscript audience draws insights and conclusions that are consistent with approved political values. Many of the films shown in military units deliberately emphasize military glory. Some are produced directly by the MoD Film Studio; in addition, the MPA exerts pressure on nonmilitary film-makers to incorporate approved military themes into their products.[77] Other films are intended to instill Soviet patriotism. Films such as *Cities of our Motherland* are explicitly designed to highlight Soviet growth and achievements—an important source of the political leadership's legitimacy.[78]

Radio is seen as another important medium for political socialization in the military.[79] The unit club provides broadcasts on both national and local stations, with special efforts to facilitate the serviceman's access to special national broadcasts aimed at military personnel. Local unit radio stations publicize the activities of the unit; programs are keyed to current training activities. For example, immediately before and during a tactical exercise the unit's radio stations will present programs with such themes as "Use the combat experience of the great motherland war on maneuvers." Group radio-listening and television-viewing are organized to maximize the educational effect of these activities. The periodical press also plays an important role in cultural work. Again emphasis is on controlling the soldier's access to the press through a careful screening of available items. The club and Lenin Room are also tasked with ensuring the proper use of art and literature for education work: arranging special concerts and dance exhibits for the draftees, and equipping the club library and Lenin Room with appropriate books.[80]

The program described above is a highly centralized and formalized program. How does the Soviet socialization program compare to those in other national settings? Perhaps the most striking point of contrast with nonsocialist armed forces is the consistency of the Soviet program. Mandatory political training classes were introduced in the Soviet Union in 1920 and have continued to the present.[81] By contrast, in the U.S. military education programs have been devised in response to war or crisis, only to be dismantled or refocussed toward recreation and welfare goals when the crisis passed.[82] During World War I the War Department established a short-lived Morale Branch that set up a program of recreational activities, movies and lectures, but these efforts were terminated soon after the war's end. The Army's Morale Branch was reestablished in 1940 to administer the "Why we fight" program. After the war, however, other training was gradually substituted. During the Korean War the program content became much more indoctrinational in tone, but since 1964 the army has taken a series of steps to make the command information program progressively less so in content, and more decentralized in administration. These changes contrast sharply with the continuity of Soviet programs. While content and format of the political training classes in the USSR have shifted over time, the message has always been explicitly political in content, and its tone one of indoctrination.

Another point of contrast is the level of resources devoted to the program. Nonsocialist armies that have civic education programs for their soldiers devote far fewer hours of training-time to them than do the Soviets. In West Germany, for example, the fifteen-month tour of duty involves only twelve hours of civic education during basic training and forty-eight hours during postbasic training. This includes all components of the program—political-type education classes (twenty hours), troop information (twenty-five hours), and films on the Bundeswehr (fifteen hours). Moreover, this (by Soviet standards)

modest expenditure of training time is not actually allocated in practice.[83] Even
the Israeli Defense Forces, which have been assigned an important political
socialization role, allocate only a week for formalized civic-training programs
for draftees. This training takes place at specially designed schools at which
students perform no other military functions. This "education series" program
is supposed to be supplemented by lectures and weekly "conversation hours"
on current affairs, but most commanders reportedly fail to schedule the conversation hour or use it for nonpolitical material such as discussion of unit
problems.[84]

Another point of contrast is the extent to which the message of the USSR's
military socialization program is integrated and coordinated with the civilian
media and educational systems. Such coordination is not feasible in Western
democracies where the media are independent of the government or, in
countries like the United States, where the educational system is highly
decentralized. In the Soviet Union, however, the MPA is part of a much larger
network of socialization institutions that all receive basic guidelines on edi-
torial policy and course coverage from the CC Secretariat. Both the content
and the tone of the message aimed at the young draftee are similar to those he
received previously in school and from the civilian mass media.

Another major difference is the extent to which the Soviet program is
centralized and standardized within the military. The U.S. program is a highly
decentralized one. "Command information" is no longer a mandatory subject.
The DoD's Armed Forces Information Service provides instruction aids, but
its service analogues are free to determine their own needs and the individual
company commander has almost total autonomy in deciding how the program
is applied in his unit.[85] Most of the instructional material currently provided to
U.S. commanders involves nonpolitical issues, such as health and personal
finance.[86] Both the Israeli and West German militaries offer more politicized
programs.[87] The lesson on "battle traditions" in the Israeli program has its
counterpart in the Soviet curriculum's stress on combat traditions and Red
Army military history. West German programs, like those of the Soviets,
include lessons on the rights and duties of the soldier; they also provide
material on the nature of the West German political system and the role in it of
the Bundeswehr—similar to Soviet lessons on the nature of socialism and the
functions of the armed forces.

The Soviet political socialization program, then, differs from its counterparts
in nonsocialist militaries in several significant ways. The Soviet military has
consistently devoted far more training time and manpower resources to political
education. Its programs are more formalized, intensive, and centralized, and
the message is both explicitly political in content and propagandistic in tone.

Program Effectiveness

Evaluating the effectiveness of the Soviet program is a difficult task, primarily
because there is no direct evidence. Studies of the military as a socializer in

other national settings are inconclusive.[88] For example, a 1969 survey of attitudes of army veterans toward military service found that the majority of World War II, Korean, and Vietnam-era veterans felt that military service had a "good effect" on character, and most claimed that the service experience helped develop a sense of responsibility and self-confidence.[89] An earlier (1952) study of the impact of basic training revealed an increase in self-esteem and social solidarity.[90] A 1970 longitudinal study of attitude change and morale during basic combat training found that basic training had a favorable effect on the morale of trainees.[91] Other studies of social and political attitudes among both career and noncareer personnel, however, suggest that military service *per se* results in only marginal changes in attitudes.[92] To be sure, ex-servicemen frequently perceive their military service as a generally maturing experience, promoting self-discipline and responsibility. As a group, former soldiers may have a somewhat more traditional view in civic virtues and military institutions, and they are more likely to participate in community projects.[93] However, on the whole they are more similar in attitudes and values than different from their nonveteran counterparts on many of the values measured.[94] Even these modest findings cannot be applied with assurance to the Soviet case because the socialization program is so different from those of its nonsocialist counterparts. Many of the attitudes and behaviors measured in those studies have little direct relevance to the USSR. There are virtually no studies, for example, that attempt to measure attitudes toward work—an important goal of the USSR's military socializers.

Another potential source of insight into the effectiveness of socialization in the Soviet military is material on the effectiveness of other socialization agents in the USSR. Information on deviance within civilian society and on the civilian socialization program is far more abundant than material on the army's socialization activities. Western observers who have examined this material correctly note that the typical Soviet citizen falls far short of the ideal—the New Soviet Man.[95] It is, of course, scarcely surprising that the Soviet program has failed to produce a nation of paragons. This observation, however, does not address the issue of whether the USSR's socialization efforts have produced any change in social and political values and behaviors.

Another approach to evaluating the effectiveness of Soviet political socialization programs is to examine the extent to which those programs modify attitudes and behavior. The problem here is that the published results of Soviet studies of effectiveness are quite frequently irrelevant. Most are focussed on the impact of formal political courses or lectures and evaluate the educator's speaking skills, knowledge, and experience, or the student's interest in Marxist–Leninist philosophy and knowledge of course content.[96] Other studies that do focus on some aspect of public opinion, such as attitudes toward the law, do not relate those attitudes to any particular aspect of the socialization programs.[97] Still other studies that claim a strong correlation between attendance at political study courses and approved attitudes and behavior (diligence, participation in factory and civic affairs, fulfillment of social obligations) fail to show causality in a convincing way.[98]

There is, of course, abundant evidence that many political lectures are boring, that some students attend only because of external pressures, and that most are more interested in current affairs and sports than in philosophy. Despite the fact that these data are not relevant to issues of regime support, one Western critic of Soviet socialization programs concluded from such studies that Soviet socialization efforts are largely ineffective in promoting commitment to Soviet political institutions.[99] In sum, Soviet studies on the effectiveness of "ideological" training provides little useful insight into the utility of the army's socialization program.

There are, however, several indirect types of evidence bearing on the issue of program effectiveness. One approach is to examine the techniques used by the USSR's military socializers against the background of Western socialization research. Soviet socialization specialists single out four aspects of military service that are viewed as crucial to socialization effectiveness: the regimented, stressful nature of the service environment; a repetitive, consistent message; manipulation of peer-group pressure within the military "collective"; and manipulation of the authority of the socializers. Each will be examined in the context of Western socialization research.

One of the most important aspects of military service from the standpoint of socialization is the military environment itself. Soviet educators view all labor as a vehicle for education; however, they see special advantages in military service in instilling patriotism, developing discipline, and promoting maturity.[100] First-term draftees provide an almost totally captive audience. Once they exchange their civilian clothing for a military uniform, the conscripts enter a highly regimented life with little opportunity for independent activity.

Tightly organized training fills most of the conscript's waking hours. The regimentation, routine, and discipline of the two- or three-year service hitch are similar in some ways to the U.S. army's much shorter basic-training course. For the typical Soviet draftee, the daily schedule usually begins with reveille at 6 a.m., followed by thirty minutes of physical training (usually calisthenics and running).[101] There is generally time allotted for area clean-up, followed by morning inspection by the company first sergeant.[102] Then the troops are marched in formation to the mess hall for breakfast. Each squad usually eats at its own table.[103] Morning formation, at which time work and training assignments are announced, follows breakfast. The rest of the morning is taken up with drill, work details, and other training sessions. There is usually a brief period (thirty minutes) allotted for rest after the midday meal, followed by another three to four hours of work details and training. There may be another hour or two of free time after dinner, plus an organized walk. Lights-out (generally at 10 p.m.) is preceded by evening inspection, again by the company first sergeant.[104] Saturday schedules follow the same general pattern, although the afternoon agenda often includes weapon and equipment maintenance, general clean-up and maintenance around the barracks and post, and a communal trip to the bath house. There may be an on-post movie in the evening to which the conscripts are marched in formation.[105] Lights-out on Saturday night is one hour later, as is Sunday morning reveille. Sunday offers somewhat more free time. Conscripts who have performed particularly well during the week may be rewarded with a pass authorizing them to spend several hours off-post.[106] The frequency with which pass privileges are provided varies from unit to unit. In some units most conscripts can expect a pass every month or so. In others passes are granted far less frequently either because of the propensities of the command and political hierarchy or because of potential problems with the civilian populace. The effect of the tightly organized schedule is to minimize free time.

Moreover, in most units little of the "free" time is spent without direct supervision. For example, those soldiers without a Sunday morning pass generally are required to attend lectures at the post theater. Those recreational opportunities that are available to the draftee are controlled by the unit political officer. This effort to harness leisure activities to politically productive ends is a reflection of the general Soviet propensity to inject approved political and social messages into all aspects of recreation.[107] The free time of the Soviet draftee is of particular concern to Soviet educators since young men of draft age are viewed as being particularly susceptible to boredom.[108] Soviet educators estimate that the typical conscript has about 1,180 hours of free time per year, and they are determined to fill every minute with as much political and military training as possible.[109] The soldier, then, provides a twenty-four-hour-a-day subject for the closely integrated network of political training programs.[110]

This regimented environment is both physically and psychologically stressful for the typical Soviet conscript—a point noted by both former Soviet soldiers and Soviet researchers.[111] Studies of draftees' physical development and fitness in the early weeks of service reveal that several key indices of physical fitness decline in the first two to four weeks of service.[112] Not suprisingly, Soviet soldiers are most vulnerable to illness during this period of adjustment. Recent studies of the incidence of acute pneumonia, for example, reveal that conscripts who contract the disease are most likely to do so in the first six months of service, with the highest incidence occurring in the first month.[113]

The early months of service are stressful from a psychological standpoint as well. Conscript life styles are spartan, even by Soviet standards. Conscripts are housed in open-bay barracks, and generally are not allowed to individualize their sleeping area or even to keep personal items with their gear.[114] Privacy is minimal. Mess hall food ranges from drab to downright unpalatable. The training routines are often physically grueling, with a heavy accent on rote and repetition to develop rapid, automatic responses to orders. Poor performance leads to extra duty assignments, which often reduce the hours available for sleep.

Many conscripts who have been spoiled by permissive parents find it hard to adapt to the rigid discipline of military life.[115] Nearly one-half of the draft-age youths surveyed in one Soviet study anticipated that they would have problems adjusting to the harsh discipline of army life.[116] This finding parallels the conclusions of the U.S. studies of attitudes at the beginning of basic training: about one-half of the U.S. trainees surveyed anticipated at least moderate difficulty in adjusting to army discipline.[117] Not surprisingly, Soviet medical researchers have found that morale and sense of well-being drops sharply during the first month of service. Physical and psychological adaptation to military life takes from one to four months.[118]

The psychological and physical stress of the rigidly regimented service environment appears to make the typical conscript more susceptible to socialization. Certainly, many Soviets who have been through the experience credit their service years with contributing to the development of maturity and self-discipline. This point is noted by Soviet researchers as well. One Soviet survey queried servicemen about which aspects of military service had influenced them most. Although one-third cited the formal system of political and recreational programs, an even larger number (40 percent) mentioned the discipline of army life as a prime factor in their personal development.[119]

The insulated military environment also affords an opportunity to reinforce approved messages through repetition. As noted by Soviet émigrés, the typical conscript finds the mandatory political education classes dull and uninspiring. The instructors, usually line officers for whom the teaching assignment is an extra (and often unwelcome) duty, are frequently ill-prepared lecturers. As with most classroom training in the USSR, the emphasis is on rote and memorization.[120] Paradoxically the repetitive nature of the message, which produces numbing boredom among the draftees, is seen by Soviet military socializers as a positive factor. Soviet socialization research places particular stress on reinforcement of the message through well-coordinated socialization channels. Their studies show that the average serviceman is exposed to the mass media for an hour and a half per day. Surveys further reveal high levels of awareness of current events among soldiers—a finding researchers attribute to the multiple exposure to one piece of information across several media channels (television, radio, newspapers).[121]

Western socialization research suggests that this repetition may be one of the more effective aspects of the Soviet program. By presenting a consistent message across all types of information channels, the Soviets exclude contrary views. The conscript is exposed to a coordinated set of themes in formal political training classes and across all of the media. Since leisuretime is organized and free time minimized, opportunities for "cross-pressuring" or dissonance-inducing messages are minimized.[122] During his school years the young Soviet may have been exposed to contradictory attitudes and values from family or friends. For Soviet draftees, however, conflicting messages are minimized simply because military authorities have more opportunities than their civilian counterparts to control communication activity. Moreover, the goal of the military's socialization program—the ideal Soviet soldier—is fully compatible with the New Socialist Man, the ideal toward which the Soviet civilian socialization program is working. In other words, the Soviet conscript is not expected to exchange civilian behavioral and attitudinal patterns for military ones: the ideal Soviet soldier is simply the New Socialist Man in uniform. This consistency between military and civilian socialization goals minimizes discontinuity between military and civilian life.

Émigré reports too suggest that the Soviet strategy of rote and repetition may well be an effective one. Virtually all ex-Soviet soldiers comment on the political passivity of the typical conscript, and the crushing boredom which most political lessons produce.[123] However, in spite of the universal lack of enthusiasm for political lessons, many of the images presented in those lessons appear to be internalized. Interviews with Soviet soldiers held by Afghan guerrillas reveal that many Soviet soldiers believed, as they had been told, that they were being sent to Afghanistan to fight "American and Chinese agents."[124] Like the American consumer targeted by a repetitive advertising campaign, the Soviet soldier may ridicule the medium but he seems to absorb the message.

A third factor assigned a key role in the socialization process is use of peer-group pressure within the military "collective."[125] Systematic manipulation of peer groups is a unique feature of Soviet socialization programs, evident in Soviet treatment of collectives from kindergarten to workplace.[126] Military collectives, however, have special features that greatly facilitate socialization:[127]

> The relative stability, duration and continuity of an individual's service in one collective may be considered one of the specific features of a military collective which has educational significance. A soldier's work, everyday life, and leisure time are all spent among one group of comrades.

The typical Soviet conscript fulfills his service obligation in an environment that is relatively insulated from civilian life. As noted above, there are no automatic leave benefits for draftees. One ten-day leave (for two-year conscripts) may be awarded as a reward for good behavior and performance, but many conscripts serve their entire terms without receiving one.[128] Moreover, there is no automatic weekend liberty. Conscripts must remain within the unit area unless they have been awarded a pass, allowing them to leave post for a few hours at a time on Sunday. This restricted access to the civilian environment means that many conscripts experience a strong sense of isolation.

This isolation is reflected in data on friendship patterns in the military. Surveys of personal contacts between soldiers indicate that most have four or five friends and that most of those friendships (70 percent) are between individuals in the same company; one out of three soldiers has friends within his own squad or tank crew; another one in three has a friend in the same platoon.[129] The military unit, then, plays a key role in the soldier's socialization because it encompasses so many different aspects of his life.[130] Because the environment of the military collective has such a great impact on the conscript, both the commander and the political officer are trained to use the collective as a socializing agent.

The Soviet use of the collective as a socializing agent is based on the conviction that peer-group influences can be controlled and manipulated for desired outcomes. Harnessing the influence of the military collective and directing it in ways that reinforce politically approved values begins with precise information about opinions and friendship groups within the unit.[131] Soviet officers are instructed to analyze individual attitudes and interpersonal behavior within their unit. The recommended strategy is to compile a record of each soldier, noting general information (age, place of birth, education, social class, nationality); motivations (interests, attitudes toward service); character (initiative, work attitudes); social activity (participation in unit activities, interest in national and international affairs); and relationships with other soldiers. This material is supplemented by data on the unit as a whole: distribution of soldiers by age, social origin, year of service, and nationality; the state of unit morale (respect for command personnel, discipline, the role of party and Komsomol activists); and unit solidarity (interpersonal relations, cooperation).[132] The extent to which Soviet officers comply with these recommendations is not known, but survey results suggest that the vast majority of officers attend—at least in a perfunctory way—to interpersonal relations in their unit and their effects on unit solidarity.[133]

Aiding the military professionals in their efforts to monitor and manipulate public opinion in military units are the unit "activists." All military units have Komsomol organizations, and the most enthusiastic of the Komsomol members provide a core of reliable and responsive soldiers to assist the socializers. The choice of activists is a crucial one because maximum control requires that they enjoy not only the confidence of the socializers, but also the respect of their comrades. Some officers are apparently prone to choosing activists rated highly by command personnel but who have little real authority among their fellows.[134] One study of "unofficial" authority patterns in military units revealed the existence of peer-group leaders who were not part of the unit's "official" leadership. In general, however, the officially designated unit activists were rated by both officers and men as enjoying relatively high authority in the units.[135] The most desirable unit, from the standpoint of the socializers, is one in which the official and unofficial leaders coincide. In other words, soldiers who are willing to assist the command personnel in monitoring and controlling opinions and behavior within the unit should be well respected by other soldiers.

How effectively do Soviet military socializers produce cohesive military units that can be effectively manipulated to influence the attitudes and behavior of the conscripts? Certainly, there is abundant anecdotal evidence that the Soviets have not been spared the sort of predictable personnel problems that trouble most other peacetime military organizations: alcohol abuse, difficulties in adjusting to military life, disciplinary infractions, and so on. Poor food, unheated barracks, and the sheer discomfort of military life may undermine unit morale in some units. Excessive hazing of newly arrived conscripts or ethnic or racial hostilities may degrade unit cohesion in others. Such evidence, however, provides very little insight into the extent of these problems. Material drawn from both the Soviet military press and the comments of ex-Soviets who have served in the army suggests that unit cohesion in the Soviet military, as in other military systems, varies enormously from unit to unit and over time within a single unit, depending on the leadership ability and interpersonal skills of the junior officers and warrant officers in command. Unit cohesion, then, is a dynamic characteristic that is fairly amenable to remedial measures. Unit solidarity is highest in high-priority combat units, where chronic disciplinary infractions and ineffective leadership are less tolerated. Solidarity is lowest in low-priority service and support units, particularly construction units, that get a disproportionate share of both incompetent officers and "problem" conscripts—youths with physical, educational, and language deficiencies, or a history of juvenile delinquency.

This sort of anecdotal evidence, of course, does not allow us to measure unit cohesion in the Soviet Union in a way that would permit either comparisons with Western armies or an assessment of how well the typical Soviet small unit measures up to the ideal of controlled and manipulated peer groups presented in the Soviet military press. However, additional insight into the use of peer groups in the military socialization process may be gleaned from Western research. Western studies on the influence of peer groups in the socialization process have isolated three factors which increase group cohesiveness and hence the influence of the group on the individual member.[136] Those factors are:

(1) Attractiveness—the more attractive the group, the greater the socializing impact of the group.
(2) Endurance—the more enduring the group, the greater the influence of modal group opinion.
(3) Homogeneity—the smaller the size of discordant groups, the less the influence -of the subgroup; as the size of the subgroup approaches a majority, conformity to the subgroup increases.

Soviet programs aimed at the educational uses of the primary military collective—the draftee's peer group—have tended to maximize all three factors. First, Soviet authorities attempt to make the unit of which the conscript is a member as important and meaningful to him as possible. The use of heroic traditions, meeting with war veterans, visits to battlefields where the unit played an important role, all tend to idealize the unit.[137] Another mechanism for promoting pride in the unit is to encourage friendly rivalry between units. Such 'socialist competition' schemes are a favorite Soviet technique for boosting performance and *esprit de corps* in the civilian economy. They fulfill a similar function in the military.[138] Finally, Soviet educators see the very rigorous training and physical demands placed on the conscript as promoting unit solidarity—a view that is echoed by U.S. sociologists and, interestingly, former Soviet servicemen now living in the West.[139]

Second, Soviet military leaders attempt to keep subunits stable, without wholesale shifting of personnel. Soldiers assigned to particular units after being drafted or having completed specialist training are also assigned to specific posts. They generally serve out their entire service obligation within that unit. Although they may be promoted to a more responsible post or demoted to a lower one, transfers are deliberately kept to a minimum.[140] Surely some conscripts are transferred between platoons and companies; but the greater the personnel stability in a subunit, the more meaningful the unit will be to the individual soldier and the more susceptible he will be to peer-group pressures.

Finally, Soviet socialization programs in the military involve measures to manipulate peer groups in military units. Soviet military educators recognize the importance of informal friendship groups. They contend that most such groups are not intrinsically harmful to the unit and, indeed, can be skillfully manipulated to promote desired attitudes and behaviors.[141] An example of the use of informal subgroups both to maintain control over unit behavior and attitudes and to promote unit solidarity is the use of the informal seniority system. Soviet studies of authority patterns within units reveal that soldiers in the final six months of duty are perceived (by both the command personnel and other conscripts) as commanding higher authority and respect than newly arrived draftees. Moreover, soldiers tend to interact more with people who were inducted at the same time. A Soviet study of unit friendship patterns revealed that about one-half of a soldier's personal contacts were with individuals in his own tenure group, another one-quarter to a third were with soldiers inducted in the six months immediately before or after his induction. This pattern held for the conscript sergeants as well. Conscripts promoted to sergeant tend to have more friends among their tenure group (regardless of rank) than with other sergeants from different tenure groups.[142] Socialization and authority patterns based on tenure can easily lead to excessive hazing of the less experienced draftees and hence to the discipline problems discussed in Chapter 5. Properly channeled, however, these friendships can be useful in socializing the new inductees; the authority of the "senior" soldiers can be skillfully harnessed to shape the behavior and attitudes of new draftees and to enforce service regulations from within.[143]

Another mechanism for facilitating unit homogeneity is the use of peer-group pressure to neutralize harmful subgroups. Unit activists help Soviet officers to identify deviant subgroups. The recommended Soviet strategy for dealing with deviant attitudes is to isolate the leader of the subgroup, alter the attitudes of his friends, and use them to instill conformist values in him. Unit activists are assigned to work with individuals or small groups that display "incorrect" attitudes. With more serious cases, the political worker can hold a unit meeting to condemn the troublemaker, but would do so only after having prepared unit activists to articulate a "correct" attitude at the meeting, in order to sway popular opinion. These methods are designed to ensure both homogeneity of group opinion and the formation of group values that are consistent with military goals.[144]

Soviet sources shed little direct light on how effective these methods are in practice. Much depends on the ability of the commander and political officer to recruit cooperative and well-respected unit activists. Soviet studies have claimed that some officers, particularly political officers, devote insufficient time to working with unit activists. One survey revealed that the average political officer devoted only thirty-five to forty minutes per day to this task.[145] On the other hand, the typical, upwardly mobile Soviet youth who is active in Komsomol affairs and who is eager to return to his civilian career or studies has a strong incentive to cooperate with unit authorities intent on using him to manipulate unit opinion.

A fourth aspect of the socialization process stressed by Soviet educators is the relationship between the socializer's authority and prestige and the susceptibility of the target group to pressures to conform.[146] This emphasis is supported by Western socialization research that indicates that successful socialization is facilitated when the socializers are perceived as powerful authority figures, who control meaningful rewards and punishments.[147] The Soviet officer does, in fact, control most aspects of the soldier's life. Control of the draftee's leave privileges, for example, is a powerful tool in promoting conformity. Gifts, cash awards, and glowing letters to family and former employers are also used as motivating devices. Although the primary goal of these measures is to maximize training effectiveness, the officer's control of rewards and punishments also tends to make the young soldier more susceptible to the pressures to conform to desired attitude and behavior patterns.

A second approach to evaluating the effectiveness of the military's socialization program is to examine the historical record. Service in the Red Army was used very early in the Soviet regime as a means to produce more "Sovietized" citizens. During the 1920s and early 1930s the Soviets embarked on a massive program to strengthen Bolshevik control over rural areas by reorganizing the peasantry into party-dominated collective farms. Demobilized soldiers played a key role in this program. Peasant resistance to collectivization was intense; but as Merle Fainsod concluded from captured Smolensk Party Archives,[148]

The Red Army functioned as a particularly important school for the preparation of rural Communists and Komsomols. The period of military service isolated the peasant soldiers from the influences of the village and exposed them to Communist indoctrination ... [They] provided the regime with a nucleus of local support without which the task of controlling the countryside would have been rendered infinitely more difficult.

Soviet authorities too credit the "ideological tempering" of the service experience with preparing the demobilized soldier for organizing work on the newly formed collective farms.[149] A 14 October 1927 Central Committee resolution calling for greater use of demobilized troops in rural administrative work described the Red Army as "one of the most important sources of ... fully Sovietized peasant activists."[150] On 12 April 1929 another CC resolution tasked the army's political administration to devise special "kolkoz" preparatory courses for 15,000–20,000 soldiers. Special credits and advantages were offered to collective farms organized with the participation of demobilized soldiers. Special programs were also set up to train ex-soldiers for government and cultural work in the countryside.[151] In 1930 the Revolutionary Military Council issued a special resolution "on the Participation of the Red Army in Kolkoz Development." The resolution required 100,000 demobilized soldiers be trained for work in the countryside.[152] Soldiers willing to help organize collective farms in the far eastern regions (and thus help secure the USSR's far eastern borders) were provided special benefits.[153] Demobilized minority soldiers played a very similar role in the USSR's southern periphery.[154] The role of demobilized soldiers in the collectivization campaigns of the 1920s and 1930s demonstrates the strong impact of military service on attitudes and behavior.[155] It is particularly relevant to the increasing laborforce distribution problems the Soviets face in the 1980s. For young men from the labor-surplus areas of Central Asia, military service in the labor-deficit far east could be the first step in a permanent change of residence.

The limited Soviet press reports of surveys examining the impact of service on military personnel reinforce the insights gained from the historical record. Such surveys indicate at least a minimal level of socialization effectiveness. Soviet military sociologists have found significant changes in the behavior and attitudes of draft personnel over their military tour of duty. For example, several studies report that second-year soldiers commit far fewer disciplinary infractions than first-year soldiers.[156] One survey revealed that 89 percent of soldiers being discharged into the reserves spoke favorably of the role of their service experience in their personal development. After five years, virtually all (98 percent) gave high marks to army service in their socialization. Another study showed that 90 percent of Soviet servicemen finishing their two-year conscript tour claim that the service experience helped them develop discipline and persistence. More than one-half reported that military service had made them more physically fit. Four out of five said that army life helped them get along better with other people.[157] These findings are in close accord with analogous data on American servicemen.[158]

Other Soviet studies have found that civic awareness increased with military experience. The proportion of active participants in volunteer work increased from 32 percent before induction to 46 percent after the first year of service, and to 70 percent at the end of the service obligation. Nearly 40 percent reported that military service had increased their interest in civic affairs. Soviet researchers have also discovered that college students who have completed military service before beginning their college studies have higher levels of participation and patriotic values than students without prior military service.[159]

Sociologists have also found that military service increased the prestige of industrial and agricultural (blue-collar) work among the conscripts.[160] Attitudes toward these occupations are an area of growing concern to Soviet authorities because far more young people aspire to white-collar status than are needed for the economy. One Soviet study found that while 37 percent of draft-age youths expressed a preference for occupations of "qualified worker" or "agricultural machinist," more than 50 percent of those in the service expressed such preferences.[161] Similar findings were reported in a study of the Polish army.[162] These data are not, of course, conclusive, but they reinforce the impression gleaned from a survey of the Red Army's historical record as a socializing agent: military service tends to produce somewhat greater conformity with Soviet standards of citizenship.

Conclusions

During the 1970s when many Western military sociologists were noting the decline of the mass army in the West, the Soviet Union remained committed to conscription as the basis of its military personnel procurement system. Part of the explanation for this long-term reliance on conscription is the socialization which military service provides. The importance assigned to the army's social role explains the USSR's significant investment of conscript training time for political education.

This is not to say that the political socialization process has no relevance for combat performance. Certainly one component of the socialization process in the military—the use of peer-group pressure—has direct implications for combat effectiveness. Studies of personnel effectiveness by Western military sociologists have found that interpersonal relationships within the small unit are a powerful predictor of combat performance. Effective combat performance depends on a high degree of social integration in the small combat unit.[163] To the degree that Soviet military socializers are successful in promoting small-unit solidarity they will also be maximizing not just the military's socialization role, but combat effectiveness as well.

The military's political socialization role also has relevance for the Soviet leadership's perception of the "military burden." The USSR's political elite views the costs and benefits of maintaining a large conscript army from a broader standpoint than that of the armed forces military capabilities alone. Although the military factor may be uppermost in the minds of Soviet leaders, the utility ascribed to the military as a socialization agent may make the costs associated with a massive army somewhat more palatable. It may also add to their reluctance to cut back military manpower in response to civilian labor shortages in the late 1980s and 1990s.

Moreover, available evidence relating to program effectiveness suggests that the high regard that the Soviets have of their military socialization program is fairly realistic. Two years in a strict military environment may not reshape the typical Soviet youth into an ideal Soviet citizen, but the discharged draftees are more mature, disciplined, and socially responsible. In short, they are generally "better" Soviet citizens after military service than before.

Notes: Chapter 6

Portions of this chapter were adapted from Ellen Jones and Fred W. Grupp, "Political Socialization in the Soviet Military," *Armed Forces and Society*, Vol. 8, No. 3, Spring 1982, pp. 355–87.

1 *Report of the President's Advisory Commission on Universal Training*, p. 92, quoted in James Alden Barber, Jr., "The social effects of military service," in Stephen E. Ambrose and James A. Barber, Jr. (eds.), *The Military and American Society: Essays and Readings* (New York: The Free Press, 1973), pp. 151–65.
2 Victor Azarya, "The Israeli armed forces," in Morris Janowitz and Stephen D. Wesbrook (eds.), *The Political Education of Soldiers* (Beverly Hills, Calif.: Sage, 1983), pp. 99–127.
3 Ralf Zoll, "The German armed forces," in ibid., pp. 209–48.
4 The armed forces' socialization role was noted by then party General Secretary Konstantin Chernenko at the May 1984 All-Army Conference of Secretaries of Komsomol Organi-

zations: "The Soviet army is also a school of patriotic growth," *KZ*, 29 May 1984, p. 1. See also Chernenko's remarks at the June 1983 plenum, "Our army and navy is correctly called a school for courage, love of work, and high morals": K. U. Chernenko, "Pressing questions of ideological and mass political work of the party," *Partiynaya zhizn*, no. 13 (July 1983), pp. 15–34; the reference to the military's socialization role is on p. 30. The 1979 party resolution on ideology and socialization claimed that military service was a school for "work and military training, moral purity and courage, patriotism and comradeship": *O dal'neyshem uluchshenii ideologicheskoy politiko-vospitatel'noy raboty*, 26 April 1979 (Moscow: Politizdat, 1979), p. 14. See also A. Kuzovnikov and N. Ustyakin, "An important social task," *KZ*, 15 January 1981, pp. 2–3; V. Manilov, "Military service and the formation of personality," *KVS*, no. 20 (1980), pp. 23–31; A. A. Yepishev (ed.), *Partiya i armiya* (Moscow: Politizdat, 1977), pp. 292–3; and B. P. Utkin, "The socialization role of the Soviet armed forces in conditions of developed socialism," *Voprosy filosofii*, no. 1 (1984), pp. 26–38.

5   Gayle Durham Hollander, *Soviet Political Indoctrination: Developments in Mass Media and Propaganda since Stalin* (New York: Praeger, 1972), pp. 7–21; Martin K. Whyte, "Child socialization in the Soviet Union and China," *Studies in Comparative Communism*, vol. X, no. 3 (Autumn 1977), pp. 235–59; and Robert W. Clawson, "Political socialization of children in the USSR," *Political Science Quarterly*, vol. 88, no. 4 (December 1973), pp. 684–712.

6   James A. Nathan and Richard C. Remy, "Comparative political socialization: a theoretical perspective," in Stanley A. Renshon (ed.), *Handbook of Political Socialization* (New York: The Free Press, 1977), pp. 85–111.

7   D. Volkogonov, "The spiritual makeup of a Soviet fighting man," *Politicheskoye samoobrazovaniye*, no. 2 (1976), pp. 93–100; and O. Kulishev, "A school of patriotism, collectivism, and citizenship," *Zarya vostoka*, 7 August 1980, pp. 2–3.

8   Calculated from *Itogi vsesoyuznoy perepisi naseleniya 1970 goda* (Moscow: Statistika, 1972), Vol. II, pp. 12–15.

9   *Programma kommunisticheskoy partii sovetskogo soyuza* (Moscow: Politizdat, 1976), pp. 116–32; and V. N. Solov'yev, "Moral upbringing of predraft youth," in N. A. Kostikov (ed.), *Kompleksnyy podkhod k vospitaniyu doprizyvnoy molodezhi* (Moscow: DOSAAF, 1980), pp. 84–113.

10 L. A. Bublik *et al.*, *Partiyno-politicheskaya rabota v sovetskoy armii i voyenno-morskom flote* (Moscow: Voyenizdat, 1982), pp. 88–96; A. Yepishev, "The question of moral–political and psychological training of troops," *Voyennaya mysl'*, no. 12 (1968); and N. I. Smorigo (ed.), *Ideologicheskaya rabota v chasti. Soderzhaniye, organizatsiya, metodika*, 2d ed. (Moscow: Voyenizdat, 1983), pp. 3–11.

11 See, for example, "Kodeks o brake i sem'ye ukrainskoy SSR," in *Sbornik zakonov ukrainskoy SSR, 1938–1979* (Kiev: Izdatel'stvo Politicheskoy Literatury Ukrainy, 1980), Vol. 2, pp. 245–82; the relevant articles are 61 and 70. The family codes in the other republics follow the same pattern.

12 Clawson, 1973.

13 See, for example, T. A. Markova (ed.), *Vospitaniye doshkolnika v sem'ye* (Moscow: Pedagogika, 1979), *pass.*

14 A. Ya. Sobolev, *Vzaimodeystviye shkoly, sem'i i obshchestvennosti v kommunisticheskom vospitanii uchashchikhsya (na materiale uzbekskoy SSR)* (Tashkent: FAN, 1979), pp. 102–40.

15 A model program for "pedagogical knowledge for parents" is provided in A. G. Khripkova *et al.* (eds.), *Vzaimodeystviye shkoly, sem'i, obshchestvennosti v kommunisticheskom vospitanii (iz opyta vospitatel'noy raboty)* (Moscow: Pedagogika, 1978), pp. 137–75.

16 Clawson, 1973, p. 701.

17 Markova, 1979, pp. 94–5.

18 "O narodnom obrazovanii," *Sbornik zakonov ukrainskoy SSR*, Vol. 1, pp. 569–90; see especially article 17.

19 Clawson, 1973.

20 "O narodnom obrazovanii," articles 24, 44, and 51, which cover the general education school, the vocational school, and the specialized secondary school respectively.

21 G. K. Mosolov and V. G. Kolychev, "Voyenno-patrioticheskoye vospitaniye," *SVE*, Vol. 2, pp. 245–6.

22 Felicity Ann O'Dell, *Socialisation through Children's Literature: The Soviet Example* (Cambridge: Cambridge University Press, 1978), pp. 76, 86–8. See also Charles D. Cary, "Martial-patriotic themes in Soviet school textbooks," *Soviet Union*, vol. 6, pt. 1 (1979), pp. 81–98.

23 O'Dell, 1978, pp. 148–55.
24 "Zarnitsa," *SVE*, Vol. 3, pp. 409–10; A. Isayev and V. Sergeyev, *"Zarnitsa"-pionerskaya igra* (Moscow: Molodaya Gvardiya, 1983), pp. 8–9; and L. A. Pesterev, "Orlenok," *SVE*, Vol. 6, p. 115.
25 A. A. Shatov, "The Komsomol and military–patriotic socialization," in *V. I. Lenin i kommunisticheskoye vospitaniye molodezhi* (Perm: Permskiy Gosudarstvennyy Pedagogicheskiy Institut, 1971), pp. 32–9; V. Lomakin, "In the glorious traditions of the Far Easterner," *KZ*, 31 May 1978, p. 2; N. Zakharov, "The stars of heroes shine for us," *KZ*, 19 August 1982, p. 2; V. Safronov, "We grow patriots," *Voyennyye znaniya*, no. 11 (November 1980), pp. 6–7; and "Ob opyte voyenno-patrioticheskoy raboty v obshcheobrazovatel'nykh shkolakh kurskoy oblasti," 1 July 1983, *Byulleten' normativnykh aktov ministerstva prosveshcheniya SSSR*, no. 10 (1983), pp. 33–8.
26 V. Balazh, "Patriotic and international socialization," *NO*, no. 1 (1980), pp. 21–5.
27 V. Drugov, "Military–patriotic socialization of workers—one of the most important tasks of today," *VIZh*, no. 9 (1979), pp. 3–8.
28 See, for example, Hedrick Smith, *The Russians* (New York: Ballantine, 1976), pp. 402–34; and David K. Shipler, *Russia: Broken Idols, Solemn Dreams* (New York: Times Books, 1983), pp. 108–10, 277–300.
29 V. K. Konoplev, "Social results of scientific–technical progress in military affairs," *SI*, no. 2 (1975), pp. 12–20.
30 N. N. Yefimov and Yu. I. Deryugin, "Ways to increase the effectiveness of military–patriotic socialization of youth," *SI*, no. 1 (1980), pp. 60–6.
31 A. M. Danchenko and I. F. Vydrin, *Voyennaya pedagogika* (Moscow: Voyenizdat, 1973), trans. by the U.S. airforce as *Military Pedagogy: A Soviet View*, pp. 95–101. See also M. M. Lisenkov, *Kul'turnaya revolyutsiya v SSSR i armiya* (Moscow: Voyenizdat, 1977), pp. 55–6; N. A. Kostikov, "The essence and content of a complex approach to the upbringing of pre-draft youth," in Kostikov, 1980, pp. 7–18; N. Stasenko, "Prepare schoolboys for military service," *Vospitaniye shkolnikov*, no. 2 (1981), pp. 21–3; and V. Mitropov, "Moral climate of the collective," *Znamenosets*, no. 12 (1980), pp. 14–15.
32 D. Orlova and I. Bykova, "One? Two? Three?" *Zdorov'ye*, no. 9 (1978), pp. 2–4; K. K. Bazdyrev, *Yedinstvennyy rebenok* (Moscow: Finansy i Statistika, 1983), pp. 111–12; V. M. Sokolov, "Forming a communist world view in youth," *SI*, no. 2 (1976), pp. 29–37; and A. Markhay, "Ideological work," *KZ*, 5 October 1983, p. 2.
33 K. Bazdyrev, "In search of harmony," *Trud*, 16 July 1982, p. 4.
34 In 1978 about 79 percent of the primary and secondary school teachers were female; the comparable figure for the U.S. public schools was about 65 percent: *Narodnoye khozyaystvo SSSR v 1978 g* (Moscow: Statistika, 1979), p. 470; and U.S. Department of Commerce, Bureau of the Census, *Statistical Abstract of the United States, 1981*, p. 152.
35 *Komsomolskaya pravda*, 21 January 1976, p. 4; and "Vladimir, 20—serving in the Soviet Union's Red Army," *Varnpliktsnytt*, June 1977, section 2.
36 Yu. I. Deryugin and N. N. Yefimov, "Socializing role of the Soviet armed forces," *SI*, no. 4 (1981), pp. 104–9.
37 *Sovetskaya estoniya*, 27 August 1983, pp. 1, 2; V. F. Farforovskiy, *Patrioticheskoye i internatsional'noye vospitaniye shkolnikov* (Kiev: Radyanska Shkola, 1978), pp. 93–4; P. N. Reshetov, "The ideological struggle and certain problems in bringing up youth," *Kommunist ukrainy*, no. 8 (August 1981), pp. 62–70; and V. Kovalev, "Disco-mania," *Komsomolskaya pravda*, 7 June 1981, p. 4.
38 *Military Pedagogy*, p. 98; and N. Mashovets, "Our own pride," *Pravda*, 31 October 1983, p. 7.
39 K. Vayno, "With an exact knowledge of the situation," *Kommunist*, no. 4 (1983), pp. 51–60.
40 Yu Lutkin, "Art and political culture of the individual," *Sovetskaya kul'tura*, 16 April 1983, pp. 2–3; and D. F. Ustinov, "Example of selfless service to the motherland," *KZ*, 15 December 1983, pp. 1–2.
41 N. V. Ogarkov, *Vsegda v gotovnosti k zashchite otechestva* (Moscow: Voyenizdat, 1982), p. 65; see also A. Sorokin, "A school for the ideological tempering and indoctrination of the motherland's defenders," *Politicheskoye samoobrazovaniye*, no. 2 (1984), pp. 28–35.
42 A. I. Sorokin, "The armed forces of developed socialism," *Voprosy filosofii*, no. 2 (1983), pp. 3–17.
43 On differential access to Soviet mass media see Lisenkov, 1977, pp. 59–60.
44 A. Dedushev, "To be a militant atheist," *Voyennyy vestnik*, no. 1 (1984), pp. 11–13;

N. Kushner, "Using party ideological weapons," *KZ*, 23 May 1982, p. 2; V. Sal'nikov, "Atheist socialization of troops," *Morskoy sbornik*, no. 7 (1983), pp. 42–3; and K. Payusov, "Atheist indoctrination of military personnel," *KVS*, no. 3 (1982), pp. 53–8.

45 S. Shatov, "The road to truth," *Znamenosets*, no. 7 (1982), pp. 18–19.

46 Ye. Dvoryanskiy, "Atheist propaganda must take the offensive," *KVS*, no. 4 (1972), pp. 55–61.

47 F. I. Dolgikh and A. P. Kurantov, *Kommunisticheskiye idealy i ateisticheskoye vospitaniye voinov* (Moscow: Voyenizdat, 1976), pp. 31–2, 70.

48 V. Marchenko, "Enlightenment," *KZ*, 11 June 1983, p. 2.

49 A. Yu. Snechkus, "In the spirit of loyalty of the multinational Soviet motherland," in *Armiya bratstva narodov* (Moscow: Voyenizdat, 1972), pp. 136–47; see also *Military Pedagogy*, p. 95.

50 G. V. Sredin, "Ideologicheskaya rabota," *SVE*, Vol. 3, pp. 493–5. On political socialization in the Eastern European armed forces see Dale R. Herspring and Ivan Volgyes, "The military as an agent of political socialization in Eastern Europe," *Armed Forces and Society*, vol. 3, no. 2 (February 1977), pp. 249–69; and Ivan Volgyes, "Political socialization in Eastern Europe." *Journal of Political and Military Sociology*, vol. 1, no. 2 (1973), pp. 261–77.

51 N. A. Petrovichev *et al.*, *Partiynoye stroitel'stvo. Uchebnoy posobiye* (Moscow: Politizdat, 1981), p. 230.

52 F. S. Stepanov *et al.*, *Zamestitel' komandira polka (korablya) po politicheskoy chasti*, 2d ed. (Moscow: Voyenizdat, 1975): on Marxist–Leninist training for officers see pp. 77–91; on political training for warrant officers see pp. 92–109; on conscript political training see pp. 110–29; on agitation and propaganda see pp. 130–53; on recreational programs see pp. 260–84; on contact with the local party see pp. 315–29; on work with military families see pp. 301–14.

53 *Military Pedagogy*, p. 212.

54 V. N. Kovalev, *Sotsialisticheskiy voinskiy kollektiv. Sotsiologicheskiy ocherk* (Moscow: Voyenizdat, 1980), p. 231.

55 V. F. Klochkov and N. A. Platonov, "Metodika politicheskoy podgotovki," *SVE*, Vol. 5, pp. 264–6.

56 Smorigo, 1983, pp. 18–20, 22; and "Marksistsko-leninskaya podgotovka," *SVE*, Vol. 5, pp. 152–3.

57 Smorigo, 1983, pp. 20–2; and Bublik, 1982, pp. 117–19.

58 "Polozheniye o vechernikh partiynykh shkolakh sovetskoy armii i voyenno-morskom flote," *Spravochnik politrabotnika* (Moscow: Voyenizdat, 1973), pp. 181–2; and M. V. Ruban, "Partiynoye obrazovaniye," *SVE*, Vol. 6, p. 237.

59 M. G. Sobolev *et al.*, *Partiyno-politicheskaya rabota v sovetskikh vooruzhennykh silakh* (Moscow: Voyenizdat, 1974), pp. 253–63; and M. M. Korolev and I. S. Mareyev, *Armeyskiy propagandist* (Moscow: Voyenizdat, 1975), pp. 44–59.

60 In some units where the regular schedule is not feasible a weekly three-hour session may be substituted instead. This change, however, must be authorized by the service commander in chief and service political chief. In construction and railway units political classes are held once a week for three hours in the winter, once a week for two hours in the summer: N. I. Smorigo (ed.), *Ideologicheskaya rabota v chasti* (Moscow: Voyenizdat, 1978), pp. 70–1.

61 Stepanov, 1975, pp. 110–29.

62 *Spravochnik politrabotnika*, p. 177.

63 KVS lesson plans for the years 1972–83 were compiled and examined to isolate changes and continuities in the political training program over the twelve-year period.

64 For the five-lesson plans in 1981, for example, see *KVS*, no. 16, pp. 68–74; no. 17, pp. 68–75; no. 18, pp. 78–84; no. 19, pp. 71–5, 76–83; analogous lesson plans for 1983 are in *KVS*, no. 16, pp. 78–83, 84–9; no. 17, pp. 73–8, 79–83; no. 18, pp. 68–73.

65 "Heroic past of our motherland," *KVS*, no. 10, 1983, pp. 75–82.

66 Sobolev, 1974, p. 281.

67 "Agitatsionno-massovaya rabota," *SVE*, Vol. 1, pp. 97–8; A. A. Yepishev, "Agitators—the political warrior of the party," *Agitator armii i flota*, no. 1 (January 1977), pp. 1–19; and I. S. Mareyev, *Propagandisty armii i flota* (Moscow: Voyenizdat, 1980), pp. 171–81.

68 N. Chebykin, "An active form of ideological education," *KVS*, no. 12 (June 1978), pp. 60–5; and *Spravochnik propagandista i agitatora armii i flota* (Moscow: Voyenizdat, 1983), pp. 111–14.

69 "The wall press," *KVS*, no. 23 (December 1977), p. 84.

70 "Komnata boyevoy slavy," *SVE*, Vol. 4, pp. 284–5.

71 *Kul'turno-prosvetitel'naya rabota v armii i na flote* (Moscow: Voyenizdat, 1977), pp. 3–8; and *Spravochnik politrabotnika*, p. 187.
72 The Central House of the Soviet Army publishes a regular bulletin providing guidelines for political workers participating in management of recreational and cultural activities: *Spravochnik propagandista i agitatora armii i flota* (Moscow: Voyenizdat, 1973), pp. 148–9, 151; and Y. E. Vostokov, "Kul'turno-prosvetitel'naya rabota," *SVE*, Vol. 4, pp. 520–4.
73 *Kul'turno-prosvetitel'naya rabota v armii i na flota*, p. 271.
74 ibid., pp. 271–94.
75 V. F. Klochkov, "Leninskaya komnata," *SVE*, Vol. 4, p. 620.
76 S. V. Koloko'tsev, "Kinoiskusstvo," *SVE*, Vol. 4, pp. 175–8.
77 A. Sabelnikov, "An important art," *KVS*, no. 12 (June 1978), pp. 66–71; and V. Spiridonov, "The objective—army and fleet life," *KVS*, no. 12 (1979), pp. 52–7.
78 *Kul'turno-prosvetitel'naya rabota v armii i na flote*, pp. 73–124, 166–86.
79 *Sprachovnik politrabotnika*, pp. 188–9.
80 *Kul'turno-prosvetitel'naya rabota v armii i na flote*, pp. 259–69; "Klub voinskoy chasti," *SVE*, Vol. 4, p. 210.
81 I. M. Butskiy, "Politicheskiye zanyatiya," *SVE*, Vol. 6, p. 420; *VES*, p. 571; and Bublik *et al.*, 1982, pp. 120–1.
82 Stephen D. Wesbrook, "Historical notes," in Janowitz and Wesbrook, 1983, pp. 251–84; Amos A. Jordan, Jr., "Troop information and indoctrination," in Roger W. Little (ed.), *Handbook of Military Institutions* (Beverly Hills, Calif.: Sage, 1971), pp. 347–71; and Thomas A. Palmer, "Why we fight: a study of indoctrination activities in the armed forces," in Peter Karsten (ed.), *The Military in America. From the Colonial Era to the Present* (New York: The Free Press, 1980), pp. 383–96.
83 Zoll, 1983.
84 Azarya, 1983.
85 Information provided by the Armed Forces Information Service; see also Marge Holz, "AFIS: providing information to first class citizens," *Direction* (Summer 1983), pp. 14–18.
86 Stephen D. Wesbrook, "Historical notes," in Janowitz and Wesbrook, 1983, pp. 251–84.
87 Zoll, 1983; and Azarya, 1983.
88 One study of the impact of military service in the Bundeswehr on the attitudes of West German youth found that the service experience promotes personality development and civic awareness, while another study (which relied on participatory observation) concluded that the draftee's experience increases fear, uncertainty, and accommodation. A panel study of Bundeswehr draftees conducted in the early 1970s found that draftees are less insecure at the end of their military service and that military service results in strengthened democratic awareness in the draftee: Ekkehard Lippert, Paul Schneider, and Ralph Zoll, "The influence of military service on political and social attitudes: a study of socialization in the German Bundeswehr," *Armed Forces and Society*, vol. 4, no. 2 (February 1978), pp. 265–82; see also *International Journal of Political Education*, vol. 1 (1977–8), pp. 225–40. This latter finding, however, could not be replicated five years later: Roland Wakenhut, "Effects of military service on the political socialization of draftees," *Armed Forces and Society*, vol. 5, no. 4 (1979), pp. 626–41.
89 Opinion Research Corporation, *The Image of the Army* (Princeton, N.J.: Opinion Research Corporation, 1969), pp. 73, 77, as cited in Peter Karsten (ed.), *Soldiers and Society: The Effects of Military Service and War on American Life* (Westport, Conn.: Greenwood Press, 1978), pp. 156–7.
90 Morris Janowitz, "Basic education and youth socialization in the armed forces," in Little, 1971, pp. 167–210.
91 Eugene H. Drucker, *A Longitudinal Study of Attitude Change and Alienation during Combat Training* (Human Resources Research Organization, 1974), HumRRO-TR-74-15.
92 For example, one study of political attitudes among Vietnam-era veterans found that military service had no measurable effect on the individual's sense of political trust and personal competence; military experience was found to decrease political efficacy. Barber, 1973, pp. 151–65. A study of the impact of military service on foreign policy beliefs also revealed only marginal differences between veterans and nonveterans; veterans, for example, were slightly more likely to support U.S. military intervention to protect other countries. They were also somewhat more supportive of the government rationale for U.S. involvement in Vietnam: Samuel A. Kirkpatrick and James L. Regens, "Military experience and foreign

policy belief systems," *Journal of Political and Military Sociology*, vol. 6 (Spring 1978), pp. 29–47, and James L. Regens, "Political attitudes and Vietnam-era service," *Social Science Journal*, vol. 14, no. 3 (1977), pp. 83–92.

93 A panel study that compared trends in political attitudes of veterans and nonveterans in 1965 and 1973 found only modest differences between the two groups. Veterans measured somewhat higher on indices of political trust and were somewhat more likely to support the U.S. entry in the Vietnam War; the service experience had little effect on civic tolerance: M. Kent Jennings and Gregory B. Markus, "The effect of military service on political attitudes: a panel study," *American Political Science Review*, vol. 71, no. 1 (1977), pp. 131–47. Another analysis of the same data revealed that veterans and nonveterans had about the same images of a good citizen. Those who had served in Vietnam, however, were more likely to stress the importance of loyalty and obedience (that is, obey laws, pay taxes), as opposed to "activist" duties (that is, vote, contact officials). Turning from civic values to reported levels of political activity, the researchers also found that military sevice had a depressing effect on some types of political participation such as voting, taking part in a demonstration, sit-in, or protest march. By contrast, military service experience was associated with increased levels of community participation such as working with others to solve a neighborhood or community problem: M. Kent Jennings and Gregory B. Markus, "Political participation and Vietnam War veterans: a longitudinal study," in Nancy L. Goldner and David R. Segal (eds.), *The Social Psychology of Military Service*, War, Revolution, and Peacekeeping research series (Beverly Hills, Calif.: Sage, 1976), Vol. 11, pp. 175–200.

94 A 1973 survey of residents in the Detroit area found few major differences in attitudes on the draft, international relations, and U.S. foreign policy. Veterans were somewhat more traditional than nonveterans in support for the draft and a continued U.S. military presence in Europe. David R. Segal and Mady Wechsler Segal, "The impact of military service on trust in government, international attitudes and social status," in ibid., pp. 201–11. The hypothesis that military service fosters violent or authoritarian attitudes has been tested in a variety of settings, but has received little empirical support: Allan J. Lizotte and David J. Bordua, "Military socialization, childhood socialization, and current situation: veterans' firearms ownership," *Journal of Political and Military Sociology*, vol. 8 (Fall 1980), pp. 243–56.

95 Joel J. Schwartz, "The elusive 'New Soviet Man'," *Problems of Communism*, vol. 22 (1973), pp. 39–50. For a more balanced treatment see Walter D. Connor, "Generations and politics in the USSR," *Problems of Communism*, vol. 24 (1975), pp. 20–31.

96 Yu K. Fishevskiy, "Sociological investigations of the effectiveness of lecture propaganda," *SI*, no. 4 (1975), pp. 109–16; and G. T. Zhuravlev, "Methodological principles of sociological research in ideological work," *SI*, no. 1 (1975), pp. 19–29.

97 A. V. Mitskevich, "The investigation of the state of legal education of workers," *SI*, no. 3 (1976), pp. 107–12; "Formation of respect for socialist law," *Sovetskoye gosudarstvo i pravo*, no. 4 (1975), pp. 37–46; and *Lichnost' i uvazheniye k zakonu. Sotsiologicheskiy aspekt* (Moscow: Nauka 1979), *pass*.

98 V. Krylov, "Aspects of the scientific approach," *Partiynaya zhizn (Kazakhstan)*, no. 5 (1978), pp. 80–5; and G. T. Zhuravlev, *Sotsiologicheskiye issledovaniya effektivnosti ideologicheskoy raboty* (Moscow: Mysl', 1980), pp. 12–15, 193, 229–30; N. N. Bokarev, *Sotsiologicheskiye issledovaniya effektivnosti lektsionnoy propagandy* (Moscow: Znaniye, 1980), pp. 46–7, 58–65. Soviet writers frequently attempt to gauge the effectiveness of socialization programs by asking the target population how they evaluate such programs. See, for example, the sample questionnaire in *Kommunisticheskoye vospitaniye. Metodicheskiye rekomendatsii dlya planov sotsial'nogo razvitiya proizvodstvennykh kollektivov* (Moscow: Profizdat, 1981), pp. 133–62.

99 Stephen White, "Political socialization in the USSR: a study in failure?" *Studies in Comparative Communism*, vol. X, no. 3 (Autumn 1977), pp. 328–42; Stephen White, "The effectiveness of political propaganda in the USSR," *Soviet Studies*, vol. XXXII, no. 3 (July 1980), pp. 323–48; and Stephen White, "The USSR: patterns of autocracy and industrialism," in Archie Brown and Jack Grey (eds.), *Political Culture and Political Change in Communist States* (New York: Holmes & Meier, 1977), pp. 25–65.

100 *Military Pedagogy*, pp. 215–18; and V. V. Shelyag et al., *Voyennaya psikhologiya* (Moscow: Voyenizdat, 1972), trans. by the U.S. airforce as *Military Psychology: A Soviet View*, pp. 194–5.

101 "Ustav vnutrenney sluzhby vooruzhennykh sil SSSR," articles 188–91, in *Svod zakonov SSSR*

(Moscow: Izvestiya, 1982), Vol. 9, pp. 278–346 (hereafter cited as Internal Service Regulations); see also "Fizicheskaya zaryadka," *VES*, p. 777.

102 During morning inspection conscript personnel are checked to ensure that they are present and observing established regulations governing uniforms and personal hygiene: "Osmotr lichnogo sostava," *VES*, p. 525; and Internal Service Regulations, articles 192–3.
103 Internal Service Regulations, articles 201–2.
104 Regulations specify six hours of training exercises; at least thirty minutes must elapse after the noon meal before work details or exercise can begin again: Internal Service Regulations, article 188.
105 Internal Service Regulations, article 200; and "Parkovo-khozyaystvennyy den'," *VES*, p. 539.
106 A pass entitles the serviceman to leave the regimental area (or ship), but he must stay within the garrison borders: Internal Service Regulations, articles 204–7; "Uvol'neniye iz raspolozheniya chasti," *VES*, p. 760; "Uvol'neniye iz raspolozheniya chasti," *SVE*, Vol. 8, p. 165; and *Znamenosets*, no. 7 (1977), p. 32.
107 As then General Secretary Brezhnev noted, "Free time is not time which is free of responsibility before society," quoted in A. I. Kitov *et al.*, *Sovremennaya armiya i distsiplina* (Moscow: Voyenizdat, 1976), p. 196.
108 *Military Psychology*, p. 349.
109 *Kul'turno-prosvetitel'naya rabota v armii i na flote*, p. 231.
110 D. Volkogonov, "Complex approach to agitational mass work," *Agitator armii i flota*, no. 4 (1977), pp. 8–14.
111 Viktor Suvorov, *Inside the Red Army* (New York: Macmillan, 1982), pp. 221–31; and *Military Pedagogy*, pp. 102–4.
112 L. A. Kustov and I. I. Barzhelenko, "Peculiarities of adaptation of young soldiers to military service," *Voyenno-meditsinskiy zhurnal*, no. 8 (1981), pp. 45–7; and Kh. A. Izakson, "Adaptation of young soldiers to service in dependence on the degree of their physical preparation," *Voyenno-meditsinskiy zhurnal*, no. 11 (1977), pp. 81–2.
113 Ye. V. Gembitskiy *et al.*, "To the question of prevention of acute pneumonia among short term servicemen," *Voyenno-meditsinskiy zhurnal*, no. 4 (1982), pp. 29–33. See also G. K. Alekseyev, "Diagnosing and preventing acute pneumonia," *Voyenno-meditsinskiy zhurnal*, no. 3 (1981), pp. 61–3; and I. K. Asaulyuk, "Clinical peculiarities of the course of acute pneumonia among young people," *Voyenno-meditsinskiy zhurnal*, no. 1 (1984), pp. 61–3.
114 "Kazarma," *SVE*, Vol. 4, pp. 31–2; M. Ponomarev, "The military life of your sons," *KZ*, 9 September 1975, p. 4; and Internal Service Regulations, articles 142–76.
115 *Military Pedagogy*, pp. 102–4; and A. Markhay, "Talking figures," *KZ*, 5 October 1983, p. 2.
116 Yu. I. Deryugen and N. N. Yefimov, "The effectiveness of military–patriotic socialization of youth," *SI*, no. 3 (1983), pp. 121–5; see also Yefimov and Deryugen, 1980.
117 Eugene H. Drucker, *The Effects of Basic Combat Training on the Attitudes of the Soldier* (Human Resources Research Organization, 1974), HumRRO-TR-74-17, pp. 21–2.
118 L. A. Kustov and I. I. Barzhelenko, "Significance of physical exercises for adaptation of young soldiers to military service," *Voyenno-meditsinskiy zhurnal*, no. 11 (1982), pp. 53–5.
119 A. V. Barabanshchikov *et al.*, *Problemy psikhologii voinskogo kollektiva* (Moscow: Voyenizdat, 1973), pp. 69–70.
120 Mikhail Tsypkin, "The conscripts," *Bulletin of the Atomic Scientists* (May 1983), pp. 28–32.
121 Kovalev, 1980, pp. 147–8.
122 On cross-pressures see H. McCloskey and L. Dahlgren, "Primary group influence on party loyalty," *American Political Science Review*, vol. 53 (1947), pp. 757–76; on the effects of dissonant messages see L. Festinger, *A Theory of Cognitive Dissonance* (Palo Alto, Calif.: Stanford University Press, 1957), *pass*.
123 See, for example, Robert Bathurst and Michael Burger, "Controlling the Soviet soldier: some eyewitness accounts", Occasional Paper No. 1, The Texas A&M University System Center for Strategic Technology; and Robert Bathurst, Michael Burger, and Ellen Wolffe, *The Soviet Sailor: Combat Readiness and Morale*, Ketron Inc., KFR 382–83, 30 June 1982, pp. 18–27.
124 Tsypkin, 1983.
125 *Military Psychology*, pp. 279–93; and K. Bochkarev, "Support of the collective is an important condition for the further strengthening of troop discipline," *Voyennaya mysl'*, no. 3 (1967).
126 On school collectives see Urie Bronfenbrenner, *Two Worlds of Childhood: U.S. and USSR*

178   *Red Army and Society*

(New York: Basic Books, 1973), pp. 15–73. On work collectives see *Sotsial'no-psikhologicheskiy klimat kollektiva* (Moscow: Nauka, 1979), *pass*.

127 *Military Pedagogy*, p. 239; see also Barabanshchikov *et al.*, 1973, pp. 63–4.

128 "Polozheniye o prokhozhdenii deystvitelnoy srvochnoy voyennoy sluzhby v sovetskoy armii i voyenno-morskom flote," article 63, *Spravochnik po zakonodatel'stvu dlya ofitserov sovetskoy armii i flota* (Moscow: Voyenizdat, 1970), pp. 132–45; see also *Sovetskiy voin*, no. 22 (1980), p. 27.

129 Kovalev, 1980, pp. 4–5.

130 *Military Psychology*, pp. 324–9, 331–2.

131 *Military Psychology*, pp. 277–355; and V. Lazarev, "On criteria of solidarity of military units," *Vestnik PVO*, no. 10 (1982), pp. 49–52.

132 I. G. Pavlovskiy (ed.), *Psikhologo-pedagogicheskiye osnovy deyatel'nosti komandira* (Moscow: Voyenizdat, 1978), pp. 74–8; and S. Mokrousov, "Improving political socialization work in subunits," *Morskoy sbornik*, no. 11 (1979), pp. 13–17.

133 Barabanshchikov *et al.*, 1973, pp. 134–7, 190; "The military collective: problems of social control," *KVS*, no. 7 (1980), pp. 50–7.

134 Kovalev, 1980, p. 134.

135 Kovalev, 1980, pp. 134–6; and A. Kitov, "Methodological questions of applied sociological research in the armed forces," *Voyennaya mysl'*, no. 10 (1968); and *Military Psychology*, pp. 287–8.

136 See Sara Silbiger, "Peers and political socialization," in Renshon, 1977, pp. 172–89.

137 *Military Psychology*, pp. 334–40.

138 ibid., pp. 287–8.

139 Kovalev, 1980, pp. 4, 81. See E. Aronson and J. Mills, "The effect of severity of initiation on liking for a group," *Journal of Abnormal and Social Psychology*, vol. 59 (1959), pp. 177–81, for an explanation of why severe initiation to a group increases loyalty and devotion to the group, much like boot camp increases commitment to the U.S. Marine Corps.

140 "Polozheniye o prokhozhdenii deystvitelnoy srochnoy voyennoy sluzhby," articles 29, 39–45.

141 Barabanshchikov *et al.*, 1973, pp. 134–7, 190; G. A. Bronevitskiy, Yu. P. Zuyev, and A. M. Stolyarenko, *Osnovy voyenno-morskoy psikhologii* (Moscow: Voyenizdat, 1977), p. 111; and S. S"yedin, "In the interests of solidifying the military collective," *KVS*, no. 7 (1982), pp. 50–5.

142 Kovalev, 1980, pp. 138–41.

143 V. Ovcharov, "My mother, my father, my master sergeant, and I," *Komsomolskaya pravda*, 21 January 1976, p. 4; and *Military Pedagogy*, pp. 102–7.

144 *Military Psychology*, pp. 326–7.

145 Kovalev, 1980, pp. 232–3.

146 K. Ambarov, "Concern about the moral atmosphere in military collectives," *Morskoy sbornik*, no. 1 (1980), pp. 8–11.

147 M. Garnier, "Power and ideological conformity: a case study," *American Journal of Sociology*, vol. 79, no. 2 (1973), pp. 343–63.

148 Merle Fainsod, *Smolensk under Soviet Rule* (Cambridge, Mass.: Harvard University Press, 1958), p. 452.

149 G. A. Konyukhov, "Kolkhozy krasnoarmeyskiye," *SVE*, Vol. 4, pp. 248–9.

150 "Ob ispol'zovanii demobilizovannykh iz krasnoy armii na nizovoy sovetskoy, kooperativnoy, i obshchestvennoy rabote," Central Committee resolution of 14 October 1927, in N. I. Savinkin and K. M. Bogolyubov (eds.), *KPSS o vooruzhennykh silakh sovetskogo soyuza. Dokumenty 1917–1981* (Moscow: Voyenizdat, 1981), pp. 243–4.

151 "O podgotovke otpusknikov v RKKA," Central Committee resolution of 12 April 1929, in ibid., pp. 256–7.

152 *SVE*, Vol. 4, pp. 248–9.

153 *Krasnoznamennyy dal'nevostochnyy. Istoriya krasnoznamennogo dal'nevostochnogo voyennogo okruga* (Moscow: Voyenizdat, 1971), pp. 128–9.

154 G. Abishev, *Kazakhstan v zashchite sotsialsticheskogo otechestva* (Alma Ata: Kazakhstan, 1969), p. 156; see also I. B. Berkhin, *Voyennaya reforma v SSSR* (Moscow: Voyenizdat, 1958), pp. 140–1.

155 John Erickson, *The Soviet High Command: A Military–Political History, 1918–1941* (London: Macmillan, 1962), p. 313.

156 Kovalev, 1980, p. 224.

157 A. A. Yepishev (ed.), *Ideologicheskaya rabota v vooruzhennykh silakh SSSR. Istoriko-*

teoreticheskiy ocherk (Moscow: Voyenizdat, 1983), pp. 312–13; and Yu. I. Deryugen and N. N. Yefimov, "The socialization role of the Soviet armed forces," *SI*, no. 4 (1981), pp. 104–9.

158 *The Image of the Army.*

159 B. Sapunov and Yu. Fedorov, "Scientific communism and military sociological research," *Voyennaya mysl'*, no. 12 (1972); and Yefimov and Deryugin, 1980.

160 Sapunov and Fedorov, 1972.

161 Deryugun and Yefimov, 1981.

162 Sapunov and Fedorov, 1972.

163 Arie Shirom, "On some correlates of combat performance," *Administrative Science Quarterly*, vol. 21 (September 1976), pp. 419–32.

7

Minorities in Uniform

Ethnic identity is an important source of social and political cleavage in plural societies—both industrialized and developing, both socialist and nonsocialist.[1] Ethnicity (defined here as the basis for groups whose membership is determined by ties of kinship, language, religion, race, or culture) interacts with other sources of identification—gender, class, occupation, and institutional affiliation—to produce the complex fabric of social and political life. Military institutions in plural societies provide a particularly intriguing focus for the study of both ethnopolitics (the political consequences of ethnicity) and of the interaction between ethnic trends and socioeconomic modernization.

The study of "ethnic soldiers" ideally asks two sets of closely related questions. The first focusses on the consequences of ethnicity on the military itself: what role does ethnicity play in the broader society and polity and how does this factor influence the armed forces? Have specific ethnic groups been excluded from the manpower procurement pool or been assigned specific roles within the military?[2] A related issue is the impact of ethnicity on the state's military potential and, in a narrower sense, on the combat capability of military units.

The issue can also be examined from the opposite direction: how have military institutions affected ethnicity? In the narrow sense this question focusses on whether the armed forces serve as a vehicle for political integration or as one which exacerbates ethnic polarization. The military in some societies may promote the breakdown of ethnic cleavages and the development of supraethnic affiliation. In other cases the military reinforces and reinvigorates ethnic identity, hence promoting ethnic polarization. A third alternative, of course, is neutrality: the armed forces may simply have no effect at all on ethnic relationships in the larger society.[3]

To understand ethnic–military relations it is necessary to understand the role which ethnicity plays in civilian society and in the military. Analysis of ethnic soldiers in the USSR must begin, then, with an examination of the role ethnicity plays in the larger society and polity. This chapter is an analysis of ethnic-military relations in the Soviet Union treated within the context of Soviet nationality policy, and ethnopolitics in a socialist state.

The USSR provides a particularly fruitful case study of a military institution in a multiethnic society. By any standard the Soviet Union's ethnonational problem is immense. The Bolshevik leaders inherited from their tsarist predecessors an empire with dozens of nationalities and substantial social, economic, religious, and linguistic diversity. Many of the ethnic minorities that populated the borderlands were separated from the Slavic majority not only by language, but also by differences in socioeconomic development, life styles, and basic values. To cope with this heterogeneous population, Soviet leaders developed a nationality policy, which at present includes two basic tactics: (1) acceptance of ethnicity as a primary element of personal identity and of those cultural differences perceived as compatible with the party-dominated system; and (2) programs to reduce socioeconomic differences between minority groups and geographic regions and to promote a common Soviet value system. The implicit assumption undergirding this approach is that fuller socioeconomic development of the less modernized minorities will produce a common Soviet value system. Moreover, the Soviet leaders obviously feel that both processes—ethnic convergence in socioeconomic level and in values—will, when coupled with regime tolerance of selected minority differences, enhance political cohesion.[4]

In essence, then, the USSR's ethnonational strategy is based on the belief that certain dimensions of ethnic integration are interconnected. To evaluate this assumption it is important to distinguish the various aspects of ethnic integration:

(*a*) identity assimilation—the erosion and disappearance of ethnic consciousness or identity (what the Soviets call *sliyaniye*);

(*b*) social assimilation—the extent to which group members socialize freely with outgroup members;

(*c*) convergence (*sblizheniye*)—equalization of socioeconomic and political status (what Rothschild refers to as "life chances" integration);[5]

(*d*) Sovietization—the process of accepting basic Soviet values (acculturation);

(*e*) political integration—minority acceptance of the legitimacy of the political system.

The Soviet leaders do not now see *identity assimilation* as a reasonable near-term goal. Soviet discussions of nationality policy refer to cultural homogeneity (*sliyaniye*) as a condition that must await "the final victory of communism." *Social assimilation* is certainly viewed with official approval. Interethnic mixing in the school, workplace, and community is strongly endorsed and "friendship of peoples" is a favorite theme in socialization programs. The linchpin of Soviet nationality policy, however, is convergence in socioeconomic level. The Soviet leadership believes that this will promote erosion of ethnonational differences in life styles and values and, ultimately, enhance political integration.

The general goal of "life chances" integration or *sblizheniye* is implemented through more specific programs affecting the educational systems, language policy, access to prized occupations and jobs, and recruitment to political roles.[6] In general this has meant that Soviet programs have attempted to equip ethnic minorities with the linguistic, educational, and skill qualifications they need to compete effectively with the dominant Russians for jobs and status. At the same time, the distribution of roles has not been "color-blind." Ethnic preferences have been used to promote social and political mobility for ethnic groups which would otherwise not be able to compete with the more urbanized Russians. In other words, both efficiency and equality have been used as criteria for allocating socioeconomic and political roles. These two criteria are often in conflict; and the history of ethnicity in the USSR is, in part, a history of a constantly shifting balance between the two goals.

The application of Soviet nationality policy to the armed forces has in many ways mirrored the essential conflict between the USSR's ideological commitment to ethnic equality and its pragmatic need for efficiency. The goal of ethnic equalization requires that all minorities be endowed with full citizenship; and this, given the close connection between citizenship and military service, requires that all ethnic groups serve in the armed forces on an equal basis. Equalization of life chances means also that minority soldiers be assigned on the same basis as ethnic Russians and that minorities be provided with equal opportunity within the military's career force. In practice, however, these goals have frequently come into conflict with the competing goal of military efficiency, and with traditional ethnic stereotypes that have operated to perpetuate some of the ethnic practices of the tsarist empire. To analyse current ethnic policies in the armed forces, then, we must begin with the tsarist past.

The Historical Experience

The imperial Russian manpower system excluded many minorities from the military service obligation.[7] The eighteenth-century manpower levies embraced only the Russians; Ukrainians and Belorussians were called to the colors only in the last quarter of the century.[8] When the manpower levies were replaced by a universal military service obligation in 1874, the original intent was to include all elements in the draft, but certain Asian minorities (including the Kazakhs, Caucasian nationalities, and the Central Asian ethnic groups) were excluded because of their "low level of civic development."[9] Many such exclusions were still in force on the eve of World War I.[10]

The tsarist exclusion of many ethnic groups was to have important consequences for Bolshevik ethnic policies. The Bolshevik leadership relied heavily on army veterans as a source of military manpower during the civil war;[11] and many of the ethnic groups that had been exempt from conscription in the tsarist period were excluded from the draft in the early years of Soviet rule. In May 1922 the Council of Labor and Defense decreed that all citizens of non-Russian nationality in Siberia, Turkistan, and other outlying regions were subject to conscription. Local authorities could, however, apply to the Council for temporary exemptions for individual nationalities and groups. This exclusionary clause was used to postpone implementation of the draft law in many regions. At the end of 1923 the regular draft applied only to Russians,

Ukrainians, Belorussians, Poles, Jews, Germans, Latvians, Chuvash, Bashkirs, and certain Tatar communities. Georgians, Armenians and Azeris were drafted only in the numbers required to man nationality units in the Caucasian republics. Other minority groups were exempt entirely from the regular draft.[12] The primary reason for these exclusions was the hostility of these groups to military service—a factor Soviet writers attribute to traditional attitudes, a "low political level," and the influence of "bourgeois–nationalist" elements. The "more progressive" minority blue-collar workers could volunteer for service and were assigned to both mixed and national units.[13] The latter were set up by national military commissariats within minority regions, according to procedures laid down by a 2 May 1918 special resolution of the Commissariat for Nationality Affairs. National units, including Ukrainian, Moldavian, Armenian, Kirgiz, Azeri, and Tatar units, were not segregated exclusively along ethnic lines, but an Armenian unit, for example, would normally have a higher concentration of Armenians than a regular (mixed) unit.[14]

The early Bolshevik attitude toward these units was ambivalent. On the one hand, the Bolshevik leaders were desperate for military manpower. On the other hand, they feared that the units might be susceptible to nationalist appeals and might be used against Soviet authorities.[15] One of the main concerns of the political leadership in the early years of the civil war was to ensure the political reliability of the nationality units. Military commissariats in the minority regions were required to coordinate their activities with the Commissariat for Nationality Affairs.[16] But military mobilization officials were so anxious to generate units that they overlooked this requirement and some of the newly formed national units fell under the influence of the anti-Soviet nationalists.[17] The Commissariat for Nationality Affairs apparently used such cases to enhance its control over the military use of minorities. Military sections attached to the nationality affairs offices at both national and provincial levels began taking a more active role in forming the units, and political programs targeted at minority soldiers were stepped up. As the civil war drew to a close the Bolshevik leadership gradually moved to expand and regularize the use of minorities in the Red Army. Between 1920 and 1922 national units were set up in Azerbaydzhan, Armenia, and Georgia.[18]

The early use of ethnic minorities in the Red Army, then, met with mixed success. The Bolshevik leadership was ideologically committed to reversing the tsarist policy of excluding the less modernized minorities, but practical questions of minority reliability (to say nothing of the complicating fact that much of the old tsarist empire lay outside of Bolshevik military control) severely limited minority participation in the Red Army. The mainstay of the fighting force remained ethnic Russian. In October 1922 non-Russians constituted only 21 percent of the servicemen called into the Red Army.[19]

The army's nationality policy was strongly affected by the mid-1920s military reform program.[20] An important aspect of the 1924 reform was a five-year plan to develop nationality formations.[21] The major purpose of the nationality formations was to extend the military service obligation to as many ethnic minority groups as possible.[22] The program called for strengthening the existing formations and setting up new ones. The pace of the program in each minority area was keyed to the region's level of economic and cultural development, the state of native command cadres, and the comprehensiveness of the population registry.[23] Ukrainians, Belorussians, Tatars, and Bashkirs, along with other minorities with some tradition of military service, were conscripted on the same basis as ethnic Russians. Nationalities that lacked this background were recruited voluntarily through party, Komsomol, and trade unions. Efforts were also made to improve the registry of draft-eligibles; between the spring and fall of 1924, the proportion of non-Russians in the military registry grew from 26 to 37 percent. The proportion of non-Russians actually in uniform increased from 21 percent in 1922 to 39 percent in October 1925.[24] Many of these minority soldiers, however, served in regular units; in 1925 nationality formations comprised only 10 percent of the overall armed forces manpower.[25]

Manpower procurement in the Soviet southern tier posed a much more difficult problem for Bolshevik authorities.[26] The native populations in this region had long been exempt from the tsarist draft. Indeed, when imperial authorities tried in 1916 to conscript Central Asians into labor battalions, they touched off a bloody uprising that took several months to quell.[27] Opposition to the Bolshevik takeover was particularly strong here. The anti-Bolshevik Basmachi revolt was not suppressed until the mid-1920s. Pockets of resistance held out until 1933.[28] Even after Bolshevik forces had succeeded in pacifying these areas, non-Russians in Central Asia and Kazakhstan remained stubbornly resistant to all efforts to lure them into the Red Army.[29] Moreover, the supply of military professionals needed to command the nationality units was almost nonexistent. In addition, the complex apparatus needed to identify and register military-aged males was not in place; Bolshevik authorities lacked even the basic data on age composition necessary to begin a comprehensive registry.[30]

In May 1918 the Commissariat for Nationality Affairs established a Central Muslim Military Collegium headed by a Tatar, Vakhitov. Its mission was to establish nationality units in the Muslim regions. The Collegium had the right to hire and fire command and political cadres in such units. By early 1919 there were 50,000 Muslims on active duty in the Red Army. The units they served in were integrated into larger Russian-dominated units. The Collegium provided native-language agitprop materials for political work among Muslim soldiers. Still, the bulk of the fighting force, even on the Turkistan front, was ethnic Russian. Data from 1920 indicate that Russians comprised 78 percent of the troops there, "local nationalities" only 12 percent.[31]

With the close of the civil war, Bolshevik authorities stepped up their efforts to bring the Muslim minorities into military service. The "Five-year plan to develop nationality formations" envisioned national units in Uzbekistan, Turkmenistan, Tadzhikstan, Kirgizia, Kazakhstan, and Azerbaydzhan. At the same time, local authorities moved to extend the draft to local Asian minorities. In April 1925 Kazakhstan began a registration drive that included all nationali-

Table 7.1   *Ethnic Representation in the Red Army (1926)*

Nationaltiy	Red Army personnel (%)	20–29-year-old males (%)	Index number
Slavic			
Russian	64·8	52·72	123
Ukrainian	17·4	21·27	82
Belorussian	4·2	3·03	139
Polish	0·9	0·49	184
Muslim			
Tatars	2·0	1·86	108
Bashkirs	0·2	0·44	45
Azeri	0·4	1·00	40
Uzbeks	0·4	2·95	14
Turkmen	0·1	0·56	18
Other			
Jews	2·1	1·95	108
Georgians	1·3	1·12	116
Armenians	1·1	0·98	112
Germans	0·9	0·87	103
Komi	0·3	0·12	250
Udmurts	0·3	0·30	100
Mari	0·2	0·26	77
Mordva	0·8	0·79	101
Karelians	0·1	0·13	77
Chuvash	0·7	0·66	106

Note: The index number is computed by dividing column 1 by column 2 and multiplying by 100; a score of 100 indicates perfect representation of the ethnic group in the military. See n. 35.

ties.[32] In 1926 the Uzbekistan Communist Party organization bureau began preparations to introduce the draft.[33] In Turkmenistan a Red Army Assistance Committee (attached to the republic Council of Ministers) began preliminary work to set up a comprehensive military registration apparatus. A resolution introducing obligatory military service for the native population was introduced in Turkmenistan in mid-1927. Obligatory military service was extended to the native populations of Azerbaydzhan in 1927 and Uzbekistan and the Muslim areas in the northern Caucasus and Dagestan in the following year. Implementation, however, was piecemeal; the draft was not extended to all minorities in these areas until 1931.[34]

As the historical record makes clear, the Muslim minorities from the Soviet southern tier represented a severe challenge to Bolshevik nationality policy in the Red Army. On the one hand, Soviet authorities were in desperate need of additional manpower. Moreover, they saw Red Army service as an important mechanism for breaking down regional, ethnic, and tribal loyalties. But the low educational attainments, the language barrier, the lack of command cadres, and the reality of widespread Muslim resistance to military service forced military authorities to move slowly. The goal was the incorporation of Muslim minorities in the military on the same basis as the dominant Russians, but it was achieved only gradually and with great difficulty. As Table 7.1 makes clear, with the exception of the Tatars, Muslim minorities were significantly under-represented in the Red Army during the 1920s.[35] The historical record of the integration of Muslim minorities in the Red Army during the first decade and a half of Soviet rule has direct relevance for the current employment of minorities from Soviet Asia in the Soviet armed forces. In neither case have the Soviets shown a willingness to sacrifice combat capability to achieve the goals of CPSU nationality policy.

In the mid-1930s the Soviet leadership decided to phase out the territorial units and with them the existing national units, both Muslim and non-Muslim. The transfer to an integrated system was formalized by a joint CC–Council of Ministers resolution of 1938.[36] Minority soldiers were assigned to multiethnic units together with the dominant Slavs; national units and schools were transferred to the regular army. Soviet efforts to integrate their armed forces were temporarily halted by the German invasion of June 1941. The wartime leadership (through a State Defense Committee order) hurriedly resurrected the national units. For much of the war, many non-Russian nationals—particularly Soviet Asians—were overrepresented in the military.[37] This was due primarily to the fact that German forces occupied much of the western USSR. In the fall of 1941 German-occupied territories included about 40 percent of the prewar Soviet populace.[38] In effect, the Soviet mobilization base shifted eastward. Like their civil war counterparts, the World War II national units were really an ethnic mix with perhaps a strong concentration of the titular nationality. Units formed in Kazakhstan, for example, were 20–40 percent Kazakh. Only about 10 percent of the non-Russians who served in the war were assigned to national units; the remainder served in regular (mixed) units.[39]

Assessing the military performance of non-Russian troops in the war is complicated by the lack of reliable data. Both Soviet and German sources, however, indicate that the World War II experience in the use of minority soldiers was not without problems. Many soldiers knew so little Russian that they could not absorb military training and remedial language programs were hastily devised.[40] Wehrmacht officials, attempting to exploit these vulnerabilities, began a recruiting program among Soviet prisoners of war (POWs) that was specifically targeted at the non-Slavic "border people."[41] Recruiting was conducted under the slogan "Crusade against Bolshevism." The POWs of Caucasian and Turkic stock were singled out for the program, which also promised the liberation of the southern-tier borderlands. The entire campaign was based on the assumption that large numbers of these POWs would respond to nationalist and ideological appeals by volunteering for service (in both rear-service labor units and combat units) on the German side. But the program produced few idealists. Many prisoners volunteered enthusiastically, but only a small proportion were motivated by anti-Russian idealism. The great bulk of the volunteers took advantage of the German offer simply to escape the horrendous conditions of the German camps. The main motive was not anti-Soviet fervor, but a desire for personal survival.[42] Moreover, German officials found that the prisoners' willingness to collaborate depended on German prospects for winning the war. The proportion of POWs volunteering to serve the German cause decreased as reverses on the German front became known.[43] Some of the intellectuals in the camps who took advantage of the German offer also hoped to parlay their participation into a leading political role in the future states the Germans promised to create from their homelands. Many were more preoccupied with sorting out future political positions than fighting the Soviets. One former German officer who served with several volunteer units recounts a wild brawl that erupted in the fall of 1942 between Armenian volunteers who could not agree on the allocation of positions in the future "free" Armenia.[44] The Bolsheviks exploited the potential for unrest by infiltrating the volunteer units with spies who fomented mutiny. The Wehrmacht officials—secure in the questionable assumption that their volunteer POWs were motivated by nationalist fervor—neglected to screen their recruits carefully enough. Similar difficulties were encountered in 1943 when German authorities decided to recruit Soviet POWs of Russian nationality. This effort was also greeted by great enthusiasm initially and for the same reason: the volunteers grasped any opportunity that meant release from the POW camps.[45]

In short—according to the accounts of former Wehrmacht officers closely associated with the POW program—the Germans appear to have derived little net benefit from their efforts to exploit anti-Russian sentiment among minority prisoners by recruiting them into pro-German combat units. Many prisoners of all Soviet nationalities were clearly willing to collaborate if it meant release from German POW camps, as indeed many German prisoners collaborated with their Soviet captors.[46] But the assumption that the Soviet POWs could be organized into effective fighting units proved fallacious. The POW program appears to have been much more useful in producing labor units that could be used to release German soldiers for front-line duty.

In spite of the problems the Germans encountered trying to employ minority POWs in combat units, Soviet authorities appear to have been seriously concerned about their receptivity to German offers. One Soviet Azeri division had to be withdrawn from the front lines, apparently because of reliability problems. In the fall of 1942 the army's political administration launched a series of programs targeted at non-Russian soldiers, in particular Caucasian and Central Asian troops. The post of "instructor for work among non-Russian soldiers" was introduced at front and army level. Efforts were made to recruit more minority political officers and agitators and to publish ideological material in native languages.[47] All of these programs indicate a high level of concern for minority reliability.

Still, it is important to remember that minority soldiers played a significant role in Soviet military efforts during World War II. Non-Russians comprised 30 percent of the military personnel on the southern front in July 1942. Almost one-third of the troops on the Stalingrad front were minority soldiers.[48] A

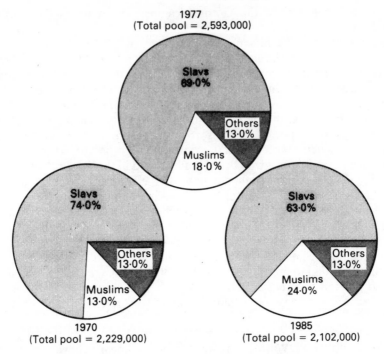

Figure 7.1 *Ethnic composition at the Soviet draft pool.*

Sources: Estimates computed from age-specific nationality data in 1970 Census; for more detailed figures and specific steps used see Ellen Jones and Fred Grupp, "Exploiting Soviet census data: some methodological considerations," unpublished paper, September 1979.

sample of 200 infantry divisions in July 1943 indicated that minorities constituted a hefty 36·2 percent. By July 1944 a survey of 100 infantry divisions revealed that the proportion of non-Russians had risen to 48 percent, primarily due to an influx of Ukrainians as the Soviet armies recaptured territory in the Western USSR lost in the early months of the war.[49] In short, the USSR could not have won World War II without substantial military participation by both non-Russian and non-Slavic troops.[50]

As World War II drew to a close nationality units were once again phased out. The current military policy towards minorities is one of integration. Minorities are subject to the draft on the same basis as other draft-age males; once drafted, they are assigned to regular mixed (that is, multinational) units. This doesn't mean that manpower procurement policies have the same impact on all nationalities. As we shall see, differences in educational attainment and linguistic ability, particularly among the older generation, have resulted in predictable patterns of assignment and officer recruitment.

The Minority Draftee

Current estimates of the ethnic breakdown of the conscript pool indicate that the proportion of dominant Slavs is declining (see Figure 7.1). Slavs constituted 74 percent of the 18-year-old males in 1970. By 1985 the Slavic share had declined to an estimated 63 percent.[51] These trends are due to the slowing population growth rates of both Slavs and other "European" nationalities. Small families with one or two children have become increasingly popular among Europeans, while Soviet Muslims have only very recently begun to limit family size.[52] These wide differences in fertility are reflected in the draft-age cohort. The fast-growing Muslim minorities increased from 13 percent of the draft pool in 1970 to 24 percent in 1985. How has this trend affected the "quality" and reliability of the Soviet soldier? Four aspects of ethnicity-related change in the Soviet military are covered here: minority educational attainments, the impact of language problems on combat capability, the level of ethnic tensions within military units, and minority reliability.

Western observers have suggested that the relatively low educational levels of the non-Slavic minorities, particularly those from the less modernized minorities in Central Asia, are having a detrimental effect on the education levels of the manpower pool as a whole.[53] Available data suggest otherwise. It is true that the overall educational levels of some of the fast-growing Asian minorities lag far behind the Russians, but overall minority scores are dragged down by the very low attainments of middle-aged women and senior citizens—none of whom are subject to the draft.[54] The younger generation has enjoyed increasing access to educational programs. As a result, educational differences between Slavs and non-Slavs are much narrower among young people. In fact, for the 16–19-year-old group, the 1970 Census indicates that many minority nationalities were ahead of the Russians in completed secondary school graduates, including all six of the Muslim minorities who are now registering large increases in the draft pool. These figures suggest that the changing ethnic breakdown of the draft pool has not had a negative effect on average conscript educational attainment. In part, these trends are due to Soviet efforts (summarized in Chapter 3) to achieve "universal secondary education." Although precise data on the percentage of high school graduates among minority youth must await release of detailed results from the 1979 Census, it is reasonable to conclude that the average minority youth of the 1980s brings into the military about the same general educational qualifications as his ethnic Russian counterpart.

Another aspect of minority performance in the military is level of technical skills. Data permitting a comparison of minority access to technical programs are very limited. One key element is exposure to formalized premilitary training programs, which were designed to offset the decrease in service terms introduced by the 1967 Law on Universal Military Service. Until the mid-1970s when the compulsory premilitary programs were phased in throughout the USSR, it seems likely that the less urbanized ethnic groups may have been disproportionately affected by the slow introduction of the programs in the rural areas. By about the mid-1970s, however, virtually all but a few schools had the required programs. Nearly all 16–17-year-old males, regardless of nationality, are probably now receiving basic premilitary training.[55] Moreover, the programs are fairly well standardized, with basic texts and curricula set at MoD level.[56] Unevenness in quality of teaching staff, facilities, and equipment remains. Examiners reviewing military courses in Ministry of Education high schools gave 36 percent of the schools good and excellent ratings, 60 percent satisfactory, and 5 percent unsatisfactory.[57] However, there is little evidence to suggest that non-Russians are any more likely than Russians to attend the poorer-quality programs. In fact many of the schools singled out for praise by the inspectors were in the Asian areas of the Soviet Union.[58] Similar comments apply to DOSAAF specialist courses, which are offered throughout the USSR.[59]

Nor does the available data suggest that minority males necessarily have less exposure to technical and specialist programs. It is true that vocational and specialist school enrollments are substantially lower in much of the Soviet southern tier, suggesting that minorities living here may have less access to such programs.[60] Here, however, the aggregate data are misleading. Traditional cultural values restricting female roles, although declining under the impact of modernization, are still strong among Soviet Muslims, limiting female enrollments in vocational and specialist programs. For specialized secondary schools, for example, female enrollments exceed those of males for many of the European nationalities; the reverse is true in Central Asia. Age- and sex-specific data on specialized secondary enrollees reveal that the *male* Muslim participation rate is virtually even with the Soviet average. More precise assessments of minority technical skills must await publication of comparative data on vocational, factory/farm training, and DOSAAF specialist graduates. However, the data that are available suggest that differences in access to technical programs for young Soviet males may, in fact, be quite narrow.

It may be argued, of course, that educational data are not really comparable across ethnic groups because of regional differences in educational quality. However, both educational programs and (to a lesser extent) curricula are fairly well standardized throughout the USSR.[61] Second, indicators of educational quality by republic suggest a fairly narrow spread. Across indicators such as student–teacher ratios, expenditures per pupil, the educational credentials of the teaching staff, and percent of full-time day students, the RSFSR generally falls in the lower third. Of course, none of these indicators address directly the issue of student performance, but they do embody factors seen by both Soviet and Western educators as key elements in quality schooling. Even accounting for possible qualitative differences not captured by available statistical indicators, the Soviet military can continue to expect a relatively well-educated draft pool.

The biggest problem in absorbing the expected increase in non-Russians in the decades to come is not education, but the language barrier. The command language of the Soviet armed forces is Russian. A minimal level of Russian fluency is necessary to understand commands and absorb basic military training. Here again, however, the problem should not be overstated. Even among those minority populations with very low Russian fluency, the fluency levels of draft-age youth tend to be much higher than those of their parents and

Figure 7.2 *Russian language fluency of the draft pool, 1970.*

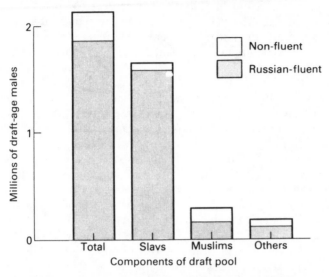

Source: Language data used are for both males and females and probably understate male fluency; fluency rates and age-group data are computed from *Itogi*, vol. IV, 1970, pp. 360–82.

grandparents. The increasing levels of Russian fluency among the younger generation is a tribute to the persistence of Soviet language policy. It is aimed at maximizing the proportion of minorities who are fluent in Russian. One of the most important vehicles for Russian language training is the school system.[62] Students can attend three types of schools: national schools where the instruction is in the native language; Russian-language schools; and mixed schools, with parallel programs in two or more languages. Many minority students, particularly smaller ethnic groups and individuals residing outside their titular republic, have little opportunity for native language schooling beyond the grades one to three.[63] For larger minority groups, the trend appears to be one in which an increasing proportion of students receive instruction in Russian. For those who do not, Russian is taught as a second language beginning in preschool or elementary classes. Frequency of instruction varies from four to six hours per week, with additional hours to be added as the 1984 educational reform is implemented. Rural youngsters who have few opportunities to use their Russian outside the language class are, of course, at a disadvantage relative to their urban counterparts; this is the one aspect of rural non-Russian schooling that is consistently noted in the Soviet educational press.

Enhanced minority access to education and expanded Russian training within the school system over the past decade or so help to account for the substantial generational differences in Russian fluency. Young people in virtually all ethnic groups are more fluent than the older generations. Estimates based on the 1970 Census, the latest period for which detailed data are available, show that over seven out of every ten draft-age non-Russians reported either native or "fluent command." Almost 90 percent of the total 1970 draft pool was fluent in Russian (Figure 7.2). With regard to current fluency levels, an estimated 80–85 percent of the current draft pool is fluent in Russian. Most of the remainder can speak it haltingly.

What are the military implications of the 15–20 percent of the draft pool that is not fluent in Russian? Unless the Soviet military-political leadership opts to exclude such individuals from the draft (and there are no indications to date that they are doing so), draftees who are not fluent in Russian must be absorbed in positions not requiring fluency. They cannot be assigned to positions requiring formal classroom training (provided in Russian) or high levels of communication skills. A unit-by-unit examination of the language requirements of conscript posts in the USSR's armed forces indicates that some 45–55 percent of the conscript posts require some level of Russian-language capability (although perhaps not complete fluency). These findings suggest that the 15–20 percent of the pool that is not fluent can be absorbed without undue difficulties.

This does not mean that the Soviet military is satisfied with the current language situation. Although as Soviet officials note there has been a "perceptible fall" in the number of draftees with poor mastery of Russian,[64] the increased complexity of conscript training has increased fluency requirements.[65] Naturally the military leadership's preference would be to maximize the proportion of servicemen fluent in the command language. Language problems have been singled out by top Soviet military leaders, including former General Staff chief Nikolay Ogarkov, as a serious impediment to training. Main Political Administration chief Yepishev, noting the difficulties some draftees from the Caucasus, Central Asia, and Kazakhstan have in studying weapons and military equipment, pointedly called on the school system and the military commissariat hierarchy to take steps to remedy the problem.[66] Several republics have already set up special required courses, Russian-language camps, and study groups for draft-age minority males with language problems.[67] In 1981 the USSR's educational publishing house produced a Russian-language textbook for draftees which focussed on basic military terminology. In 1982 Voyenizdat, the military publishing house, published another Russian-language textbook for soldiers with poor Russian. It was designed to increase verbal skills, particularly in technical subjects. Educators are also concerned that some youngsters lack the necessary military vocabulary to absorb the predraft initial military training (NVP) courses. They have now begun to develop programs to remedy that deficiency.[68] These activities indicate that Soviet authorities recognize the problem that the language barrier poses to mastery of military technology.

A third aspect of ethnicity-related change in the military is the possibility of widespread interethnic tension within military units that could conceivably degrade combat cohesion, and with it combat capability. Soviet military officials are well aware of this possibility, and they have taken steps to minimize ethnicity-related morale problems. How well have they succeeded in containing ethnic tensions in the armed forces? Evidence on this issue is incomplete. Soviet discussions readily admit that ethnic loyalties can lead to friction, but they depict such situations as isolated instances, amenable to prompt remedial action by the commander and political officer.[69] The testimony of émigrés who have served in the Soviet military, although probably biassed in the opposite direction, would suggest wide variation in ethnic relations from unit to unit. Occasional manifestations of ethnic friction have been reported, particularly in the low-prestige components of the armed forces, such as the construction troops. These incidents range from private expressions of ethnic prejudice to ethnic name-calling and fistfights. It is clear, moreover, that ethnic antagonism may exacerbate existing difficulties in those units with serious discipline and morale problems (such as alcohol abuse, poor NCO–draftee relations, bad living conditions).

It is easy, however, to read too much into such anecdotes. Many other ex-Soviet servicemen report that they could recall no ethnic problems in their unit and a few even repeat the contention of Soviet military authorities that multiethnic soldiers serve together in friendship and harmony. On balance information from this kind of evidence would suggest that most Soviet minority soldiers fit in fairly well to the integrated units. As a source of interpersonal conflict nationality tensions appear to be less significant than, for example, excessive hazing of newly arrived soldiers by the "veteran" draftees. Effective small-unit leadership and decent food are more important determinants of good morale than the unit's ethnic composition.

If the Soviet military authorities can claim modest success in containing what could be an explosive source of conflict in military units, it is only partly due to policies aimed in that direction. It is true that the official military line is one of equal opportunity; and exhibiting ethnic prejudice is a punishable offense. The importance of ethnic harmony is promoted in political training classes, television and radio broadcasts, and lectures. More important than the formal programs to promote ethnic harmony, however, is the *esprit de corps* generated by the hardships of military life. Western social scientists have found that personal contacts between members of different ethnic or racial groups can lead, under certain conditions, to a lessening of prejudice. Social interaction based on common goals is most likely to produce favorable attitude changes. A study of white attitudes toward integrated companies during World War II revealed differences in attitude depending on the respondents' own experience with integrated units. Infantrymen who were themselves serving in companies with black platoons had a much more favorable attitude toward them than those serving in all-white units. Similar findings were reported in a study of Korean War soldiers.[70] These studies suggest that the shared tasks and hardships of integrated units might have a similar effect on interethnic attitudes in the Soviet military as well. The testimony of émigrés who have served in the Soviet military suggest that this is indeed the case.

The most common reflection of ethnic diversity in mixed units is a tendency, noted by both ex-Soviet soldiers and Soviet military sociologists, for soldiers of the same nationality to socialize together in the off-duty hours. Émigré reporting indicates that such patterns are more common during the early months of military service. A Soviet study of friendship patterns within military units confirms these comments; the study found that the role of ethnicity as a determinant of friendships declines the longer the draftee serves. Common nationality or region of origin was an important aspect in about one-half of the friendships formed in the first six months of duty. At the end of the two-year obligation 60–65 percent of the friendships between soldiers were based on common personal interests or tenure of service. In other words, as the young soldier nears the end of his tour of duty shared ethnic or regional origins are much less important in his choice of friends.[71]

A final aspect of the growing non-Slavic presence in the draft pool is the question of minority reliability. Some Western observers have hypothesized that certain ethnic groups are deemed by the military hierarchy to be of inherently questionable reliability and hence are restricted completely to nonsensitive or noncombatant posts. A detailed examination of conscription, stationing, and assignment policies, however, does not support this hypothesis. Draftees of all nationalities are evaluated on the basis of individual educational, language, technical, and security qualifications. There do not appear to be separate policies differentiated by ethnic group, but rather one set of standards that may affect different ethnic groups in different ways.

For example, there is no evidence of differential conscription policies based on ethnicity *per se*. An overwhelming majority of former Soviet citizens report that all young Soviet males are subject to the draft, regardless of nationality. However, the impact of the exemption/deferment provisions in the 1967 Universal Military Service Law does not necessarily fall evenly on all ethnic groups. For example, educational deferments provide those young men who have been accepted into selected colleges or universities with an opportunity to put off, if not avoid entirely, service as a draftee. Minorities, such as Moldavians and Mordvinians, with relatively low student participation rates, would tend to be underrepresented among young men receiving such deferments. Security considerations also fall unevenly on some ethnic groups. Most individuals with relatives who have resettled outside the USSR or those who have applied to emigrate are apparently considered something of a security risk. Young men who were born or resided outside the USSR are also affected by the security checks made during the predraft screening. These considerations would tend to fall heavier on nationalities, such as the Germans and Jews, who have received selective permission to emigrate.

Stationing policy is another barometer of leadership perception of minority reliability. Ex-Soviet citizens indicate that non-Russian draftees are often assigned to units far from their hometowns and often on the other side of the country. However, this general policy of distant stationing applies to all ethnic groups, Russians included; it is an adaptation of imperial Russian practices. The tsarist army (which was itself following a practice dating to the Roman army) had traditionally assigned soldiers of one region to serve in distant units. A soldier of Polish origin, for example, would typically be posted to serve in the Urals (and vice versa). The rationale for this policy was that it helped to prevent soldiers from establishing close ties with the civilians in regions adjacent to their units. Tsarist authorities frequently used the troops to quell peasant outbreaks; and the distant stationing system made it less likely that soldiers would refuse to act against local civilian participants in disturbances.[72] This consideration helps to explain its retention by Soviet authorities, who apparently concur with their tsarist predecessors that local soldiers from any region might be hesitant about using force against citizens from their home territory. Distant stationing also helps to break down regional isolation. The urban conscript is exposed to rural and provincial life styles and vice versa. Finally, desertions and unauthorized leave are minimized when the draftee is posted far from home. These considerations suggest that current Soviet stationing policy is based on military and political considerations not directly relevant to the issue of minority reliability *per se*.

Unit assignment policy is another example of how military authorities try to balance goals arising from Soviet nationality policy with military requirements. Draftees are assigned to units and positions based on individual aptitude and qualifications. There is little evidence to suggest that ethnicity itself is part of the service and unit assignment procedures. Former Soviet servicemen reporting on the ethnic composition of their unit indicate that non-Russians, including ethnic Germans, Jews, and Muslims, are assigned to virtually every sort of post, including technical units, the Strategic Rocket Forces, elite airborne units, and specialist training programs. They are not restricted to menial tasks or nonsensitive posts.[73]

Nor are non-Slavs barred from assignment outside the USSR. Ex-Soviet soldiers describing the ethnic composition of their unit report that Soviet units based in Eastern Europe include sizable proportions of non-Slavs, particularly Soviet Muslims. This pattern is probably a reflection of the Soviet "distant-stationing" policy rather than doubts about the loyalty of Slavic troops. Western eyewitnesses in Afghanistan noted the presence of Asian troops in the initial invasion force.[74] Because some of the initial troops were in units from nearby MDs fleshed out with "local" reservists, it is likely that Muslim minorities were overrepresented among Soviet troops involved in the invasion. When the mobilized reservists were replaced with active duty troops, however, the ethnic composition of the troops in Afghanistan apparently shifted to one closely resembling the ethnic mix of normal active duty units, following a pattern noted in earlier Soviet interventions in Eastern Europe.[75] In sum, if Soviet military authorities have had reservations about the reliability of non-Slavic troops, it has not interfered with unit assignment policy.

The Soviet military leadership, however, feels no compulsion to ensure proportional ethnic representation in every unit. Linguistic, specialist, educational, and security requirements emanating from purely military needs sometimes act to underrepresent some ethnic groups in certain types of units and overrepresent others. It is reasonable to assume, then (although available data limitations preclude testing this assumption), that those minorities with low levels of Russian fluency are probably overrepresented in construction units and ground force infantry units where the requirements for language fluency are less stringent.

The Military as Vehicle for Socializing Minority Soldiers

Soviet concerns about minority draftees go beyond the potential impact on combat capability. Soviet authorities view the special environment within the military as an opportunity to attenuate competing nationalist loyalties and to instill approved "Soviet" values in minority soldiers.[76] There is no direct method to measure the effectiveness of the military as a socialization device. However, insight into the potential value of military service in "Sovietizing" young Soviet males may be gleaned from Western social science research. Western socialization research suggests that the very repetitive nature of the USSR's highly intensive political socialization program may be most effective with minority soldiers. A study of the effects of civics classes on the political attitudes of American high school students revealed few shifts in attitudes among white students; more significant attitude changes were found among black students. The researchers interpreted these findings as evidence that civics classes were more effective for black students (for whom the message was new) than for white students who had already absorbed the message elsewhere, in their homes or among peers.[77] These findings suggest that the repetitive messages of the Soviet political socialization program may be the most effective in producing desired attitude change among those soldiers who are least well socialized, including minority conscripts.[78]

Western research underlines the importance of another Soviet socialization technique: the use of peer-group pressure. In the military unit the minority draftee is insulated from the traditional cultural views of family and community and exposed to peer-group pressures to conform with more urbane, "Soviet" values and behavioral patterns. An example of how controlled and manipulated peer groups can influence minority attitudes is provided by a Soviet press description of one such manipulation. The incident involved a unit screening of a documentary about the treatment of women in the Caucasus. The film centered on the ethnic custom of kidnapping one's bride, a tradition that Soviet authorities frown on as a reflection of "feudal" attitudes toward women. In the discussion following the film only one soldier, a draftee of apparent Muslim origin called Mamedov, expressed approval of the custom. His comrades disagreed; in a well-organized discussion one soldier pointed out that approval of such traditions reflected not only the man's disrespect of his bride-to-be, but his own insecurity and weakness as well. Stung by this slur from his comrades, Mamedov retracted his opinion. At this point the officer presiding over the discussion intervened, congratulated the soldiers for coming to the approved view, and redirected the discussion to the issue of interethnic marriages (strongly endorsed by Soviet authorities).[79]

The incident, an idealized one which was no doubt related as an example of appropriate use of peer-group manipulation, reflects several aspects of the application of peer-group pressure to remold minority values. First, the officer directed but did not overly dominate the discussion. Second, the rebuke to Mamedov came from his fellow soldiers. The incident demonstrates how powerful peer-group disapproval can be in reshaping "incorrect" values and opinions. In those cases where soldiers like Mamedov are in the minority they may in fact be quite susceptible to pressures to adopt the values and behavioral patterns of the dominant group.

This hypothesis is supported by historical material on the Red Army's socialization role in the interwar period. As Merle Fainsod's analysis of captured Soviet documents from Smolensk makes clear, demobilized soldiers played a key role in strengthening Bolshevik control over the rural areas during the chaotic collectivization campaigns in the 1930s.[80] Demobilized minority soldiers were used in a similar capacity to help consolidate Bolshevik control of the Soviet periphery:[81]

> The demobilized [Muslim] Red Army soldiers returned to their villages, auls, and kishlaks politically and culturally matured. They became the initiators of socialist undertakings sponsored by the Communist Party and Soviet government.

The military is also seen as a useful supplement to the school as a teacher of Russian.[82] As noted above, considerable numbers of draft-age youths from some of the Central Asian and Caucasus areas enter the military with low levels of Russian fluency. The Soviet leadership is clearly anxious to use the Russian-language environment of the military unit as a means to promote Russian bilingualism among such draftees. Some premilitary training programs include special Russian-language instruction for predraft males identified as having problems with Russian. The local military commissariats and DOSAAF groups also provide remedial Russian instruction.[83] Once drafted, those soldiers with language problems may be assigned to remedial Russian programs organized by the political officer and conducted by bilingual teachers.[84]

How well does the military function as a vehicle to promote Russian fluency? The use of the military in the 1920s campaign against illiteracy suggests that the military experience has, in the past at least, provided a very useful vehicle for educational programs.[85] Additional evidence comes from ethnographic and linguistic surveys. Results of these surveys indicate that military service was an important source of Russian language training. Most of those who claimed Russian as a second language reported that school was a major factor. But for five out of six groups surveyed (urban Moldavians, Estonians, and Uzbeks, rural Georgians, Estonians, and Uzbeks), the next most important factor in Russian-language learning was the army. Rural residents and middle-aged respondents were more likely to have learned Russian while in the service. These data suggest that the military has served as an important supplement to the school system as a vehicle for promoting bilingualism. Even those individuals whose first exposure to the language came through the schoolroom seem to benefit from the two-year exposure to a Russian-language environment in the military. Most non-Russian draftees complete their service obligation with considerably better Russian than they had prior to induction.[86]

The material presented above on the effectiveness of the armed forces' socialization role *vis-à-vis* minorities is far from being as complete as one would like. The available evidence, however, suggests that the armed forces have served the Soviet leadership fairly well in helping to socialize minority soldiers. The hardships of military life and the common goals involved in training within a military unit help to minimize ethnic tensions in most units and make the minority soldier more susceptible to peer-group pressures to conform to mainstream "Soviet" values.

The Minority Military Professional

The discussion above centered on the problems involved in adjusting to the increased proportion of non-Slavs in the draft pool. A related issue is the extent to which non-Slavs have been recruited into the body of military professionals: commissioned officers, warrant officers, and long-term enlistees. This is an important issue because an increase in the proportion of non-Slavic conscripts might logically lead to increasing pressure on the military leadership to recruit minority military professionals.

As the historical record makes clear, the early Soviet policy of concentrating the less modernized minority soldiers in nationality units led to efforts to recruit minority officers to command them. Although many minority units, particularly those in the southern tier, were at first commanded by bilingual Russians and Ukrainians, the Bolshevik military leadership remained firmly committed to the goal of developing a cadre of minority military professionals to assume command and political posts in nationality formations.[87] Implementing this policy was not without difficulty. For some ethnic groups, the recruiting base was virtually illiterate. Minority military schools had to be established; and military textbooks and regulations had to be translated into minority languages. It was difficult to find instructors who had both the necessary military qualifications and fluency in the native languages.[88]

The first step was to organize short command and political courses for local minorities. By October 1923 24 percent of the students in Soviet military schools were non-Russians.[89] In the spring of 1924 six new national military schools were established. By the end of the year eighteen minority military colleges were operating, with three-year command/staff training programs for Ukrainians, Belorussians, Armenians, Georgians, Azeris, Tatars, and Central Asians. The Central Asian Command and Staff School, for example, had separate sections for Tadzhiks, Turkmen, Uzbeks, and so on. The low educational level of the students remained a stumbling-block. In the mid-1920s 94 percent of the students entered with lower or "home" education. To train faculty for these schools nationality sections had to be formed in military pedagogical schools.

The five-year plan for the development of nationality formations, approved in 1925, envisioned an expansion of the minority command training programs. By the mid to late 1920s the military cadre of the Red Army had become more representative of the ethnic composition of the military as a whole (Table 7.2). Thirty-six percent of the Red Army, compared to 33 percent of the military

Table 7.2   *Ethnic Composition of the Red Army (1926)*

Nationality	Red Army (%)	Junior commanders and rank-and-file (%)	Military cadres (%)	Of which			
				command (%)	administration (%)	political (%)	medical (%)
Slavic							
Russians	64·0	63·1	66·8	72·0	72·6	61·9	59·4
Ukrainians	17·6	19·2	11·4	10·1	9·4	11·6	9·3
Belorussians	4·4	4·2	5·3	5·0	5·2	4·3	4·4
Poles	0·9	0·8	1·5	1·6	1·3	0·9	1·1
Balts							
Latvians	0·3	0·1	1·3	1·5	1·2	1·6	0·6
Muslim							
Tatars	2·1	2·4	0·9	0·7	0·4	1·6	—
Bashkirs	0·3	0·3	0·1	—	—	0·2	—
Turks (Azeri)	0·5	0·5	0·7	0·5	0·3	0·9	—
Uzbeks	0·4	0·4	0·4	0·1	—	0·2	—
Others							
Jews	2·1	1·6	4·4	2·1	3·9	10·3	18·6
Udmurts	0·3	0·3	—	—	—	—	—
Komi	0·3	0·3	0·1	0·1	—	0·1	—
Chuvash	0·7	0·9	0·2	0·2	0·1	0·4	—
Germans	0·9	0·9	0·6	6·6	1·1	0·5	1·1
Armenians	1·1	1·0	1·4	1·0	1·3	1·6	2·1
Georgians	1·3	1·2	1·7	1·6	1·1	1·8	1·6
Mordvinians	0·9	1·0	0·2	0·1	—	0·2	0·1
Other	1·9	1·8	3·0	2·8	2·1	1·9	1·7

Source: Ye. Ioseliani, "Social–demographic composition of the RKKA," *Statisticheskoye obozreniye*, no. 7, 1929, pp. 97–105.

cadre, were non-Russians. By the early 1930s native military professionals dominated the nationality formations, at least in the political officer positions. In 1932 96 percent of the political staffers in the Central Asian military district were "local" minorities.[90] Data from the Independent Kazakh Cavalry division revealed that 63 percent of the mid- and senior-level officers in 1930 were Kazakh; 90 percent of the unit political officers and virtually all the junior commanders were Kazakh.[91]

The data from the interwar period, then, suggests that the Soviet use of nationality units accelerated the development of the minority officer corps. Politically reliable minority-group members were trained in special native-language command schools and were not forced to compete with the better-educated ethnic Russians. The result was an ethnically heterogeneous officer corps. The less modernized nationalities may have been somewhat under-

Table 7.3   *Ethnic Composition of Supreme Soviet Military Delegation*

Ethnic group	Military members of Supreme Soviet* (%)	Relevant age cohort† (%)
Russian	80·7	57·1
Ukrainian	14·0	19·1
Belorussian	3·5	3·7
Armenian	1·8	1·2

*The nationality of each delegate is provided in the official biography: *Deputaty verkhovnogo soveta SSSR*, Moscow, Izvestiya, 1979, *pass*.
†The average age of the military delegates in 1979 was 61; ethnic composition of the relevant age cohort was computed from the 40–59-year-old cohort in the 1970 Soviet Census: *Itogi vsesoyuznoy perepisi naseleniya 1970 goda*, vol. IV, Moscow, Statistika, 1973, pp. 360–82.

represented, but less so than would have been expected given the substantial educational and linguistic disadvantages they suffered *vis-à-vis* the dominant Slavs.

The phase-out of the nationality units envisioned by the 1938 decree marked a reversal of Soviet nationality policy in the armed forces. The decree included plans to disband the minority officer candidate schools and to integrate minority training into the regular network of candidate schools. The German invasion of the Soviet Union forced Soviet authorities to postpone their integration plans and reintroduce nationality units. The senior commanders in these units were appointed by the Red Army Main Cadres Directorate, but mid-level officers were recruited primarily from minorities serving in "regular" units. Fluency in Russian, however, was an important qualification even for junior officers. Although political instruction was presented in the minority languages, the command language in minority formations was Russian.[92] The heavy wartime reliance on non-Russian soldiers led to special efforts to train non-Russian command cadres; most were recruited from active duty soldiers and sergeants.[93] Attention was also focussed on training native political workers and propagandists to counter German appeals to minority soldiers.[94]

How well represented were Soviet minorities in the wartime officer corps? Soviet historical treatments provide data only for certain components of the armed forces.[95] The need for Russian-fluent officers suggests, however, that minorities may have been less well represented in the officer corps than in the armed forces as a whole. The low educational attainments of many of the less modernized minorities would also contribute to their underrepresentation.

Both factors help to explain the continued Slavic dominance of the highest echelons of the MoD hierarchy.[96] Analysis of the fifty-five military members of the Supreme Soviet (Table 7.3) reveals overwhelming Slavic dominance—98 percent of this group listed a Slavic nationality. This compares with an 80 percent Slavic share of the relevant age cohort for senior officers. A similar pattern emerges from a name analysis of seventy-three key MoD officials: only two of these officers (2·7 percent compared with 7·8 percent of the relevant age cohort) are of Muslim origin. It is clear then that Slavs are overrepresented at the very highest levels of the MoD, when compared to the Slavic share of the relevant age group. Muslims and other less modernized minorities are under-represented, but not excluded.[97] But it would be wrong to conclude that this pattern necessarily results from deliberate discrimination. The very senior levels of the officer corps are dominated by men who entered the service just prior to the war when the educational levels and language capability of the more traditional minorities would have necessarily limited their access to officer posts.[98] In analyzing the ethnic composition of this group we are, in effect, examining the situation of thirty to forty years ago.

What is the current role of minority officers? During both the interwar period and World War II increased use of non-Russians was coupled with stepped-up Soviet efforts to recruit minority military professionals. Current increases in the proportion of non-Slavs in the draft pool will also create pressures on the Soviet military leadership to increase minority representation in the officer corps. Indeed, Soviet authorities have evidenced growing concern that all minority groups be "adequately represented" in the officer corps. But historical evidence also suggests that military authorities would be hesitant to sacrifice officer effectiveness for the goal of a more ethnically balanced officer corps. What is most likely, then, are programs to expand minority access to military careers by enhancing their ability to compete with ethnic Russians. Increasing convergence in educational attainments across ethnic groups has eased one barrier to fuller ethnic participation in the officer corps. The language barrier, however, will continue to limit minority opportunities. Examinations for officer candidate schools, which are given in Russian, include materials on the Russian language, and in some cases Russian literature as well. This places even the most talented minority group member at a dis-advantage. To deal with this problem several republics have established remedial Russian-language programs for boys who indicate a desire to enroll in officer commissioning school.[99]

There is also the question of the attractiveness of a military career to members of minority groups. In the United States the army has provided upward mobility for disadvantaged minorities whose access to civilian jobs may be much more limited.[100] Soviet minorities, however, have a broad range of opportunities in the civilian sphere.[101] They are less likely to view a military career as a particularly attractive opportunity for professional advancement. Moreover, as indicated above, Soviet studies of career preferences indicate that fathers who are themselves military professionals tend to esteem military careers for their sons more highly than do civilians. This suggests that past patterns of differential participation in the officer corps may be partly perpetuated through self-selection.[102]

There are, however, indications that the less modernized minorities, includ-ing the Muslims, are better represented among junior officers than among senior or general/flag rank officers.[103] Both émigré evidence and material from the Soviet military press indicate that those minorities who are fluent in

Russian can and do make the military a career. As the educational qualifications and Russian fluency of minorities increase, their role will probably
grow, even in the absence of a Soviet-style affirmative action program to
increase minority representation in the officer corps. What should not be
overlooked in this discussion, however, is the fact that Slavs account for 78
percent of the relevant age cohort for Soviet officers (of 29–59 years of age).
Even if non-Slavs achieve representation in the officer corps equivalent to their
share of the relevant age group in the general population, the Soviet officer
corps will remain a Slavic-dominated institution.

Ethnic Soldiers: a Balance Sheet

The USSR's changing ethnic mix has presented Soviet military authorities with
many of the same problems faced by other states with an ethnically mixed
military force. A review of the evidence bearing on this issue suggests we
should be cautious in accepting at face value the Soviet propaganda claim that
the ethnic diversity in their army is a source of strength. Equal caution,
however, is warranted in assessing interpretations that portray minority participation in the military as a source of insurmountable difficulty. Soviet
military authorities are well aware of the problems and potential problems of
integrating a growing percentage of non-Slavs in the Red Army. Once one gets
past the cheerful insistence that minority soldiers are a source of cohesion, the
military press provides a fairly frank and realistic (if guarded) assessment of the
problems associated with non-Slavic soldiers. The military leadership has
devised a series of programs to deal with these problems, programs which (to
judge by the comments of many ex-Soviet soldiers in the West) seem to be
working fairly well.

The most immediate difficulty facing the Soviet military with regard to the
changing ethnic mix is the growing proportion of non-Slavs in the draft pool.
Here, however, military manpower officials are benefiting from overall educational and linguistic policies. The Soviet program to extend basic education
from eight to ten years has produced a steady increase in the educational
qualifications of Red Army conscripts, during a time when the proportion of
non-Slavs in the pool increased dramatically. Soviet efforts to enhance minority access to technical education have also benefited the military by improving
the technical qualifications of the conscripts. For example, the participation
rates of young Muslim males in Soviet tekhnikums is virtually even with the
Soviet average. Language, of course, is a more difficult problem for many
Soviet conscripts, but here again the military has benefited from broader Soviet
attempts to increase Russian fluency. The 15–20 percent of the draft-age cohort
that is not fluent in Russian can easily be absorbed in slots not requiring
Russian, because the supply of young males who are fluent in Russian far
exceeds the military requirements for Russian-fluent conscripts. Nor do ethnic
tensions appear to present a major source of disciplinary problems in multiethnic units. The average draftee is anxious to satisfy his military obligation as

easily as possible and return to civilian life with a clean service record. He regards the other conscripts in his unit, including those of a different nationality, more as fellow sufferers than as adversaries.

The issue of minority representation in the Soviet officer corps presents a longer-term problem for Soviet military authorities. Although relevant statistical data are not available, it seems clear that minorities are underrepresented in the current cadre of military professionals. This is particularly true among senior officers who entered the military at a time when the low educational attainments of non-Slavs limited minority access to military careers. The coming decades are likely to see an increase in the number of minority group members in the officer corps since the improved minority educational qualifications and Russian fluency should enhance the ability of young non-Slavs to compete for military academy positions. The historical record suggests, moreover, that the Soviet military leadership may opt to accelerate this process by special programs targeted at minority youth. This is especially true of posts in the political apparatus, where Red Army officials have been particularly concerned to maximize non-Slavic representation.

This assessment raises the issue as to why the Soviet military–political leadership has chosen to cope with the problems of an integrated military. One alternative is to exclude entirely all but the most Russian-fluent and "Sovietized" minorities from military service; another is a return to partially segregated units as in the interwar and wartime systems. Recent policies cannot be adequately explained by manpower shortages; the 1979 draft pool, after all, was the largest in Soviet history. The most compelling explanation for the Soviet decision to opt for an integrated force is that the two-to-three-year service experience plays a role in helping to "Sovietize" young non-Slavic males. This explains why the Soviets routinely draft many individuals who because of language difficulties may not be desirable from a purely military standpoint. Military considerations alone might lead to efforts to minimize the number of such draftees to avoid placing pressure on the military training system. From the socialization standpoint, however, those individuals who are least desirable from a narrowly military perspective are those who are most in need of the socialization training and Russian-language environment offered by the military experience. But the Soviets apparently feel no compulsion to ensure equal representation in every unit. This has resulted in an assignment pattern where the best-educated and most Russian-fluent conscripts are overrepresented in elite units and technical posts. In this way the Soviets have attempted to balance the goals arising from military and socialization functions of their armed forces, without sacrificing the primary goal of maintaining a high level of combat capability.

Notes: Chapter 7

Portions of this chapter were adapted from Ellen Jones, "Minorities in the Soviet Armed Forces," *Comparative Strategy*, Vol. 3, No. 4, 1982, pp. 285–318.

1 See, for example, Joseph Rothschild, *Ethnopolitics: A Conceptual Framework* (New York: Columbia University Press, 1981), *pass*.

2 James F. Guyot, "Efficiency, responsibility and equality in military staffing: the ethnic

dimension in comparative perspective," *Armed Forces and Society*, vol. 2, no. 2 (February 1976), pp. 291–304.

3 Cynthia H. Enloe, *Ethnic Soldiers: State Security in Divided Societies* (Athens, Ga.: University of Georgia Press, 1980), pp. 8–12.

4 On Soviet nationality policy see "*Konstitutsiya SSSR*" in *Svod zakonov SSSR* (Moscow: Izvestiya, 1980), Vol. 1, pp. 14–42; *Pravda*, 22 December 1982, pp. 1, 2; and "Natsionalnaya politika KPSS," in *Kratkiy slovar' spravochnik agitatora i politinformatora* (Moscow: Politizdat, 1974), pp. 41–3.

5 Rothschild, 1981, p. 108.

6 Ellen Jones and Fred W. Grupp, "Modernisation and ethnic equalisation in the USSR," *Soviet Studies*, vol. XXXVI, no. 2 (April 1984), pp. 159–84.

7 D. V. Pankov, "The Russian regular army," in D. V. Pankov (ed.), *Razvitiye taktiki russkoy armii* (Moscow: Voyenizdat, 1957), pp. 3–30.

8 L. G. Beskrovnyy, *Russkaya armiya i flot v XVII veke (ocherki)* (Moscow: Voyenizdat, 1958), pp. 300–1.

9 P. A. Zayonchkovskiy, *Voyennyye reformy 1860–1970 godov v rossii* (Moscow: Izdatel'stvo Moskovskogo Universiteta, 1952), pp. 304–5. See also A. V. Fedorov, *Russkaya armiya v 50–70-x godakh XIX veka. Ocherki* (Leningrad: Izdatel'stvo Leningradskogo Universiteta, 1959), pp. 256–7.

10 UK War Office, Intelligence Division, *Handbook of the Military Forces of Russia* (London: Harrison, 1898), pp. 1–4.

11 N. I. Shatagin, *Organizatsiya i stroitel'stvo sovetskoy armii v period inostrannoy voyennoy interventsii i grazhdansky voyny 1918–1920 gg* (Moscow: Voyenizdat, 1954), pp. 33–4.

12 "Postanovleniye STO o predostavlenii mestnym organam Sovetskoy vlasti sibiri, turkestana i drugikh okrain prava vremennogo osvobozhdeniya ot prizyva v krasnuyu armiyu otdel'nykh narodnostey ili grupp grazhdan nerusskoy natsional'nosti," *Dekrety sovetskoy vlasti* (Moscow: Politizdat, 1976), Vol. 8, pp. 175–6; and N. Makarov, "The Communist Party and strengthening the multinational Red Army, 1922–1925," *VIZh*, no. 7 (1972), pp. 3–9.

13 P. M. Pakhurnyy, "The Communist Party in the struggle for Soviet power in Kazakhstan," in *Vsegda nacheku* (Alma Ata: Kazakhstan, 1971), pp. 3–24; and S. M. Klyatskin, *Na zashchite oktyabrya. Organizatsiya regulyarnoy armii i militsionnoye stroitel'stvo v sovetskoy respublike, 1917–1920* (Moscow: Nauka, 1965), pp. 183–4.

14 Shatagin, 1954, pp. 114–18; and I. B. Berkhin, *Voyennaya reforma v SSSR (1924–1925 gg)* (Moscow: Voyenizdat, 1958), pp. 119–20.

15 Yu. I. Korablev, *V. I. Lenin i sozdaniye krasnoy armii* (Moscow: Nauka, 1970), pp. 193–4; N. T. Silin, "On the participation of the peoples of the Soviet republics in the organization of the Red Army and in the defense of the socialist motherland," in *Iz istorii bor'by sovetskogo naroda protiv inostrannoy voyennoy interventsii i vnutrenney kontrrevolyutsii v 1918g* (Moscow: Gosudarstvennoye Izdatel'stvo Politicheskiy Literatura, 1956), pp. 467–91; and M. Molodtsygin and P. Nersesyan, "Lenin on the peculiarities of development of the army of the multiethnic Soviet government," *VIZh*, no. 4 (1982), pp. 3–9.

16 A. K. Afanas'yev, "To the history of the development of the Red Army in Turkistan," in *Iz istorii*, 1956, pp. 492–516.

17 Silin, 1956.

18 M. Lakhtikov, *Sovetskaya armiya—armiya bratstva i druzhba narodov* (Moscow: Gosudarstvennoye Izdatel'stvo Politicheskoy Literatury, 1952), p. 56; V. Mekvabishvili, "From the history of the Georgian Red Army," *VIZh*, no. 8 (1965), pp. 111–15; and M. Molodtsygin, "V. I. Lenin and the formation of the army of friendship and brotherhood of the peoples," *VIZh*, no. 11 (1972), pp. 12–19.

19 Makarov, 1972; see also M. Molodtsygin, "Leninist principle of internationalism in the organization of military security of socialist countries," *VIZh*, no. 9 (1974), pp. 3–10.

20 Lakhtikov, 1952, pp. 58–9.

21 Kh. M. Ibragimbeyli, "Natsional'nyye formirovaniya," *SVE*, Vol. 5, pp. 552–3.

22 P. Rtishchev, "Leninist national policy and the development of the Soviet armed forces," *VIZh*, no. 6 (1974), pp. 3–9.

23 Lakhtikov, 1952, pp. 60–1.

24 Makarov, 1972.

25 A. Plekhov, "Class and nationality in Soviet military development," *KVS*, no. 23 (1972),

pp. 14–20; and N. Abrosimov, "Army of the friendship of the peoples," *Vestnik PVO*, no. 11 (1982), pp. 6–10.

26 Makarov, 1972; and R. Akchurin, "Universal military training in the Turkistan republic," in *Vsegda nacheku*, 1971, pp. 30–7.

27 Helene Carrere d'Encausse, "The fall of the czarist empire," in Edward Allworth (ed.), *Central Asia: A Century of Russian Rule* (New York: Columbia University Press, 1967), pp. 207–23; and Ye. Yusupov and Kh. Tursunov, "To the history of the 1916 uprising," *Obshchestvennyye nauki v uzbekistane*, no. 4 (1981), pp. 26–9.

28 Michael Rywkin, *Moscow's Muslim Challenge: Soviet Central Asia* (London: Sharpe, 1982), pp. 34–44.

29 K. Ye. Voroshilov, "Defense of the country and the status of the workers' and peasants' Red Army" (Report to the 4th All-Union Congress of Soviets), 25 April 1927, in K. Ye. Voroshilov, *Stat'i i rechi* (Moscow: Partizdat TsK VKP(b), 1937), pp. 104–35; G. Abishev, *Kazakhstan v zashchite sotsialisticheskogo otechestva* (Alma Ata: Kazakhstan, 1969), pp. 149–50; and A. Zevelev, "On several questions of the history of the civil war in Central Asia," *VIZh*, no. 9 (1970), pp. 77–82.

30 Berkhin, 1958, pp. 121–2; Lakhtikov, 1952, p. 57; Ye. Romanov, "Formation of the Kazakh military commissariats," in *Vsegda nacheku*, 1971; K. R. Amanzhdov, "From the history of the formation of Kazakh national units of the Red Army in 1922–1938," *Izvestiya akademii nauk kazakskoy SSR. Seriya obshchestvennykh nauk*, no. 4 (1982), pp. 9–12.

31 "Tsentral'naya musul'manskaya voyenna kollegiya," *Grazhdanskaya voyna i voyennaya interventsiya v SSSR. Entsiklopediya* (Moscow: Sovetskaya Entsiklopediya, 1983), p. 639; Afanas'yev, 1956; and Silin, 1956.

32 Makarov, 1972.

33 O. Khudoyberdiyev, "From the history of the formation of national units of the Red Army in the Central Asian republics," *Izvestiya AN tadzhikskoy SSR. Otdeleniye obshchestvennykh nauk*, no. 4 (1976), pp. 3–9.

34 V. M. Kuz'mina, "Formation of Red Army national units in Turkmenistan," *Izvestiya akademii nauk turkmenskoy SSR. Seriya obshchestvennykh nauk*, no. 4 (1968), pp. 11–17; Khudoyberdiyev, 1976; and N. Makarov, "The development of the multinational armed forces of the USSR in 1920–1939," *VIZh*, no. 10 (1982), pp. 39–43.

35 Data on the ethnic breakdown of the Red Army in 1926 are based on a Red Army census and drawn from *X let krasnoy armii. Al'bom diagram* (Moscow: Izdatel'stvo Voyennyy Vestnik, 1928), p. 32. The percentage breakdown of the 20–29-year-old male cohort was calculated using 1926 Census data from Tsentral'noye Statisticheskoye Upravleniye SSSR: Otdel Perepisi, *Vsesoyuznaya perepis' naseleniya 1926 goda* (Moscow: Izdaniye TsSU SSR, 1929), Vol. 17, pp. 26–32, 46–87.

36 "O natsional'nykh chastyakh i formirovannyakh RKKA," 7 March 1938 Central Committee/Council of Ministers resolution, in N. I. Savinkin and K. M. Bogolyubov (eds.), *KPSS o vooruzhennykh silakh sovetskogo soyuza* (Moscow: Voyenizdat, 1981), pp. 286–7.

37 A. P. Artem'yev, *Bratskiy boyevoy soyuz narodov SSSR v velikoy otechestvennoy voyne* (Moscow: Mysl', 1975), pp. 56–9; see also V. Plyashkevich, "Friendship of the peoples of the USSR—one of the most important sources of victory in the Great Motherland War," *VIZh*, no. 6 (1972), pp. 3–11.

38 I. Timoshchenko, "Military–organizational work of the Communist Party in the period of the Great Motherland War," *VIZh*, no. 6 (1963), pp. 3–14.

39 P. S. Belan, *Kazakhstantsy v boyakh za leningrad* (Alma Ata: Kazakhstan, 1973), p. 146; and I. S. Gurvich, "To the question of the influence of World War II on the course of Soviet ethnic processes," *Sovetskaya etnografiya*, no. 1 (1976), pp. 39–48.

40 I. Pulatov, *Kommunisty, vpered* (Tashkent: Uzbekistan, 1965), pp. 5–6; E. Ye. Yusupov (ed.), *Natsional'naya politika KPSS v deystvii* (Tashkent: Uzbekistan, 1979), pp. 253–6; and Gurvich, 1976.

41 Department of the Army, Office of the Chief of Military History, "Eastern nationals as volunteers in the German Army," Foreign Military Studies, ms. no. C-043, National Archives.

42 "Propagandizing Russian POWs of the 1st Cossack Division, formerly in German custody," Foreign Military Studies, ms. no. P-018d, p. 68, National Archives.

43 "The German methods of propagandizing prisoners of war," Foreign Military Studies, ms. no. P-018d, pp. 7–29, National Archives.

44 "Caucasian and Turkic volunteers in the German Army," Foreign Military Studies, ms. no. C-043, pp. 4–34, National Archives.
45 "In the volunteer units of the German Army," Foreign Military Studies, ms. no. P-018d, pp. 30–61, National Archives. On problems with the German use of Estonian troops see "The Estonian contingent in 1944–45," Foreign Military Studies, ms. no. D-061, National Archives.
46 For two different viewpoints on German collaboration with the Soviets see "Information on the Russian Army," Foreign Military Studies, ms. no. D-304; and "The Russian program of propagandizing prisoners of war," Foreign Military Studies, ms. no. P-018c, National Archives.
47 V. A. Muradyan, *Boyevoye bratstvo* (Moscow: Voyenizdat, 1978), pp. 90–3. See also Belan, 1973, pp. 143–54; Pulatov, 1965, p. 11; O. Malybayev, *Druzhba, ispytannaya v boyakh za rodinu* (Alma Ata: Kazakhskoye Gosudarstvennoye Izdatel'stvo, 1955), p. 35; *Istoriya natsional'no-gosudarstvennogo stroitel'stva v SSSR, 1917–1978*, 3d ed. (Moscow: Mysl', 1979), Vol. 2, pp. 65–6; and N. I. Matyushkin, *Armiya druzhby narodov i proletarskogo internatsionalizma* (Moscow: Voyenizdat, 1982), pp. 77–9.
48 G. Gaynutdinov, "Agitation in the trenches," in *V boyakh za rodinu* (Alma Ata: Kazakhstan, 1966), pp. 202–25.
49 Artem'yev, 1975, pp. 57–9.
50 On the role of Kazakhs in World War II see Malybayev, 1955, pp. 19–34; G. Abishev, *Kazakhstan v velikoy otechestvennoy voyne* (Alma Ata: Kazakhskoye Gosudarstvennoye Izdatel'stvo, 1958), pp. 242–309; A. Mukhamedzhanov, *Kazakhstantsy v bitve pod moskvoy* (Alma Ata: Kazakhstan, 1968), p. 24; and S. N. Pokrovskiy, *Kazakhstanskoye soyedineniya v bitve na kurskoy duge* (Alma Ata: Nauka, 1973), *pass*. On Tadzhik participation in World War II see M. Kh. Khakimov, *Partiya i sovetskaya natsional'naya gosudarstvennost'* (Tashkent: Uzbekistan, 1980), p. 204.
51 These estimates are based on age-specific nationality data in the 1970 Census. Specific steps used in these estimates are detailed in Ellen Jones and Fred Grupp, "Exploiting Soviet census data: some methodological considerations," unpublished paper, September 1979. The basic source for the nationality data is *Itogi vsesoyuznoy perepisi naseleniya 1970 godu* (Moscow: Statistika, 1973), Vol. IV, pp. 360–82.
52 A. G. Vishnevskiy and A. G. Volkov (eds.), *Vosproizvodstvo naseleniya SSSR* (Moscow: Statistika, 1983), pp. 194–241; Maqash Tatimov, "A family with children is like a bazaar," *Madeniet Jane Turmis*, no. 10 (1980), pp. 20–31; trans. from Kazakh in JPRS 77252, 27 January 1981, pp. 58–60; and D. Valentey and A. Kvasha, "Problems of population and demographic policy," *Pravda*, 19 June 1981, pp. 2, 3.
53 See, for example, Jeremy Azrael, "Emergent nationality problems in the USSR," in Azrael (ed.), *Soviet Nationality Policies and Practices* (New York: Praeger, 1978), pp. 363–90.
54 *Itogi 1970*, vol. IV, pp. 393–433, 549–66. Data on the educational attainments of the 16–19-year-olds is provided in Ellen Jones "Soviet military manpower policy in the eighties," paper presented at 1981 International Studies Association Conference.
55 F. Shtykalo, "The high duty of the school," *Sovetskiy patriot*, 22 August 1976, p. 2; M. M. Lisenkov, *Kul'turnaya revolyutsiya v SSSR i armiya* (Moscow: Voyenizdat, 1977), p. 113; and I. Buchinskiy, "Before military service," *Sovetskaya estoniya*, 25 November 1975, p. 25.
56 "Polozheniye o nachalnoy voyennoy podgotovke molodezhi," 17 June 1968, excerpted in *Spravochnik po zakonodatel'stvu dlya ofitserov sovetskoy armii i flota* (Moscow: Voyenizdat, 1970), pp. 43–7.
57 F. Shtykalo, "To improve basic military training," *NO*, no. 5 (1981), pp. 18–21.
58 ibid.; premilitary classes are conducted primarily in Russian. See K. Polshin, "Only in Russian," *Voyennyye znaniya*, no. 12 (1980), pp. 26–7.
59 A. I. Pokryshkin, "DOSAAF SSSR," *SVE*, Vol. 3, pp. 255–7; see also Charles Taylor and Natalie Prissovsky, *Soviet Military Schools*, Defense Intelligence Agency, DDB-2680-52-78, pp. A1–A44.
60 Data on graduates of vocational schools available in *Narodnoye obrazovaniye, nauka, i kul'tura v SSSR* (Moscow: Statistika, 1977), p. 147. Data were standardized to the 15–19-year-old cohort. Data on specialized secondary enrollment provided in Ellen Jones and Fred W. Grupp, "Measuring nationality trends in the Soviet Union: a research note," *Slavic Review*, vol. 41, no. 1 (Spring 1982), pp. 112–22.
61 Jones and Grupp, 1984.
62 A brief survey of Russian-language training in the school system is available in M. N.

Guboglo, "The development of social functions of languages in the sphere of education," in *Sovremennye etnicheskiy protsessy v SSSR* (Moscow: Nauka, 1977), pp. 260–75. See also S. Sh. Shermukhamedov, "On further improvement of Russian-language teaching in republic schools," in *Russkiy yazyk—yazyk druzhby i bratstva narodov* (Tashkent: Izdatel'stvo Ukituv-chi, 1974), pp. 9–21; K. Kh. Khanazarov, *Sblizheniye natsiy i natsional'nyye yazyki v SSSR* (Tashkent: Izdatel'stvo Akademii Nauki Uzbekskoy SSR, 1963), pp. 194–9; and B. Kh. Khasanov, "Development of functions of the Russian language in Kazakhstan," in *Russkiy yazyk v natsional'nykh respublikakh sovetskogo soyuza* (Moscow: Nauka, 1980), pp. 7–18.

63 M. Z. Zakiyev and R. A. Yusupov, "The development of bilingualism in Tataria," in *Puti razvitiya natsional'no-russkogo dvuyazychiya v nerusskikh shkolakh RSFSR* (Moscow: Nauka, 1979), pp. 108–17.

64 V. Samoylenko, "The peoples' friendship—the source of the armed forces' might," *KVS*, no. 15 (1982), pp. 15–21.

65 O. A. Bel'kov, "The military–patriotic importance of the Soviet peoples' international unity," *Nauchnyy kommunizm*, no. 1 (1983), pp. 3–10.

66 N. V. Ogarkov, *Vsezda v gotovnosti k zashchite otechestva* (Moscow: Voyenizdat, 1982), p. 64; and A. A. Yepishev, *Svyashchennyy dolg, pochetnaya obyazannost'* (Moscow: DOSAAF, 1983), pp. 75–6. See also A. I. Sorokin, "The armed force of developed socialism," *Voprosy filosofii*, no. 2 (1983), pp. 3–17. Sorokin comments on the wide regional variations in actual levels of Russian mastery among non-Russian draftees; despite the fact that these soldiers have had identical forms of schooling, some enter the army with insufficient practice in Russian.

67 R. A. Abuzyarov, "An effective form of military-language training for students," *Russkiy yazyk i literatura v uzbekskoy shkole*, no. 5 (1982), pp. 36–8; S. Shermukhamedov, "The Russian language and patriotic–military upbringing of young people," *Pravda vostoka*, 15 May 1983, p. 3; G. Ismagulov, "Development of speech through mastery of military–patriotic texts," *Russkiy yazyk v kazakhskoy shkole*, no. 10 (1982), pp. 27–33; E. Kafarova, "Language of friendship—language of October," *Bakinskiy rabochiy*, 15 April 1983, p. 3; and T. Usuba-liyev, "Our common concern," *KZ*, 16 December 1983, pp. 2–3.

68 *Russkiy yazyk uchebnoye posobiya dlya prizyvnikov* (Moscow: Prosveshcheniye, 1981); *KZ*, 4 August 1982, p. 2; and R. A. Abuzyarov and Z. I. Tuayeva, *Russkiy yazyk na zanyatiyakh po nachal'noy voyennoy podgotovke v natsional'noy shkole* (Moscow: Proveshcheniye, 1983).

69 N. Shumikhin, "Multi-national army of the Soviet state," *KZ*, 9 October 1980, pp. 2, 3.

70 Samuel A. Stouffer *et al.*, *The American Soldier: Adjustment during Army Life*. Vol. 1, Studies in Social Psychology in World War II (Princeton, N.J.: Princeton University Press, 1949), p. 594. See also Arnold M. Rose, "Army policies toward Negro soldiers—a report on a success and a failure," *Journal of Social Issues*, vol. III, no. 4 (Fall 1947), pp. 26–31; and *Social Research and the Desegregation of the U.S. Army* (Chicago: Markham, 1969), pp. 76–103, 125–33. A summary of the key findings of several studies of intergroup relations in racially mixed units is available in Charles C. Moskos, Jr., "Minority groups in military organizations," in Ralph W. Little (ed.), *Handbook of Military Institutions* (Beverly Hills, Calif.: Sage, 1971), pp. 271–89.

71 V. N. Kovalev, *Sotsialisticheskiy voinskiy kollektiv. Sotsiologicheskiy ocherk* (Moscow: Voyenizdat, 1980), p. 140.

72 John Shelton Curtiss, *The Russian Army under Nicholas I, 1825–55* (Durham, N.C.: Duke University Press, 1965), pp. 273, 275–6.

73 This conclusion is based on the material provided by former Soviet soldiers reporting on the ethnic mix of the units in which they served. Soviet émigrés will commonly express the opinion that non-Russians are deemed unreliable and hence assigned primarily to nonsensitive posts, particularly the construction forces. When asked to describe the ethnic mix of their own unit, however, such informants typically reply with data that contradicts their own generalizations about minority troops. For this reason analyses that rely on émigré generalizations about the use of minority soldiers reflect common Soviet stereotypes (at least among Soviets who chose to emigrate), but not Soviet reality. See, for example, S. Enders Wimbush and Alex Alexiev, "The ethnic factor in the Soviet armed forces: preliminary findings," Rand Note, N-1486-NA, May 1980.

74 See, for example, *U.S. News and World Report*, 21 January 1980, p. 20. Western news reports that include specific percentage breakdowns of the ethnic mix of the Soviet invasion force should be treated with caution. Given the circumstances in which those observations took

place and the difficulty of determining ethnic identity by sight, it is extremely doubtful if such reports are valid. One may conclude only that soldiers of non-European appearance were present in Afghanistan, probably in numbers exceeding their share of the relevant age cohort.

75 Several Western authors have alleged that the mobilized reservists, including Soviet Asians, were withdrawn in February and March 1980 because they "developed unacceptable attachments with the Afghan population": see S. Enders Wimbush and Alex Alexiev, "Soviet Central Asian soldiers in Afghanistan," Rand Note N-1634-NA, p. 17. Alexandre Bennigsen, for example, has claimed that "Soviet authorities refused to send Soviet Uzbeks and Tajiks to Afghanistan after the first five weeks": see *Russkaya mysl'*, 23 June 1983, p. 5. I have searched in vain for evidence supporting this widely repeated contention; a more likely explanation for the replacement of reservists by active duty forces is that the ninety-day active duty period for the mobilized reservists had ended.

76 See, for example, K. U. Chernenko, "To live, work, struggle according to Lenin," *KZ*, 29 May 1984, pp. 1, 2; K. Vorob'yev, "Multinational character of the USSR armed forces," *KVS*, no. 4 (1984), pp. 24–9; and V. Voronov, "The military collective—school of maturity for defenders of the motherland," *KVS*, no. 20 (1972), pp. 47–53.

77 M. K. Jennings, K. P. Langton, and R. G. Niemi, "The effects of the high school civics curriculum," in *The Political Character of Adolescence* (Princeton, N.J.: Princeton University Press, 1974), pp. 181–206. Studies of cultural variations in political socialization in the United States abound. There have been studies that focus on the Amish, the Mennonites, Chicanos, and Appalachian whites; see Renshon, 1977, *pass.*

78 A. A. Yepishev, "In leadership by the party," *Armiya bratstva narodov* (Moscow: Voyenizdat, 1972), pp. 27–41; and "Army of the friendship of the peoples," *KZ*, 2 September 1980, p. 1.

79 V. I. Plyashkevich, *Vospitaniye voinov v dukhe druzhby narodov* (Moscow: Voyenizdat, 1973), pp. 136–9.

80 Merle Fainsod, *Smolensk under Soviet Rule* (Cambridge, Mass.: Harvard University Press, 1958), p. 452.

81 Abishev, 1969, p. 156; and Berkhin, 1958, pp. 140–1.

82 K. S. Grushevoy, "Correctness of Lenin's behests," *Armiya bratstva narodov*, 1972, pp. 280–92.

83 V. Samoylenko, "Blossoming and mutually enriching cultures of the brotherly peoples," *KVS*, no. 21, November 1972, pp. 28–33.

84 A. Overchuk, "Our brotherhood is indivisible," *KZ*, 15 August 1979, p. 2; and "The language of friendship and fraternity," *KZ*, 20 January 1973, p. 1.

85 Lisenkov, 1977, pp. 100–8.

86 M. N. Guboglo, "A study of the perspectives for developing bilingualism among the peoples of the USSR," *Istoriya SSSR*, no. 1 (1978), pp. 27–42; M. N. Guboglo, "Tendencies in the development of national-Russian bilingualism," *Polevyye issledovaniya instituta etnografii, 1976* (Moscow: Nauka, 1978), pp. 12–23; and S. I. Bruk and M. N. Guboglo, "Factors in developing bilingualism among peoples of the USSR," *Sovetskaya etnografiya*, no. 5 (1975), pp. 17–30.

87 Information on programs during the interwar period to recruit and train minority military cadres was drawn from Yu. Kislovsky, "The first red commanders," in *Vsegda nacheku*, 1971, pp. 45–52; Silin, 1956; Afanas'yev, 1956; Romanov, 1971; Berkhin, 1958, pp. 132–8; and Lakhtikov, 1952, pp. 57–61; see also N. Shumikov, "Army of the multinational Soviet state," *KZ*, 9 October 1980, pp. 2, 3.

88 K. Ye. Voroshilov, "National development in the Red Army," in Voroshilov, 1937, pp. 338–40.

89 Makarov, 1972.

90 Khudoyberdiyev, 1976.

91 Abishev, 1969, p. 153. See also Kh. Mambetkaziyev, "Army of friendship and brotherhood of the peoples," in *Vsegda nacheku*, 1971, pp. 217–30.

92 Gurvich, 1976.

93 N. H. Kilyayev (ed.), *KPSS i stroitel'stvo sovetskikh vooruzennykh sil* (Moscow: Voyenizdat, 1967), pp. 302–3.

94 Artem'yev, 1975, pp. 64–94; and Belan, 1973, pp. 143–54.

95 One historical treatment of World War II provides data on the raw numbers of officers for selected non-Russian groups in the airforce and also for officers in the armoured and mechanized troops: see *Istoriya velikoy otechestvennoy voyny sovetskogo soyuza, 1941–1945*

(Moscow: Voyenizdat, 1964), Vol. 3, p. 220. Rtishchev provides additional data for selected non-Russian artillery officers: see Rtishchev, 1974, pp. 7–8. Neither source provides total figures or data on ethnic Russians, so it is impossible to compute an ethnic percentage.

96 The Soviets have not, to my knowledge, published a nationality breakdown for its postwar officer corps. The 1959 Census does provide data "in the ranks of the Soviet Army" broken out by republic. These data are further broken down by sex and "social group" (workers, white-collar employees, collective farmers, and peasants). There are many problems in interpreting these data. First, there are indications that some portions of the uniformed personnel are counted under other occupational headings. Second, it is unclear how various categories of service personnel were assigned to "social-group" categories. Third, there is some confusion as to how the uniformed personnel were counted. The Census indicates that soldiers were enumerated at the place where their units were located, but counted as residing at the place where they were drafted. It is not clear how this rule applies to career personnel. These problems make the 1959 data virtually useless from the standpoint of determining nationality participation in the military.

97 See National Foreign Assessment Center, *Directory of Soviet Officials. National Organizations*, CR 81-11343, May 1981, pp. 69–73.

98 There are, however, certain military agencies where minority officers appear to be actively recruited such as the civil defense and military commissariat (manpower training and procurement) network. The military commissar of Uzbekistan, for example, is an Uzbek who has worked his way up the Uzbekistan commissariat system: see *Deputaty verkhovnogo soveta uzbekskoy SSSR* (Tashkent, Uzbekistan 1976), p. 221.

99 Ye. Nikitin, "The triumph of Lenin's national policy," *Agitator armii i flota*, no. 23 (1982), pp. 10–14; and O. Bel'kov, "An army of friendship and fraternity of the peoples," *KVS*, no. 12 (1981), pp. 9–16. On remedial programs see A. Melkumyan, "To bring up defenders of the motherland," *Kommunist*, 17 February 1980, p. 2; V. Koshelchenkova, "Language of brotherhood and mutual understanding," *Turkmenskaya iskra*, 25 October 1983, p. 4; and Shermukhamedov, 1983.

100 Charles C. Moskos, "The American dilemma in uniform: race in the armed forces," *The Annals of the American Academy of Political and Social Science*, March 1973, pp. 94–106.

101 Jones and Grupp, 1984.

102 Ye. Ye. Levanov, "Family socialization: status and problems," *SI*, no. 1 (1979), pp. 115–18.

103 This conclusion is based on an analysis of surnames of a sample of Soviet officers drawn from the military press. Conclusions drawn from this analysis must remain tentative because the sample could not be drawn scientifically.

8

The Armed Forces in Contemporary Soviet Society

Both the Red Army of the interwar period and the Soviet armed forces of the 1980s are heirs to the imperial Russian military tradition.[1] Many of the organizational institutions, basic elements of the manpower procurement system, and key aspects of personnel management are all modifications of tsarist practices. One of the most obvious continuities between the Soviet military and its tsarist predecessors is organization. The structure and organizational principles underlying the contemporary Soviet Ministry of Defense (as indeed virtually all Soviet ministries) are derived from the tsarist model. The roots of the contemporary MoD Collegium can be traced to the tsarist Military Council—an advisory committee attached to the War Ministry and roughly paralleling civilian ministry councils.[2] The contemporary territorial system for administering troop units is a variation on a theme established in 1862, when Milyutin attempted to rectify the overcentralization of the War Ministry by delegating selected functions to a new territorial structure. Like the current version of the military district, Milyutin's district administration was set up as a microcosm of the national-level War Ministry, with a district staff and a collegial entity (the MD Council) to broaden decisionmaking.

Another continuity is the manpower system itself. When the Bolshevik leaders abandoned the short-lived experiment with a volunteer military in 1918 in favor of conscription, they were returning to an imperial Russian practice. The Soviet army, like its tsarist predecessor, serves as a "school for the reserves." Soviet soldiers, again like those under the tsar, serve part of their military obligation as active duty servicemen, then are discharged into the reserves where they are subject to periodic training musters. The Soviet military adopted the tsarist distant-stationing policy to minimize draftee contact with civilian life. Military units in both tsarist and Soviet periods have been used for civilian construction projects.

There are other parallels between military life in the imperial and Soviet armies. Westerners commenting on the prerevolutionary Russian army were often struck by the harsh living conditions of the average soldier; as one English observer noted: "What with hard toil, constant drill, poor pay and not overpleasant food [the soldier] has usually a not good time of it in barracks."[3] This comment applies equally well to the contemporary Soviet soldier as compared to his European or American counterpart. The tsarist soldier, like his modern Soviet counterpart, was very fond of escaping the harsh living conditions and physically grueling drill through drinking-bouts.

The strict discipline of the Soviet army also finds its roots in tsarist precedent. Disciplinary regulations in the tsarist army were much stricter than in West European militaries of the day. Even in the late tsarist period when disciplinary codes were far less stringent than previously, there was a much higher reliance on physical coercion to enforce order. This is still true to some extent today. In the late 1960s and early 1970s the United States and several West European states experienced major countercultural challenges, opposed to both military values and life styles and to the service obligation. In response the armed forces in several countries adopted a series of changes in military regulations (for example, relating to uniforms, domiciling, and restrictions on marital status) and in the role of individual soldiers in the military decisionmaking structure (for example, the right to appeal an order to civilian authorities).[4] While the Soviet Union has attempted some marginal improvements in the military life style, Soviet military authorities have thus far eschewed the kinds of disciplinary concessions adopted in Western Europe and the United States. The Soviet military remains a far more strictly regimented environment.

Costs and Benefits of the Current Military System

The continuities between the contemporary Soviet military and its tsarist predecessor, important as they are, should not be overdrawn. The military of the 1980s operates in a very different socioeconomic and political environment from either its nineteenth-century predecessor or the Red Army of Stalin's day. The final years of this century will bring still more changes—changes that may call into question the long-term commitment to the conscript army inherited from the tsars.

One of the most serious of these changes is in the economic environment: the Soviet manning system faces an era of increased economic constraints. Soviet economic growth rates fell from 5·2 percent average annual growth in the last half of the 1960s to 3·7 percent between 1970 and 1975, and to 2·7 percent between 1976 and 1980.[5] The causes of this trend are diverse. It is associated, in part, with the maturing of the Soviet economy: the depletion of the resource base and the aging of capital stock. Intrinsic weaknesses in the economic system (for example, barriers to innovation, the cumbersome nature of centralized economic planning) have had a progressively more deleterious effect on growth rates as the economy matures. The economy was also hard-hit by an above-average incidence of bad weather that contributed to low agricultural output in the late 1970s.[6] Western commentators have suggested that long-term solutions to these problems may well involve increased emphasis on investment and consumption and a consequent shift in resource allocation away from the defense sector.[7] A manpower system based on maintaining a large standing army and relying on active duty military service for reserve training is extremely costly. As economic constraints tighten less expensive alternatives are almost certain to become more attractive.

International consequences of the current manning system represent still another consideration. The massive peacetime force produced by the current procurement system influences how the USSR's Western rivals perceive Soviet intentions. Adoption of an alternative procurement system involving a smaller standing force might well help counteract NATO's suspicions of the USSR's foreign policy intentions.

The most immediate threat to the draft army, however, is demographic. Manpower procurement is closely linked with the size of the 18-year-old male cohort; and this pool, as discussed, has varied substantially over the last three decades. The outlook for the final years of the twentieth century is one of substantial declines in the size of the draft pool. What options do the Soviets have? One policy option is to decrease the size of the standing force, mitigating the potentially detrimental impact on combat capability by a selective reduction in unit manning levels. Manning levels within the Soviet armed forces vary widely with the mission and status of the unit. Some units are maintained during peacetime at essentially wartime strength; this includes those ground forces predesignated for initial wartime operations (units now deployed in the Warsaw Pact countries and in the border areas); the strategic rocket forces; most of the air defense forces; and some naval forces (that is, submarines). The remaining units are maintained at lower-than-wartime strength. Some are designated for quick mobilization during times of crisis or war. Others are maintained in peacetime at greatly reduced strength. This group includes many divisions in the internal military districts. Each unit has an authorized strength for peacetime and another for wartime, although the actual manning may, of course, vary from authorized strength. The manning level represents the percentage of wartime authorized personnel that are present during peacetime. These levels can be adjusted—through General Staff directive—depending on the foreign or domestic situation.[8] The reduced strength units, primarily ground force, comprise the "core" about which the mobilized reservists would be assembled during war or emergency.

During the 1970s when Soviet military authorities were faced with an increased draft-age pool, the authorized strengths for understrength units may have been selectively increased to absorb additional conscripts. The Soviet manning system thus provides a mechanism for dealing with an unusually large influx of draftees. During the 1980s when the situation is reversed and the Soviets must adapt to a declining draft-age cohort, they are quite likely to apply this mechanism in reverse—decreasing the manning levels of selected units. Marginal shifts in manning levels would provide a way of absorbing a net decrease in the active duty force without significantly undermining military capability. The attractiveness of this option is limited, however, by the potentially detrimental effect of large decreases in manning levels for combat readiness. As suggested above, the larger the proportion of reservists needed to bring a unit up to wartime strength, the more difficult it becomes to make that unit battle-ready. Marginal changes might be relatively easy to absorb, but major shifts would be undertaken only with great reluctance.

Another way of cushioning the effects of a force cutback is through an increase in the proportion of civilians in the MoD. Civilians now constitute an estimated 12 percent of the total MoD manning. Selected posts now filled by conscripts could be civilianized to accomplish decreases in the size of the uniformed force but no drop in total MoD manning. There are several disadvantages to this approach. First, civilian posts are more expensive. Second, as noted above, the Soviets view the draft as both a training and socialization experience—functions that are not served by radically increased civilianization of conscript posts. For these reasons, although selective increases in the use of civilians may occur, it is unlikely that this mechanism would be used to absorb entirely the impact of reduced manpower supplies in the coming decades.

A more attractive alternative is that of selective transfers of support troops to regular combat status. This would involve shifting some auxiliary troops, such as construction and railway troops, to more directly combat-related roles. This shift would not be without economic costs. As noted above, railway and construction forces work on both civilian and military projects; some of these projects, like the Baykal Amur railway, are of high priority. There would naturally be some resistance to wholesale transfers of these troops. Moreover, these units provide a convenient place to assign conscripts of lower-than-average quality. Apparently these units are able to absorb easily individuals with minor mental or physical disabilities, those of questionable reliability (such as former criminals), and those non-Slavs with Russian-language difficulties. It should be pointed out, by way of a caveat, that many other support, service, and combat units have a high percentage of slots requiring rather low levels of technical skills or language competency; the construction troops are by no means the only useful outlet for such draftees. These considerations do suggest, however, that the Soviets would avoid wholesale transfers of slots currently assigned to such forces. The MoD would more likely transfer such slots selectively; a transfer of, for example, one-third of the construction and railway troops would release over 100,000 conscripts for service in the regular combat, service, and service-supported units.

Given the current international environment and the post-Andropov leadership's apparent determination to present a hardline response to NATO's force-modernization programs, the Soviets may be reluctant to accept the decrease in the active duty force associated with a declining manpower supply. If the Soviets decided to maintain current force levels, they have several options. One is to simply increase the length of conscript service. In 1977 the basic service tour obligation of university graduates was extended from twelve to eighteen months. The Soviets may well decide to return to the basic three-year tours in effect before the 1967 service law changes. This approach to coping with the decreasing draft pool of the 1980s and 1990s does entail some economic costs, because it prolongs the draftee's absence from the civilian laborforce at a time of increasing manpower constraints. Counterbalancing these considerations, however, is the fact that these young men are being removed from the laborforce at a period of time when their civilian productivity is low; most are between 18 and 21 and have certainly not reached their peak in terms of civilian skill and experience.

Another way to cushion the impact of draft pool declines while avoiding decreases in the level of uniformed military personnel is to tighten up deferment practices to achieve an increase in the conscription rate (defined here as the percentage of 18–26-year-old males who actually serve in a conscript status). The utility of this option rests on the current conscription rate. If the rate is estimated at, say, 90 percent, an increased rate could be achieved only with great difficulty. If, however, we estimate that the Soviets are conscripting only 70 percent, rather substantial increases in conscription could be achieved by tightening deferment and raising the percentage actually drafted. An increase of ten percentage points, for example, would translate into over 200,000 additional conscripts per year. In effect, stable force levels can be maintained (within certain limits) by adjusting conscription rates up and down with the changing supply of draft-age males. As indicated in Chapter 3, we do not know what proportion of the draft-age pool is actually drafted. Our estimates suggest (and it is important here to stress again the uncertainties involved in this and all other estimates of conscription rates) that between 65 and 75 percent of the 18-year-old pool is drafted; an additional 5–10 percent is added from those who initially escape service but are drafted after educational, health, or family deferments run out. It is quite likely that these percentages shift from year to year (and from region to region). During years when the supply of 18-year-olds is plentiful, educational deferments can be increased, providing an increased number of 21–27-year-olds to augment manpower supplies in leaner years. This practice in effect mutes the sharp increases and decreases in the size of the 18-year-old pool and facilitates the military's efforts to adjust to changing supplies.

The entire system of deferments is responsive to policy choices; educational and family deferments can be selectively tightened. Even health standards can be selectively lowered to minimize the percentage who escape service through this provision. Current force levels (5·2 million, assuming a 70:30 conscript–career ratio and a two-year service term) require an annual conscript intake of 1·8 million men, or 81·5 percent of the 1983 pool of 18-year-olds. The force could be maintained through 1988 (the lowest year for the draft pool) by increasing the conscription rate to about 90 percent, with no other policy revisions. The Soviets may choose to increase conscription rates by perhaps five or six percentage points as part of a larger package of options. This approach might be especially attractive to them because it dovetails nicely with the goal of exposing the largest possible number of young males to the socialization experience of the two-year service term, as well as providing intensive military training to future reservists.

Steps in this direction have already been taken. As noted in Chapter 3, the December 1980 revision of the 1967 Universal Military Service Law included a change in the previous deferment system for specialized secondary and higher educational students. After January 1982, the only students who receive deferments are those admitted to institutions on an approved list. This provides the Soviets with a great deal of flexibility since they can add to or subtract from the list, adjusting the proportion of 18-year-old males affected by the educational deferment in the process.

Still another of the policy options available to the Soviets, should they decide to maintain forces at current levels, is to increase the proportion of the career military in the total force. Again some caveats about the size of the career force are in order. For convenience sake a career–conscript mix of 25:75 has often been assumed, particularly in computing the number of draftees required annually. This estimate, however, is not the result of a careful, comprehensive unit-by-unit examination of manning practices; and studies of individual unit types suggest that the estimate of 75 percent for the conscript share, which is generally used as a rule-of-thumb, is probably too high. The actual career–conscript ratio is probably closer to 30:70. This ratio could be shifted further in favor of the career component, to, say, 35:65. Given a total uniformed force of 5·2 million men, an annual conscript intake of 1·8 million is required if the career–conscript ratio is 30:70; less than 1·7 million draftees are required if the ratio shifts to 35:65. Use of this option would also be in line with the trend already under way to strengthen the career enlisted component of the armed forces.

Increasing the size of the career force is not without problems, however. First, it would remove additional and potentially skilled and well-educated individuals from the civilian laborforce at a time of increasing demand for labor. In addition, there are also direct costs to the MoD. Conscripts are a relatively inexpensive source of manpower; they are paid only a small monthly allowance, fed, clothed, and housed at a fairly austere level, certainly well under prevailing civilian living standards. Every career serviceman, particularly an officer, represents a sizable financial commitment. He is relatively well paid and the infrastructure of support (for example, housing, recreation, pensions) is also far more expensive. The attractiveness of a military career in the officer corps suggests that recruitment of additional officer candidates would not be very difficult. Recruitment of additional career enlisted personnel presents greater difficulties and might require enhanced pay, amenities, and other benefits. An additional drawback to significant increases to the career force is the fact, noted above, that the Soviets see a high payoff for conscript service in terms of both socialization and intensive military training of future reservists. Any option that involved selective increases in the career force would probably also maintain conscription rates at fairly high levels. In any case, it is likely that an increased career force would be achieved by some combination of increases in the number of officers, warrant officers, and extended servicemen with only marginal increases in the use of servicewomen, whose role in the peacetime military is much more limited.

The most likely Soviet response to the environmental constraints of the coming decades is some combination of the measures summarized above. For example, the Soviets might opt to increase the career component of their force to 35 percent; cut back deferments to bring the conscription rate to, say, 85 percent; and increase the proportion of civilian positions from 12 to 13 percent. This approach would be consistent with the tendency of Soviet policymakers to adopt compromise solutions that avoid reliance on a single strategy. There is certainly a historical precedent for such an approach. In the decades that .followed World War II the Soviets faced changes in the manpower supply that were far more abrupt than those that will face them in the final years of the twentieth century. They responded to these changes by adapting the existing procurement system. It would not be surprising, then, if they adopted a similar strategy now.

The strategy outlined above, of course, entails considerable costs to an already strained civilian economy. But the Soviet leadership will be evaluating the economic sacrifices entailed by this option within the larger framework of the costs and benefits of the Soviet armed forces. The costs of training a massive reservist base go well beyond the obvious one of maintaining large numbers of young men under arms. The current system also means that a large portion of career force efforts are focussed toward training the continuing waves of new conscripts who cycle through the services. To be sure; all military organizations are closely involved with training; even volunteer systems, especially those in which retention rates are low, must be concerned with training programs for new enlistees. However, the Soviet system of twice-yearly replacement of one-quarter of their draftees ensures that training activities will assume an even greater share of attention from the career force.

Another military cost of the current system is the particular pattern of personnel management problems with which the career force must deal. A majority of the uniformed force consists of postadolescent males who have not freely chosen to serve and who have no expectation of making the military a career. They clearly regard the two-year service experience as an interruption of their normal life plans. The prevalence of discipline problems relating to homesickness and adjustment difficulties is a natural outgrowth of these patterns. These problems are exacerbated by the extreme isolation, regimentation, and strict discipline of Soviet military life. Clearly, those military organizations that allow off-post housing for young recruits will not, by definition, share the Soviet army's problem of soldiers who slip out of barracks after bed-check. The Soviets have retained the rigidly disciplined environment because they believe it is conducive to both political and military socialization. Such rigid controls, however—in the absence of a selection process to filter out individuals who are not predisposed to accept them—inevitably pose a strain on the disciplinary system.

Use of active duty service as a method of reservist training, in the USSR as in other national settings, also places very real limits on technology. Soviet design philosophy has traditionally placed heavy emphasis on rugged, straightforward equipment design. This is partly because much of the equipment, particularly in the ground forces, will be used by draftees; technologically sophisticated operation and maintenance routines would be difficult for the conscript army to absorb. This doesn't necessarily mean, of course, that the ideal weapon system for a conscript army is a technically primitive one. Indeed, some relatively simple designs can require extremely long training and high skill levels to operate effectively. Conversely, some of the most technically sophisticated designs produce weapons that are extremely easy to operate. Many such weapons, however, are highly susceptible to breakdown, and maintenance procedures are complex. The ideal weapon for a conscript army, from the Soviet view, is one that combines relative ease of operation with reliability, ruggedness, and ease of maintenance.[9] In sum, reliance on a conscript army to produce a large reserve, in contrast to the use of long-term military professionals, places direct constraints on weapons technology.

The Soviet experience with mobilized reservists also raises questions as to how well the system works on the battlefield. The effectiveness of units manned by reserves probably varies greatly, depending on the proportion of slots designated for reserve fills, quantity and quality of reserve equipment, how recent the reservists' active duty training, the time available for refresher training before commitment to battle, and the rapidity of changes in military technology. A former Soviet officer involved in the mobilization preparations for the Czech invasion noted that artillery, infantry (motorized rifle), and tank units fleshed out with reservists—even reservists whose active duty service had taken place ten years before mobilization—were ready for battle after a short training period; but air defense, antitank rocket, and chemical units that were filled up with reservists were not battle-ready, even after four months of intensive training.[10] The Soviet mobilization system, then, does not produce uniformly well-trained, well-equipped, and battle-ready units.

Moreover, the utility of the current system—using the two-year active duty service term for reservist training—hinges, in part, on the longevity of weapons systems and tactics. While some skills learned during the draft tenure are transferable to new weapons designs, a reservist whose active duty tour was spent learning to operate a weapon of a particular design will clearly contribute less to modernization potential once that design has become obsolete. This is particularly true of weapons that require lengthy training to master. As Soviet military scientists have noted, the average length of a weapons system generation has decreased steadily in recent decades. If this trend continues, it may well undermine the military justification for the current reliance on a two-year draft tour as a form of reserve training; while enhancing the attractiveness of alternate systems such as the mixed cadre–militia arrangement that was used in the 1920s and early 1930s.

What, then, are the military benefits of the current system? First of all, it produces the massive standing force that the Soviets are convinced they need. Unless the Soviet leadership becomes convinced that the next war can be fought and won by a small, well-equipped, professional force, it is not likely that the Soviets will opt for this alternative. Second, the system produces a massive body of reservists to create huge numbers of ground force divisions.

Readiness and training levels of divisions created in this way may be low, but the sheer masses of men were used effectively (if not efficiently) in World War II to defeat a much better-trained adversary. As noted by Franz Halder, the German Chief of Staff, in 1941: "Even though these [mobilized Soviet] divisions were not as well organized, equipped, or led as the German ones, they nevertheless existed and had to be defeated."[11] This historical experience helps account for the continued Soviet reliance on the reserve and mobilization system.

The current system has political benefits as well. One of the most important is that it produces both a massive standing force and a large reserve base— factors that contribute greatly to the image of the USSR as a military super-power. This image must surely be a source of satisfaction among Soviet leaders and at least some portion of the Soviet citizenry. The Soviets have been able to compete effectively with the West in the military arena when—judged by either economic efficiency or living standards—the USSR trails far behind many other industrialized nations. Military power is the chief justification for the USSR's claim to great power status. Soviet military power has been used to buy a place in the world diplomatic community for the contemporary Soviet leadership that their tsarist predecessors could only dream about. This status in the international arena is, in turn, an important point of pride for many Soviet citizens and a critical source of legitimacy for the current Soviet leadership. A major retreat from current force levels, or a return to the militia system, would certainly not be undertaken lightly.

There are socioeconomic reasons as well for the Soviet unwillingness to abandon either conscription or the large standing army that it produces. The military as currently configured provides a package of economic and social benefits whose importance is likely to grow in the future; and one of the major explanations for the Soviet unwillingness (thus far) to abandon either conscription or the mass standing army is the package of economic and social benefits derived from the current system of personnel recruitment. Future laborforce trends, for example, mean that demand for military labor is likely to grow. As noted above, there are few reasons to believe that the spot labor shortages that afflicted the Soviets in the 1970s will disappear in the 1980s and 1990s. Of the several options the Soviet leadership has available to deal with such problems (that is, expanded use of prison labor, an increase in incentives to encourage migration to labor-deficient areas), use of military support units is perhaps the most desirable. Reliance on such units is relatively inexpensive and far less politically sensitive than expanding the prison or laborcamp population, parti-cularly in an era when the leadership has shown increasing concern for cultivating the image of an orderly, law-abiding system. These considerations suggest that the military's contribution to laborforce needs may well assume greater importance over the coming decade.

The military's social role is also likely to grow. Soviet military officials arguing for the utility of military service as a socializing agent can point to expected increases in the size of two groups most in need of the homogenizing and toughening benefits of service life: non-Russian minorities and consumer-conscious urbanites. For the first group, military service provides needed exposure to a mixed-ethnic peer group and a Russian-language environment. Military service is also a means of temporarily transplanting the fast-growing Muslim minorities out of the labor surplus areas of Central Asia. The Soviets are clearly hoping that at least some minority soldiers, armed with job skills and enhanced Russian fluency acquired during military service, will choose not to return to their home village. Military service, then, dovetails with Soviet nationality and migration policy and will likely assume increasing importance as the share of non-Slavs increases, particularly among the cohort of laborforce entrants. These considerations argue against a return to a territorially based militia system that would undermine the socialization potential of military service for non-Russian draftees.

Rural ethnic minorities are not the only group with a special need for the socialization benefits of military service. An increasing proportion of more consumer-oriented youth, unwilling to tolerate the hardships their parents' generation took for granted, has caused growing concern among Soviet educators. Military officials argue that for these youths, often the product of the small nuclear families increasingly common in Soviet urban areas, military service provides an almost unique opportunity to instill discipline and maturity, and to counteract what some bemoan as the "feminization" of young Soviet males. Given the steady growth of the social and economic factors that produce this pattern of attitudes, the share of Soviet youth so afflicted is likely to increase. The role of military service in toughening and disciplining such individuals in a highly regimented, all-male environment may well grow in importance.

Permeability of Military-Civilian Boundaries

Perhaps one of the most important social benefits of a conscript v. a volunteer army is the high level of permeability between military and civilian institutions. Western observers of contemporary Soviet reality are often struck by the extent to which the civilian world has absorbed the outlook and vocabulary of the military. The reverse observation is also valid: the USSR's military is, in a very real sense, a civilianized institution. Certainly, the institutional boundaries between the Soviet Ministry of Defense and the civilian world count for less than they do in the West. The MoD's internal arrangements and bureaucratic culture are similar to those in virtually all entities in the USSR's government hierarchy. The relationship between the military and various party organs charged with military-related missions is but a subset of the larger party–government relationship. The value system held up as ideal for the Soviet military officer is a variation on that of the ideal civilian manager; and many of the characteristics valued in Soviet military officers are the same qualities prized in civilian managers. Both the military and civilian manager must operate in an authoritarian, hierarchical system that touts the virtues of innovation and flexibility while rewarding rigidity and subservience. These considerations mean that the gulf that separates the military officer from his civilian counterpart is far smaller in the USSR than in many Western industrial societies.

Perhaps the major difference between the military management system and its civilian analogues is the sexual segregation of the military profession. Females in the USSR, unhampered by the stereotype of feminine fragility that has reinforced occupational barriers in the West, have moved into many jobs that remain virtual male monopolies in Europe and the United States. While Soviet women are underrepresented in the management hierarchies in many fields (including those, like medicine, where they dominate the rank-and-file positions), the avenues for professional advancement remain open. The one area in which this is not true is the Soviet armed forces. For a variety of reasons females have been almost totally excluded from the peacetime army. The decision to exclude over one-half of the USSR's citizens from the peacetime military has important societal implications. Because security issues are so important and the armed forces play such a crucial role in foreign policy, the exclusion of women from the military has had a more detrimental impact on the access of Soviet women to political elite status than is the case in most Western democracies.

The interdependence of military and civilian institutions is based on much more than shared values. Use of conscription maximizes the connections between military and civilian environments. In the USSR the pressures to achieve a "real universality" in military service have meant that many young men with major physical or mental disabilities—individuals who in most national settings would be quickly filtered out of the conscription pool—are in fact called up for service. Relatively few adult males escape military service in some capacity. The universality of military service serves to blur the boundaries between civilian life and military institutions. On the one hand, the majority of Soviet service personnel are civilians in uniform who bring the values, strengths, and weaknesses of the larger social setting into the military with them. The discipline and regimentation of the military environment— strict by Western standards—are acceptable in the Soviet military because such an environment is but a more rigid version of the USSR's regimented civilian life style. Soviet soldiers are able to adjust eventually to the harsh living standards of barracks life, because the material amenities of Western industrial society are virtually unknown to all but the very elite in the Soviet system. The citizen-soldiers also bring with them the patterns of deviance and social cleavages of the larger civilian society. The prevalence of alcohol use and abuse in the Soviet military, for instance, is a reflection of a more pervasive social problem in civilian life.

The large number of young civilians cycling into the military system to serve as conscripts also means that there is a constant flow of ex-soldiers returning to civilian life, bringing with them the outlook, vocabulary, and values of the two years of military service. This factor is reinforced by the fact that the behaviors and values sponsored by the military's socialization program, to which the draftee has been exposed, are compatible with those of the New Socialist

Man—the ideal of the civilian socialization program. The typical demobilized soldier leaves his military unit more mature, more pliable, and more passively obedient than when he was drafted. These qualities will help him adjust to adulthood in a civilian world that expects, indeed demands, those characteristics.

Notes: Chapter 8

1 Walter M. Pintner, "The Russian Army and Russian society," Final Report to the National Council for Soviet and East European Research, 10 May 1982.
2 Ellen Jones, "Committee decision making in the Soviet Union," *World Politics*, vol. XXXVI, no. 2 (January 1984), pp. 165–88.
3 William Barnes Steveni, *The Russian Army from Within* (New York: Doran, 1914), pp. 49–50.
4 Catherine McArdle Kelleher, "Mass armies in the 1970s: the debate in Western Europe," *Armed Forces and Society*, vol. 5, no. 1 (Fall 1978), pp 3–30.
5 Kate L. Tomlinson, "Plan and performance: overview," in *Soviet Economy in the 1980s: Problems and Prospects*, Selected Papers Submitted to the Joint Economic Committee, Congress of the United States, pt. 1 pp. 147–52.
6 Herbert S. Levine, "Possible causes of the deterioration of Soviet productivity growth in the period 1976–1980," in ibid., pp. 153–68.
7 John P. Hardt, "Highlights: problems and prospects," in ibid., pp. vii–xv.
8 "Boyevoy i chislennyy sostav," *VES*, p. 88; and A. A. Il'in, "Boyevoy i chislennyy sostav," *SVE*, Vol. 1, pp. 528–9.
9 I. Tsygankov, "Soviet military technology: the development of design thought," *Tekhnika i vooruzheniye*, no. 11 (1974), pp. 6–9; and Viktor Suvorov, *Inside the Soviet Army* (New York: Macmillan, 1982), pp. 181–211.
10 Viktor Suvorov, *The Liberators: My Life in the Soviet Army* (New York: Norton, 1981), p. 140.
11 Diary of Franz Halder, Chief of Staff of the German Army, 11 August 1941, quoted in Mitzi Leibst, "Soviet Mobilization," in *The Soviet Military District in Peace and War: Manpower, Manning, and Mobilization* (GE TEMPO, GE 79 TMP-30), appendix I, pp. I-1–I-19.

Index